James Muirhead

Historical Introduction to the Private Law of Rome

James Muirhead

Historical Introduction to the Private Law of Rome

ISBN/EAN: 9783744765961

Printed in Europe, USA, Canada, Australia, Japan

Cover: Foto ©Suzi / Pixelio.de

More available books at **www.hansebooks.com**

LAW OF ROME.

All Rights Reserved.

HISTORICAL

INTRODUCTION

TO THE PRIVATE

LAW OF ROME

BY

JAMES MUIRHEAD, LL.D. (GLASG.)
PROFESSOR OF ROMAN LAW
IN THE UNIVERSITY OF EDINBURGH

EDINBURGH
ADAM AND CHARLES BLACK
MDCCCLXXXVI

PRINTED BY BALLANTYNE, HANSON AND CO.
EDINBURGH AND LONDON.

PREFATORY NOTE.

THE following pages were written originally for the ENCYCLOPÆDIA BRITANNICA, but had to be very much abridged in order to bring them within the limits of space the Editor could afford to devote to their subject. He did me the honour to express the opinion that their publication *in extenso* would prove of service to various classes of readers; and the Publishers of the "Encyclopædia" were so good as to urge me to adopt his suggestion. This book is the result.

I think it right to prefix this explanation; for the plan and execution might have been somewhat different had an independent volume been in contemplation from the first.

EDINBURGH,
    1st *October* 1886.

PRINTED BY BALLANTYNE, HANSON AND CO.
EDINBURGH AND LONDON.

PREFATORY NOTE.

THE following pages were written originally for the ENCY-CLOPÆDIA BRITANNICA, but had to be very much abridged in order to bring them within the limits of space the Editor could afford to devote to their subject. He did me the honour to express the opinion that their publication *in extenso* would prove of service to various classes of readers; and the Publishers of the " Encyclopædia " were so good as to urge me to adopt his suggestion. This book is the result.

I think it right to prefix this explanation; for the plan and execution might have been somewhat different had an independent volume been in contemplation from the first.

EDINBURGH,
1st *October* 1886.

CONTENTS.

PART I.

THE REGAL PERIOD.

CHAPTER I.

SOCIAL AND POLITICAL CONDITION OF ROME AND ITS POPULATION DOWN TO THE TIME OF SERVIUS TULLIUS.

SECT. 1. *Genesis of the Roman State* (pp. 3–5).—Different races. Different customs. Dualistic result.
SECT. 2. *The Patricians* (pp. 5–8).—They alone ranked as citizens or *Quirites*. Their *gentes* or clans. Gentile organisation. Relation between the *gentes* and their constituent families.
SECT. 3. *The Clients* (pp. 8, 9).—How clientage arose. Relation between patron and client.
SECT. 4. *The Plebeians* (pp. 9–13).—Origin of the *plebs*. Accessions to its ranks. Different races and customs represented. Some of the plebeians belonged to guilds of craftsmen. The greater number engaged in agriculture. Had no gentile institutions and no share in government.

CHAPTER II.

REGULATIVES OF PUBLIC AND PRIVATE ORDER.

SECT. 5. *Absence of any Definite System of Law* (pp. 14, 15).—Pomponius's account of the early law. Errors in it. *Fas, jus,* and *boni mores*.
SECT. 6. *Fas* (pp. 15–18).—What understood by it. Its behests. Their enforcement. The *homo sacer*.

viii   CONTENTS.

SECT. 7. *Jus* (pp. 18-21).—Meaning and etymology. Its sources: custom and statute. The *leges regiae.*
SECT. 8. *Boni Mores* (pp. 31-34).—Their function: restraining *jus* and supplementing it. Illustration: influencing faithfulness to engagements.

CHAPTER III.

INSTITUTIONS OF THE PRIVATE LAW.

SECT. 9. *The Family Organisation* (pp. 24-36).—The *familia* and its head and members. The patrician family (25-34). Its perpetuation a religious duty (25). Confarreate marriage (26). The husband's resulting *manus* over his wife (27). His *patria potestas* over issue of the marriage (27-29). Recruitment of a family by adoption when marriage fruitless (29). Conjugal and parental (as distinguished from dominical) position of the *paterfamilias* (30-32). How and when the *pat. potestas* came to an end (32, 33). Guardianship of wife, daughters, and pupil sons on death of *paterfamilias* (33). The family clients and slaves (33, 34). Plebeian family relationships (34-36). No *justae nuptiae*. Their formless unions only *matrimonia*. Exercised a *de facto pat. potestas*. Having no *gentes*, set more store than the patricians on *cognati* and *adfines*.

SECT. 10. *Distribution of Land and Law of Property* (pp. 36-42).— Varro's *bina jugera* (36, 37). Gentile settlements (37, 38). *Possessiones* in *ager publicus* (38). Grants of land to plebeians (39). Were the *heredia* inalienable? (39, 40). *Dominium ex jure Quiritium* (40). Property in movables (40-42).

SECT. 11. *The Order of Succession* (pp. 43-49).—Patrician practice (43-47). By law a man's wife and children, if *in manu* and *in potestate* at his death, were his proper heirs (*sui heredes*); failing them his *gens* succeeded (43). Children who had quitted the family by marriage or otherwise were not *sui heredes* (44). By law no preference of sex or age (44, 45). Splitting-up of a *heredium* avoided by testamentary arrangement (45, 46). Testaments made with sanction of curies (47). Plebeian order of succession (48, 49). *De facto* a plebeian's children *in potestate* succeeded (48). Having no gentiles, and being unable to make a testament, his succession was *de jure* vacant on failure of children (48). Its *de facto* appropriation by a kinsman,—the foundation of the later *usucapio pro herede* (48, 49).

SECT. 12. *Breach of Contract, and Private and Public Offences* (pp. 49-55).—Social arrangements left narrow range for contractual engagement (49). The guarantees for good faith: invocation of *Fides, jusjurandum*, and *de facto* pledge (50, 51). Redress for breach (51). Redress for wrongs outside contract (52). Private vengeance (52, 53). *Expiatio, supplicium, sacratio capitis* (53, 54). Compositions (55).

CHAPTER IV.

THE SERVIAN REFORMS.

SECT. 13. *Effect of the Reforms of Servius Tullius on the Law of Property* (pp. 56-64).—The census, and the necessity for regulating conveyances of censuable property (56, 57). *Mancipium* or mancipation,—its origin and reformation by Servius (57-60). Meaning of *mancipium* (61, 62). *Res mancipi* and *nec mancipi* (62-64).

SECT. 14. *Their Incidental Effects on the Law of the Family, of Succession, and of Contract* (pp. 64-69).—Employment by plebeians of *mancipium*, under the name of *coemptio*, as a civil form of marriage and means of acquiring *manus* over their wives (64, 65). Their employment of it for *mortis causa* disposal of their estates as a makeshift for a testament (65, 66). Its employment, under the name of *nexum*, in contracting money loans (67, 68). Its employment in emancipation and adoption of a *filiusfamilias*, and in release of a nexal debtor (68). In all those applications it involved acquisition of *manus* (69).

SECT. 15. *Servian Amendments on the Course of Justice* (pp. 69-77).—The state of matters before Servius (69-73). The king's criminal jurisdiction (69). Those of the *paterfamilias* and the *gens* (70). Origin of the king's jurisdiction *inter privatos* (71-73). Servian reforms (73-77). The centumviral court (75, 76). The *unus judex* (77).

PART II.

THE JUS CIVILE.

(*From the Establishment of the Republic till the Subjugation of Central and Southern Italy.*)

CHAPTER I.

HISTORICAL EVENTS THAT INFLUENCED THE LAW.

SECT. 16. *The Change from King to Consuls* (pp. 81-83).—The strife between patricians and plebeians and its causes.

SECT. 17. *Political Inequalities Removed* (pp. 83-88).—The first secession and the tribunate (83, 84). The *concilium plebis* and its *plebiscita* (84). The second secession and the *comitia* of the tribes (84-86). The third secession and the Hortensian law (86). The Canuleian law and repeal of the prohibition of intermarriage of patricians and plebeians (86, 87). The Licinian laws, admission of the plebeians to the consulate, and institution of the prætorship (87, 88). Plebeians in all the magistracies (88).

SECT. 18. *Uncertainty of the Law* (pp. 88–90).—The Terentilian rogation, the Decemvirate, and the XII Tables.

SECT. 19. *The Public Lands* (pp. 90–92).—How these were dealt with. Patrician monopoly. The Cassian law of 268 u.c. The Licinian laws. Later agrarian legislation.

SECT. 20. *The Law of Debt* (pp. 92–96).—Causes of plebeian poverty and patrician wealth (92). Nexal loans and sufferings of the *nexi* (93). Measures in relief (94). Poetilian law abolishing *nexum* (95). Subsequent enactments in aid of debtors (96).

CHAPTER II.

THE TWELVE TABLES.

SECT. 21. *Their Compilation* (pp. 97, 98).
SECT. 22. *Their Sources* (pp. 98, 99).
SECT. 23. *Their Remains and Reconstruction* (pp. 99–103).
SECT. 24. *General Characteristics of the Laws contained in them* (pp. 103–106).

CHAPTER III.

THE PRIVATE LAW WITHIN AND BEYOND THE TABLES.

SECT. 25. *Citizen and Non-Citizen* (pp. 107–113).—Early law personal, not territorial (107). Position of foreigners (107, 108, 110). *Conubium*, *commercium*, *actio* (108, 109). *Amicitia* and *hospitium* (110, 111). *Conubium*, *commercium*, and *recuperatio* under treaty arrangements (111–113).

SECT. 26. *The Gens or Clan* (pp. 113, 114).—Effect of the XII Tables on gentile institutions.

SECT. 27. *The Family Relations Proper* (pp. 115–121).—Husband and wife (115–117). *Manus*-less marriage, and *manus* superinduced by a year's *usus* (115). The wife's *dos* or dowry (116). Divorce (117). Parent and child (117–120). The *patria potestas* (118). "Si paterfamilias ter filium venum duit, filius a patre liber esto" (119). Adoption (119, 120). Master and slave (120, 121). *Statu liberi* (120). *Noxae deditio* (120, 121).

SECT. 28. *Guardianship and Introduction of the Order of Agnates* (pp. 121–126).—Impossibility of extending the gentile guardianships of the patricians to the citizens generally (121, 122). Agnatic guardianship substituted by the Decemvirs (122). Agnation defined and illustrated

(123, 124). Order of devolution of tutory over females and male pupils under the Tables (124, 125). The office of a tutor (125). Curatory of lunatics and spendthrifts (125, 126).

SECT. 29. *Capitis Deminutio* (pp. 126-131).—*Caput* and *capitis deminutio*—what? (126, 127). Various degrees of *capitis deminutio* (127). *Cap. dem. minima* in particular (128-131). It was change of family, but not necessarily of *status* in the family (129). It dissolved *patria potestas* and agnation (130), and extinguished claims of creditors of the *capite minutus* (131).

SECT. 30. *Mancipation and the Law of Property* (pp. 131-149).—Was there under the Tables any quiritarian ownership (*manus*) of *res nec mancipi*? (131, 132). Natural and civil modes of acquiring property (133). Mancipation of *res mancipi* (133-143). Changes on the Servian *mancipium* consequent on the introduction of coined money (134, 135). Effect of mancipation in passing property (135). Transferrer's *auctoritas* or obligation to maintain his title (136-138). Statutory limitation of the *auctoritas* (138). *Leges mancipii* or concurrent engagements of transferrer and transferee (139). The *fiducia* or *lex fiduciae* in particular (140-142). *Usureceptio fiduciae* (142, 143). Did mancipation avail to transfer ownership of *res nec mancipi*? (143). In *jure cessio* (144). Adjudication (145). Usucapion (145, 146). Offences against property (146-148). *Jura in re aliena* (148-149).

SECT. 31. *Nexum and the Law of Obligations* (pp. 149-166).—Sources of obligation, and preponderance in the XII Tables of obligations *ex delicto* (149). Mere agreement, unclothed in legal word and form, not creative of civil obligation (150, 151). Conservatism in matters of form (151). The contracts of the earliest *jus civile* (151). *Nexum* in particular (152-162). Its origin (152). The ceremonial (153). Effects of the nexal contract (154-157). The creditor's right of *manus injectio* under the XII Tables (157, 158). The *nexus* (or nexal debtor) in detention (158-160). Abuses of the system (160). Its practical abolition by the Poetilian law (161, 162). Ordinary engagements,—how their fulfilment was guaranteed (163-165). Obligations *ex re* (166).

SECT. 32. *The Law of Succession* (pp. 166-180).—Testamentary succession (166-172). The old forms of testament and the "uti legassit" of the Tables (166, 167). The testament *per aes et libram* in its inchoate condition (167-169). Its second and third stages (169, 170). Application to it of the "uti legassit" (171). Necessity of institution or disherison of the testator's *sui heredes* (171). Intestate succession,—*sui heredes, adgnati, gentiles* (172). Succession of agnates introduced by the Decemvirs to meet the case of non-patrician citizens (172). Limitations (173). *Résumé* (173, 174). Necessary and voluntary heirs, and how an inheritance vested in them (174, 175). Representation, *consortium*, and accrual (175, 176). "Heres eadem persona cum defuncto" (177). The heir and the family *sacra* (178). *Usucapio pro herede* (179, 180).

CHAPTER IV.

JUDICIAL PROCEDURE UNDER THE DECEMVIRAL SYSTEM.

SECT. 33. *The Legis Actiones generally* (pp. 181-186).—Gaius's account of them (181, 182). The five *genera agendi* (183). Preliminary *in jus vocatio* (183, 184). Proceedings *in jure* and *in judicio* (184, 185). Centumviral court, *unus judex*, and *tres arbitri* (185, 186).

SECT. 34. *The Legis Actio Sacramento* (pp. 186-197).—General idea (187). The procedure in vindication of land (179-191). The *manus consertio* (188-190). The *sacramento provocatio*, &c. (190, 191). The judgment (190). What did it all mean? (192-194). Effect of the judgment (194, 195). Application of the sacramental action in other cases (195-197).

SECT. 35. *The Legis Actio per Judicis Postulationem* (pp. 197-201).

SECT. 36. *The Legis Actio per Manus Injectionem* (pp. 201-214).—Gellius's description of it (201-203). Against whom employed (203-205). Procedure when against a judgment-debtor (205-207). "Capite poenas dabat" and "partis secanto,"—meaning (207-210). Attempted reconstruction of provisions of XII Tables on subject (211). Effect of the Poetilian law (211, 212). *Man. injectio pro judicato* and *pura* (213, 214)]

SECT. 37. *The Legis Actio per Pignoris Capionem* (pp. 214-217).

SECT. 38. *Judicial and Quasi-Judicial Procedure outside the Legis Actiones* (pp. 217-225).—Magisterial intervention in exercise of the *imperium* (217-219). Plebeian processes before the *judices decemviri* (219, 220). Pontifical jurisdiction (221, 222). Censorial, familiar, and gentile intervention (222, 223). International *recuperatio* (223-225).

CHAPTER V.

THE STIPULATION AND THE LEGIS ACTIO PER CONDICTIONEM.

SECT. 39. *Introduction of the Stipulation* (pp. 226-229).—Its importance in the history of the law (226, 227). Theories as to its origin (227, 228). Its forms—*sponsio* (σπένδειν and σπονδή), *promissio*, &c. (228, 229). A formal contract (229).

SECT. 40. *The Silian and Calpurnian Laws* (pp. 229-232).—The Silian law apparently a result of the Poetilian. Its *sponsio et restipulatio tertiae partis* the earliest statutory sanction of stipulation. The Calpurnian law.

SECT. 41. *The Legis Actio per Condictionem* (pp. 232-235).—Introduced by the Silian and Calpurnian laws. Its advantages. Procedure.

PART III.
THE JUS GENTIUM AND JUS HONORARIUM.
(*Latter Half of the Republic.*)

CHAPTER I.

THE INFLUENCES THAT OPERATED ON THE LAW.

SECT. 42. *Growth of Commerce and Influx of Foreigners* (pp. 239-242). — Necessary consequence,—commencement of a *jus gentium*. This chiefly in contract, but more or less affected all branches of the law. Illustrations.

SECT. 43. *Institution of the Peregrin Prætorship* (pp. 242-244).—The urban prætorship. Date of, and reasons for, the introduction of the peregrin prætorship. Relation of the new magistrate to his urban colleague.

SECT. 44. *Simplification of Procedure and Introduction of New Remedies under the Aebutian Law* (pp. 244, 245).—Probable purpose of the Aebutian law. Result,—the formular system of procedure. Characteristic of the new system.

SECT. 45. *Provincial Conquests* (pp. 245, 246).—Roman officials brought face to face with new institutions. Some of these imported to Rome.

SECT. 46. *Spread of Literature and Philosophy* (pp. 246, 247).—Aided equity. This not confined to prætors and their edict.

SECT. 47. *Decline of Religion and Morals* (pp. 248-251).—Effects on domestic relations (248-250). Divorce and *judicium de moribus*. Inofficious testaments and introduction of the law of legitim. Effects in social and mercantile life (250, 251). New guarantees in contracting. Bankruptcy arrangements. Measures for repressing fraudulent dealings.

CHAPTER II.

FACTORS OF THE LAW.

SECT. 48. *Legislation* (p. 252).—Paucity of legislative enactments affecting the private law. Some of the more important (in foot-note).

SECT. 49. *Edicts of the Magistrates* (pp. 253-258).—Antiquity of practice of publishing edicts (253). The urban prætor's edict (253-257). *Edicta repentina* and *perpetua*. *Edictum tralaticium*. Its gradual enlargement. Edict proper and appendix of styles. Forms of the edictal provisions. The edicts of the peregrin prætor, the provincial governors, and the curule ædiles (257, 258).

SECT. 50. *Consuetude, Professional Jurisprudence, and Res Judicatae* (pp. 258-264).—The making of custom (258-261). The pontiffs and their "interpretatio" (261, 262). The *Jus Flavianum*, Tiberius Coruncanius, and the *Jus Aelianum* (262). The "veteres" of the later republic (263, 264).

CHAPTER III.

SUBSTANTIVE CHANGES IN THE LAW DURING THE PERIOD.

SECT. 51. *Citizens, Latins, and Peregrins* (pp. 265, 266). *Jus Latii* and colonial latins. Peregins of lower grade.

SECT. 52. *The Law of Property and the Publician Edict* (pp. 266-271). —Changes in the law of property and of *jura in re aliena* generally (266-268). The Publician edict and the defects it was introduced to remove (268-271). Results,—the introduction of the *in bonis* (or bonitarian) tenure of *res mancipi* (269, 270), and of *bonae fidei possessio* as a fictitious property (271).

SECT. 53. *Development of the Law of Contract* (pp. 271-287).—Development of the law of obligation generally (272). Popularisation of the stipulation (273). Indefinite stipulations, the *stipulatio Aquiliana*, and prætorian and judicial stipulations (274). The *nomen transscripticium* or *literarum obligatio* (275-278). Evolution of the purely consensual contracts (278). Sale as an example: its beginnings (279). Sale in the XII Tables (280). How aided *per aes et libram* (280, 281). How aided by *nomina transscripticia*, ancillary stipulations, &c. (282, 283). The *actio empti* originally an *actio ex stipulatu* (284). It becomes a *bonae fidei* action (285). Thereby sale becomes an independent consensual contract (285, 286). The real contracts (286, 287).

SECT. 54. *Amendments on the Law of Succession* (pp. 288-294).— Changes effected by legislation, *interpretatio*, and practice of the centumviral court (288). Prætorian *bonorum possessio* (289-294). Nature and probable origin (289). *Bonor. poss. secundum tabulas* (289-291). *Bonor. poss. contra tabulas* (291, 292). *Bonor. poss. ab intestato* (292). Prætorian order of intestate succession (293). Admission of *cognati* (293, 294). How *bonor. possessio* obtained (294). Its immediate effect (294).

CONTENTS. xv

PART IV.
THE JUS NATURALE AND MATURITY OF ROMAN JURISPRUDENCE.
(*The Empire until the Time of Diocletian.*)

CHAPTER I.
CHARACTERISTICS AND FORMATIVE AGENCIES OF THE LAW DURING THE PERIOD.

SECT. 55. *Characteristics generally, and Recognition of a "Jus Naturale" in Particular* (pp. 297-301).—Nature of the changes on the law during the period (297, 298). Many of them not to be accounted for by advance of *jus gentium*, but due to growth of *jus naturale* (298, 299). Characteristics and fundamental principles of latter (299-301). *Naturalis ratio* (301).

SECT. 56. *Influence of Constitutional Changes* (p. 302).

SECT. 57. *Legislation of Comitia and Senate* (pp. 302-307).—Comitial legislation of Augustus regarding marriage (and herein of the *lex Julia et Papia Poppaea*), manumission, and judicial procedure. Legislation of the senate from time of Tiberius onwards.

SECT. 58. *The Consolidated Edictum Perpetuum* (pp. 307-310).—History of the Julian consolidation. Its contents and arrangement.

SECT. 59. *Responses of Patented Counsel* (pp. 310-312).—Origin of the *jus respondendi*. Value of the *responsa*. Their regulation by Hadrian.

SECT. 60. *Constitutions of the Emperors* (pp. 312-314).—*Edicta*, their character at this time. *Rescripta* and *decreta*.

CHAPTER II.
JURISPRUDENCE.

SECT. 61. *Labeo and Capito, and the Schools of the Proculians and Sabinians* (pp. 315-318).

SECT. 62. *Julian, Gaius, and the Antoninian Jurists* (pp. 318-323).— Salvius Julianus (318, 319). Sextus Pomponius (319). Sextus Caecilius Africanus (320). Gaius (320-322). Q. Cervidius Scævola (322, 323).

SECT. 63. *Papinian, Ulpian, and Paul* (323-326).—Æmilius Papinianus (323, 324). Domitius Ulpianus (325). Julius Paulus (326).

SECT. 64. *Modestine and the Post-Severan Jurists*(326-328).—Herennius Modestinus. Paucity of jurisprudential literature after reign of Alexander Severus. Excellence of many of the rescripts of Gordian and Diocletian.

SECT. 65. *Remains of the Jurisprudence of the Period* (pp. 328-335).— The Institutes of Gaius and the Verona Codex (328-331). Part of

Ulpian's *Liber Regularum* (331). Paul's "Sentences" (332). The *Notae Juris* of Valerius Probus, the *Assis distributio* of Maecianus, the Dosithean fragment on manumissions, and the *Fragmentum de jure fisci* (333, 334). Minor fragments (334, 335).

CHAPTER III.

SUBSTANTIVE CHANGES IN THE LAW DURING THE PERIOD.

SECT. 66. *Citizenship, Junian Latinity, and Peregrinity* (336–341).— The inductive cause of the Aelia-Sentian law (336, 337). Its provisions (337). The Junia-Norban law and the Junian latins (338, 339). Caracalla's grant of citizenship to all his free subjects (340, 341).

SECT. 67. *Concession of Peculiar Privileges to Soldiers* (341–345).— Exceptional position of soldiers (341). The *testamentum militare* (342–344). The *peculium castrense* (344, 345).

SECT. 68. *The Family* (pp. 345–349).—Husband and wife, and the disappearance of marital *manus* (345, 346). Parent and child, and relaxation of the *patria potestas* (346, 347). Tutory, and disappearance of that of women (348). Curatory, and institution of that of minors (348, 349).

SECT. 69. *Possession, Property, Real Rights, and Obligations* (pp. 349–351).

SECT. 70. *The Law of Succession, and particularly Testamentary Trusts* (pp. 351–356).—Testamentary succession (351). Legacies and the *Senatusconsultum Neronianum* (352). *Fideicommissa* (*mortis causa* trusts), universal and singular (353, 354). Codicils (355). Intestate succession and the Tertullian and Orphitian senatusconsults (335, 336).

CHAPTER IV.

JUDICIAL PROCEDURE.

SECT. 71. *The Formular System* (pp. 357–367).—Characteristic (357). The Aebutian and Julian laws (357). Transition from earlier system,— in personal actions by simplification of the procedure *per condictionem* (358–360), and in *vindicationes* by the introduction of that *per sponsionem* (360), paving the way for the *formula petitoria* (361). *Formulae in jus* and *in factum conceptae* (361, 362). *Actiones utiles* (362). *Actiones ficticiae* (362, 363). *Actiones in factum* (364). *Actiones arbitrariae* (364, 365). *Exceptiones*, &c. (366, 367). Elasticity of the *formula* (367).

SECT. 72. *Procedure "Extra Ordinem"* (pp. 368, 369).—The *extraordinaria cognitio* and what occasioned it.

SECT. 73. *Jural Remedies Flowing Directly from the Magistrate's Imperium* (pp. 369–375).—Interdicts (370–372). *Uti possidetis* and *utrubi* in particular (371, 372). Prætorian stipulations (372, 373). *Missione in possessionem* (373, 374). *In integrum restitutio* (374, 375).

PART V.
THE PERIOD OF CODIFICATION.
(Diocletian to Justinian.)

CHAPTER I.
HISTORICAL EVENTS THAT INFLUENCED THE LAW.

SECT. 74. *Supremacy of the Emperors as Sole Legislators* (pp. 379–381). —The *leges generales* or *edictales* of the later empire.
SECT. 75. *Establishment of Christianity as the State Religion* (pp. 381–384).—Its influence generally (381, 382). Repeal of the caduciary provisions of the Julian and Papia-Poppaean law (382). Legislation about divorce (382, 383). Institution of the bishop's courts (383, 384).
SECT. 76. *Social and Agrarian Changes* (pp. 384–387).—In particular, the recognition and regulation of the colonate (or servitude of the glebe).
SECT. 77. *Abandonment of the Formular System of Procedure* (pp. 387–390).—Abolition of the two-staged procedure (1) *in jure* and (2) *in judicio*, and remit to a *judex* allowed only exceptionally (387, 388). The ordinary *fora* (388). The new procedure *per libellum conventionis*, &c. (389). Execution (389, 390).
SECT. 78. *The Valentinian "Law of Citations"* (pp. 390, 391).—Scientific jurisprudence gives place to mechanical.

CHAPTER II.
ANTE-JUSTINIANIAN COLLECTIONS OF STATUTE AND JURISPRUDENCE.

SECT. 79. *The Gregorian and Hermogenian Codes* (pp. 392, 393).
SECT. 80. *The Theodosian Code and Post-Theodosian Novels* (pp. 393–395).
SECT. 81. *The "Collatio," the Vatican Fragments, and the "Consultatio"* (pp. 395–397).—The *Collatio Legum Mosaicarum et Romanarum* (395). The Vatican Fragments (396). The *consultatio veteris jurisconsulti* (397).
SECT. 82. *The Romano-Barbarian Codes* (pp. 397–399).—The *Edictum Theodorici* (397). The *Breviarium Alaricianum* or *Lex Romana Visigothorum* (398). The *Lex Romana Burgundionum* (399).
SECT. 83. *Oriental Collections* (401, 402).—Bernardakis's Sinaitic papyri. The Syrian "*Leges Constantini, Theodosii, et Leonis.*"

b

CHAPTER III.

THE JUSTINIANIAN LAW.

SECT. 84. *Justinian's Collections and his own Legislation* (pp. 402–414). —Justinian (402). Chronology of his collections (403). His first Code of statute-law (403, 404). His commission for preparation of the Digest (404–406). The *Quinquaginta Decisiones* (406). The Institutes (406, 407). Publication of the Digest (407). Its divisions, and the sources drawn upon (408, 409). The order of sequence of books, titles, and fragments (409–411). The *Codex Repetitae Praelectionis* or second edition of his Code of statute-law (411). Its relation to the Digest (412). Its sources (413). The Novels (413). Characteristics of Justinian's own enactments (414).

SECT. 85. *Changes in the Law of the Family* (pp. 414–419).—Husband and wife—marriage, divorce, *dos*, and *donatio propter nuptias* (415, 416). Parent and child—still greater relaxation of the *patria potestas*, personally and patrimonially (416–418). Amendments in other branches of the law of the family—adoption, legitimation, emancipation, tutory, slavery, manumission (418, 419).

SECT. 86. *Changes in the Law of Property and Obligation* (pp. 419–422).—Abolition of distinction between *res mancipi* and *nec mancipi* and quiritarian and bonitarian ownership, and simple tradition made the universal mode of conveyance (419, 420). Usucapion and long possession remodelled (420). Emphyteusis sanctioned and regulated (420, 421). Changes in the law of obligation (421).

SECT. 87. *Changes in the Law of Succession* (pp. 422–426).—Testaments and codicils (422, 423). Amendments in the law of intestate succession prior to the publication of the Code (423). The 118th and 127th Novels, eradicating agnation and settling a new order of succession on intestacy (423, 424). Declaration of a child's right to be his parent's heir in a certain share of his estate, and practical abolition of *bonorum possessio contra tabulas* (424, 425). Other amendments (425, 426).

CHAPTER IV.

THE JUSTINIANIAN LAW-BOOKS.

SECT. 88. *Their Use in the Courts and the Schools* (pp. 427–430).— Translations, abridgements, &c., of Digest and Code (427, 428). New course of study for the law-schools (429). Greek paraphrase of the Institutes imputed to Theophilus (430).

SECT. 89. *Their Fate in the East* (pp. 430–432).—The Byzantine jurisprudence, and particularly the Basilica.

SECT. 90. *Their Fate in the West* (pp. 432–443).—The Romano-Barbarian Codes the earliest instructors of Central and Western Europe in Roman law (432). Transmission of Justinian's collections to Italy (432, 433). Literary indications of their currency there and elsewhere in Southern Europe between the sixth and eleventh centuries (433, 434). Revival of their study at Bologna, and their treatment by the glossarists (434, 435).

SECT. 91. *The Principal Manuscripts, Texts, and Editions of the Justinianian Books* (pp. 435–439).

APPENDIX.

NOTE A. On the use of the word *cognati* by the lay writers (p. 441).
NOTE B. On *coemptio* (pp. 441–443).
NOTE C. On the definitions of *nexum* by Mamilius, Quint. Mucius, and Ael. Gallus (pp. 443 *sq.*)
NOTE D. Ihering on the effect of the *lex Papiria* (*de sacramentis exigundis*) on the sacramental procedure (pp. 444 *sq.*)
NOTE E. On the deposit of the sacramental sheep, cattle, or money *ad pontem* (p. 445).
NOTE F. Argument from the *L. colon. Juliae Genetivae* that the *aes confessum* of the XII Tables meant nexal loan (p. 445 *sq.*)
NOTE G. Kohler on the *partis secanto* of the XII Tables (p. 446 *sq.*)
NOTE H. Cicero's anecdote of Canius and Pythius, as illustrative of the operation of the *nomen transscripticium* (pp. 447 *sq.*)

ADDENDUM.

On p. 186, l. 13, after "however," *insert*—" unless, perhaps, when they arose under a *lex mancipii* (p. 139)."

ABBREVIATIONS IN REFERENCES TO LITERATURE.

Arch. Giurid.—Archivio Giuridico, diretto di Filippo Serafini (Prof. in Pisa). Bologna, and now Pisa, 1868-86; vol. xxxvii. current.
Baron, *Gesch. d. R. R.*—Geschichte des Römischen Rechts, von Dr. J. Baron (Prof. in Berne). Erster Theil: Institutionen u. Civilprozess. Berlin, 1884. Vol. ii. not yet published.
Bekker, *Aktionen* (or *Akt.*)—Die Aktionen des Röm. Privatrechts, von Dr. E. I. Bekker (Prof. in Heidelberg). 2 vols. Berlin, 1871, 1873.
Bekker u. Muther's Jahrb.—Jahrbuch d. gemeinen deutschen Rechts, herausg. von Bekker, Muther, u. Stobbe. 6 vols. Leipsic, 1857-63.
Bethmann-Hollweg, *Röm. CP.* (or *Gesch. d. CP.*)—Der Röm. Civilprozess, von (†) Dr. A. v. Bethmann-Hollweg. 3 vols. Bonn, 1864-66. (They form the first three of his 6 vols. on the Civilprozess des gemeinen Rechts, Bonn, 1864-74.)
Bruns (or Bruns, *Fontes*).—Fontes Juris romani antiqui ed. (†) Car. Geo. Bruns. 4th ed. Tübingen, 1879.
Buonamici, *Procedura.*—La Storia della Procedura civile Romana, per Francisco Buonamici (Prof. in Pisa). Vol. i. Pisa, 1886. Vol. ii. not yet published.
Burckhard-Glück.—Glück's Ausführliche Erläuterung d. Pandekten ... fortgesetzt von ... Dr. Hugo Burckhard (Prof. in Würzburg). Serie d. Bücher 39. u. 40. (As yet 3 vols.) Erlangen, 1871-81.
Clark, *Early Rom. Law.*—Early Roman Law : the Regal Period, by E. C. Clark, LL.D. (Prof. in Cambridge). London, 1872.
Clark, *Pract. Jurisprud.*—Practical Jurisprudence : a Comment on Austin, by the same author. Cambridge, 1883.
Cod. (or *Cod. Just.*)—Codex Justiniani Augusti. See *infra*, p. 438.
Collatio.—Lex Dei, sive Mosaicarum et Romanarum legum collatio. See *infra*, p. 396.
Collect. libror. jur. antejust.—Collectio librorum juris antejustiniani in usum scholarum. Edid. P. Krueger, Th. Mommsen, G. Stude-

ABBREVIATIONS. xxi

mund. (As yet 2 vols.) Vol. i., 2d ed., Berlin, 1884 ; vol. ii., 1st ed., Berlin, 1878.
Corp. jur. rom. antejust.—Corp. Juris Romani Antejustiniani, consilio Böckingii, Bethmann-Hollwegii, Puggaei, aliorumque institutum. Bonn, 1831-44.
Danz, *Gesch. d. R. R.*—Lehrbuch der Geschichte d. Röm. Rechts, von (†) Dr. H. A. A. Danz. 2d ed., 2 vols. Leipsic, 1871, 1873.
Danz, *Sacrale Schutz.*—Der sacrale Schutz im Röm. Rechtsverkehr, by the same author. Jena, 1857.
Dig.—Digesta (or Pandectae) Justiniani Augusti. See *infra*, p. 438.
Dirksen, *Hinterlass. Schrift.* — Heinrich Ed. Dirksen's Hinterlassene Schriften zur Kritik u. Auslegung d. Quellen Römischer Rechtsgeschichte, herausg. von Dr. Fr. D. Sanio. 2 vols. Leipsic, 1871.
Ferrini, *Fonti.*—Storia delle Fonti del Diritto Romano, e della Giurisprudenza Romana, di Contardo Ferrini (Prof. in Pavia). Milan, 1885.
Fustel de Coulanges.—La Cité Antique : étude sur le culte, le droit, les institutions de la Grèce et de Rome. 7th ed. Paris, 1879.
Gai.—Gaii Institutionum libri iv. See *infra*, p. 330.
Gaii Epit. — Gaii Epitomes Institutionum libri ii. In the Lex Romana Visigothorum ; see *infra*, p. 398.
Genz.—Das Patricische Rom, von Dr. Hermann Genz. Berlin, 1878.
Glück-Burckhard. See Burckhard-Glück.
Glück-Leist.—Glück's Erläuterungen d. Pandekten . . . fortgesetzt von Dr. Burkard Wilh. Leist (Prof. in Jena). Serie d. Bücher 37. u. 38. (As yet 5 vols.) Erlangen, 1870-79.
Grünhut's ZSchr.—Zeitschrift für das privat- und öffentliche-Recht der Gegenwart, unter Mitwirkung d. Wiener jurist. Facultät, herausg. von Dr. C. S. Grünhut. Vienna, 1874-86. Vol. xiii. current.
Hölder, *Erbrecht.*—Beiträge zur Geschichte d. Röm. Erbrechts, von Dr. Ed. Hölder (Prof. in Erlangen). Erlangen, 1881.
Huschke, *Jurisprud. Antejust.*—Jurisprudentiae Antejustinianae quae supersunt. In usum max. academ. compos. recens. adnot. (†) Ph. Ed. Huschke. 4th ed., Leipsic, 1879.
Huschke, *Multa.*—Die Multa u. das Sacramentum in ihren verschiedenen Anwendungen, by the same author. Leipsic, 1874.
Huschke, *Nexum.*—Ueber das Recht des Nexum u. d. alte röm. Schuldrecht, by the same author. Leipsic, 1846.
Huschke, *Studien.*—Studien des Römischen Rechts, by the same author. Breslau, 1830.
Ihering, *Geist.*—Geist d. röm. Rechts auf d. verschiedenen Stufen seiner Entwickelung, von Dr. Rudolph von Ihering (Prof. in Göttingen). As yet 4 vols., in several editions. Made use of in the following pages :—Vol. i., 3d ed., Leips., 1873 ; vol. ii., 2d ed., 1866 ; vol. iii., 2d ed., 1869 ; vol. iv., 2d ed., 1871. There is a French translation by Meulenaere, revised by the author, in 4 vols., Paris, 1877-78.

ABBREVIATIONS.

Ihering, *Scherz u. Ernst.*—Scherz und Ernst in der Jurisprudenz, by the same author. 2d ed. Leipsic, 1885.
Ihering, *Zweck.*—Der Zweck im Recht, by the same author. (As yet) 2 vols. Leipsic, 1877, 1883.
Inst.—Justiniani Institutiones. See *infra*, p. 436.
Jurisprud. Antejust. See Huschke.
Karlowa, *Röm. CP.*—Der römische Civilprozess zur Zeit d. Legisactionen, von Dr. Otto Karlowa (Prof. in Heidelberg). Berlin, 1872.
Karlowa, *Röm. Ehe.*—Die Formen d. Röm. Ehe u. Manus, by the same author. Bonn, 1868.
Karlowa, *Röm. RG.*—Römische Rechtsgeschichte, Erster Band : Staatsrecht u. Rechtsquellen. By the same author. Leipsic, 1885. (Vol. ii. not yet published.)
Keller, *Röm. CP.*—Der Röm. Civilprocess u. die Actionen, von (†) Dr. Fried. Lud. von Keller. 1st ed., 1852 ; 6th ed., by Wach, Berlin, 1883.
Kohler, *Shakespeare.*—Shakespeare vor dem Forum der Jurisprudenz, von Dr. Jos. Kohler (Prof. in Würzburg). Würzburg, 1884.
Krit. VJS. (or *VJSchr.*)—Kritische Vierteljahrsschrift für Gesetzgebung u. Rechtswissenschaft, herausg. von Windscheid, Bekker, Brinz, Seydel, &c. Munich, 1853–86. Vol. xxiii. (ix. of new series) current.
Kuntze, *Cursus.*—Cursus des Röm. Rechts, von. Dr. Joh. Emil Kuntze (Prof. in Leipsic). 2d ed., Leipsic, 1879.
Kuntze, *Excurse.*—Excurse über Röm. Recht, by the same author. 2d ed., Leipsic, 1880.
Lange, *Röm. Alt.*—Römische Alterthümer, von Dr. Ludwig Lange. 3 vols. Berlin, 1863–71, and subsequently.
Leist, *Bonor. Poss.*—Die Bonorum Possessio : ihre geschichtliche Entwickelung, &c., dargestellt von Dr. Burkhard Wilh. Leist (Prof. in Jena). 2 vols. Göttingen, 1844.
Leist-Glück : see Glück-Leist.
Leist, *Graeco-ital. RG.*—Graeco-italische Rechtsgeschichte, by the same author. Jena, 1884.
Lenel, *Beiträge.*—Beiträge zur Kunde des Praetorischen Edicts, von Dr. Otto Lenel (Prof. in Kiel). Stuttgart, 1878.
Lenel, *Edict.*—Das Edictum Perpetuum : ein Versuch zu dessen Wiederherstellung, by the same author. Leipsic, 1883.
Maine, *Anc. Law.*—Ancient Law : its Connection with the Early History of Society, &c., by Sir Henry Sumner Maine (1st ed., 1861), 9th ed., London, 1883.
Marculf.—Marculfi monachi Formularum libri ii. Lut. Par., 1513. (Many editions.)
Marquardt, *Röm. Staatsverwalt.* — Römische Staatsverwaltung, von Joachim Marquardt. 3 vols. Leipsic, 1873–78. (Vols. iv.-vi. of his and Mommsen's Handbuch d. Röm. Alterthümer.)

Mommsen, *Röm. Forsch.*—Römische Forschungen, von Th. Mommsen. 2 vols. Berlin, 1864, 1879.

Mommsen, *Röm. Staatsrecht* (or *SR.*)—Römisches Staatsrecht, by the same author. 2 vols. (Vol. iii. not yet published.) Leipsic, 1871–75, and later editions. (Vols. i. and ii. of Marquardt and M.'s Handbuch d. Röm. Alterthümer.)

Moyle, *Inst.*—Imp. Just. Institution. libri iv. with English commentary, &c., by J. B. Moyle, B.C.L. 2 vols. Oxford, 1883.

Nouv. Rev. Hist.—Nouvelle Revue Historique de Droit Français et Étranger, publ. sous la direction de Laboulaye, de Rozière, Dareste, Gide, Esmein, &c. (Continuation of the Revue de Législation, &c.) Paris, 1877–86. Vol. x. current.

Nov.—Novellae Constitutiones Justiniani. See *infra*, p. 439.

Paul.—Pauli Sententiae. See *infra*, p. 332.

Pernice, *Labeo.*—Marcus Antistius Labeo : das röm. Privatrecht im ersten Jahrhunderte d. Kaiserzeit, von Dr. Alfred Pernice (Prof. in Greifswald). (As yet) 2 vols. Halle, 1873, 1878.

Puchta, *Inst.*—Cursus der Institutionen d. Röm. Rechts, von (†) Dr. G. F. Puchta ; 8. Aufl., besorgt von Dr. Paul Krüger (Prof. in Königsberg). 2 vols. Leipsic, 1875.

Rev. de Législat.—Revue de Législation ancienne et moderne, publ. sous la direction de Laboulaye, de Rozière, et Dareste. (Continuation of the Revue Historique de Droit Français et Étranger.) 6 vols. Paris, 1870–76.

Richter's Krit. Jahrb. (or *JB.*).—Kritische Jahrbücher für deutsche Rechtswissenschaft, herausg. von Dr. Aem. Lud. Richter. 12 vols. Leipsic, 1837–48.

Rivier, *Introd.*—Introduction historique au Droit Romain, par Dr. Alphonse Rivier (Prof. in Brussels). 2d ed. Brussels, 1881.

Roby, *Introd.*—An Introduction to the Study of Justinian's Digest, &c., by H. J. Roby, M.A. (formerly Prof. of Jurisprud. in Univ. Coll., London). Cambridge, 1884.

Rossbach, *Röm. Ehe.*—Untersuchungen über die röm. Ehe, von Dr. Aug. Rossbach, Stuttgart, 1853.

Rudorff, *Röm. RG.*—Römische Rechtsgeschichte zum akademischen Gebrauch, von (†) Dr. Ad. Fr. Rudorff. 2 vols. Leipsic, 1857, 1858.

Savigny, *Gesch.*—Geschichte d. Röm. Rechts im Mittelalter, von Fried. Carl von Savigny. 2d ed., 7 vols. Heidelberg, 1834–51.

Savigny, *System.*—System des heutigen Röm. Rechts, by the same author. 8 vols. Berlin, 1840–49.

Savigny, *Verm. Schr.*—Vermischte Schriften, by the same author. 5 vols. Berlin, 1850.

Sohm, *Inst. d. R.R.*—Institutionen des Röm. Rechts, von Dr. Rudolph Sohm (Prof. in Strasburg). Leipsic, 1884, (2d ed. 1886).

Theod. Cod.—Theodosianus Codex. See *infra*, p. 395.

Theoph.—Theophili Antecessoris Paraphrasis Graeca Institutionum

Caesarearum. Standard edition that of Reitz, 2 vols., Hag. Com., 1751. New ed. by E. C. Ferrini (Prof. in Pavia), 2 vols., Berlin, 1884–85 ; (2d not yet completed).

Ulp.—Ulpiani Fragmenta ex libro singulari Regularum. See *infra*, p. 331.

Vat. Frag.—Vaticana Fragmenta. See *infra*, p. 396.

Voigt, *Jus nat.*—Das jus naturale, aequum et bonum, und jus gentium der Römer, von Dr. Moritz Voigt (Prof. in Leipsic). 4 vols. Leipsic, 1856–75.

Voigt, *XII Tafeln.*—Die XII Tafeln. Geschichte u. System d. Civil-und Criminal-Rechtes, wie Processes, der XII Tafeln, nebst deren Fragmenten, by the same author. 2 vols. Leipsic, 1883.

Z. d. Sav. Stift., R. A.—Zeitschrift der Savigny Stiftung für Rechtsgeschichte, herausg. von Bruns, Bekker, v. Roth, Böhlau, Pernice, &c. (Continuation of the *Z. f. RG.*) Weimar, 1880–86. Vol. vii. current. Each vol. contains a Romanistische and a Germanistische Abtheilung, separately paged ; R. A. stands for the former.

Z. f. gesch. RW.—Zeitschrift für geschichtliche Rechtswissenschaft, herausg. von F. C. v. Savigny, Göschen, Rudorff, &c. 15 vols. Berlin, 1815–50.

Z. f. RG.—Zeitschrift für Rechtsgeschichte, herausg. von Rudorff, Bruns, v. Roth, &c. 13 vols. Weimar, 1861–78.

Z. f. vergl. RW.—Zeitschrift für vergleichende Rechtswissenschaft, herausg. von Bernhöft, Cohn, Kohler, &c. Stuttgart, 1878–86. Vol. vii. current.

PART I.
THE REGAL PERIOD.

PART I.
THE REGAL PERIOD.[1]

CHAPTER FIRST.
SOCIAL AND POLITICAL CONDITION OF ROME AND ITS POPULATION DOWN TO THE TIME OF SERVIUS TULLIUS.

SECTION 1.—GENESIS OF THE ROMAN STATE.

THE union of the Latin, Sabine, and, to a small extent, Etruscan bands that, as conquerors or conquered, old settlers or new immigrants, together constituted the first elements of the Roman people, did not necessarily involve contemporaneous adoption of identical institutions or identical notions of law. Though descended from the same Indo-European stock, and inheriting the same primitive ideas about religion and government, yet those ideas must have been more or less modified in the course of centuries of separate and independent development.[2] It is said that the

[1] See especially Puchta, *Cursus der Institutionen d. Röm. Rechts* (1st ed., Leipsic, 1841), 8th ed. by Krüger, Leipsic, 1875, vol. i. §§ 36-50 ; Clark, *Early Roman Law: Regal Period*, London, 1872 ; Genz, *Das Patricische Rom*, Berlin, 1878 ; Kuntze, *Cursus der Institutionen*, 2d ed., Leipsic, 1879, §§ 47-68 ; Bernhöft, *Staat und Recht der Röm. Königszeit im Verhältniss zu verwandten Rechten*, Stuttgart, 1882.

[2] The Aryan origin of several of the most important religious notions and public and private institutions of early Rome, and their resemblance to corresponding ones in India and Greece, have been shown by Fustel de Coulanges, *La Cité Antique* (1st ed., Paris, 1857), 7th ed., 1879 ; Sir H. S. Maine, *Ancient Law* (1st ed., London, 1862), 9th ed., 1883 ; Bernhöft, as above ; Leist, *Graeco-Italische Rechtsgeschichte*, Jena, 1884.

characteristic of the Latin race was its sense of the importance of discipline, and the homage it paid to power and might; that of the Sabines, their religious feeling and their reverence for the gods; that of the Etruscans, their subservience to forms and ceremonies in matters both divine and human. Corresponding influences are very manifest in the growth of Rome's early public institutions, civil, military, and religious. It does not seem too much to say that they are traceable also in the institutions of the private law. The *patria potestas*, with the father's power of life and death over his children; the *manus* and the husband's power over his wife; the doctrine that those things chiefly was a man entitled to call his own which he had taken by the strength of his arm;[3] the right which a creditor had of apprehending and imprisoning his defaulting debtor, and, if need were, reducing him to slavery,—all these seem to point to a persuasion that might made right. The religious marriage ceremony, and the recognition of the wife as mistress of the household and participant in its sacred offices as well as its domestic cares; the family council of kinsmen, maternal as well as paternal, who advised the *paterfamilias* in the exercise of the domestic jurisdiction; the practice of adoption, on purpose to prevent the extinction of a family and deprivation of its deceased members of the prayers and sacrifices necessary for the repose of their souls,—these seem to have flowed from a different order of ideas, and to bear evidence of Sabine descent. Etruscan influence could make itself felt only at a later date; but to it may possibly be attributed the strict regard that came to be required to the observance of ceremonials and words of style in the more important transactions both of public and private life.

While the result of the union of Latins and Sabines was

[3] "Maxime sua esse credebant quae ex hostibus cepissent" (Gai, iv. 16),—a doctrine rather pre-Roman than Roman.

that regulations were at once adopted which should apply to their public life as a united people, yet it is not only conceivable but probable that, as regarded the private relations of its members, each tribe continued for a time to accord a preference to its own ideas and traditions of right and law, and that the amalgamation was a gradual process, partly silent, partly due to regal or pontifical intervention. Just as there is little reason to believe in any nicely organised constitution down at least to the time of the Servian reforms, so is there little reason to believe in the existence of any very definite system of private law. Mixed races must, in minor matters at least, have made mixed customs and usages; and, though there is lack of material for establishing with certainty the coexistence of different systems among different branches of the population, yet it is difficult to resist the conviction that something at all events of the dualism [4] so marked in many of Rome's early institutions may be accounted for by ethnical considerations.

SECTION 2.—THE PATRICIANS.[1]

There was part of the law of Rome that got the distinctive

[4] Ihering, *Geist*, vol. i. § 19 (while tracing it to another source), has thus tabulated some of its more prominent manifestations:—

	Religious System. *Fas.*	Profane System. *Jus, vis.*
Symbol	*Aqua et ignis.*	*Hasta* (*quiris*), *manus.*
Representative . .	Numa.	Romulus.
Marriage	*Confarreatio* (*far, aqua et ignis*).	*Coemptio* (*hasta coelibaris*).'
Contract	Oath, *sacramentum, sponsio, foedus.*	Public guarantee, *mancipatio, nexum.*
Procedure . . .	*Legis actio sacramento.*	Private justice, *vindicatio, manus injectio, &c.*
Criminal law . .	*Homo sacer.*	*Vindicta publica.*
	Poena, a means of expiation.	*Poena*, a means of reparation.

[1] Ihering, *Geist*, vol. i. § 14; Genz, as above, p. 1 *sq.*; Voigt, *XII Tafeln* vol. ii. §§ 169, 170.

name of *jus Quiritium*, the law of the Spearmen. The *Quirites* were the members of the gentile houses, organised in their curies, primarily for military, and secondarily for political purposes. They alone of the settlers around the *urbs quadrata* ranked as citizens, down at least to the time of Servius Tullius. They alone could consult the gods through the medium of *auspicia*, and participate in the services offered to the tutelary deities of Rome. From their number the king drew his council of elders, and they alone could take part in the curiate comitia, the assembly of the warriors. They alone could contract a lawful marriage and make a testament; in a word, it was they alone that were entitled directly to the benefit of Rome's peculiar institutions.

But those prerogatives of the patrician burgesses were theirs as members of the gentile houses. Patrician Rome was a federation of *gentes* or clans; the clans aggregations of families, bearing a. common name, and theoretically at least tracing their descent from a common ancestor. Whether or not the traditional account of the numerical proportion of families to clans and of clans to curies have any substantial historical foundation, and whatever may be the explanation of the method by which the symmetry on which the old writers dwell with so much complacency was attained, it is beyond doubt that the gentile organisation was common to the two races at least that contributed most largely to the citizenship of Rome, and that it was made the basis of the new arrangements. Federation necessitated the appointment of a common chieftain, and common institutions, religious, military, political, and judicial. But it was long before these displaced entirely the separate institutions of the federated *gentes*. Every clan had its own cult, peculiar to its own members; this was the universal bond of association in those early times. It had its common property (p. 38) and˗ its common burial-place. It must have had some common council or assembly; for we read not only of special gentile customs, but of gentile statutes and decrees. Instances are on record of wars waged by individual *gentes;* so they must have had the right to require military service alike from their *gentiles* and *gentilicii*.[2] Widows and orphans of deceased clansmen were under the guardianship of the *gens*, or of some particular member of it to whom the trust was specially confided. If a clansman left no heirs, his property passed to his fellow-gentiles. Over the morals of its members the *gens* exercised supervision and discipline; interfering to prevent prodigality and improvidence, restraining abuses of the domestic authority, and visiting with censure, and probably in grave cases with punishment, any breach of faith or other dishonourable conduct. It is said that there is no evidence of the exercise by it of any proper jurisdiction; but, in the presence of all those other powers that it undoubtedly possessed, it is difficult to suppose that, within its own limits, it was not constantly called upon, through the medium of its chief, to act the part of peacemaker and arbiter. Finally, its members were always entitled to rely upon its assistance, to have maintenance when indigent, to be ransomed from captivity, to be upheld in their just disputes and quarrels, to be avenged when killed or injured.

How all this was worked out in detail it is impossible to say. We do not know even whether the chieftainship or presidency of a clan was hereditary or elective, and if the latter, whether for life or for a shorter term. Probably in this, as well as in other matters, there was no uniform practice. But in the gentile system there was undoubtedly an *imperium in imperio* that must for two or three centuries have exercised a powerful influence on the private law, and

---

[2] It was the heads of the constituent families of a *gens* that were properly *gentiles;* the dependent members of those families and the clients attached to them were only *gentilicii*.

that must not be lost sight of in noting the conditions that accelerated or retarded its progress.[3]

SECTION 3.—THE CLIENTS.[1]

It was very early in its history that Rome gave promise of its future eminence. Successful in one petty war after another, it deprived many small communities of their independent existence, leaving their members bereft alike of their religion, their territory, and their means of existence. These had to turn elsewhere for protection, and in large numbers they sought it from their conquerors. To many others, both voluntary immigrants and refugees from other cities, the new settlement proved a centre of attraction. It was quite ready to receive them; but as subjects only—not as citizens. Following a custom familiar to both Latins and Sabines, the new-comers invoked the protection of the heads of patrician families of repute, to whom they attached themselves as free vassals. The relationship was known as that of patron and client. It made the latter an independent member of his patron's *gens*, and thus indirectly brought him into relation to the state. But it was to his individual patron that he looked primarily for support and maintenance, and to him that his allegiance and service were due in the

[3] It deserves to be kept in mind that, with a very few exceptions, the individual patrician *gentes* were not numerically strong. Whatever may be the explanation, it seems to be the fact that, notwithstanding the admission to their ranks of the principal Alban families by Tullus Hostilius, and the creation of the *minores gentes* by the elder Tarquin, they died out so rapidly that by the end of the regal period the original three hundred had been reduced by more than a half (see Genz, *l.c.*, p. 9 *sq.*) The reported great strength of the Tarquinian and Claudian *gentes* was due to their clients; that of the Fabian may have been due to the rule in observance amongst them prohibiting the exposure of infants, and requiring all their men to marry.

[1] See Mommsen, "Die röm. Clientel," in his *Röm. Forsch.*, vol. ii. p. 355 *sq.*; Voigt, "Ueber die Clientel u. die Libertinität," in the *Berichte d. phil.-hist. Classe d. K. Sächs. Gesellsch. d. Wissensch.*, 1878, pp. 147-219; Marquardt, *Privatleben d. Römer* (Leipsic, 1879), p. 196 *sq.*; Voigt, *XII Tafeln*, vol. ii. pp. 667-679.

first instance. Dionysius describes the relation between them as of the most sacred character, the duty the patron owed to his client coming next in order to that he owed to his children and his wards. He had to provide his vassal with all that was necessary for his sustenance and that of his wife and children; and, as private holdings increased in extent, it was not unusual for the patron or his *gens* to give a client during pleasure a plot of land to cultivate for himself. The patron had, moreover, to assist his client in his transactions with third parties, obtain redress for him for his injuries, and represent him before the tribunals when he became involved in litigation. The client, on the other hand, had to maintain his patron's interests by every means in his power. What Dionysius says of his contributing to endow his patron's daughters, and the like, obviously refers to an advanced period of the history of Rome, when it sometimes happened that the position of parties, so far as wealth was concerned, was reversed; for the relation was hereditary on both sides; and there may have been instances of families that had risen to good social position and ample fortune recognising at the distance of many generations that they were still clients of patrician houses in embarrassed circumstances, and rendering them assistance as in duty bound. But in the regal period the advantage must have been chiefly on the side of the client, who, without becoming a citizen, obtained directly the protection of the patron and his clan, and indirectly that of the state.

SECTION 4.—THE PLEBEIANS.

The plebs included all those freemen who, being neither patrician citizens nor clients, had settled in Rome as permanent residents, hoping to make a living within her bounds, and enjoy *de facto* at least the benefit of her institutions. The commencement of this body, as distinct from that of the clients, is usually associated with the overthrow of Alba; the idea being that those of its population who were not of sufficient distinction to be admitted into the ranks of the patriciate, and yet were too independent to brook submission to a private patron, put themselves under the direct protection of the sovereign, and thus, as Cicero says,—though he no doubt meant the words only in a popular sense,—became royal clients. Their number is said to have been largely augmented in the ensuing reign by the conquest of many Latin towns that had broken the treaty made with them after the fall of Alba, and the removal of their inhabitants to Rome. It is very doubtful, however, whether it be possible to condescend upon any particular settlement as the origin of the plebs. It seems more consistent with history to regard them as a heterogeneous mass of non-gentile freemen, small probably in numbers at first, but augmenting with ever-greater rapidity, who had of choice or compulsion made Rome their domicile, but declined to subject themselves to a patron. Some may have been on the spot when Rome was founded, others were voluntary immigrants in pursuit of trade; some may have been refugees, exiles from earlier homes because of their misdeeds; many had been driven to seek their new shelter by the hard fate of war, which had subverted their native cities and left them godless, landless, and houseless; while in course of time there were accessions to their numbers from amongst the descendants of clients, who either were disinclined to continue their allegiance, or were relieved from it by the extinction of their patronal *gentes*.

That there was any general cohesion amongst them before the time of Servius there is not the slightest reason to believe. They were of different races, settling in Rome from different motives, practising in many matters different customs. If Livy be right in the statement he makes with every appearance of assurance that the worship of Hercules at the *ara maxima* was Greek, we may almost infer that among the earliest representatives of this class of unattached non-citizen subjects may have been some of Hellenic descent. The existence at a very early date of a *vicus Tuscus* in the valley below the Palatine speaks of the presence of a contingent from Etruria. The bulk of them, however, were undoubtedly Latins, with traditions and customs much the same as those of the greater number of the patrician houses; and this it was that in time caused the triumph of Latinism, and the predominance of the masterful spirit in the *jus Quiritium*.

History attributes to Numa the distribution of the artisans and craftsmen into guilds, eight or nine in number (*collegia opificum*).[2] In view of the accounts we have of later date as to the relations that subsisted between guild brethren, this action of Numa's is of special interest and significance. It was the creation of associations among the plebeians that to some extent compensated for the absence among them of gentile organisation. Those associations did not affect their position politically, but they conferred upon them advantages in private life which otherwise they would not have enjoyed. They got a common cult, and possibly a common burial-place, with a master and his council to manage their affairs, consolidate customs, and arrange disputes. Between the brethren there was a bond, not indeed of descent, real or fictitious, from a common ancestor, but of close alliance and interdependence, each owing duty to the other similar to what might be claimed from him by a ward, a guest, or a kinsman.[3] The Latin contingents that helped to swell the

[2] Plut., *Numa*, 17. Mommsen, in his treatise *De collegiis et sodaliciis Romanorum* (Kiliæ, 1843), spoke of this as a fable; but in his history he accepts it as fact to this extent,—that the guilds must have been established in the earliest years of the City.

[3] See in Mommsen, *De collegiis*, p. 3, various extracts from Cicero illustrating the closeness of the relationship between *sodales*. M. Albert Gérard, in his *Etude sur les corporations ouvrières à Rome* (Montbéliard, 1884), p. 4, is of opinion that the guilds were no invention of Numa's, but only a reproduction

ranks of the plebeians in the reigns of Numa's immediate successors were more addicted to rural pursuits than to trade, but they seem to have been treated by the sovereign in the same indulgent spirit as the craftsmen had been previously. Not that they were incorporated in any way; that in their case was not so necessary as in that of the traders, and might politically have been inexpedient. But they got— what to them was of most importance—allotments of lands for culture, and a weekly market was established in Rome, at which they might dispose of their produce. The accounts are conflicting as to the tenure on which they held their farms; but whatever may have been the case originally, and whether the lands they occupied had been derived from the king individually or from the state, and whether acquired by assignation or purchase, it is clear that by the time of Servius they were freeholders; for they were enrolled in his "classes" in large numbers, and the qualification was ownership of real estate on quiritarian title. It is in view of this that some authorities are disposed to regard the plebeians, even before the Servian reforms, as half-fledged citizens—*cives sine suffragio;* but the application to them of such an epithet seems to put their right too high. Admitted that they had the right to hold property both movable and immovable, to transfer it by quiritarian modes of conveyance, and to have the protection for it of the tribunals, yet not only had they no share in the government of the city, but they were denied any participation in its religion. As men to whom the *auspicia* were incompetent, their intermarriage with the gentile houses was out of the question; while by the more unbending of the patricians their unions

by him in Rome of an institution already well known elsewhere. There is a passage in Livy (iv. 9) in which, speaking of the revolt in 311 U.C. of the *plebs* of Ardea against the optimates, he says that, after the former had withdrawn from the city, the *opifices*.resolved to side with them in hope of plunder; his language suggests that the craftsmen had an independent organisation, and were to some extent a separate class.

amongst themselves were often decried as wanting in the effects of lawful marriage, because unhallowed by the religious ceremony to which the higher order was accustomed (p. 26). *Gentes* they had none during the first four centuries of Rome,—a fact which placed them at a disadvantage in the matter of inheritance and guardianship (§§ 9, 11); but there are indications that for certain purposes the circle of near kinsfolk and connections by marriage held amongst the plebeians the same place that fellow-gentiles did amongst the patricians (p. 35).

CHAPTER SECOND.

REGULATIVES OF PUBLIC AND PRIVATE ORDER.

SECTION 5. — ABSENCE OF ANY DEFINITE SYSTEM OF LAW.

POMPONIUS,[1] who was a contemporary of Gaius's, describes the state of the law in regal Rome as follows:—

"In the early years of our City the people lived for a time without actual statute or any definite law; in everything they were subject to the uncontrolled power (*manus*) of the kings. But it is related that after the City had grown somewhat, Romulus divided the populace into thirty parts, which he called *curiae*, because it was in accordance with the opinions expressed by them that he managed the guardianship of the state (*reipublicae curam per sententias earum expediebat*). He himself carried some enactments through the curiate assembly; so did the subsequent kings; all of which are extant in the collection of Sextus Papirius, who was one of the leading citizens in the time of Tarquin the Proud, the son of Damaratus of Corinth. His book bears the name of *jus civile Papirianum;* not because Papirius contributed to it anything of his own, but because the previously isolated laws it contains were arranged by him in a sort of order. On the expulsion of the kings by the Junian law (*lege tribunicia*) all those royal laws fell aside, and the people once more began to be governed by undefined law and usage, rather than by legislative enactment. This state of matters lasted for about twenty years."

Such is the account of the beginnings of Roman law, which Justinian places in the forefront of the chief part of the *Corpus Juris*. It abounds in historical errors; yet is interesting as the record of what a jurist of the time of the Antonines believed to be fact, and which Justinian nearly 400 years later was content to accept as accurate. The only part of it that can be received without reserve is the

[1] Pomp., *lib. sing. Enchiridii*, in *Dig.* i. 2, fr. 2, §§ 1-3.

statement that originally the law was far from definite. It may at once be admitted also that much of what there was fell short of the conditions which philosophical jurists hold essential to the conception of law. There was no single sovereign authority that set it; its quality was not always the same; its sanctions were often such as would be resented by modern jurisprudence; and in many cases their enforcement was the care of individuals rather than of the state. But, whether in the shape of *fas* or *jus*, or merely precepts of *boni mores*, there were rules in very considerable number for defining men's rights and preventing their infringement, —regulatives, in a word, of public and private order, out of which was to be evolved in the course of centuries the matured jurisprudence of the *Corpus Juris Civilis*.

SECTION 6.—FAS.[1]

While the very frequent references to *fas* as distinct from *jus* bear testimony to its importance as one of the factors of early Roman law, yet it is extremely difficult to define its nature and limits. This may to some extent be accounted for by the fact that much of what was originally within its domain, once it had come to be enforced by secular tribunals, and thus had the sanction of human authority, was no longer distinguishable from *jus*; while it may be that others of its behests, once pontifical punishments for their contravention had gone into desuetude, sank to nothing higher than precepts of *boni mores*.

By *fas* was understood the will of the gods,—the laws given by heaven for men on earth.[2] Among a people that

---

[1] Iherlng, *Geist*, vol. i. §§ 18, 18a; Voigt, *XII Tafeln*, vol. i. §§ 19, 46.
[2] Isid., *Orig.*, v. 2,—"Fas lex divina, jus lex humana est;" Serv. *ad Georg.*, i. 269,—"Fas et jura sinunt, *i.e.*, divina humanaque jura permittunt; nam ad religionem fas, jura pertinent ad homines." These definitions are comparatively modern, and hardly express the idea. Ausonius identifies *Fas* and *Themis*,—"Prima Deum Fas, Quae Themis est Graecis." Certainly *fas* was

believed so profoundly as did those early Romans that in the gods they lived and moved and had their being, it could not fail to be regarded with the utmost consideration, and to exercise an influence more potent than any merely human rules. So far as can be gathered from the scattered references to it, it occupied a higher platform and had a wider range than these last.[3] There were but few of its commands, prohibitions, or precepts that were addressed to men as citizens of any particular state; all mankind came within its scope. It forbade that a war should be undertaken without the prescribed fetial ceremonial; otherwise it was not a *purum piumque bellum*, but an act of violence by the invaders, which their gods had not sanctioned, against others who were equally god-protected. It required that faith should be kept even with an enemy when a promise had been made to him under sanction of an oath. It enjoined hospitality to foreigners, because the stranger guest was presumed, equally with his entertainer, to be an object of solicitude to a higher power. It punished murder, for it was the taking of a god-given life; the sale of a wife by her husband, for she had become his partner in all things human and divine; the lifting of a hand against a parent, for it was subversive of the first bond of society and religion,—the reverence due by a child to those to whom he owed his existence; incestuous connections, for they defiled the altar; the false oath and the broken vow, for they were an insult to the divinities invoked. To displace a boundary or a landmark was a most heinous offence, not so much because the act was provocative of feud, as because the march-stone itself, as the guarantee of peaceful neighbourhood, was especially under the guardianship of the gods.

sometimes personified, especially in the *formulae* employed by the fetials, *e.g.*, Liv., i. 32. See Bréal, " Sur l'origine des mots désignant le droit en Latin," *Nouv. Rev. Hist.*, vol. vii. (1883), p. 607 *sq.*

[3] *Fas* sometimes allowed what *jus* forbade,—" transire per alienum fas est, jus non est " (Isid., *Orig.*, v. 2, 2, in Bruns, p. 326).

No *locus sacer* whatever could be interfered with without a breach of the *fas*; and on a day that the ministers of religion had declared holy it was a sin for a magistrate to exercise any branch of his jurisdiction in which he required to pronounce one of the three solemn words of style—*do, dico, addico*.[4]

To give an answer to the question, How were those rules of the *fas* enforced? is beset with difficulties. Breach of any of them rendered the offender *impius*; but his sin was sometimes expiable, sometimes not. Expiation required a peace-offering to the offended deity (*piacularis hostia*), accompanied possibly with satisfaction to any injured third party. What happened in consequence of an inexpiable breach of the *fas* depended apparently on circumstances. Take the case of the perjurer. He had solemnly invoked the wrath of heaven upon himself and all that belonged to him in the event of his knowingly swearing falsely. It was for the pontiff to say whether he had done so, or whether his offence was attributable to his imprudence and therefore expiable. If it was not, what then? Did the pontiffs content themselves with their finding, abstaining from any express sentence, and leaving the party injured to be the instrument of the irate deity in punishing the offender by reprisals?[5] Or did they formally excommunicate the sinner, declaring him *sacer*, *i.e.*, devoting him to the infernal gods, and forfeiting his estate to the service of the deity he had primarily offended. This was expressly

[4] The above are illustrations merely, and not intended as an exhaustive enumeration of what fell within the *fas*. Such an enumeration is impossible. Cicero speaks of the adoption of the elder by the younger as not only *contra naturam* but *contra fas*; and Paul uses the same expression in speaking of the purchase of a freeman to take effect in the event of his becoming a slave. It is doubtful, however, whether they meant more than that the acts they were condemning were contrary to the unwritten law of nature. The same dubiety arises in other instances of the employment of the word by the later writers.

[5] This is the view of Danz, *Sacrale Schutz*, p. 47 *sq*. He lays considerable stress on the words of Livy (v. 11),—" Numquam deos ipsos admovere nocentibus manus; satis esse, si occasione ulciscendi laesos arment."

B

the penalty of several of the contraventions referred to above,—selling a wife, striking a parent, removing a landmark, &c. (p. 54). The *homo sacer* was in every sense of the word an outcast,—one with whom it was pollution to associate, who dared take no part in any of the institutions of the state, civil or religious, whose life the gods would not accept as a sacrifice, but whom, nevertheless, any one might put to death with impunity as no longer god-protected.[6] Those precepts of the *fas*, therefore, were not mere exhortations to a blameless life, but closely approached to laws, whose violation was visited with punishments none the less effective that they were religious rather than civil.

Section 7.—Jus.

There is no word in the vocabulary of Roman law that had more meanings than *jus*,—" law " as the rule of action (*norma agendi*), " right " as the faculty conferred by the rule (*facultas agendi*), " right" as opposed to wrong, " strict law " as opposed to equity, " justice " as in the phrase *jus reddere* (to dispense justice), " the place where justice was dispensed," as in the phrase *in jus vocatio*, and so on.[1] It can admit of little doubt that the first of these was the original idea the word conveyed; and it has been well said that if we can ascertain the meaning of the name *jus* we shall thus have an unconscious definition of what the Romans understood by law.[2] The older form of it was *jous;* and Ennius is said to have regarded it as connected with Jove.[3] Some modern authorities entertain the same opinion.[4] Recent philology derives it from the Sanscrit *ju*, to join, bind, or unite; from which some deduce as the signification of *jus*

[6] Festus, v. *Sacer* (Bruns, p. 288). See § 12, notes 12, 13.
[1] See *Dig.* i. 1, frs. 11, 12.   [2] Clark, *Pract. Jurisprud.*, p. 14.
[3] Apuleius, *De deo Socratis*, 5.
[4] *E.g.*, Lasaulx, *Ueber den Eid bei den Römern*, Würzburg, 1844, p. 9; Huschke, *Das alte Römische Jahr*, Breslau, 1869, p. 214.

"that which binds," "the bond of society," others "that which is regular, orderly, or fitting."[5] The latest inquirer (M. Bréal) identifies it with the *jos, jaos,* or *jaus* of the Vedas, and the *jaes* of the Zend-Avesta,—words whose exact meaning is controverted, but which he interprets as "the divine will."[6] *Jubeo* is generally allowed to be a contraction of *jus hibeo*, hold or take as *jus*. If Bréal's definition can be adopted we obtain a very significant interpretation of the words addressed by the presiding magistrate to the assembled comitia in asking them whether they assented to a law proposed by him,—*Velitis, jubeatis, Quirites,* &c., "Is it your pleasure, Quirites, and do you hold it as the divine will, that," and so on. As legislation by the comitia of the curies and centuries was regarded as a divine office, and their vote might be nullified by the fathers on the ground that there had been a defect in the *auspicia*, and the will of the gods consequently not clearly ascertained, this explanation of Bréal's seems not without support,—*vox populi vox dei*. If it be right, then the only difference between *fas* and *jus* was this,—that the will of the gods, which both embodied, was in the one declared by inspired and in the other by merely human agency.

This *jus* might be the result either of traditional and inveterate custom (*jus moribus constitutum*) or of statute (*lex*).[7]

---

[5] See references in Clark's *Pract. Jurisprud.*, pp. 16-20. He himself adopts the latter definition.

[6] Bréal (as in § 6, note 2), p. 606.

[7] There is controversy about the etymology of the word *lex*. It was used by the jurists in two distinct senses—(1) as meaning a comitial enactment (Gai., i. 3), and hence occasionally called *lex publica* (Gai., ii. 104, iii. 174); (2) as meaning an obligation, restriction, condition, declaration, or what not, expressly incorporated in a private deed (*lex privata*), as in the phrases *lex mancipii, lex contractus, lex testamenti*, &c. Its most likely derivation is from λέγειν, to say or to speak. The *lex publica* was originally always put to and voted by the comitia by word of mouth; and the XII Tables, in declaring the binding effect of a *lex privata* when engrafted on a conveyance or contract *per aes et libram* (§ 13), use in reference to it the phrase *uti lingua nuncupassit* (Festus, v. *Nuncupata*, Bruns, p. 23).

We look in vain for any legislative enactment establishing such an institution, for example, as the *patria potestas*, or fixing the early rules of succession on death. Statute may have regulated some of their details; but they had taken shape and consistency before Rome had its beginnings. It can well be believed, however, that in the outset the customs in observance may have been far from uniform,—that not only those of the different races but those also of the different *gentes* may at first have varied in some respects, but undergoing a gradual approximation, and in course of time consolidating into a general *jus Quiritium*.[8] That the bulk of the law was customary is universally admitted. But Pomponius speaks of certain laws enacted by the comitia of the curies, which he calls *leges regiae*. The opinion of the best authorities is that it is a mistake to attribute those so-called "royal laws"[9] to that assembly. According to the testimony of the old writers it had very little share in the work of legislation. Romulus *jura dedit* at his own hand,—not *jura tulit*. As Bernhöft remarks, we read not a word of the co-operation of the people when he united the old Romans and Sabines, when Numa regulated the cult, when Tullus Hostilius admitted the Alban *gentes* to the patriciate and

[8] Yet without necessarily extinguishing particular customs. *E.g.*, the common law conferred upon a parent a qualified right to abandon his offspring, while the *gens Fabia* required its members to rear all their children (Dion., ix. 22). " There can be no community without rules,—law in the widest sense ; family, clan, &c., all must have them ; but even when the state is reached, state law does not necessarily overwhelm the rules of the lesser communities " (Bekker, *Z. f. vergleich. RW.*, vol. i. p. 109).

[9] The most recent and comprehensive treatise on the subject of the so-called Royal Laws, and containing references to the earlier literature, is that of Voigt, *Ueber die Leges Regiae*, Leipsic, 1876, 1877 (republished from the *Transactions* of the Saxon Academy). A collection of them from Livy, Dionysius, Plutarch, Servius, Macrobius, &c., will be found in Bruns, p. 1 *sq.* Of the *Jus Papirianum* referred to by Pomponius no remains are extant ; but Paul (*Dig.* l. 16, fr. 144) mentions incidentally that it was commented by one Granius Flaccus (who was of the time of Julius Cæsar). Marliani's Laws of Romulus, in his *Topographia urbis Romae*, lib. 2, cap. 8 (*Graevii Thes.*, vol. iii. p. 86 *sq.*), are now on all hands regarded as apocryphal.

reorganised the army, when Ancus Marcius formulated the fetial law, when the elder Tarquin augmented the senate, or when Servius Tullius created the centuries. Tarquin's attempt to double the strength of each century of the cavalry had to be abandoned; but that was because it had been fixed by Romulus *auspicatim*, and his proposal therefore an interference with divine arrangements; he got over the difficulty by doubling the centuries themselves. When the king did consult the comitia it was in minor matters of a semi-private nature, and probably as matter of policy,— the sanctioning of testaments, adrogations, and the like.[10] Mommsen is probably near the mark when he describes the *leges regiae* as mostly rules of the *fas*, which were of interest not merely for the pontiffs but for the public,— with which it was of importance the latter should be acquainted, that they might know the risks they incurred from their contravention.[11] Instead of remaining buried in the pontifical books, along with the more esoteric rules of ritual, &c., they were published in some form or other; but whether by the kings whose names they bear, or by the pontiffs under their direction, can only be matter of speculation. It is not to be assumed that there was no legislation beyond this; some of the laws of which we have record were of a different character. But on the whole it seems beyond doubt that it was custom rather than statute that was the main factor of the *jus* of the regal period.

SECTION 8.—BONI MORES.

As something different from the *jus moribus constitutum* mention must be made of *boni mores* as one of the regu-

[10] Bernhöft, *l.c.*, pp. 116, 117. See also Karlowa, *Röm. RG.*, vol. i. p. 52.
[11] Mommsen, *Römisches Staatsrecht*, vol. ii. 1, p. 41. Clark (*Pract. Jurisprud.*, p. 284) thinks that the pontiffs, as "the repositories of those primeval customs which formed the first Roman law," threw "into the form of general rules such applications of general custom and opinion as required declaration or penal enforcement."

latives of public and private order.[1] Part of what fell within their sphere might also be expressly regulated by *fas* or *jus;* but there was much also that was only gradually brought within the domain of these last, and even down to the end of the republic not a little that remained solely under the guardianship of the family tribunal or the censor's *regimen morum.* Its function was twofold: for sometimes it operated in restraint of law by condemning—though it could not prevent—the ruthless and unnecessary exercise of legal right, as, for example, that of the head of a house over his dependants; and sometimes it operated supplementarily, by requiring observance of duties that could not be enforced by any compulsitor of law. Dutiful service, respect, and obedience (*obsequium et reverentia*) from inferiors to superiors, chastity (*pudicitia*), and fidelity to engagements express or implied (*fides*), were among the *officia* that were thus inculcated, and whose neglect or contravention not only affected the reputation but often entailed punishments and disabilities, social, political, or religious.[2] To increase the respect for such virtues, and make their observance in a manner a religious duty, some of them were deified and provided with a temple and a cult. *Fides* was one of them (p. 50). There was none of the minor *numina* for which the ancient Roman had greater reverence. Whether in public or private life, an engagement in his eyes was sacred.[3] An avoidable breach of it

---

[1] See Voigt, *XII Tafeln*, vol. i. § 15.

[2] The constant reference in the pages of both the lay and professional writers to *infamia, ignominia, turpitudo, improbitas,* &c., as imposing disqualifications, shows how much store continued to be set, theoretically at least, on integrity of character. Even in the Justinian law we find ingratitude regarded as justifying a donor in revoking a donation, a patron in again reducing his freedman to slavery, a parent in disinheriting his son, and a court of law in refusing to allow an heir to take an inheritance left him by testament.

[3] "Populus Romanus . . . omnium [virtutum] maxime et praecipue Fidem coluit sanctamque habuit tam privatim quam publice" (Gell., xx. 1, 39).

is said to have been extremely rare. If he failed the *jus* had no punishment for him. It might reach a man if he had engaged *per aes et libram* (§§ 14, 30) or by a formal *sponsio* (§ 39); but then the ground of action was the *nexum* or *sponsio* in which his engagement was clothed, not the engagement itself. " He agreed, but has not stood to his agreement," was a plaint of which the ordinary civil tribunal took no cognisance. Whether the pontiffs ever did so, viewing it as a dishonour of *Fides*, does not appear; but as a contravention of *boni mores* it was undoubtedly a matter for the animadversion of those who exercised the *regimen morum*,—the king over the citizens generally, the *gentes* over their members, and probably the *collegia opificum* over their *sodales*.

"Fides, *i.e.*, dictorum conventorumque constantia et veritas" (Cic., *De off.*, i. 7, 23). See also *De off.*, iii. 31, 11. On Numa's institution of the cult of Fides, see Liv., i. 4; Dion., ii. 75. See also *infra*, p. 50.

CHAPTER THIRD.

INSTITUTIONS OF THE PRIVATE LAW.

SECTION 9.—THE FAMILY ORGANISATION.[1]

IN describing the domestic organisation of the Romans it would be pedantic to be always using the Latin word *familia* instead of the English "family."[2] Yet there would be reason for it; for the ideas they respectively convey are by no means identical. Husband, wife, and children did not necessarily constitute an independent family among the Romans, nor were they all necessarily of the same family. Those formed a family who were all subject to the right or power—originally *manus*,[3] but latterly *jus*—of the same family head (*paterfamilias*). He might have a whole host dependent on him,—wife and sons and daughters, and daughters-in-law, and grandchildren by his sons, and possibly remoter descendants related through males; so long as they remained subject to him they con-

---

[1] See Schupfer, *La Famiglia secondo il diritto Romano*, Padua, 1876.

[2] *Familia* and "family" are used in this section solely to designate the group of persons subject to the same *paterfamilias*. Occasionally they meant (1) a *gens* or group of families in the stricter sense; or (2) the family estate proper, as in the provisions of the XII Tables about succession—*adgnatus proximus familiam habeto;* or (3) the family slaves collectively, as in the phrases *familia urbana, familia rustica*.

[3] This word *manus*, though in progress of time used chiefly to express the power a husband had over the wife who had become a member of his family, was originally the generic term for all the rights exercised not only over the things belonging but also the persons subject to him; for a slave when enfranchised was said to be "manumitted," and the same phrase was also employed occasionally to express the condition of a *filiusfamilias* released from the *potestas*, although "emancipated" was the usual one.

stituted but one family, that was split up only on his death or loss of citizenship. But if his wife had not passed *in manum*—and that was common enough even during the republic and universal in the later empire—she did not become a member of his family; she remained a member of the family in which she was born, or, if its head was deceased, or she had been emancipated, was the sole member of a family of her own. Both sons and daughters on emancipation ceased to be of the family of the *paterfamilias* who had emancipated them. A daughter's children could never under any circumstances be members of the family of their maternal grandfather; for children born in lawful marriage followed the family of their father, while those who were illegitimate ranked from the moment of birth as *patresfamilias* and *matresfamilias*. It is very evident, therefore, that the Roman *familia* was an association of which the word "family" in its ordinary acceptation conveys but an imperfect and inaccurate representation.

With the early Romans, as with the Hindus and the Greeks, marriage was a religious duty,[4]—a duty a man owed alike to his ancestors and himself. Believing that the happiness of the dead in another world depended on their proper burial, and on the periodical renewal by their descendants of prayers and feasts and offerings for the repose of their souls, it was incumbent upon him above all things to perpetuate his race and his family cult.[5] In taking to himself a wife, he was about to separate her from her father's house and make her a partner of his family mysteries. With the patrician at least this was to be done only with divine approval, ascertained by *auspicia*. His choice was limited to a woman with whom he had *conubium* ($\epsilon\pi\iota\gamma\alpha\mu\iota\alpha$)

[4] See Fustel de Coulanges, *La Cité Antique*, pp. 41–54.
[5] "Sacra privata perpetua manento. Deorum manium jura sancta sunto. Sos (=suos) leto datos divos habento" (Cic., in his draft of a code, *De leg.*, ii. 9, 22). "Animas placare paternas" (Ov., *Fast.*, ii. 533). See also Cic., *De leg.*, ii. 22, § 55; Aug., *De Civ. Dei*, viii. cap. 26.

or right of intermarriage.[6] This was a matter of state arrangement; and in the regal period Roman citizens could have it outside their own bounds only with members of states with which they were in alliance, and with which they were connected by the bond of common religious observances. A patrician citizen, therefore, if his marriage was to be reckoned lawful (*justae nuptiae*), had to wed either a fellow-patrician or a woman who was a member of an allied community. In either case it was essential that she should not be one of his sobrinal circle, *i.e.*, of kin to him within the seventh degree;[7] second cousins, therefore, being related in the sixth degree according to Roman computation, could not intermarry.[8]

The ceremony itself was a religious one, conducted by the high priests of the state, in presence of ten witnesses, representatives probably of the ten curies of the bridegroom's tribe, and known as *confarreatio*;[9] for it may be affirmed with all but absolute certainty that it was not until after the Canuleian law (309 U.C.) had legalised intermarriage with a plebeian, that a patrician condescended to any less sacred form of completing the bond of marriage. Its effect was to dissociate the wife entirely from her father's house and to make her a member of her husband's; for confarreate marriage involved what was called *in manum conventio*, the

[6] It was the want of *conubium* between the early settlement of Romulus and the neighbouring cities and villages that, according to the story (Liv. i. 9), caused the abduction of the Sabine maidens. Romulus is said to have sued for it in the first instance; but his overtures were repulsed with the advice to open an asylum for women as well as men, as his only chance of finding equal mates for his followers; and it was only then that they resorted to their rough mode of wooing and wedding.

[7] According to the old phraseology there could be no intermarriage within the circle of the *jus osculi*. On this old institution, "the right of kiss," see Klenze, *Das Familienrecht der Cognaten und Affinen nach Röm. u. verwandten Rechten* (Berlin, 1828), p. 16 *sq*.

[8] In time this was relaxed, and eventually marriage permitted even between first cousins, Just., *Inst.*, i. 10, 4.

[9] Gai., i. 112. See Rossbach, *Die Römische Ehe* (Stuttgart, 1853), p. 95 *sq.*; Karlowa, *Die Formen d. Röm. Ehe u. Manus* (Bonn, 1868) p. 5 *sq*.

passage of the wife into her husband's "hand" or power, (but this always on the assumption that her husband was himself *paterfamilias;* if he was not, then, though nominally in his hand, she was really subject like himself to his family head). Any property she had of her own—which was a possible state of matters only if she had been independent before marriage—passed to him as a matter of course; if she had none, her *paterfamilias* provided her a dowry (*dos*), which shared the same fate. Whatever she acquired by her industry or otherwise while the marriage lasted also as a matter of course fell to her husband. In fact, so far as her patrimonial interests were concerned, she was in much the same position as her children; and on her husband's death (according to Gaius) she had a share with them in his inheritance, as if she had been one of his daughters. In other respects *manus* conferred more limited rights than *patria potestas;* for Romulus is said to have ordained that if a man put away his wife except for adultery or one of two or three other very grave offences, he forfeited his estate half to her and half to Ceres;[10] while if he sold her he was to be given over to the infernal gods.[11]

The *patria potestas* was the name given to the power exercised by a father, or by his *paterfamilias* if he was himself *in potestate*, over the issue of such *justae nuptiae*. The Roman jurists boasted that it was a right enjoyed by none but a Roman citizen,[12] — a statement not strictly accurate, seeing that in the early empire the Latin municipalities of Spain and some other western provinces, though their burgesses were not Roman citizens, yet had *manus*

---

[10] One wonders how in such a case children were provided for.
[11] Plut., *Rom.*, 22 (Bruns, p. 6). On the subject of the early law of divorce, see von Wächter, *Ueber Ehescheidungen bei dem Römern* (Stuttgart, 1822), p. 1 *sq.;* Berner, *De divortiis apud Romanos* (Berolini, 1842), p. 1 *sq.;* Schlesinger, *Z. f. RG.*, vol. viii. (1867), p. 58 *sq.*
[12] "Jus proprium civium Romanorum" (Gai., i. §§ 55, 189; Just., *Inst.*, i. 9).

and *patria potestas* modelled on those of Rome.[13] But it certainly was peculiar to the Romans in this sense, that nowhere else, except among the Latin race from which they had sprung, did the paternal power attain such an intensity. It seems originally to have entitled a father, or his *paterfamilias* if he was himself in domestic subjection, to decide —not arbitrarily, of course, but judicially—whether or not he should rear the child with which his wife had presented him. But this right of his was very early restricted; for Romulus has the credit of having ordained (1) that he should rear all his male descendants, and at least his firstborn daughter; (2) that he should not put any child to death before it had reached its third year, unless it was grievously deformed, and then he might expose it at once, after showing it to his neighbours; and (3) that if he transgressed he should forfeit half of his estate, and submit to other undefined penalties, probably religious.[14] But this did not affect his right to determine whether or not he should admit the child whose life was thus secured to membership in his family (*liberi susceptio*), with all its privileges, social and religious; apparently it was not until in the early empire that he was deprived of his power to decide himself the question of his child's legitimacy.[15]

The practical omnipotence of the *paterfamilias* and condition of utter subjection to him of his children *in potestate* became greatly modified in course of centuries; but originally the latter, though in public life on an equality with the house father, yet in private life, and so long as the *potestas* lasted, were subordinated to him to such an extent as, according to the letter of the law, to be in his hands little better than his slaves. They could have nothing of their own,—all they earned was his; and though it was quite

---

[13] *Lex Salpensana* (temp. Domit.), cap. 22 (Bruns, p. 131).
[14] Dion. Hal., ii. 26, 27 (Bruns, p. 7).
[15] See Voigt, *Leges Regiae* (as in § 7, note 9), p. 24, note.

common, when they grew up, for him to give them *peculia*, "cattle of their own," to manage for their own benefit, yet these were only *de facto* theirs but *de jure* his. For offences committed by them outside the family circle, for which he was not prepared to make amends, he had to surrender them to the injured party, just like slaves or animals that had done mischief. If his right to them was disputed he used the same action for its vindication that he employed for asserting his ownership of his field or his house: if they were stolen, he proceeded against the thief by an ordinary action of theft; if for any reason he had to transfer them to a third party, it was by the same form of conveyance he used for the transfer of things inanimate. Nor was this all; for according to the old formula recited in that sort of adoption known as adrogation,[16] he had over them the power of life and death, *jus vitae necisque*. This power, as already noticed, was subject to certain restrictions during the infancy [17] of a child; but when he had grown up, his father, in the exercise of the domestic jurisdiction, might visit his misconduct, not only in private but in public life, with such punishment as he thought fit, even banishment, slavery, or death.[18]

It might happen that a marriage was fruitless, or that a man saw all his sons go to the grave before him, and that the *paterfamilias* had thus to face the prospect of the extinction of his family and of his own descent to the tomb without posterity to make him blessed. To obviate so dire a misfortune two alternatives were open to him,—either to give himself in adoption and pass into another family, or to adopt some one as a son, who should perpetuate his own. The latter was the course usually followed. If it was a

---

[16] Aul. Gell., v. 18, 9.
[17] In the Roman, not the English, sense of the word.
[18] A law attributed to Numa forbade a man to sell a son he had permitted to marry (Dion. Hal., ii. 20, Bruns, p. 9).

paterfamilias that he adopted, the process was called adrogation (*adrogatio*); if it was a *filiusfamilias*, it was simply *adoptio*. The latter, unknown probably in the earlier regal period, was a somewhat complicated conveyance of a son by his natural parent to his adopter, the purpose of course being expressed; its effect was simply to transfer the child from the one family to the other. But the former was much more serious; for it involved the extinction of one family [19] that another might be perpetuated. It was therefore an affair of state. It had to be approved by the pontiffs, who probably had to satisfy themselves that there were brothers enough of the adrogatee to attend to the interests of the ancestors whose cult he was renouncing; and on their favourable report it had to be sanctioned by the vote of a comitia of the curies, as it involved the possible deprivation of his *gens* of their right of succession to him. If it was sanctioned, then the *adrogatus*, from being himself the head of a house, sank to the position of a *filiusfamilias* in the house of his adoptive parent; if he had had wife or children subject to him, they passed with him into his new family; and so did everything that belonged to him and that was capable of transmission from one person to another. The adopting parent acquired *potestas* and power of life and death over the adopted child exactly as if he were the issue of his body; while the latter enjoyed in his new family the same rights exactly that he would have had if he had been born in it.

The *manus* and the *patria potestas* represent the masterful aspects of the patrician's domestic establishment. Its conjugal and parental ones, however, though not so prominent in the pages of the jurists, are not to be lost sight of. The Roman family in the early history of the law was governed quite as much by *fas* as *jus*. It was an association

---

[19] A *paterfamilias* who had no person subject to him constituted a "family" in his own person.

hallowed by religion, and held together not by might merely but by conjugal affection, parental piety, and filial reverence.[20] The purpose of marriage was to rear sons who might perpetuate the house and the family *sacra*. In entering into the relationship the wife renounced her rights and privileges as a member of her father's house; but it was that she might enter into a lifelong partnership with her husband, and be associated with him in all his family interests, sacred and civil.[21] The husband was priest in the family; but wife and children alike assisted in its prayers, and took part in the sacrifices to its lares and penates. As the Greek called his wife the house-mistress, δέσποινα, so did the Roman speak of his as *materfamilias*, the housemother.[22] She was treated as her husband's equal. As for their children, the *potestas* was so tempered by the natural sense of parental duty on the one side and filial affection on the other, that in daily life it was rarely felt as a grievance;

[20] "Matrem et patrem . . . venerari oportet" (Ulp., in *Dig.* xxxvii. 15, fr. 1, § 2). "Patria potestas in pietate debet, non in atrocitate consistere" (Hadr., in *Dig.* xlviii. 9, fr. 5). Cicero (*Cato Maj.*, 11, 37), speaking of App. Claudius Caecus, thus depicts the ancient household *régime:* "Quattuor robustos filios, quinque filias, tantam domum, tantas clientelas Appius regebat et caecus et senex. . . . Tenebat non modo auctoritatem, sed etiam imperium in suos; metuebant servi, verebantur liberi, carum omnes habebant; vigebat in illa domo mos patrius et disciplina." Dénis, in his *Histoire des idées morales dans l'antiquité* (vol. ii. p. 112), says: "Instead of that terrible power (the *patria potestas*) of which the historians of Roman law speak so much, we read rather in the writers of the early empire of nothing but the sacred duties of father and mother. . . . I might cite from Quintilian, and Pliny, and Tacitus, and Juvenal the most beautiful passages on the necessity and importance of education in the family, the inconvenience and mistake of confiding children to slaves, the respect due to the innocence of their infancy and youth, the tenderness that ought to be displayed towards them, and which forbids the use of the rod in training them as if they were mere animals."

[21] Dion. Hal. (ii. 25) says that so it was expressly declared by Romulus. The old idea still survived in the imperial jurisprudence, when technically, in consequence of the disuse of *in manum conventio*, husband and wife were no longer members of the same family; as, for instance, in the words of the emperor Gordian (*Cod. Just.*, ix. 32, 4), "uxor, quae socia rei humanae atque divinae domus suscipitur." See also Modest., in *Dig.* xxiii. 2, fr. 1.

[22] *Materfamilias* is used in the texts in two distinct senses, (1) a woman *sui juris*, i.e., not subject to any family head, and (2) a wife *in manu mariti*.

while the risk of an arbitrary exercise of the domestic jurisdiction,[23] whether in the heat of passion or under the impulse of justifiable resentment, was guarded against by the rule which required the *paterfamilias* to consult in the first place the near kinsmen of his child, maternal as well as paternal. Even the incapacity of the subject members of the family to hold property of their own cannot in those times have been regarded as any serious hardship; for, though the legal title to all their acquisitions was in the house-father, yet in truth they were acquired for and belonged to the family as a whole, and he was but a trustee to hold and administer them for the common benefit.[24] What had come to him by descent, the *bona paterna avitaque*, he was in a peculiar manner bound to preserve for his children, any squandering of them to their prejudice entitling them to have him deprived of his administration.[25]

In Greece the *patria potestas* never reached such dimensions as in Rome, and there it ceased, *de facto* at least, when a son had grown up to manhood and started a household of his own. But in Rome, unless the *paterfamilias* voluntarily put an end to it, it lasted as long as the latter lived and retained his status. The marriage of a son, unlike that of a daughter passing into the hand of a husband, did not release him from it, nor did his children become subject to him so long as he himself was *in potestate*. On the contrary, his wife passed on marriage into the power of her father-in-law, and their children as they were born fell under that of

---

[23] Seneca speaks of the *paterfamilias* as *judex domesticus* (*Controv.*, ii. 3), and *domesticus magistratus* (*De benef.*, iii. 11).

[24] Under the Servian constitution the valuation of a man's freehold was really the valuation of the family freehold,—his *filiifamilias* as well as he had political and military rights and duties in respect of it. See Paul. Diac., v. *Duicensus* (Bruns, p. 266).

[25] Paul., *Sent.*, iii. 4a, 7. There can be little doubt that in regal Rome the interdiction of a patrician proceeded from his *gens*, who were his children's proper guardians, and on their failure his own heirs. The Greeks manifested the same solicitude for the preservation of the πατρῷα παππῷα.

their paternal grandfather; and the latter was entitled to exercise over his daughter-in-law and grandchildren the same rights he had over his sons and unmarried daughters. But there was this difference,—that, when the *paterfamilias* died, his sons and daughters who had remained *in potestate*, and his grandchildren by a predeceased son, instantly became their own masters (*sui juris*), whereas grandchildren by a surviving son simply passed from the *potestas* of their grandfather into that of their father.

The acquisition of domestic independence by the death of the family head frequently involved the substitution of the guardianship of tutors (*tutela*) for the *potestas* that had come to an end. This was so invariably in the case of females *sui juris*, no matter what their age; they remained under guardianship until they had passed by marriage *in manum mariti*.[26] It was only pupil males, however, that required tutors, whose office came to an end when puberty was attained. It is doubtful whether during the regal period a testamentary appointment of tutors by a husband or parent to wife or children was known in practice,—probably not. If so the office devolved upon the *gens* to which the deceased *paterfamilias* belonged; and it may reasonably be assumed that it delegated the duties to one of its members in particular, retaining in its collective capacity a right of supervision.

The position of the clients attached to a family has already been referred to (§ 3). The only persons belonging to it that have not been mentioned were its slaves. In the regal period they were socially more intimately related to the family than in later centuries; few in num-

[26] Gaius (i. 190) makes the extraordinary statement that it was not easy to assign any sufficient reason for the perpetual tutory of females *sui juris*. No doubt by his time its stringency had been much relaxed; but the manifest reason originally was to put it out of the power of such women to dispose of any part of their family estate to the prejudice of their *gens* without its cooperation (see p. 44).

C

ber, sitting at table with their masters, and treated with a consideration due to them as reasonable human beings, rather than as the mere chattels that they were in contemplation of law. The existence of slavery and its enormous expansion in the latter half of the republic not only told on the social and political institutions of Rome, but exercised a very considerable influence on the complexion of many branches of the private law. But this can be better indicated in dealing with later periods than that of the kings.

The preceding observations on the early organisation of the family refer for the most part to the state of matters amongst the patricians. In the debates that took place about the proposal of C. Canuleius to repeal the declaration in the XII Tables that intermarriage between the orders was unlawful, it was urged by patrician orators, in language of supremest contempt, that the plebeians in practice knew nothing of marriage; that their unions amongst themselves were promiscuous,—no better than those of the beasts of the field, and could not possibly be creative of any of the rights that resulted from *justae nuptiae*.[27] The picture was over-drawn and over-coloured by the prejudice of caste; for, although the plebeians were strangers to the religious marriage *confarreatione*, and it could not have been until after the Servian reforms that they became familiar with the civil one effected *coemptione*,[28] yet they had amongst themselves alliances completed by interchange of consent, and doubtless accompanied by customary social observances, which they regarded as marriages. In the eye of law, it is true, these were not creative either of *manus* or *potestas;* neither did they bring the wife into her husband's family. Nay, more, as a plebeian was not esteemed a citizen, and could not therefore have *conubium* in the sense of the right to contract

[27] Liv., iv. 2.   [28] On coemption, see p. 65.

a lawful marriage,[29] his children were in patrician estimation illegitimate,—not so much his as their mother's.[30] In this may be discovered the origin of *matrimonium* as distinguished from *justae nuptiae*,—alliance with a woman in order to make her a mother of children, but that did not make her—still from the patrician's point of view—"a partner in all the affairs of the household, human and divine."[31] Being of different races, and the traditions of some of them, for instance the Etruscan, tinctured more or less with gynæocratic notions,[32] the domestic customs and institutions of the plebeians may well have varied; but the majority being of Latin origin, it is reasonable to assume that *de facto* they regarded their children as *in patria potestate*,[33] and asserted in respect of it the same powers as their patrician superiors. They were at a disadvantage as compared with the latter, however, in having no *gentes* to stand by them in emergencies, to avenge their quarrels and their deaths, and to act as guardians of their widows and orphans. To compensate for this they seem to have set more store than did the patricians upon the circle of their relatives by blood and marriage (*cognati et adfines*). It is remarkable that, notwithstanding the preeminence given to agnates by the XII Tables in matters of tutory and succession (§§ 28, 32), the law reserved to the cognates as distinguished from the agnates certain rights and duties that in patrician Rome must have belonged to

[29] "Uxoris jure ducendae facultas" (Ulp., v. 3).
[30] Gai., i. 67 ; Ulp., v. 8.
[31] This accounts also for the grammatically untenable explanation of *patricii* in Liv., x. 8, 10, "Qui patrem ciere possunt"; *i.e.*, patricians were father's sons, while plebeians, before they were admitted to citizenship and *conubium*, were only reckoned mother's sons.
[32] Bachofen, *Das Mutterrecht*, Stuttgart, 1861, p. 92.
[33] Their recognition of *manus* may not have been so general. While the XII Tables declared that it should be the legal result of a year's matrimonial cohabitation, they reserved power to a wife and her family to prevent it; which would hardly have been the case had not some at least of the plebeians had a preference for marriage without it.

the *gens;* for example, the duty of acting as assessors in the *concilium domesticum*, the duty of prosecuting the murderer —originally of avenging the death—of a kinsman, and the right of appeal against a capital sentence pronounced upon the latter.[34] This can only have been because in olden times, when agnation was unknown as distinct from the *gens*, it was plebeian practice to entrust those rights and duties to the sobrinal circle of cognates.[35]

SECTION 10.—DISTRIBUTION OF LAND AND LAW OF PROPERTY.[1]

The distribution of land amongst the early Romans is one of the puzzling problems of their history. The Servian constitution classified the citizens and determined their privileges, duties, and burdens according to the extent of their freeholds; and yet we know very little with certainty of the way in which these were acquired.

The story goes that Romulus divided the little territory of his original settlement into three parts, not necessarily of equal dimensions, one of which was intended for the maintenance of the state and its institutions, civil and religious, the second (*ager publicus*) for the use of the citizens and profit of the state, and the third (*ager privatus*) for subdivision among his followers. Varro and Pliny[2] relate that to each of these he assigned a homestead (*heredium*) of two jugers, equal to about an acre and a quarter, to be held to him and his heirs (*quae heredem sequerentur*); Pliny adding

[34] See Klenze (as in note 7), pp. 43, 46, and *passim*.
[35] See Appendix, note A.
[1] Giraud, *Recherches sur le droit de propriété chez les Romains*, Aix, 1838 (only first vol. published); Macé, *Histoire de la propriété, du domaine public, et des lois agraires chez les Romains*, Paris, 1851; Hildebrand, *De antiquissimae agris Romani distributionis fide*, Jena, 1862; Voigt, Ueber die bina jugera d. ältesten Röm. Agrarverfassung, in the *Rhein. Mus. f. Phil.* vol. xxiv. (1869), p. 52 *sq.*, the opinions in which are somewhat modified in his *XII Tafeln*, vol. i. § 102; Karlowa, *Röm. RG.*, vol. i. § 15.
[2] Varro, *De R.R.*, x. 2 (Bruns, p. 309); Plin., *H.N.*, xviii. 2, 7.

that to none of them did the king give more. The credibility of this statement is disputed on two grounds,—that so small a plot was utterly inadequate to supply the wants of a family, and that there is evidence elsewhere that the practice was to assign lands, not to an individual or a family, but to a *gens*.[3] But it is not to be lost sight of that this distribution is spoken of as made in the very first days of Rome, amongst a handful of adventurers, the nuclei of future *gentes*, but as yet without family ties; whose occupations as herdsmen were carried on upon the open hills, and for whom an acre and a quarter afforded ample space for a dwelling for themselves, shelter for their herds, and tillage ground for their personal requirements.

It is not necessary, however, to assume, nor do Pliny's words imply, that this first distribution was a final one. The Sabines and others who from time to time threw in their lot with the new settlement, recognised rights of property either in the *gens* or the family,—it was from the former, we are told, that came the worship of Terminus and the idea of the sacredness of the landmark; and most of them when they formed their union with the followers of Romulus must have had their own lands and possessions, which had possibly descended to them through many generations. It would be unreasonable to suppose that, joining Rome, as some of them did, as equals rather than conquered, they would be content to resign their hereditary possessions for so inconsiderable a substitute. The majority of the Servian local tribes bore the names of well-known patrician *gentes;* whence it may be inferred that the families of the various clans did not disperse, but continued settled alongside each other, either in their original localities or on estates newly assigned to them. This view is confirmed by the fact mentioned by Livy, that when Appius Claudius and his followers came to Rome they were drafted as a body to a district north

[3] See Mommsen, *Hist.*, vol. i. p. 194 *sq.*

of the Anio, which was afterwards known as the *tribus Claudia*.

It is highly probable that, as the surviving Romulian families developed into *gentes*, they also acquired gentile settlements proportioned to their numerical strength and expectations. In their subdivision the practice may not have been uniform; but apparently there was a reserve retained in the hands of the *gens* as a corporation as long as possible, from which allotments were made from time to time to new constituent families as they arose, and which were held by them in independent ownership under the old name of *heredia*. As agriculture gained ground these must have been of greater extent than those originally granted by Romulus. Seven jugers, about 4½ acres, seem to have been the normal extent of royal grants to plebeians, and a patrician's freehold is not likely to have been less; probably in the ordinary case it was larger, seeing the minimum qualification for the third Servian class was ten jugers, and for the first twenty.[4] To enable him to make grants during pleasure to his clients he must have held more than seven. But he did not necessarily hold all his lands by gratuitous assignation either from the state or from his *gens*; purchase from the former was by no means uncommon; and it may have been on his purchased lands, outside his *heredium* proper, that his clients were usually employed. Those dependents were also employed in large numbers upon those parts of the *ager publicus* which were occupied by the patricians under the name of *possessiones*. It was these, and not their *heredia*, that were the great source of wealth to

[4] At the same time the writers of the empire frequently refer to the early *heredium* of seven jugers, as having been amply sufficient for its frugal owner, content to till it himself with the aid of his sons. The case of Cincinnatus in the year 293 U.C. is often mentioned: having a freehold of just that extent, he had to sell three jugers to meet engagements for which he believed himself in honour responsible, and yet found the remaining four ample to enable him to maintain himself with all the dignity of a man who had been consul and became dictator.

the patricians in the early republic, and that formed such a fertile cause of contention between the orders. But as their monopolisation by the former did not begin to manifest itself ostentatiously or to be felt as a grievance during the period of the kings, further reference to it may be reserved for a subsequent section (§ 19).

The accounts of the early distributions of land amongst the plebeians are even more uncertain than those we have of its distribution amongst the patricians. They had undoubtedly become freeholders in large numbers before the Servian reforms. But they probably attained that position only by gradual stages. There are indications that their earliest grants from the kings were only during pleasure; but latterly, as they increased in numbers and importance, they obtained concessions of *heredia*, varying in extent from two to seven jugers. That those who had the means also frequently acquired land by purchase from the state may be taken for granted. In fact, there is good reason to believe that by the time of Servius the plebeians were as free to hold land in private property as the patricians, although the stages by which they reached equality in this respect are uncertain and difficult to follow.

The language of Varro in reference to the *heredia*—two jugers which should follow the heir (*quae heredem sequerentur*)—is sometimes interpreted as implying that those of them at least which were acquired by gratuitous grant from the state were declared inalienable.[5] Such an interpretation is not inadmissible; for the Sempronian law of 621

[5] Schwegler (vol. ii. p. 444 *sq.*) and Rudorff (*Gromatische Institutionen*, Berlin, 1852, p. 303) are of this opinion, and base it to some extent on the consideration that until the time of Servius there was no process by which lands could be alienated. But this is assumed. There may possibly have been something akin to the *resignatio in favorem* of the feudal law—resignation of them into the hands of the king for re-grant to an alienee. There may even have been already in practice the surrender in court (*in jure cessio*), which we are told was confirmed by the XII Tables, and which is explained on p. 144.

expressly declared inalienable the allotments of thirty jugers which it authorised.[6] It is very likely that sale of them was never contemplated; they were assigned to families rather than individuals; and it has been observed already (p. 32) that a man was not allowed to alienate recklessly the estate that had come to him from his ancestors and ought to descend to his children. At the same time the interpretation seems somewhat strained. A grant to the original grantee and his heirs is all that the words fairly cover, in contradistinction to a more limited grant during pleasure or for life. It was a grant in absolute ownership,—what came to be called *dominium ex jure Quiritium*. The epithet was not applied from the first; for *dominium* was not a word in early use, the owner being originally spoken of as *herus*,[7] and his right as *manus*.[8] The qualification *ex jure Quiritium* was derived from the words of style employed in an action for vindication of a right of property; the condition of the vindicant's obtaining the protection of the state through its ordinary tribunals being that he held on a title which the state, *i.e.*, the Quirites, regarded as sufficient.

It is sometimes said that the law of the regal period anterior to the reign of Servius Tullius knew no property in movables. The proposition is startling. How could it be that men who held separate property in land should be indifferent to the distinction between mine and thine in other things! It is inconceivable that a man's slaves and cattle and sheep, his plough and other instruments of husbandry or trade, the crops he raised from his farm and the

---

[6] The restriction, however, was found unworkable, and had to be removed.

[7] The word is common in Plautus as a form of address by a slave to his master, and occurs in the Aquilian law of 467 U.C. (*Dig.*, ix. 2, fr. 11, § 6) in the sense of owner (*dominus*). Paul. Diac., v. *Heres* (Bruns, p. 269), and Justinian (*Inst.*, ii. 19, 7) declare that with the ancients *heres* had the same meaning. Corssen (*Beiträge*, p. 40) connects them with the Sanscrit *har*, to take.

[8] As evidenced by the *manum conserere* (p. 188) of the *actio sacramenti in rem*, and other considerations referred to in § 13.

wares he manufactured by his industry, were not regarded by him as just as much his, *de facto* at least, as the lands he tilled or the house he occupied. The proposition is maintained on the strength of a dictum of Gaius's, in which, referring to the distinction that arose in the later republic between quiritarian ownership and the inferior tenure which he designates as *in bonis habere*,[9] he says that formerly (*olim*) matters were different,—that a man was either owner *ex jure Quiritium* or was not owner at all.[10] But from the standpoint of Gaius his *olim* refers only to the state of the law immediately before this bonitarian tenure of *res mancipi* (§ 13)—for it was to them only that it applied—was introduced; and does not exclude the possibility that at a still earlier period the law recognised a distinction between natural and legal or civil ownership.[11] The fact that the prætors and the jurists of the early empire strove successfully to mitigate the rigour of the pure *jus civile* by leavening it with principles of natural law, is apt to induce the belief that this element was altogether novel. Yet Justinian warns us to the contrary. "Natural law," he says, "is clearly the older, for it began with the human race; whereas civil laws commenced only when states began to be founded, magistracies to be created, and laws to be written."[12]

It is quite conceivable that the law might refuse a real

[9] The rule of the *jus civile* was that what were called *res mancipi* could be transferred in full or quiritarian ownership only by mancipation or surrender in court (p. 63). The result was that a transfer by simple delivery left the legal title in the transferrer; so that the transferee was unable to maintain a real action for vindication of his right until he had cured his defective title by prescriptive possession upon it. This was amended by a prætorian edict, which, on certain conditions, allowed him an action even before the prescriptive period had expired (§ 52). The transferrer was not thereby divested of his quiritarian title; but, by concession to the transferee of an action *in rem*, the latter was also recognised as owner on an inferior title, which got the name of *in bonis habere* (Gai., ii. 40). Hence the epithet of δεσπότης βονιτάριος which Theophilus applies to the equitable owner.

[10] Gai., ii. 40.
[11] Ἔστι φυσικὴ καὶ ἔννομος δεσποτεία (Theoph., i. 5, 4).
[12] Just., *Inst.*, ii. 1, § 12.

action for determining a question of legal right over a thing to a man who was unable to found on a title that conferred quiritarian ownership, and yet have no hesitation in protecting his possession of it when disturbed, or allowing him a remedy when he was deprived of it by theft or violence; indeed, such a state of matters is not only conceivable but manifest beyond possibility of dispute. There can be little doubt that it was so down to the time of the introduction of the bonitarian tenure,—that just as the possession of an occupant of the *ager publicus*, who notoriously was not a quiritarian owner, was protected by an interdict, so was that of the purchaser of a few acres of *ager privatus* who had been content to take conveyance by simple delivery, at least against any one but the quiritarian vendor; and that if a movable *res mancipi*, acquired by purchase without mancipation or surrender in court, was stolen from the purchaser, the latter would have his penal action against the thief. It comes, therefore, to be very much a question of words. If by ownership or *dominium* be meant quiritarian ownership, such as was sufficient for a real action in a court of law, then it may be admitted that, down to the time of Servius, with exception perhaps of captured slaves and cattle, there was no property in movables; but if no more be meant than a right in a man to alienate by tradition what he held as his own, and to protect himself, or have protection from the authorities, against any attempt to deprive him of it by theft or violence, then the existence of an ownership of movables—a natural ownership—cannot well be denied.[13] Theft was theft, even though the stolen article had been acquired only by natural means,—by barter in the market, by the industry of the maker, or as the product of something already belonging to its holder.

[13] By the reforms of Servius Tullius certain movables came to be classed along with lands and houses as *res mancipi*, and thus became objects of quiritarian right.

Section 11.—Order of Succession.

The story of the grant by Romulus of little homesteads that were "to follow the heir" indicates clearly that from earliest times the Romans recognised inheritance and an order of succession. Imposing, as they did, on a man's descendants the duty of perpetuating the family and its *sacra*, it would have been strange if those descendants had been deprived of their estate.

The difference of the family organisation of patricians and plebeians necessarily involved a divergence to some extent in their rules of succession. Amongst the former the order was this,—that on the death of a *paterfamilias* his patrimony devolved upon those of his children *in potestate* who by that event became *sui juris*, his widow taking an equal share with them, and no distinction being made between movables and immovables, personalty and realty; and that, failing widow and children, it went to his *gens*.[1] The notion that between the descendants and the *gens* came an intermediate class under the name of agnates does not seem well founded as regards the regal period;[2] they were introduced by the XII Tables to meet the case of the plebeians, who, having no *gentes*, were without legal heirs in default of children (p. 172).[3]

[1] Although the words of the XII Tables were "gentiles familiam habento" (Ulpian, in *Collat.* xvi. 4, 2), yet Cicero's reference to the *cause célèbre* between the Claudii and Claudii Marcelli (*De Orat.*, i. 39, 176) seems to indicate that the *gens* took as a corporation. But opinions differ; and Göttling (*Röm. Staatsverfassung*, p. 71 *sq.*) may be right in thinking practice varied.

[2] The supposed mention of agnates in a law attributed to Numa rests simply on a conjecture of I. G. Huschke's (*Analecta litteraria*, Leipsic, 1826, p. 375). The law is preserved in narrative by Servius *in Virg. Eclog.* iv. 43, which runs thus: "In Numae legibus cautum est, ut si quis imprudens occidisset hominem, pro capite occisi et natis ejus in cautione (Scalig. concione) offerret arietem." Huschke's substitution of *agnatis* for *et natis* is all but universally adopted; but, even were it necessary, need mean nothing more than the deceased's children *in potestate* or his *gens*. See next note.

[3] It is quite true, nevertheless, that from the first the order of succession was agnatic; for it was those only of a man's children who were agnate as

In India, as it was sons alone that could perpetuate a family, daughters had no right of succession. And so was it also in Athens,—in presence of a son daughters were excluded. There are some historical jurists who maintain that so it must have been in patrician Rome.[4] The texts, however, afford no support to this theory.[5] Justinian more than once refers to the perfect equality of the sexes in this matter in the ancient law. But it was nominal rather than real. A daughter who had passed into the hand of a husband during her father's lifetime of course could have no share in her father's inheritance, for she had ceased to be a member of his family. One who was *in potestate* at his death, and thereby became *sui juris*, did become his heir, unless he had prevented such a result by testamentary arrangements; but even then the risk of prejudice to the *gens* was in their own hands to prevent. For she could not marry, and so carry her fortune into another family without their consent; neither could she without their consent alienate any of the more valuable items of it; nor, even with their consent, could she make a testament disposing of it in prospect of death.[6] Her in-

well as cognate that had any claim to his inheritance; and the *gens* was, theoretically at least, just a body of agnates.

[4] Genz (p. 11) holds this opinion very decidedly. M. Fustel de Coulanges (p. 80 *sq.*) is of opinion that, if not expressly, yet practically, women were excluded.

[5] The Voconian law of 585 avowedly introduced something new in prohibiting a man of fortune instituting a woman, even his only daughter, as his testamentary heir; but it did not touch the law of intestacy.

[6] Cic., *Top.*, iv. 18. The primary reason of this disability may have been that a woman had no admission to the curies, and so could not make a testament in the only way known in the regal period, however willing her tûtors might have been to consent. But in time it came to be represented as a disability peculiar to women in the legal tutory of their agnates or their *gens*,— as a disability of the guardians rather than of the ward, that might be avoided by the substitution of fiduciary for legal tutors. It was, as Cicero says (*Pro Mur.*, xii. 27), a gross subversion of the spirit of the law while adhering strictly to its letter. The tutors-at-law, knowing quite well what was the object in view, gave their authority to their ward to pass herself, by coemption, into the hand (*in manum*) of a man she had no intention of regarding as her husband,

heritance, therefore, was hers in name only; in reality it was in the hands of her guardians.

Daughters *in potestate* having been admitted to participate along with sons, *a fortiori* there was no exclusion of younger sons by the first-born. There is not a trace of the existence in Rome at any time of a law of primogeniture, even to the extent, as in India, of entitling the elder to some trifling share beyond that of his younger brothers. And yet we find record of *heredia* remaining in a family not for generations merely but for centuries,—a state of matters that would have been impossible had every death of a *paterfamilias* involved a splitting up of the family estate. It is conceivable that this was sometimes avoided by arrangement amongst the heirs themselves. The practice was by no means uncommon for brothers to abstain from dividing their patrimony, continuing to possess it as partners (*consortes*).[7] We have no details about it; but it is quite possible that by some understanding amongst them the *heredium* eventually remained in the hands of one only, who in turn transmitted it to his posterity. The practice of drafting younger members of a family to colonies may also have aided; and no doubt a *paterfamilias* often withheld his consent to the marriage of younger sons, and so prevented the multiplication of heirs in a later generation. But the simplest plan was the regulation of his succession by testament. This was had recourse to, not so much for instituting a stranger

---

on the understanding that he was at once to remancipate her (Gai., i. 137) to a person of her own selection, it might be one of the very tutors-at-law of whom she was getting rid. The latter was bound at once to manumit her, whereby she again became *sui juris*, and her manumitter *ipso jure* became her fiduciary tutor, bound in honour to comply with all her wishes, and even to sanction her testament (Gai., i. 115; ii. 112).

[7] Gell., i. 9, 12, "Societas inseparabilis, tamquam illud fuit antiquum consortium, quod jure atque verbo Romano appellatur 'ercto non cito.'" Serv. *in Aen.*, viii. 642, "Ercto non cito, *i.e.*, patrimonio vel hereditate non divisa." See Leist, *Zur Gesch. der Röm. Societas*, Jena, 1881, p. 20 *sq*. Festus, v. *Sors*, says *sors* meant *patrimonium;* hence *consortium*. But literally it was the allotment of land—what was assigned by lot—to its original owner.

heir when a man had no issue,—according to patrician notions his duty then was to perpetuate his family by adopting a son,—as for partitioning the succession when he had more children than one. There was more than one way in which in the later law a settlement of a particular part of the inheritance might be made upon a particular heir, with substitution of another on failure of the first; and there is no reason to suppose that a similar device was not resorted to when necessary in the oral testament of the regal period.

During the republic and afterwards it was held to be within the power of a *paterfamilias* testamentarily to disinherit any or all of his children *in potestate*, and so with his last breath to deprive them of their interest in the family estate. We have no evidence of this having ever been done by the early patricians. The practice seems rather to have crept in on the strength of the *uti legassit* [8] *suae rei, ita jus esto* of the XII Tables,—" as a man shall settle in reference to his estate (*res = res familiaris*), so shall it be law"; words, we are told, which were interpreted with the utmost latitude, as sanctioning and confirming every provision in a testament that dealt either with the interests of the subject members of the testator's family or the disposal of his property. But so repugnant was it to the ideas entertained of the relation of a *filiusfamilias* to the family estate as one of its joint-owners, that it was in every way discountenanced. Nothing short of express disherison could deprive him of his birthright (p. 171). The omission by his father either to institute or disinherit him in a testament conceived in favour of a stranger was not *legare* in the sense of the statute; consequently it did not deprive him of his inheritance, but, on the contrary, rendered the will ineffectual (p. 171). And so

---

[8] *Legare* in the XII Tables did not, as in later times, bear the limited signification of bequeathing to a legatee, but embraced the whole expression of will of a testator. It meant *legem dicere de re sua mortis causa*. Justinian, in *Nov.* xxii. cap. 2, renders it by νομοθετεῖν.

impressed was Justinian with the undutifulness of disherison of children, that he forbade it except on the ground of gross misconduct specially narrated in the testament (p. 424).

It is hardly credible, therefore, that the practice could have found acceptance amongst the patricians of the time of the kings. It was foreign to early Aryan notions. A testament was unknown to the Hindus. There was no such thing in Sparta. There was none in Athens until introduced by the legislation of Solon, and it could never prejudice the inheritance of a son; while, if made by a man who had none, it was substantially a *mortis causa* deed of adoption, artificially supplying the descendant that nature had not seen fit to grant. That the Romans had testaments from very early times is probably the fact: those made in the comitia of the curies and in presence of the army on the eve of battle bear the impress of antiquity.[9] But the first at least—and the second was just a substitute for it on an emergency—had in it nothing of the *uti legassit ita jus esto*. For, though in the course of time the curies may have become merely the recipients of the oral declaration by the testator of his last will (p. 167), in order that they might testify to it after his death, it is impossible not to see in the comitial testament what must originally have been a legislative act, whereby the testator's peers, for reasons which they and the presiding pontiffs thought sufficient, sanctioned in the particular case a departure from the ordinary rules of succession.[10] The pontiffs were there to protect the interests of religion, and the curies to protect those of the testator's *gens*; and it is hardly conceivable that a testament could have been sanctioned by them which so far set at nought old traditions as to deprive a *filiusfamilias* of his birthright, at least in favour of a stranger.

[9] *Calatis comitiis* and *in procinctu*, Gai., ii. 101. Comp. Gell., xv. 27, 3.
[10] Mommsen, *Röm. Staatsrecht*, vol. ii. p. 37; Ihering, *Geist*, vol. i. § 11 b.

It may be assumed that, *de facto* at all events, the children *in potestate* of a plebeian becoming *sui juris* by his death took his succession in the same way as the children of a patrician; (or rather, in regard to both, acquired by that event the free administration of the family estate, from which they had been excluded during their parent's lifetime).[11] But as a plebeian was not a member of a *gens*, there was no provision for the devolution of his succession on failure of children. The want of them he could not supply by adrogation, as for long he had no access to the assembly of the curies; and it is very doubtful if adoption of a *filiusfamilias* was known before the reforms of Servius Tullius. The same cause that disqualified him from adrogating a *paterfamilias* disqualified him for making a testament *calatis comitiis*;[12] and even one *in procinctu* was impossible, since, even though before the time of Servius plebeians may occasionally have served in the army, yet they were not citizens, and so had not the requisite capacity for making it.[13] Until, therefore, the Twelve Tables introduced the succession of agnates (p. 172), a plebeian unsurvived by children *in potestate* was necessarily heirless,—that is to say, heirless in law. But custom seems to have looked without disfavour on the appropriation of his *heredium* by an outsider,—a brother or other near kinsman would have the earliest opportunity; and if he maintained his possession of it in the character of heir for a reason-

[11] "Domestici heredes sunt, et vivo quoque parente quodammodo domini existimantur" (Gai., ii. 157); "itaque post mortem patris non hereditatem percipere videntur, sed magis liberam bonorum administrationem consequuntur" (Paul., in *Dig.* xxviii. 2, fr. 11). See *infra*, § 32.

[12] Gellius (as in note 9) says that there were *calata comitia* of the centuries as well as of the curies; but that, according to the general opinion, cannot have been until after the establishment of the republic.

[13] Citizenship was, and to the last continued to be, the fundamental requisite of testamentary capacity: see Gai., ii. 147; Just., *Inst.*, ii. 17, 6. "Testamenti factio est juris publici," says Papinian; it had originally been the act of a citizen in his public character as a member of the comitia, and, although the reason probably was forgotten, the consequences remained.

able period, fixed by the XII Tables at a year,[14] the law dealt with him as heir, and the pontiffs in time imposed upon him the duty of maintaining the family *sacra*. This was the origin, and a very innocent and laudable one, of the *usucapio pro herede* (p. 179), which Gaius condemns as an incomprehensible and infamous institution, and which undoubtedly lost some of its *raison d'être* once the right of succession of agnates had been introduced.

SECTION 12.—BREACH OF CONTRACT, AND PRIVATE AND PUBLIC OFFENCES.

To speak of a law of obligations in connection with the regal period, in the sense in which the words were understood in the later jurisprudence, would be a misapplication of language. It would be going too far to say, as is sometimes done, that before the time of Servius, Rome had no law of contract; for men must have bought and sold, or at least bartered, from earliest times,—must have rented houses, hired labour, made loans, carried goods, and been parties to a variety of other transactions inevitable amongst a people engaged to any extent in pastoral, agricultural, or trading pursuits. It is true that a patrician family with a good establishment of clients and slaves had within itself ample machinery for supplying its ordinary wants, and was thus to some extent independent of outside aid; but there were not many such families; and the plebeian farmers and the artisans of the guilds were in no such fortunate position. There must therefore have been contracts and a law of contract; but the latter was very imperfect. In barter,—for at that time money was not in use,—with instant exchange and delivery of one commodity against another, the transaction was complete at once without the creation of any obligation. But in other cases, such as

[14] Gai., ii. §§ 53, 54.

those alluded to, one of the parties at least must have trusted to the good faith of the other. What was his guarantee, and what remedy had he for breach of engagement? His reliance in the first place was on the probity of the party with whom he was dealing,—on the latter's reverence for Fides (p. 22), and the dread he had of the disapprobation of his fellows should he prove false, and of the penalties, social, religious, or pecuniary, that might consequently be imposed on him by his *gens* or his guild.[1] If the party who had to rely on the other's good faith was not satisfied with his promise, and the grasp of the right hand that was its seal,[2] he might require his solemn oath (*jusjurandum*). Cicero speaks again and again of the sanctity of an oath, and its potency in holding men to their word;[3] and Gellius remarks on the extreme rarity of failure to perform an undertaking entered into in sight and hearing of a deity (*deo teste*).[4] Dionysius mentions that the altar of Hercules (*ara maxima*) in the cattle-market, and which is said to have existed before Rome itself, was the resort of those who desired to bind each other by covenant;[5] and it can hardly be doubted that, whatever may have been the case at a later period, in the time of the earlier kings he who forswore himself was amenable to pontifical discipline.

[1] Such as debarment from gentile or guild privileges, exclusion from right of burial in the gentile or guild sepulchre, fines in the form of cattle and sheep, &c.

[2] Some of the old writers (*e.g.*, Liv., i. 21, § 4, xxiii. 9, 3 ; Plin., *H.N.*, xi. 45 ; Serv. *in Aen.*, iii. 687) say that the seat of Fides was in the right hand, and that to give it (*promittere dextram*,—is this the origin of the word "promise"?) in making an engagement was emphatically a pledge of faith. See a variety of texts illustrating the significance of the practice, and testifying to the regard paid to Fides before foreign influences and example had begun to corrupt men's probity and trustworthiness, in Lasaulx, *Ueber d. Eid bei d. Römern* (Würzburg, 1844), p. 5 *sq.* ; Danz, *Sacrale Schutz*, pp. 139, 140 ; Pernice, *Labeo*, vol. ii. p. 408 *sq.*

[3] *E.g.*, *De off.*, iii. 31, § 111.

[4] "Jusjurandum apud Romanos inviolate sancteque habitum servatumque est. Id et moribus legibusque multis ostenditur" (*Noct. Att.*, xi. 18, 1).

[5] Dion. Hal., i. 40.

If the promisee desired a more substantial security, he took something in pledge or pawn from the other contractor; and though he had no legal title to it, and so could not recover it by judicial process if he lost possession, yet so long as he retained it he had in his own hand a *de facto* compulsitor to performance. Upon performance he could be forced to return it or suffer a penalty; not by reason of obligation resulting from a contract of pledge, for the law as yet recognised none, but because, in retaining it after the purpose was served for which he had received it, he was committing theft and liable to its punishment.

At this stage breach of contract, as such, founded no action for damages or reparation before the tribunals; but it is not improbable that, where actual loss had been sustained, the injured party was permitted to resort immediately to self-redress by seizure of the wrongdoer or his goods. Self-help was according to the spirit of the time; not self-defence merely, in presence of imminent danger, but active measures for redress of wrongs already completed. Vindication of a right of property (p. 192) was originally, and possibly still in the first days of the kings, an actual display of force,—a fight between the contending parties; and *manus injectio* (§ 36) and *pignoris capio* (§ 37), arrest of a debtor and distraint on his goods, both of them acts not of officers of the law but of the creditor himself, survived, under statutory or customary restrictions, all through the republic.

For anything like a clear line of demarcation between crimes, offences, and civil injuries we look in vain in regal Rome. Offences against the state itself, such as trafficking with an enemy for its overthrow (*proditio*) or treasonable practices at home (*perduellio*), were of course matter of state concern, prosecution, and punishment from the first. But in the case of those that primarily affected an individual or his estate, there was a halting between, and to some extent a confusion of the three systems of private vengeance, sacral atonement, and public or private penalty.[6] The coexistence of those systems has been attempted to be explained by reference to the different temperaments of the races that constituted united Rome;[7] and this certainly is a consideration that cannot be left out of view. But the same sequence is observable in the history of the laws of other nations whose original elements were not so mixed, the later system gradually gaining ground upon the earlier and eventually overwhelming it.

The remarkable thing in Rome is that private vengeance should so long not only have left traces but continued to be an active power. It must still have been an admitted right of the *gens* or kinsmen of a murdered man in the days of Numa; otherwise we should not have had that law of his providing that where a homicide was due to misadventure, the offering to them of a ram should stay their hands.[8] To avenge the death of a kinsman was more than a right—it was a religious duty, for his *manes* had to be appeased; and so strongly was this idea entertained, that, even long after the state had interfered and made murder a matter of public prosecution, a kinsman was so imperatively bound to set it in motion that, if he failed, he was not permitted to take anything of the inheritance of the deceased. Private vengeance was lawful too at the instance of a husband or father who surprised his wife or daughter in an act of adultery; he might kill her and her paramour on the spot, though, if he allowed his wrath to cool, he could afterwards deal with her only judicially in his domestic tribunal. The talion we read of in the Twelve Tables[9] is also redolent of the *vindicta*

---

[6] See Abegg, *De antiquissimo Romanorum jure criminali* (Regiom. 1823), p. 36 *sq.*; Rein, *Das Criminalrecht der Römer* (Leipsic, 1844), p. 24 *sq.* ; Clark, *Early Roman Law*, p. 34 *sq.*

[7] Rein (as in last note), p. 39 *sq.*

[8] See § 11, note 2; Clark, *Early Rom. Law*, p. 47 *sq.*

[9] Gell., xx. 1, 14.

privata, although practically it had become no more than a compulsitor to reparation. And even the nexal creditor's imprisonment of his defaulting debtor (§ 31), which was not abolished until the fifth century of the city, may not unfittingly, in view of the cruelties that too often attended it, be said to have savoured more of private vengeance than either punishment or procedure in reparation.

Expiatio, supplicium, sacratio capitis, all suggest offences against the gods rather than against either an individual or the state. But it is difficult to draw the line between different classes of offences, and predicate of one that it was a sin, of another that it was a crime, and of a third that it was but civil injury done to an individual.[10] They ran into each other in a way that is somewhat perplexing. Apparently the majority of those specially mentioned in the so-called *leges regiae* (p. 20) and other records of the regal period were regarded as violations of divine law, and the punishments appropriate to them determined upon that footing. Yet in many of them the prosecution was left to the state or to private individuals. It is not clear, indeed, that there was any machinery for public prosecution except in treason and murder,—the former because it was essentially a state offence, the latter because it was comparatively early deemed expedient to repress the blood-feud, which was apt to lead to deplorable results when friends and neighbours appeared to defend the alleged assassin.[11]

[10] Voigt (*XII Tafeln*, vol. i. p. 484) observes that the patrician looked upon every offence as committed at once against gods and men, and held that the punishment should be one that satisfied both; hence the *deo necari, sacratio capitis*, and *consecratio bonorum*. The plebeians regarded its two moments as separable; and (as appears from the spirit of the XII Tables) left it to the pontiffs to protect the gods, putting it on the state to protect itself by ordinary death punishment, addiction into slavery, declaration of *improbitas* or intestability, talion, and pecuniary penalties.

[11] On murder (*parricidium*) in regal Rome see Osenbrüggen, *Das altrömische Paricidium* (Kiel, 1841), and review by Dollmann in Richter's *Krit. Jahrb.*, vol. xi. (1842), p. 144 *sq.*; Clark, *Early Roman Law*, p. 41 *sq.*

Take some of those offences whose recognised sanction was *sacratio capitis*. Breach of duty resulting from the fiduciary relation between patron and client, maltreatment of a parent by his child, exposure or killing of a child by its father contrary to the Romulian rules, the ploughing up or removal of a boundary stone, the slaughter of a plough-ox,—all these were capital offences; the offender, by the formula *sacer esto*, was devoted to the infernal gods. Festus says that, although the rules of divine law did not allow that he should be offered as a sacrifice to the deity he had especially offended (*nec fas est eum immolari*), yet he was so utterly beyond the pale of the law and its protection that any one might kill him with impunity.[12] But, as the *sacratio* was usually coupled with forfeiture of the offender's estate or part of it to religious uses, it is probable that steps were taken to have the outlawry or excommunication judicially declared, though whether by the pontiffs, the king, or the curies does not appear;[13] such a declaration would, besides, relieve the private avenger of the incensed god of the chance of future question as to whether or not the citizen he had slain was *sacer* in the eye of law.

That there must have been numerous other wrongful acts that were regarded in early Rome as deserving of punishment or penalty of some sort, besides those visited with death, sacration, or forfeiture of estate total or partial, cannot be doubted; no community has ever been so happy as to know nothing of thefts, robberies, and assaults. The XII Tables contained numerous provisions in reference to them; but it is extremely probable that, down at least to the time

[12] Festus, v. *Sacer mons* (Bruns, p. 288). This penalty is thought by Niebuhr and others to have been a survival of actual human sacrifice in pre-Roman Italy. The matter is discussed by Rein (as in note 6), p. 33 *sq*. On the position of the *homo sacer* see Ihering, *Geist*, vol. i. § 18.

[13] Festus (as in last note) says the *sacratio* was a sentence by the assembly of the people. But he is referring specially to the *sacratio* resulting from a contravention of the *leges sacratae* of the early republic. In time it was displaced by "interdiction of fire and water,"—practically a sentence of exile.

of Servius Tullius, the manner of dealing with them rested on custom, and was in the main self-redress, restrained by the intervention of the king when it appeared to him the injured party was going beyond the bounds of fair reprisal, and frequently bought off with a composition. When the offence was strictly within the family, the *gens*, and perhaps the guild, it was for those who exercised jurisdiction over those corporations to judge of the wrong and prescribe and enforce the penalty.

CHAPTER FOURTH.

REFORMS OF SERVIUS TULLIUS.[1]

SECTION 13.—EFFECT OF HIS REFORMS ON THE LAW OF PROPERTY.

THE aim of the constitutional, military, and financial reforms of Servius was to promote an advance towards equality between patricians and plebeians. While it may be an open question whether the institution of the comitia of the centuries was of his doing, or only a result of his arrangements in after years, yet it seems clear that he had it in view to admit the plebeians to some at least of the privileges of citizenship, imposing on them at the same time a proportionate share of its duties and burdens. Privileges, duties, and burdens were alike to be measured by the citizen's position as a freeholder; the amount of the real estate with its appurtenances held by him on quiritarian title was to determine the nature of the military service he was to render, the extent to which he was to be liable for tribute, and, assuming Servius to have contemplated the creation of a new assembly, the influence he was to exercise in it.

To facilitate his scheme he established a register of the citizens (*census*), which was to contain, in addition to a record of the strength of their families, a statement of the value of their lands and appurtenances, and which was to be revised periodically. In order to ensure as far as possible certainty of title, and to relieve the officials of troublesome

[1] Huschke, *Die Verfassung d. Königs Servius Tullius*, Heidelberg, 1838.

investigations of the genuineness of every alleged change of ownership between two valuations, it was declared that no transfer would be recognised which had not been effected publicly, with observance of certain solemnities, or else by surrender in court before the supreme magistrate (*in jure cessio*).[2] The form of conveyance thus introduced got the name of *mancipium*, and at a later period *mancipatio*, while the lands and other things that were to pass by it came to be known—whether from the first or not is of little moment —as *res mancipi*. Hence arose a distinction of great importance in the law of property (and which was only abolished by Justinian more than a thousand years later)[3] between *res mancipi*, transferable in quiritarian right only by mancipation or surrender in court, and *res nec mancipi*, transferable by simple delivery.

Mancipation[4] is described by Gaius, but with particular reference to the conveyance of movable *res mancipi*, as a pretended sale in presence of five citizens as witnesses and a *libripens* holding a pair of copper scales. The transferree, with one hand on the thing being transferred, and using certain words of style, declared it his by purchase with an *as* (which he held in his other hand) and the scales (*hoc aere aeneaque libra*); and simultaneously he struck the scales with the coin, which he then handed to the transferrer as figurative of the price.[5] The principal variation when it was an immovable that was being transferred was that the mancipation did not require to be on the spot;[6] the land was

---

[2] The nature of *in jure cessio* is explained on p. 144.
[3] *Cod. Just.*, vii. 31 (de usucap. transform., et de sublata differentia rerum mancipi et nec mancipi).
[4] Leist, *Mancipation und Eigenthumstradition* (Jena, 1865), §§ 2-39, and rev. by Bekker, in *Krit. VJS.*, vol. ix. (1867), p. 232 *sq.*; Ihering, *Geist*, vol. ii. § 46; Maine, p. 318 *sq.*; Clark, *Early Roman Law*, p. 108 *sq.*; Bechmann, *Gesch. d. Kaufes im Röm. Recht* (Erlangen, 1876), §§ 5-36; Voigt, *XII Tafeln*, vol. i. § 22, vol. ii. §§ 84-88, 126.
[5] Gai., i. 121.
[6] Gai., i. 121; Ulp., *Frag.*, xix. 6.

simply described by its known name in the valuation roll. Although in the time of Gaius only a fictitious sale,—in fact the formal conveyance upon a relative contract,—yet it was not always so. Its history is very simple. The use of the scales fixes its introduction to a time when coined money was not yet current, but raw copper nevertheless had become a standard of value and in a manner a medium of exchange. That, however, was not in the first days of Rome. Then, and for a long time, values were estimated in cattle or sheep, fines were imposed in them,[7] and the deposits in the *legis actio sacramento* (§ 34) took the same form.[8] The use of copper as a substitute for them in private transactions was probably derived from Etruria. But, being only raw metal or foreign coins, it could be made available for loans or payments only when weighed in the scales; it passed by weight, not by tale.[9] There is no reason for supposing that the weighing was a solemnity,—that it had any significance beyond its obvious purpose of enabling parties to ascertain that a vendor or borrower was getting the amount of copper for which he had bargained.

It was this very simple practice of every-day life in private transactions that Servius adopted as the basis of his mancipatory conveyance, engrafting on it one or two new features intended to give it publicity and as it were state sanction, and thus render it more serviceable in the transfer of censuable property. Instead of the parties themselves using the scales, an impartial balance holder, probably an

[7] "Romulus . . . multae dictione ovium et bovum—quod tum erat res in pecore et locorum possessionibus, ex quo pecuniosi et locupletes vocabantur— non vi et suppliciis coercebat" (Cic., *De rep.*, ii. 9, § 16). The Aternian law of 300 U.C., in fixing the maximum of magisterial mulcts, still did so in sheep and oxen; it was only by the *lex Julia Papiria* of 324 that they were converted into money (Marquardt, *Röm. Staatsverwalt.*, vol. ii. p. 6). *Pecus* gave its name to *pecunia* (Varro, *De L.L.*, v. 95, Bruns, p. 301).

[8] Huschke, *Die Multa und das Sacramentum* (Leipsic, 1874), p. 387. The XII Tables fixed the amount of those deposits in money.

[9] Gai., i. 122.

official,[10] was required to undertake the duty, and five citizens were required to attend as witnesses, who were to be the vouchers to the census officials of the regularity of the procedure. They are generally supposed to have been intended as representatives of the five classes in which Servius had distributed the population, and thus virtually of the state; and the fact that, when the parties appealed to them for their testimony, they were addressed not as *testes* but as *Quirites*,[11] lends some colour to this view. Servius is also credited with the introduction of rectangular pieces of copper of different but carefully adjusted weights, stamped by his authority with various devices (*aes signatum*),[12] which are supposed to have been intended to come in place of the raw metal (*aes rude*)[13] formerly in use, and so facilitate the process of weighing.[14] If so, it is not easy to understand why weighing should have continued to be the characteristic feature of the transaction down to the time of the XII Tables; for what could be gained by passing through the scales ten bars which were known to weigh each a certain number of pounds? It is more likely that they were cast and stamped as standards, which were put into one scale

---

[10] Danz (*Gesch. d. R.R.*, § 143, note 6) refers to an inscription in which two persons are designated "IIviri libripendes ex decreto decurionum." The scales, too, may have been state scales; for Varro (*De L.L.*, v. 183, Bruns, p. 303) mentions that in his day a pair was still preserved in the temple of Saturn.

[11] Gai., ii. 104.

[12] Plin., *H.N.*, xviii. 3, "Servius rex ovum bovumque effigie primus aes signavit." Specimens exist in many museums.

[13] Varro, *De L.L.*, v. 163 (Bruns, p. 302); Festus, v. *Rodus* (Bruns, p. 288).

[14] Mommsen (*Gesch. d. Röm. Münzwesens*, Leipsic, 1860) suggests that the stamping was a guarantee not of the weight but of the purity of the metal. The notion is entertained by some jurists that the solemn weighing of the copper, whether stamped bars, rough lumps, or foreign coins, converted it into money. This is as meaningless as it is fanciful. The metal was no more money after it was weighed and handed to a vendor or borrower than it had been before,—it was still just so many pounds' weight of copper. If he had to use it next day in a transaction *per aes et libram* it would have to be weighed afresh.

while the raw metal whose weight was to be ascertained was put into the other.

Instead, therefore, of being a fictitious sale as Gaius describes it, and as it became after the introduction of coined money early in the fourth century (p. 134), the *mancipium* or mancipation, as regulated by Servius, was an actual completed sale in the strictest sense of the term. What were the precise words of style addressed by the transferree to the transferrer, or what exactly the form of the ceremonial, we know not. But, as attendance during all the time that some thousands of pounds perhaps of copper were being weighed would have been an intolerable burden upon the five citizens convoked to discharge a public duty, it may be surmised that it early became the practice to have the price weighed beforehand, and then to reweigh, or pretend to reweigh, before the witnesses only a single little bit of metal (*raudusculum*),[15] which the transferree then handed to the transferrer as "the first pound and the last," and thus representative of the whole.[16] Whatever may have been its form, however, its effect was instant exchange of property against a price weighed in the scales. The resulting obligation on the vendor to maintain the title of the vendee, and the qualifications that might be superinduced on the conveyance by agreement of parties,—the so-called *leges*

---

[15] Hence the request the scale-bearer made to the transferrer, "touch the scales with a small piece of the metal" (*rausdusculo libram ferito*),—words, says Festus, that were still used after coined money (which was counted, not weighed) had taken the place of the raw copper, and when it was with a coin and not a bit of metal that the scales were struck.

[16] The conjecture is suggested by the words of style in the *solutio per aes et libram*, Gai., iii. §§ 173, 174. There were some debts from which a man could be effectually discharged only by payment (latterly fictitious) by copper and scales, in the presence of a *libripens* and the usual five witnesses. In the words addressed to the creditor by the debtor making payment these occurred —*hanc tibi libram primam postremamque expendo* ("I weigh out to you this the first and last pound"). The idea is manifestly archaic, and the words in their letter quite inappropriate to the transaction in the form it had reached long before the time of Gaius.

mancipii,—will be considered in connection with the provisions of the XII Tables on the subject (§ 30).

Why this form of conveyance got the name of *mancipium* or *mancipatio,* why those things, to whose effectual transfer by a private party in quiritarian right either it or surrender in court was essential, were called *res mancipi,* and what were the considerations that determined the selection of the things that should or should not be included in this class, are questions that have been much discussed. The explanation of Gaius,[17] that mancipation was so called because in the process the transferree took with his hand the thing that was being transferred to him (*quia manu res capitur*), has been accepted in many quarters much too readily. Great as is the authority of Gaius, he was not infallible, least of all in a question of etymology. If there was one point on which Roman jurists and grammarians displayed weakness it was this, as witness their derivation, apparently in all seriousness, of *testamentum* from *testatio mentis, mutuum* from *de meo tuum, oratio* from *oris ratio.*[18]

The fundamental mistake lies in supposing that the notion embodied in the word is *manu capere* instead of *manum capere.*[19] There was no taking with the hand when land or a house was being conveyed, for the parties did not require to be near them;[20] and there could be none in the mancipation of a prædial servitude, for it was intangible. As already observed, the early law had no word that specially denoted ownership. The generic *manus* answered the purpose. By it was understood the power or right of the head of a house over the persons and things that were

---

[17] Gai., i. 121.
[18] See many other instances in Dukeri *Opusc. de latinitate JCorum veterum,* Leyden, 1711, p. 462 *sq.*
[19] No aid can be taken from *usucapere,* for that really meant *manum usu capere.*
[20] Gai., i. 121 ; Ulp., *Frag.,* xix. 6.

subject to him.[21] *Mancipere* or *mancipare*, therefore, was simply to acquire *manus*, *i.e.*, dominion or ownership. Possibly the acquirer was sometimes called *manceps*.[22] *Mancipium* (or *mancupium*) was used in three distinct though cognate senses,—(1) the power or mastery of the *manceps*, and thus synonymous with *manus*;[23] (2) the thing over which that mastery extended, but most frequently a slave;[24] (3) the process of law whereby any person and some things *in manu mancipiore* were transferred and acquired.[25] It must have been from *mancipium* in the last of these senses that the phrase *res mancipi* (*i.e.*, *mancipii*) was derived; if from the first it would more properly have been rendered *res in mancipio;* and it is out of the question that it can have been derived from the second. We reach, therefore, the same conclusion as Gaius,[26]—that *res mancipi* meant a thing passing by mancipatory process.

According to the enumeration of Gaius and Ulpian, the things included in the class of *res mancipi* were lands and houses in Italy or in those districts in the provinces enjoying

[21] See § 9, note 3. For examples of the employment of the word in reference to one and all of the subject members of the household, see Rossbach, *Die Röm. Ehe*, p. 28, and Voigt, *XII Tafeln*, vol. ii. p. 84. We have evidence of its employment in reference to things in the *manum conserere* of the sacramental action *in rem* (see § 34, note 6).

[22] The progression is the same as in *primus, princeps, principium; avis, auceps, aucupium, aucupari*, &c. *Manceps* occurs in the sense of owner in Tertull., *De idolol.*, 1. In the later republic and early empire it had many special meanings, for which see Forcellini.

[23] As in Gell., xviii. 6, 9.

[24] Just., *Inst.*, i. 3, 3.

[25] As in the famous provision in the XII Tables, "cum nexum faciet mancipiumque, uti lingua nuncupassit ita jus esto." In every case, without exception, in which the process of *mancipium* was resorted to there was acquisition of *manus* in the old meaning of the word,—mancipation of things, coemption (p. 119), giving of a *filiusfamilias* in adoption, passing a *filiusfamilias* into the hand of a third party as a *mancipium* with a view to his emancipation, the same with a woman in order to effect her release from marital *manus*, the noxal upgiving of a *filiusfamilias* or slave to the party he had wronged (p. 120), and the *familiae emptio* of the testament *per aes et libram* (p. 169).

[26] Gai., ii. 22.

jus italicum (§ 52, n. 2),—in other words, lands and houses held on quiritarian title, together with rights of way and aqueduct, slaves, and domestic beasts of draught or burden (oxen, horses, mules, and donkeys); all other things, including provincial lands generally, (their ownership being in the state), were *res nec mancipi*. In the time of Servius and during the greater part of the republic the domain land (*ager publicus*) in Italy, until it was appropriated by private owners, was also reckoned as *res nec mancipi*; like all other things of the same class it passed by simple delivery, whereas *res mancipi* could not be transferred in full ownership except by mancipation or surrender in court. Many are the theories that have been propounded to account for the distinction between these two classes of things, and to explain the principle of selection that admitted oxen and horses into the one, but relegated sheep and swine, ships and vehicles to the other.[27] But there is really little difficulty. Under the arrangement of Servius what was to determine the nature and extent of a citizen's political qualifications, military duties, and financial burdens was the value of his *heredium* (and other freeholds, if he had any), and what may be called its appurtenances,—the slaves that worked for the household, the slaves and beasts of draught and burden that worked the farm, and the servitudes of way and water that ran with the latter. It may be that in course of time slaves without exception were dealt with as *res mancipi*,—without consideration, that is to say, whether they were employed on their owner's house or farm or on any part of the public lands in his occupancy (§ 19); and reasonably, because they were often shifted from the one to the other. But the cattle a man depastured on the public meadows were no more *res mancipi* than his sheep.[28] To say that the things

---

[27] See a summary of the principal ones in Danz, *Gesch.˙d. R.R.*, vol. i. § 119.
[28] Ulpian (*Frag.*, xix. 1), in enumerating the animals that were *res mancipi*, expressly limits them to those *broken to* yoke or burden; and Gaius, though in

classed as *res mancipi* were selected for that distinction by Servius because they were what were essential to a family engaged in agricultural pursuits would be to fall short of the truth. They *constituted* the *familia* in the sense of the family estate proper;[29] whereas the herds and flocks, and in time everything else belonging to the *paterfamilias*, fell under the denomination of *pecunia*. So the words are to be understood in the well-known phraseology of a testament, *familia pecuniaque mea*.[30]

SECTION 14.—INCIDENTAL EFFECTS OF HIS REFORMS ON THE LAW OF THE FAMILY, OF SUCCESSION, AND OF CONTRACT.

In alluding in a previous section (p. 34) to the family institutions of the plebeians it was explained that prior to the time of Servius their unions were not, in the estimation of the patricians at least, regarded as lawful marriages (*justae nuptiae*), although amongst themselves they may have been held effectual, and productive, if not of *manus*, at all events of *patria potestas*. For this there were two reasons—(1) that, not being citizens, they did not possess the preliminary qualification for *justae nuptiae*, namely, *conubium*, and (2) that, not being patricians, the only ceremony of marriage known to the law was incompetent to them. The first obstacle was removed by their admission by Servius to the ordinary rights of citizenship, the second by the introduction of the civil marriage ceremony of coemption.[1] This was an adaptation of the *mancipatio* described in the preceding section. Once the efficacy of

one passage he mentions oxen without any qualification, yet in another (ii. 15) records it as the opinion of some jurists that animals did not become *res mancipi* on birth, but only when broken in, or at least when they had reached the usual age for putting them under yoke or girth.

[29] See § 9, note 2.
[30] Gai., ii. 124.
[1] See Rossbach, *Röm. Ehe*, p. 65 sq.; Karlowa, *Röm. Ehe*, p. 43 sq.; Voigt, *XII Tafeln*, vol. ii. §§ 158, 159.

the latter as a mode of acquiring *manus* over things was established, its adoption by the plebeians, now citizens enjoying *conubium*, as a method of acquiring *manus* over their wives,[2] was extremely natural. The scales, the *libripens*, and the five witnesses were all there; but, as there was no real price to be paid, the only copper that was needed was a single *raudusculum*. The words recited in the ceremonial, unfortunately not preserved, were necessarily different from those of an ordinary mancipation.[3] According to the testimony of a considerable number of ancient writers, and as the word *co-emptio* itself seems to indicate (though disputed by most modern civilians), the nominal purchase was mutual; the man acquired a *materfamilias*, who was to bear him children and enable him to perpetuate his family, while she acquired a *paterfamilias*, who was to maintain her while the marriage lasted, and in whose succession she was to share when a widow.[4] It was accompanied with other observances described by many of the lay writers, but which were matters of usage and fashion rather than law; and might be, and often was, accompanied also with religious rites, which, however, were private, not public, as in confarreation.

To the introduction of mancipation is also due a device resorted to by the plebeians for disposing of their estates in contemplation of death. Their elevation to the rank of citizens did not apparently give them admission to the comitia of the curies; and, as it was many years after the assassination of Servius before that of the centuries was ever convened, they had still no means of making testaments unless perhaps in the field on the eve of battle. So here again the expedient of mancipation was taken

---

[2] It was not necessary for creation of the *patria potestas*; that, as the history of the later marriage law amply testifies, was a necessary civil consequence of *justae nuptiae*, although there might have been neither confarreation nor coemption.

[3] Gai., i. 123. [4] On *coemptio*, see Appendix, Note B.

advantage of, not indeed to make a testament instituting an heir, and to take effect only on the death of the testator, —the form of the transaction, as an instant acquisition in exchange for a price real or nominal, could not lend itself to that without statutory intervention,—but to carry the transferrer's *familia*[5] to a friend, technically *familiae emptor*, on trust to let the former have the use of it while he survived,[6] and on his death to distribute according to his instructions whatever the transferree was not authorised to retain for himself.[7] Like so many others of the transactions of the early law, it was legally unprotected so far as the third parties were concerned whom the transferrer meant to benefit; they had no action against the trustee to enforce the trust; their sole guarantee was in his integrity and respect for Fides. This *mortis causa* but *inter vivos* alienation was the forerunner of the testament *per aes et libram*, which will be described (§ 32) in connection with the provisions of the Twelve Tables in reference to succession.

[5] The *familia* was the collective name for a man's *heredium* and other lands, with their slaves and other mancipable appurtenances (§ 13 *in fine*),—an aggregate of *res mancipi*, and therefore itself capable of mancipation. The conveyance was universal, *i.e.*, the items of the aggregate, even though movable, did not require to be conveyed separately or to be handled in conveying; and apparently the *pecunia* was carried along with the *familia* as an accessory, at least if expressly mentioned.

[6] Sir Henry Maine (*Ancient Law*, p. 206) is of opinion that, as a mancipation could not be subject to a limitation either of condition or time, there must have been not only instant but total divestiture of the transferrer. But this was not necessarily the result; for it was the commonest thing in the world for the transferrer in a mancipation to reserve a life-interest (Gai, ii. 33); and a reservation of a life-interest in one's own *familia* would possibly be construed even more liberally than an ordinary usufruct. See *infra*, p. 168.

[7] It is a question what was the exact position of the beneficiaries in relation to the deceased after the trust was fulfilled. Were they bound to maintain the *sacra* of the deceased's family? They could not be so as his heirs, for they lacked that character. Perhaps it was to meet the case of persons in their position that the pontiffs first began to modify the rules on the subject, adopting as their leading principle, "Ut, ne morte patrisfamilias sacrorum memoria occideret, iis essent ea adjuncta ad quem ejusdem morte pecunia veniret" (Cic., *De leg.*, ii. 19, 47). See p. 178.

Dionysius credits Servius with the authorship of more than fifty enactments relative to contracts and crimes, which he says were submitted to and approved by the assembly of the curies.[8] This statement can hardly be accepted as it stands. That a few such laws may have been enacted by him, either at his own hand or with the assistance of the curies, such as that imposing the penalties of confiscation of his estate, scourging, and sale beyond Tiber as a slave, upon a citizen who failed periodically to report himself at the taking of the census, can be admitted without difficulty; but the majority of them were probably nothing more than formularisations of customary law for the use of the private judges in civil causes whom he is said to have instituted. There was one contract, however, notorious in after years under the name of *nexum*, that manifestly was influenced, either directly or indirectly, by his legislation. In its normal estate it was a loan of money, or rather of the raw copper that as yet was all that stood for it. Whether before the time of Servius it was accompanied by any formalities beyond the weighing of it in a pair of scales (which was rather substance than form) we know not; and what right it conferred on the creditor over his debtor who failed to repay can only be matter of speculation. But there are indications that, in the exercise of undefined self-help, defaulters were treated with considerable severity, being taken in satisfaction and put in chains by their creditors; for Servius is reported to have promised to pay their debts himself in order to obtain their release, and to pass a law limiting execution by persons lending money at interest to the goods of their debtors.[9] Whether he fulfilled the first part of his promise we are not informed; but the second part of it was impracticable, since a debtor's failure to repay a loan was in most cases attributable to his insolvency and want of means

[8] Dion., iv. 13.   [9] Dion., iv. capp. 9, 11.

with which to satisfy his creditors. So, apparently, Servius had to be content with regulating and ensuring the publicity of the contract, and making a creditor's right of self-redress by apprehension (*manus injectio*) and confinement of his debtor conditional on the observance of the prescribed formalities of the *nexum*. These were the weighing of the copper that was being advanced in a pair of scales held by an official *libripens*; the reweighing of a single piece in the presence of five citizen witnesses, and its delivery by the lender as representing the whole;[10] and the simultaneous recital of certain words of style, which had the effect of imposing on the borrower an obligation to repay the loan, usually with interest, by a certain day. The consequence of this, one of the earliest independent contracts of the *jus civile*, will be more appropriately considered in a subsequent section (§ 31).

The extension of the solemnities of *mancipium* to such very diverse transactions as nexal contract, coemption, adoption, emancipation of a *filiusfamilias*, release of a debtor, and execution of a testament has been commented upon as manifesting great poverty of invention on the part of the early Roman jurists. But the criticism is undeserved. In one and all of them, as already remarked,[11] the same idea was involved,—acquisition of *manus* in the original meaning of the word.[12] In all of them the process was intended to ensure deliberation on the part of those engaged in the transaction, certainty as to its terms, publicity, and preservation of evidence alike of the *res*

---

[10] See § 13, note 16.   [11] See § 13, note 25.

[12] This was so even in the case of nexal contract and release of a nexal or judgment debtor. In the former, in consideration of the loan advanced, the creditor acquired a power over his debtor which entitled him to apprehend and imprison him; in the latter, in consideration of the loan repaid or judgment satisfied, the debtor acquired release from that power (*me a te solvo liberoque hoc aere aeneaque libra*, Gai., iii. 174); in other words, he reacquired over himself that *manus* which, by *nexum* or judgment, had been conferred on his creditor (see §§ 31, 36).

gestae and of the words interchanged. Those objects are attained now by writing, and subscribing, and sealing, and attesting, and recording; and these solemnities, or some of them, we resort to without reference to the particular nature of the matter dealt with. The early Romans were not in the habit of embodying their deeds in writing. But the procedure as a whole was a guarantee for deliberateness; the touching of the scales with a bit of metal was as good an index that the transaction was perfect as the adhibiting of a seal; and the performance of the whole business in presence of five citizens, as representatives of the public, who were bound by statute to testify to it when required,[13] was as fair a substitute for recording in a public register as the civilisation of the time could have provided.

SECTION 15.—AMENDMENTS ON THE COURSE OF JUSTICE.[1]

Of the course of justice in the regal period, whether in criminal or civil matters, before the time of Servius, we know little that can be relied on. Mr. Clark says, in reference to criminal procedure, fairly summarising our scanty information about the judicial functions of the king:— " The king as judge; sometimes availing himself of the aid of a council, sometimes perhaps, in cases of minor importance, delegating his judicial powers to individual *judices;* aided in his quest of capital crimes by the *quaestores parricidii;* appointing at his pleasure, in cases of treason, the

---

[13] The XII Tables, according to Gellius (xv. 13, 11), contained a provision that if a man who had suffered himself to be called as a witness, or who had acted as a *libripens*, refused to declare his testimony when required, he should be reckoned dishonourable, and be incapable in future of executing, or being a witness to, or taking any benefit under, a deed requiring the testimony of witnesses,—" Qui se sierit testarier libripensve fuerit, ni testimonium fariatur, inprobus intestabilisque esto." Probably something of the same sort had previously been enacted by Servius.

[1] Clark's *Early Roman Law*, pp. 54-108.

extraordinary *duumviri;* allowing, though perhaps not bound to do so, an appeal from the latter to the assembled burgesses,—this is all that we can recognise with any degree of confidence." It would be a mistake, however, to suppose that the king alone was invested with criminal jurisdiction. The *paterfamilias* also, aided by a council in cases of importance, was judge within the family; his jurisdiction sometimes excluding that of the state, at other times concurring with it, and not to be stayed even by an acquittal pronounced by it. He alone was competent in any charge against a member of the family for a crime or offence against the domestic order,—adultery or unchastity of wife or daughter, immorality of his sons, undutiful behaviour of children or clients; while there are instances on record of his interference judicially where an offence such as murder or theft had been committed by a member of his family against a stranger, and even when his crime had been treason against the state.[2] Death, slavery, banishment, expulsion from the family, imprisonment, chains, stripes, withdrawal of *peculium,* were all at his command as punishments; and it may readily be assumed that in imposing them he was freer to take account of moral guilt than an outside tribunal. The indications of criminal jurisdiction on the part of the *gens* are slight; but its organisation was such that it is impossible not to believe that it must occasionally have been called on to exercise such functions; as, for example, in deciding whether the penalty of *sacratio capitis* had been incurred by a clansman charged with having put one of his children to death before it had reached its third year, contrary to the law of Romulus, or with having violated his duty to his client, contrary to

[2] See a variety of examples in Voigt, *XII Tafeln,* vol. ii. § 94. They are all later than the regal period; but as, with the progress of centuries, the tendency was to relax rather than augment the powers of the *paterfamilias,* it may be assumed that in the early years of Rome his judicial authority was quite as great as during the republic.

that of Numa. And it must not be lost sight of that, as murder seems to have been the only crime in regard to which private revenge was absolutely excluded, the judicial office of the kings must thus also have been considerably lightened, public opinion approving and not condemning self-redress, so long as kept within the limits set by usage and custom.

The boundary between civil and criminal jurisdiction, if it existed at all, was very faintly defined. Theft and robbery, for example, if one may conclude from the position they held in the later jurisprudence, were regarded not as public but as private wrongs; and yet when a thief was caught plying his trade by night he might be slain, and when taken in the act by day might be sold as a slave. It can hardly be doubted that in the former case, and possibly until the time of the XII Tables, there might be instant retribution without any pretence of trial, the avenger taking his risk of the consequences if perchance he had been mistaken in imputing felonious intent to the man whose blood he had shed. In the latter, a mistake was unlikely; and here too we may assume that there was room for instant apprehension of the offender, and sale of him across the frontier by the party he had wronged, without any judicial warrant. But in both cases it may also be assumed that a practice, afterwards formally sanctioned by the XII Tables,—that of the thief compounding for his life or freedom,—was early admitted, and the right of self-redress thus made much more beneficial to the party wronged than when nothing was attained but vengeance on the wrong-doer. In assaults, non-manifest thefts, and other minor wrongs, self-interest would in like manner soon lead to the general adoption of the practice of compounding; what was originally a matter of option in time came to be regarded as a right; and with it occasional difficulty in settling the amount of the composition, and consequent necessity of an appeal to a third party. Here seems to be the origin of the king's jurisdiction in matters of this sort. He was the natural person to whom to refer such a dispute; for he alone, as supreme magistrate, had the power to use coercion to prevent the party wronged insisting on his right of self-redress, in face of a tender by the wrong-doer of what had been declared to be sufficient reparation. But that self-redress was not stayed if the reparation found due was withheld; as the party wronged was still entitled at a much later period to wreak his vengeance upon the wrong-doer by apprehending and imprisoning him, it cannot reasonably be doubted that such also was the practice of the regal period.

How the kings acquired jurisdiction in questions of quiritarian right, such as disputes about property or inheritance, is by no means so obvious. Within the family, of course, such questions were impossible; though between clansmen they may have been settled by the *gens* or its chief. The words of style used in the sacramental real action (p. 189) suggest that there must have been a time when the spear was the arbiter, and when the contending parties, backed possibly by their clansmen or friends,[3] were actual combatants, and victory decided the right. Such a procedure could not long survive the institution of a state. In Rome there seems to have been very early substituted for it what from its general complexion one would infer was a submission of the question of right to the pontiffs as the repositories of legal lore. Nor is this view in conflict with the well-known passage in which Cicero affirms that in the earlier regal period—contrary to the later practice—a private citizen never acted as judge or arbiter in a civil suit (*lis*), but that it was always disposed of in the king's court;[4] for the

---

[3] The prætor's command to the parties to go to the ground *suis utrisque superstitibus praesentibus*, "each with his seconds in attendance," which Cicero (*P. Mur.*, xii. 26) found so absurd, is manifestly a relic of it.

[4] "Nec vero quisquam privatus erat disceptator aut arbiter litis, sed omnia conficiebantur judiciis regiis" (Cic., *De rep.*, v. 2, 3). The old writers, Cicero

latter may quite well have consisted of the members of the college of pontiffs, of which the king was the official head. But their proper functions were sacred. To bring what was a question of purely civil right within their jurisdiction, they engrafted on it a sacral element, by requiring each of the parties to make oath to the verity of his contention; and the point that in form they decided was which of the two oaths was false, and therefore to be made atonement for. In substance, however, it was a finding on the real question at issue; and the party in whose favour it was pronounced was free to make it effectual if necessary by self-redress in the ordinary way.[5]

Of Servius, Dionysius says—using, as he often does, language more appropriate to the republican than to the regal period—that he drew a line of separation between public and private judicial processes; and that, while he retained the former in his own hands, he referred the latter to private judges, and regulated the procedure to be followed in causes brought before them.[6] The intrusting of the judicial office to a private citizen, chosen for each individual case as it arose, and acting on a commission from the prætor, instead of to permanent officials trained for the purpose, was one of

particularly, frequently seem to distinguish between *lites* and *jurgia;* but among moderns there is great difference of opinion as to whether the distinction was well founded, and if so, what it amounted to. If Karlowa (*Röm. CP.*, §§ 1-6) be right in his opinion (which, however, has met with little acceptance, and presents many and serious difficulties), that while *lites* were suits (1) founded either on statute or fixed and certain custom (both, according to him, included in the word *lex*), and (2) insisted in either by a *legis actio sacramenti* (*infra*, § 34), or (later) a *legis actio per condictionem* (*infra*, § 41), *jurgia* were (1) founded on undefined *jus*, of which king, consul, or prætor, in the exercise of his *jurisdictio*, was the mouthpiece, and (2) brought under his notice in the shape of a demand for appointment of a (delegated) judge (the *legis actio per judicis postulationem, infra*, § 35),—if this view be right, the field of possible intervention by the kings in matters judicial would be materially widened. But the only thing absolutely certain about the distinction is that questions litigated *per sacramentum* and (afterwards) *per condictionem* were *lites* and not *jurgia*.

[5] For details see *infra*, § 34.   [6] Dion. Hal., iv. 25.

the remarkable features of the Roman system, and contributed greatly to the development of that instinctive jurisprudential faculty which eventually produced such admirable results. It is interesting, therefore, to inquire whether Servius is really entitled to the credit of the private judge. His reforms in other directions were such as to render some change in existing judicial arrangements all but imperative. He was enormously increasing the number of the citizens,—that is to say, of those who were to enjoy in future the privileges of quiritarian right,—and multiplying the sources of future disputes that would have to be determined by the tribunals. Not improbably, too, if there be any truth in the statement that he was the author of some fifty laws about contracts and crimes,[7] he thought it right to make some regulations for further restraining self-help, and for assuring something like uniformity of practice in fixing the amount of composition or reparation for minor wrongs. All this augmented the burden of the judicial office; so that the account we have of the institution by Servius of private *judices*, acting on a reference from him when he found a good cause of action averred, is more than credible.

The question remains, however, was it his intention that those judges of his should have no official character, but should be selected from among the patrician citizens for each case as it arose, in the ordinary case sitting singly (*unus judex*)? Or was it a collegiate court or courts that he established? Pomponius alludes to two such courts, that of the *centumviri* and that of the *decemviri litibus judicandis*. The centumviral court[8] and centumviral causes

---

[7] Dion., iv. 13. It is said they were repealed by his successor on the throne; "ignored" would be a better phrase, seeing that apparently the great majority of them at least were not comitial enactments, but only instructions to the newly instituted *judices*.

[8] Literature : Schneider, *De Cvirali judicio apud Romanos*, Rostochii, 1834, and rev. by Zumpt, in Richter's *Krit. Jahrb.*, vol. iii. (1839), p. 475 *sq.*; C. G. Zumpt, *Ueber Ursprung, Form, u. Bedeutung d. Centumviralgerichts*, Berlin,

are often referred to by Cicero, and the range of their jurisdiction seems to have included every possible question of *manus* in the old sense of the word,—status of individuals, property and its easements and burdens, inheritance whether testate or intestate; in other words, all questions of quiritarian right. By the time of Gaius the only matters apparently that were brought before it were questions of right to an inheritance of the *jus civile*; but the spear, the emblem of quiritarian right generally, was still its ensign.[9] We have no distinct reference to its existence before the beginning of the sixth century;[10] but the nature of its jurisdiction, and the consideration that transition from a court of one judge to a court of a hundred is the reverse of what experience of Roman procedure would lead us to expect, induces the belief that its origin must have been comparatively early, and due probably to Servius. But it is impossible to accept the opinion, even of so eminent an authority as Bethmann-Hollweg,[11] that it was a plebeian court composed of plebeian members, and intended to administer justice only to plebeian citizens; that would be to run counter to all we read of the monopoly of the law in the hands of the patricians[12] until the publication of the Flavian collection in the middle of the fifth century (p. 262), and to render unintelligible what Livy says of the honours conferred on its author by the grateful

---

1838; Huschke, *Serv. Tullius*, p. 585 *sq.*; Bachofen, *De Romanorum judiciis civilibus*, Göttingen, 1840, p. 9 *sq.*; Puchta, *Institut.*, vol. i. § 153; Keller, *Röm. CP.*, § 6; Bethmann-Hollweg, *Gesch. d. CP.*, vol. i. § 23; Clark, *Early Roman Law*, p. 103 *sq.*; Karlowa, *Röm. CP.*, p. 247 *sq.*

[9] "Hasta signum justi dominii; . . . unde in centumviralibus judiciis hasta praeponitur" (Gai., iv. 16). Pomponius (*Dig.* i. 4, fr. 2, § 29) designates the centumviral court as *hasta*, and Suetonius (*Aug.*, 36) as *centumviralis hasta*.

[10] Paul. Diac., in his abridgment of Festus, v. *Centumviralia* (Bruns, p. 264), says that, after the increase of the tribes to thirty-five (*anno* 513 U.C.), three members were chosen from each to act as judges (*electi ad judicandum*); and that, although their number was thus 105, they were nevertheless called *centumviri* for simplicity's sake.

[11] *Gesch. d. CP.*, vol. i. p. 57 *sq.*

[12] Liv., ix. 46, 5. See also Cic., *P. Mur.*, xi. 25.

plebeians. It must have been, originally at least, a court of patricians, with a jurisdiction in questions of quiritarian right, whether arising among patricians or plebeians.

It is Pomponius who also narrates [13] that soon after the creation of the second prætorship (which was in 507 or thereabout) certain persons were appointed, under the title of *decemviri litibus judicandis*, to act as presidents of the centumviral court. It has been attempted to identify them with the *judices decemviri* mentioned in the *leges sacratae* that followed the second secession in 305 U.C., and to carry their institution likewise back to Servius. The *decemviri* of Pomponius may possibly have been the successors of those referred to in the Valerio-Horatian laws, and whose persons were therein declared inviolable, like those of the tribunes and ædiles. But there is no semblance of reason for connecting them with the Servian reforms. The Valerio-Horatian decemvirs were plebeian officials, acting under the direction of the tribunes and ædiles (p. 85), and can have had no existence until after the institution of the tribunate.[14]

That Servius should substitute for king and pontiffs a numerous court of citizens to try questions of quiritarian right on remit from himself was quite in accordance with the general spirit of his reforms. It was not mere matters of personal dispute they had to decide, but a law they had to build up by their judgments, which was to be of general and permanent application; and as it was beyond the power

---

[13] See reference in note 9.

[14] The theories maintained in reference to the centumviral and decemviral courts are very various. Some identify the *centumviri* with the Romulian senate of 100, and the *decemviri* with its *decem primi, e.g.*, Sanio, *Varroniana in d. Schriften d. Röm. Juristen* (Leipsic, 1867), p. 123, Kuntze, *Excurse*, p. 115, and (to some extent) Karlowa, p. 249. Some—*e.g.*, Niebuhr, Bachofen, and Bethmann-Hollweg—attribute the institution of both colleges to Servius Tullius. Others—*e.g.*, C. G. Zumpt—hold their establishment to have been contemporaneous with the XII Tables; while others again—*e.g.*, Puchta, Huschke, and Keller—credit Servius with the decemvirate, but postpone the establishment of the centumvirate to the sixth century at soonest.

of the king to overtake the task, what could be a more appropriate substitute than a court of his counsellors acting under pontifical guidance?[15] But there were many cases requiring judicial assistance in which no question of quiritarian right had to be determined, but only one of personal claim,—of alleged indebtedness, whether arising out of a legal or illegal act, denied either *in toto* or only as to its amount. Matters of that sort were supposed to involve no general principle of law, but to be rather mere disputes or differences about facts, which could well be decided by a single judge. To meet their case was introduced the *unus judex*, appointed for each case as it arose, and acting really as the king's commissioner. This was the beginning of a system that bore wondrous fruit in after years, and that eventually displaced altogether the more imposing court of the centumvirs.

[15] Pomponius says (*Dig.* i. 2, fr. 2, § 6) that even after the XII Tables the college of pontiffs annually appointed one of their number to preside in private judicial processes.

PART II.

THE JUS CIVILE.

From the Establishment of the Republic till the Subjugation of Central and Southern Italy.

PART II.

THE JUS CIVILE.

From the Establishment of the Republic till the Subjugation of Central and Southern Italy.

CHAPTER FIRST.

HISTORICAL EVENTS THAT INFLUENCED THE LAW.

SECTION 16.—THE CHANGE FROM KING TO CONSULS.

THE establishment of the consulate was not attended by the happy results that must have been anticipated by many of those who had rejoiced over the expulsion of the Tarquins. The retaliatory wars that followed cost Rome much of her territory. The influx of wealth from Etruria was suddenly checked; and the return of the Tuscan immigrants to their own country arrested at once the trading and mercantile spirit that had begun to develop. An important field of industry was thus closed, and the poorer classes forced to confine themselves to petty agriculture for their means of subsistence. From their betters they met with little sympathy. Although in the cities of Latium the commonalty seem generally to have ranked as citizens, and to have had a substantial share in government as well as in military service and taxation, yet in Rome they were practically denied such a position; for the constitution of the centuriate assembly was such as to make the vote to which they were nominally entitled an empty name. Patrician predominance soon became much more marked and oppressive than it had been in the time of the later kings. The consuls were not a whit less powerful than these had been. For they had the same *imperium*, conferred in the same way; and in virtue of it they might make and enforce what decrees they pleased, with little chance of impeachment on demitting office, so long as they were responsible only to the comitia of the centuries and had done nothing to impair the privileges or offend the prejudices of those by whom they had really been elected. They had much in their power in the way of alleviating the position of the plebeians, healing dissensions, and fusing the different elements of the populace into a united and cohesive community; but many did not care to take advantage of their opportunities, while, of the few who were animated by nobler sentiments, most feared to incur the enmity of their order, which usually consigned those who had courage to resist it to death or exile. The times, too, were adverse. Constant petty warfare drained the resources of the peasantry and involved them in debt, from which they found it almost impossible to free themselves,—debt contracted to patrician money-lenders. For it was the higher class that monopolised the little wealth of which Rome now could boast; amassed partly in farming their holdings of public land through the agency of their clients and slaves, and partly by their ruthless severity towards their debtors, whose mortgages were rarely redeemed, and who, as a final resource, had too often to impledge themselves to their creditors as the condition of a fresh advance.

The inevitable result of this unhappy state of matters was a bitter feeling of hostility on the part of the plebeians towards the patricians and the new order of things,—a hostility that manifested itself not merely in individual instances, but in a general and all-pervading spirit of disaffection. In fact, while their desire really was for equality in political rights and participation in the more substantial privileges enjoyed by their patrician fellow-citizens, the contumelious treatment they received at the hands of the latter drove them to band themselves together for purposes of united action. They even went so far as to form quasi-corporations within the limits of their tribes, and to establish their own tutelary divinities in Liber, Libera, and Ceres, corresponding to the divine triad of the Capitoline. They were thus in a position to make common cause; and so effectually did they do so that frequently they refused to join in a campaign, and three times seceded in a body from the city, with the threat of complete severance of their connection with Rome. On such occasions it was only the tardy promise of redress of some overpowering grievance, to be embodied in laws under sanction of oath (*leges sacratae*), and appeals to their patriotism and common interests in face of an enemy, that induced them to forego their resolution.

SECTION 17.—POLITICAL INEQUALITIES REMOVED.

It was not by any comprehensive and well-digested reform, dictated by considerations of justice, that the plebeians at last attained a position of political equality with the higher order, but by fragmentary legislation wrung from time to time from the latter against their will, and when Rome was in peril from dissensions within or hostile demonstrations from without. It was the first secession in the year 260 U.C., in resentment of the failure of M. Valerius to obtain the approval of the patricians for his proposals for alleviation of the condition of insolvent debtors, that brought about the tribunate. The enactment that established it was the result of a treaty between the two orders, as solemn almost as if it had been concluded with fetial ceremonial between two independent states. With the institution of the new office the plebeians obtained a leverage power that stood them in good stead in their subsequent contests; for in their tribunes, whose persons were declared sacred and inviolable, and whose number in course of time was increased to ten, they obtained representatives who could officially expose their grievances, and protectors who within the city could stop the execution of a decree or the levy for a campaign, could impose fines on those disobeying their orders, could bring even a consul to trial for official misdeeds, and could prevent the election of new magistrates when complaints were too long unheeded.

Still greater compactness was given to the plebeians as a power in the state by the constitutional recognition in 283 of the elective and legislative competency of their council (*concilium plebis*). It had often met before, and often passed resolutions (*plebiscita*).[1] It was now, however, that for the first time it took its place as one of the institutions of the commonwealth, and that its resolutions became of indisputable authority amongst the plebeians themselves; although they were binding upon the citizens as a whole only when —as occasionally happened—they had been sanctioned by a senatusconsult.[2]

The second secession in 305 resulted in the overthrow of the decemvirate, which had been created to give effect to the demands of the plebeians for a codification of the law; and was followed immediately by the Valerio-Horatian laws, re-establishing the previous magisterial *régime*. One of their provisions was that whoever should harm a tribune of the people, an ædile, or one of the "ten-men judges" should forfeit his head to Jupiter and his fortune to Ceres.[3] The ædiles here referred to had been first appointed on the insti-

---

[1] The Icilian law, empowering the tribune presiding at an assembly of the plebeians to prevent by very stringent means its disturbance by patricians, is attributed by Dionysius to the year 262; some historians, *e.g.*, Schwegler, doubt the accuracy of his date.

[2] As in the case of the Terentilian law, which resulted in the compilation of the XII Tables, the Canuleian law sanctioning intermarriage of patricians and plebeians, &c.

[3] Liv., iii. 55.

tution of the tribunate; they were the assistants of the tribunes, had supervision of the market in which the plebeians disposed of their produce, were keepers of the temple of Ceres,[4] and specially charged with the custody therein of senatusconsults confirmatory of plebiscits. The ten-men judges (*judices decemviri*) probably owed their institution to the tribunes themselves; they seem to have been judges in civil causes arising between plebeians, officiating on a remit from a tribune or ædile.

According to Mommsen, the creation of the comitia of the tribes was due to the same Valerio-Horatian laws.[5] If this was so, the object must have been not so much to favour the plebeians as to weaken the power of the tribunes. For while the new assembly, like the *concilium plebis*, was based on the tribal organisation with a tribal vote, yet the patricians as well as the plebeians had access to it, and its convocation and presidency were competent only to patrician magistrates. While there was in it, therefore, a semblance of concession to the plebeian preference for tribal arrangement, it was the magistrate who convoked it that had the right to say what proposals should be submitted to it. It had this advantage,—that its resolutions were *leges* even without approbatory senatusconsult; but also this disadvantage,—that, like the resolutions of the centuries, they did not take rank as *leges* without the authority of the fathers (*auctoritas patrum*), latterly, it is true, very much a matter of form, and from the time of the Publilian law of 415 conferred in advance. Whatever may have been the exact relation in which the two assemblies stood to each other constitutionally, there was difference enough between

---

[4] It has been suggested that their original official designation may have been *aediles Cereris*.

[5] Mommsen, *Röm. Forsch.*, vol. i. p. 164. He holds that the passage in Livy, "ut, quod tributim plebs jussisset, populum teneret," should read "quod tributim populus jussisset," &c. See also Karlowa, *Röm. RG.*, p. 118 *sq.*

them to prevent an amalgamation; each went its own course, the one summoned and presided over by a consul or the prætor, the other always by a tribune; the comitia of the tribes occupying itself with occasional general legislation on matters of private law, the council of the plebeians, more active than the other, devoting its attention more particularly to the redress of grievances that specially affected its own constituent members. All the latter needed to make it as efficient a legislative machinery as the former was that its resolutions should rank as *leges* without the necessity of a confirmatory senatusconsult. Livy says that the Publilian law of 415 contained a provision to that effect; but in this he is uncorroborated by any other authority. It was by the Hortensian law of 467, passed immediately after the third secession, that the amendment, if ever before proposed, was at last definitively effected; "it declared," says Gaius, "that plebiscits should be of force universally, and thus put them on an equality with comitial enactments." And from that time there can be little doubt that the patricians, now a body numerically insignificant, were free to take part in the votes of their tribes in the plebeian assembly whenever they were so minded.

Not less resolute and successful were the plebeians in asserting their claim to participate in the honours of the state. But it was a harder fight. The argument with which ever and again they were met was that the supreme government of the divinely-founded and divinely-protected commonwealth could not possibly be intrusted to men whose descent disqualified them for communion with the gods (*auspicia*); that to place the holies (*res divinae*) of the city in profane hands would be to draw down upon it the wrath of heaven. The first determined contest about the matter was in 309. A provision in the XII Tables a few years previously had declared marriage unlawful between patricians and plebeians. C. Canuleius carried in the council of the plebeians a resolution that this obnoxious enactment, a standing proclamation of social as well as political inequality, should be repealed; and to it he appended a second,—that the consulate should be opened to the plebeians. With these in his hand he presented himself before the senate (to which the tribunes had the entry, but without a vote), and demanded a confirmatory senatusconsult. After much strong language, much contemptuous denunciation of the looseness of the matrimonial relations of the lower order, sanctioned by no auspices and hallowed with no sacrifice, and much declamation more or less sincere about the divinity of the commonwealth, the senate was persuaded to accept the first resolution, but refused to adopt the second. Canuleius was disposed to rest satisfied with his victory, conceiving —and events proved he was right—that once mixed marriage should be not sanctioned merely but realised, a few years would suffice so far to efface distinctions as to render the advance to complete equality comparatively easy. His colleagues, however, insisted on proceeding with the second resolution. The result was a compromise, whereby it was arranged that for the consuls six military tribunes with consular powers should be substituted, three from each of the orders; but, though the new magistrates were elected, it was more than forty years before a plebeian had a place among them.

In 378 a still bolder proposal was made by C. Licinius Stolo, one of the tribunes, who had married a daughter of a distinguished patrician, and L. Sextius, one of his colleagues. They submitted three rogations to the plebeian assembly, the first demanding that consuls should again be elected instead of military tribunes, the second dealing with the occupancy of the state lands (§ 19), and the third with the law of debt (§ 20). His proposals were promptly passed by the plebeians, but at once rejected by the senate. For nine years did the contest last; eight times were the identical measures voted by the one body, only to be thrown out by the other. All this time Licinius and his colleagues were regularly re-elected by their grateful and determined constituents; and for the last five years of it, in the hope of bringing the senate to reason, they employed their veto to prevent the election of the supreme magistrates. It was only when a war with Velitræ became imminent that the patriotism of Licinius induced him to withdraw it. His forbearance brought its reward; for in 387 he had the satisfaction of seeing his proposals accepted, and in the year following, his colleague, L. Sextius, installed as the first plebeian consul. But the installation was to an office shorn of some of its prerogatives. For, just as the *regimen morum* and virtual control of admission to the senate (*lectio senatus*) had been severed from the consular prerogative and confided to a patrician censor when the military tribunate was established, so was the supreme judicial office (*jurisdictio*) divorced from the consulate when thrown open to plebeians, and intrusted to a patrician prætor (p. 242), the custody of the temples being at the same time committed to curule ædiles. Not for long, however, did the severance last. With the admission of the plebeians to the consulate the rest was but a matter of time. Within thirty years the dictatorship, censorship, and prætorship had ceased to be exclusively patrician offices. The last step was gained in the Ogulnian law of 454, which threw open the pontificate; although it was not until 502 that a plebeian actually reached the supreme dignity of *pontifex maximus*.

SECTION 18.—UNCERTAINTY OF THE LAW.

The later kings, with exception of the last, in their desire to conciliate the plebeians, whom Cicero says they regarded as in a manner royal clients, were careful that justice should be administered to them in their private relations, if not as citizens entitled as of right to claim the protection of the laws, yet as subjects to whom to deny it would be alike a patronal betrayal of trust and a grave mistake in policy. Servius's reputed fifty enactments about contracts and wrongs were probably nothing more than a series of instructions to those whom he deputed to act under him as judges (p. 67); but their attribution to him indicates an effort on his part to secure that the dispensation of justice should neither be neglected nor left to caprice or haphazard, one rule to-day and another to-morrow. With the consulate, and the disregard of the laws and instructions of the kings, all this was changed. The consuls, with their harassing military engagements, could have little time to devote to their judicial functions or properly to instruct those to whom they delegated the duty of investigating and adjudicating on the merits of a complaint; and the yearly change of magistrates must itself have been a serious obstacle to uniformity either of rule or practice so long as the law rested on nothing but unwritten custom. One can well believe, too, when feeling was so embittered between the orders, that it was no rare thing for a consul to use his magisterial punitive powers (*coercitio*) with undue severity when a plebeian was the object of them, or to turn a deaf ear to an appeal for justice addressed to him from such a quarter. The state of matters had become so intolerable that in the year 292 the demand was made by C. Terentilius Arsa, one of the tribunes, that a commission should be appointed to define in writing the jurisdiction of the consuls, so that a check might be put on their arbitrary, high-handed, and oppressive administration of what they were pleased to call the law. His colleagues induced him for the moment not to press his demand, which he was urging with a violence of invective that was unlikely to promote his object. But next year they made common cause with him, requiring that the whole law, public and private, should be codified, and its uncertainty thus as far as possible be removed. After a few years' delay upon one pretence or another, preliminary steps were taken for giving effect to a demand that in itself was too reasonable to be withstood; and in the years 303 and 304 the result was seen in the Twelve Tables, which became the basis of the bulk of the *jus civile*. Their history, sources, and contents will be explained hereafter (§§ 21-24).

SECTION 19.—THE PUBLIC LANDS.

The disposal of territory acquired by conquest, especially that part of it which was neither assigned gratuitously (*ager assignatus*) nor sold (*ager quaestorius*) to citizens as private property, was at all times a source of more or less bad feeling and contention. There were many ways of dealing with it. Land in cultivation at the time of its conquest, or at least so much of it as was taken from its old occupants, was usually let for short terms for a money rent (*vectigal*), while the better pasturage was dealt with in the same way, the rent (*scriptura*) being proportioned to the number of cattle put to graze upon it. Uncultivated lands (*agri occupatorii*) were left free to the occupancy of the first comer who was prepared to recognise the state's ownership by payment of a tithe of all standing crops, and half-tithe of all hanging fruits gathered by him. Lands of this sort in the occupancy of any particular individual were technically known as *possessiones*, and their holder as *possessor*. Not being private property, though capable of transfer by sale or gift, and of passing by succession just as if they were, such lands never figured in their occupants' pages in the valuation-roll (p. 56); no military service was rendered nor any tribute paid in respect of them. This was what rendered them so valuable. It was from them that the patricians derived their wealth. By the agency of clients, freedmen, and slaves, they were able to make them very productive without much personal effort. And for long they had the monopoly of them. Yet not of right, but only by force of custom and by their commanding influence. Although their exclusive occupancy of them in the early years of Rome was due to the very simple reason that they alone were citizens, yet when the plebeians were admitted to the franchise, and the territory largely increased, they refused to abate anything of their pretensions, which they sought to justify on the ground of patrician privilege. What was worse, the tithe was neglected, and the state revenues thereby so much diminished. The pasture land, too, was treated in much the same fashion,—the use of it denied to the humble citizen, and confined by the senate to the patricians and a few of the wealthier members of the lower order, who often managed to evade payment of their rent through the indulgence of the quæstors whose duty it was to exact it. And what was quite as great a hardship was this,— that while the plebeian was subject to tribute in respect of the cattle with which he worked his farm, the patrician herds grazing on those public pastures, as they were not *res mancipi*, were liable to no such burden.

The first serious attempt to redress those grievances was that made by Sp. Cassius, in co-operation with the tribunes, in the year 268. He aimed at three things,—the curtailment of the privileges asserted by the patricians, the regular collection of the dues leviable alike for the *possessiones* and the pasturage, and the instant distribution of some of the lands taken in recent conquests amongst the poorer citizens by whose prowess they had been won. His scheme miscarried; but subsequent agrarian proposals modelled upon it, and usually introduced immediately after some fresh conquest, were more fortunate. Yet on the whole they failed to ameliorate the position of those for whose benefit they had been passed. A poor plebeian was not able to cultivate to advantage anything but a small plot he could work himself with the aid of his sons; and even this fell all too soon into the hands of some capitalist, either by purchase or by foreclosure of a mortgage. And so, notwithstanding all the efforts of legislation to distribute the land, it continued to accumulate in the hands of a few. This was what led to the agrarian provisions of the Licinio-Sextian law of the year 387,—that no citizen should hold more than 500 jugers of arable land, or put to graze more than one hundred oxen and five hundred sheep upon the public pastures; while every occupant of arable land was to employ on it as much free as slave labour. Although by various devices the restrictions imposed were easily evaded, yet the passing of the enactment was in itself a declaration that gentile privilege, if it had ever existed, was no longer admitted. The object of later agrarian laws was usually to withdraw portions of the *ager publicus* from their possessors for distribution (*assignatio*) among poorer citizens as owners; the Licinian law had disposed for ever of any pretence of right on the part of the patricians to exclusive occupancy of the domain land.

SECTION 20.—THE LAW OF DEBT.

The tumults and seditions so frequent in Rome during the first two centuries of the republic are more frequently attributed by the historians to the abuses of the law of debt than to any other cause, social or political. The circumstances of the poorer plebeians were such as to make it almost impossible to avoid borrowing. Their scanty means were dependent on the regular cultivation of their little acres, and on each operation of the agricultural year being performed in proper rotation and at the proper season. But this was every now and again interfered with by wars which detained them from home at seed-time or harvest, practically rendering their farms unproductive, and leaving them and their families in straits for the commonest necessaries of life. A poor peasant, in such a case, had no alternative but to apply to a capitalist for a loan either of corn or money. But it was not to be had without security, and rarely without interest. It was not that the lender doubted the borrower's honesty and willingness to repay his debt; it was rather that there was every chance that next year a fresh war might again interfere with the latter's agricultural operations, leave him again without a crop, and thus render repayment impossible. And so, while interest accumulated and was periodically added to capital, new loans had year after year to be contracted as long as any acres remained that could serve as a security; failing all things, the debtor had to yield himself to his creditor in *de facto* servitude. This was a result of the transaction with the copper and the scales, technically known as *nexum*, whose origin has already been referred to (p. 67). It was bad enough at the best, but horrible in its abuse. For, not content with the slave's work he exacted from his debtor, the creditor too often put him in chains, and starved him and flogged him, as if really and truly a slave instead of still a Roman citizen. For that the status of the *nexi*, notwithstanding their bondage, was still that of freemen and citizens is clearly demonstrated by the fact that again and again, when there was a scarcity of fighting men to face an approaching enemy, their creditors were required to release them for the term of the campaign, reclaiming them when it was over. To such a height did the system grow, that often those free bondmen might be reckoned by thousands, and that the saying was almost justified that every patrician's dwelling had become a private prison-house.[1] For it so happened, owing to causes already explained, that for a long time it was almost exclusively in patrician hands that capital had accumulated, so that they were the lenders and oppressors, and the poor plebeians the borrowers and oppressed.

[1] Liv., vi. 36.

Many were the commotions and frequent the revolts to which such a state of things gave rise. It could hardly be otherwise. They were no fraudulent bankrupts or reckless speculators those miserable objects who appeared from time to time in the market-place, with lacerated shoulders, tattered garments, and famished countenances, to relate the story of their wrongs, but brave citizens who had been reduced to insolvency by a vicious system, which required them at a day's notice to leave their fields unsown or unreaped in order to fight the battles of the commonwealth, and that (till the year 348) at their own cost.[2] According to Livy, it was the sight of one of those wretched *nexi*, and the tale he told his old comrades of the sufferings he had endured, that was the immediate incitement to the first secession. The establishment of the tribunate was its great constitutional result; but that gave no relief so far as the treatment of a debtor by his creditor was concerned; for the tribunes could not interfere with the action of a private citizen, but only with that of an official. The same enactment, however, that created the tribunate and its *jus auxilii*, contained a provision that to many must have been even more welcome,—that all debts were to be remitted and all *nexi* to be liberated.[3] This, if not actually the first,[4] was at all events a forerunner of a long series of enactments for ameliorating the position of those who had been obliged to borrow money and by no fault of their own were unable to repay it. There were laws to repress usury: for example, a provision of the XII Tables making the *unciarium fenus*—*i.e.*, one-twelfth of the capital, or 8⅓ per cent. yearly—the maximum rate, and imposing a fourfold penalty on its contravention; a law in the year 407 reducing the rate to 4⅙

[2] Aug., *De Civ. Dei*, ii. 18.

[3] Dion., vi. 83, vii. 49. See on this, and on the silence of Livy in regard to it, Schwegler, *Röm. Gesch.*, vol. ii. p. 259.

[4] Dionysius (iv. 9) vaguely attributes some similar measures of relief to Servius Tullius.

and giving debtors three years' grace; and the Genucian law of 412, making the taking of interest altogether illegal, but which, as one might expect, soon became a dead letter. And there werè enactments remitting debt on terms that were ever varying, such as one of the Licinio-Sextian laws of 387 U.C.,—that interest already paid should be imputed to reduction of principal, provided the balance was paid off in three annual instalments.

Finally came the Poetilian law of 428.[5] Its occasion, purpose, and effect have been subjects of much discussion, and will be referred to in describing the contract of *nexum* (§ 31)—the transaction whereby a borrower gave his creditor the right to apprehend him on his failure to fulfil his obligation of repayment, and, without any process of law, carry him home and detain him, and employ his services as *de facto* (though not *de jure*) a slave. This apparently was the extent of the creditor's right, depending on consuetude rather than statute. But it had become frightfully abused; their *jus detinendi* being regarded by creditors not as affording them the means of obtaining through their debtor's industry substantial satisfaction for their pecuniary losses, but rather as entitling them to inflict as punishment every sort of cruelty and torture and indignity. It was recognised that nothing less would suffice than the total abolition of the *nexum* as a contract between lender and borrower. It was a serious matter, for it was the sacrifice of one of the most potent compulsitors to fidelity to one's engagements;[6] but no half measures would do; the root of the matter had to be reached; all the then *nexi* were liberated, and nexal contract forbidden for the future.[7]

---

[5] Liv., viii. 28 ; Cic., *De Rep.*, ii. 34, § 59.

[6] "Victum eo die ingens vinculum fidei" (Liv., viii. 28, § 8).

[7] "Propter unius libidinem omnia nexa civium liberata, nectierque postea desitum" (Cic., *De Rep.*, ii. 34, § 59). "Eo anno plebei Romanae velut aliud initium libertatis factum est, quod necti desierunt" (Liv., viii. 28, § 1).

This could not, of course, obviate the necessity for or the practice of borrowing, nor remove all chance of future agitation by the poorer classes about the burden of their debts. The right of the creditor at his own hand to apprehend and incarcerate his debtor was gone; so were the chains and hideous cruelties to which the latter had so often been subjected. But his detention as a judgment-debtor and on the warrant of a magistrate was still open to his creditor, who was still entitled to utilise his services until he had wiped off with his labour the sum of his indebtedness (§ 31). And one of indebtedness still continued to be the normal condition of the poorer plebeians, and an ever-festering source of discontent. It was this that caused the third secession, as it had caused the first; and with the Hortensian law, which was the issue of it (p. 86), was coupled a scheme of relief for insolvents. In the next period there was quite a series of measures devised for the same purpose, some of them accomplishing it by increasing the nominal value of the currency, and others, such as the Valerian law of 668, by simply wiping out the debts to the extent of a half or three-fourths. It was only by the Julian *cessio bonorum* (706 A.U.C.),[8] however, which entitled a debtor to his discharge on formally giving up everything to his creditor, that the position of insolvents was really greatly ameliorated, and their confinement or incarceration avoided.

"Ita nexi soluti, cautumque in posterum ne necterentur" (*Ib.*, 9). There were other provisions of the statute that applied to judgment-debtors (*judicati, addicti*), which are referred to in § 36.

[8] Caes., *B. C.*, iii. 1; Dio Cass., xli. 37.

CHAPTER SECOND.

THE TWELVE TABLES.

SECTION 21.—THEIR COMPILATION.

THE circumstances that occasioned the compilation of the XII Tables have been alluded to in Section 18. The first practical step towards it was taken in the year 300, in the despatch of a mission to Greece and the Greek settlements in Southern Italy, to study their statute law and collect any materials that might be of service in preparing the projected code. It may well be doubted whether the embassy ever went so far as Athens. It was quite unnecessary that it should, seeing how easily transcripts of Greek legislation were to be obtained in Cumæ and other Ionic colonies not far from home, as well as in the Greek settlements in Lower Italy and Sicily. On the return of the three ambassadors in 302, all the magistracies were suspended, and a commission of ten patricians (*decemviri legibus scribundis*) appointed with consular powers, under the presidency of Appius Claudius, for the express purpose of reducing the laws to writing. In this task they had the assistance as interpreter of one Hermodorus, an exile from Ephesus, whose presence seems to confirm the narrative of the previous collection of Greek material. Before the end of the ensuing year (303), the bulk of the code was ready, and was at once passed into law by the comitia of the centuries, and engraved or impressed on ten tables of wood, probably faced with stucco, which were displayed in the Forum. Next year the decemvirate was renewed with a slight change of *personnel*, but

G

under the same presidency as before; and in the course of a few months it had completed the supplemental matter, which was passed in due form, and displayed on two other tables, thus bringing the number up to twelve, and giving the code its official name of *Lex XII Tabularum.*

SECTION 22.—THEIR SOURCES.

There were provisions in the Tables that were almost literal renderings from the legislation of Solon; this is so stated, with reference to particular enactments, by both Cicero and Gaius.[1] Others again bore a remarkable correspondence to laws in observance in Greece, such as the provision that the conveyance following on a sale should not carry the property until the price had been paid or security given for it to the seller,[2] and the rules about theft discovered with loin-cloth and platter (*furtum linteo et lance conceptum*),[3] but which there is no authority for saying were directly borrowed.[4] By far the greater proportion of them, however, was native and original. Not that they amounted to a general formularisation of the hitherto floating customary law; for, notwithstanding Livy's eulogium of them as the fountain of the whole law, both private and public,[5] it seems clear that many branches of it were dealt with in the Tables only incidentally, or with reference to some point of detail. The institutions of the family, the fundamental rules of suc-

---

[1] Cic., *De Leg.*, ii. 23, § 59, in reference to the regulations about funerals in Table X; Gai., *lib.* 4. *ad XII Tab.*, in *Dig.*, x. 1, fr. 13, and xlvii. 22, fr. 4, in reference to other provisions.

[2] A provision attributed to the XII Tables by Justinian (*Inst.*, ii. 1, 41), which bears a close resemblance to a statement of Greek law by Theophrastus: see Hofmann, *Periculum beim Kaufe* (Vienna, 1870), p. 172, and his *Beiträge zur Gesch. d. Griech. u. Röm. Rechts* (Vienna, 1870), p. 71.

[3] Aristoph., *Nub.*, 497 *sq.*, and scholia to 499.

[4] On the whole subject see a paper by Hofmann "On the Influence of Greek Law on the XII Tables," in his *Beiträge*, p. 1 *sq.*

[5] Liv., iii. 34, where he calls them not only "fons omnis publici privatique juris," but "corpus omnis Romani juris."

cession, the solemnities of such formal acts as mancipation, *nexum*, and testaments, the main features of the order of judicial procedure, and so forth,—of all of these a general knowledge was presumed, and the decemvirs thought it unnecessary to define them.

What they had to do was to make the law equal for all, to remove every chance of arbitrary dealing by distinct specification of penalties and precise declaration of the circumstances under which rights should be held to have arisen or been lost, and to make such amendments as were necessary to meet the complaints of the plebeians and prevent their oppression in name of justice. Nothing of the customary law, therefore, or next to nothing, was introduced into the Tables that was already universally recognised as law, and not complained of as either unequal, indefinite, defective, or oppressive. Only one or two of the laws ascribed to the kings reappeared in them, and that in altered phraseology; yet the omission of the rest did not mean their repeal or imply denial of their validity; for some of them were still in force in the empire, and are founded on by Justinian in his Digest. Neither were any of the laws of the republic anterior to the Tables embodied in them, although for long afterwards many a man had to submit to prosecution under them and to suffer the penalties they imposed. In saying, therefore, that for the most part the provisions of the decemviral code were of native origin, all that is meant is that they were the work of the decemvirs themselves, operating upon the hitherto unwritten law in the directions already indicated.

SECTION 23.—THEIR REMAINS AND RECONSTRUCTION.

It is probably quite true that the original tables were destroyed when Rome was sacked and burned by the Gauls. But they were at once reproduced, and transcripts of them must have been abundant if, as Cicero says was still the case in his youth, the children were required to commit them to memory as an ordinary school task.[1] This renders all the more extraordinary the fact that the remains of them are so fragmentary and their genuineness in many cases so debatable. They were embodied in the Tripertita of Sextus Aelius Paetus (p. 262); they must have formed the basis of all the writings on the *jus civile* down to the time of Servius Sulpicius Rufus (who first took the prætor's edicts as a text), and they were the subjects of monographs by L. Acilius Sapiens in the latter half of the sixth century of Rome, by Servius Sulpicius Rufus himself in the end of the seventh or beginning of the eighth, by M. Antistius Labeo in the early years of the empire, and by Gaius probably in the reign of Ant. Pius. Yet a couple of score or so are all that can be collected of their provisions in what profess to be the *ipsissima verba* of the Tables, (though in a form in most cases more modern than what we encounter in other remains of archaic Latin). These are contained principally in the writings of Cicero, the *Noctes Atticae* of Aulus Gellius, and the treatise *De verborum significatione* of Festus, the two latter dealing with them rather as matters of antiquarian curiosity than as rules of positive law. There are many allusions to particular provisions in the pages of Cicero, Varro, Gellius, and the elder Pliny, as well as in those of Gaius, Paul, Ulpian, and other ante-Justinianian jurists. But such allusions, in the case of the later writers at least, must be accepted with caution. For it is often difficult to know whether it is the text itself that was their source of information, or not rather the readings of the interpreters (p. 262); whose rules, as is well known, were often nothing more than analogical applications of provisions of the Tables,[2]

---

[1] Cic., *De Leg.*, ii. 23, § 58.
[2] *E.g.*, the tutory-of-law of patrons; attributed to the Tables only *per consequentiam* (Gai., i. 165; Ulp., xi. 3).

or arbitrary constructions of them suggested by considerations of social policy.[3]

With such *disjecta membra* to operate upon, the work of reconstruction has been beset with difficulties. The questions that had to be encountered at the outset were these :— (1) were the provisions of the Tables arranged systematically? and (2) if they were, did they run on continuously, or was each Table in a manner complete in itself? The earlier editors, or at least some of them, seem to have assumed an answer to the first question in the negative, and accordingly adopted an arbitrary arrangement of the fragments; that of Charondas, for example, in 1578, was into public, private, and sacred law. Latterly, and ever since the appearance of the reconstruction of Jac. Gothofredus (Godefroi) in 1616, the editors have proceeded on the assumption that not only were the individual laws arranged upon a definite plan, but that each Table was complete in itself. But they are far from unanimous as to the sequence of the Tables or the proper allocation of the fragments amongst them. There are not more than four or five of the latter whose positions are expressly defined by ancient writers; and two or three more are said to have been the work of the decemvirate of 304, and therefore must have been in one or other of the two last and supplemental Tables. Beyond these much is left to the ingenuity of the reconstructors.

They have relied for guidance mainly on Gaius's commentary on the decemviral code and on Julian's consolidation of the prætorian edict. The commentary is in six books, in

---

[3] *E.g.*, the exclusion of all women except sisters of an intestate from succession as agnates. Gaius (iii. 23) says this was provided in the statute ; while Justinian, on the authority of Paul (in a commentary of his on the Tertullian senatusconsult) assures us (*Cod.*, vi. 58, 14, § 1, *Inst.* iii. 2, 3) that it was due to the restrictive interpretation of the jurists. Says Ulpian (*Dig.*, l. 16, 0), " Verbum 'ex legibus' sic accipiendum est : tam ex legum sententia, quam ex verbis."

which Gaius is supposed to have followed the order of his text, devoting one book to every two Tables; but as the excerpts from them in the Digest are few, and refer to only a small number of the matters we are assured were dealt with by the decemvirs, their value as a guide seems to have been overrated. There is a sort of tradition that, as Justinian in his Digest and Code followed the order of the Edict, so Salvius Julianus, in consolidating the latter, followed the order of the XII Tables; and of this clue the editors have availed themselves so far as it goes. The latest of them, Voigt, relies in addition on the order of matters in the various commentaries on the treatise of Sabinus (p. 318) on the *jus civile* (*Sabini libri tres juris civilis*).[4] As those commentaries run parallel throughout, he concludes that they closely follow the sequence of the treatise with which they are dealing; and this, he holds, corresponded exactly to the Tripertita of Sextus Aelius Paetus (p. 262). But the Tripertita included the XII Tables, arranged, as is supposed, in their legal order; and so, through Sabinus and his commentators, Voigt obtains a guide of some value, and which has the advantage of being a good deal earlier than those mainly followed by his predecessors in the work of reconstruction. The misfortune is that it is impossible to arrive at a generally accepted tabulation for purposes of reference; Dirksen differs from Gothofredus, Schoell to a slight extent from Dirksen, and Voigt very materially from all of them. There is unanimity as to the order and contents generally of the first three Tables, and the contents of the tenth; but as regards the others there is considerable divergence,—Dirksen, for example, placing the fragments relating to succession in the fifth Table, while Voigt places them in the fourth. It is safer, therefore, when referring to a provision

---

[4] See his paper "Ueber das Aelius und Sabinus System," in the *Abhandl.* (*Phil. Hist. Cl.*) *d. K. Sächs. Gesellsch. d. Wissensch.*, vol. vii. p. 320 *sq.;* also his *XII Tafeln*, vol. i. p. 55 *sq.*

of the Tables, to quote the ancient writer on whose authority it is said to have been contained in them, without condescending upon table or law. For, after all, the sequence is of little importance, and is throughout purely conjectural.[5]

SECTION 24.—GENERAL CHARACTERISTICS OF THE LAWS IN THE TABLES.

In form the laws of the tables were of remarkable brevity, terseness, and pregnancy, with something of a rhythmical cadence that must have greatly facilitated their retention in the memory. For example :—" Si in jus vocat, ito. Ni it, antestamino. Igitur em capito. Si calvitur pedemve struit,

---

[5] Dirksen's *Uebersicht der bisherigen Versuche zur Kritik u. Herstellung d. Zwölf-Tafel-Fragmente* (Leipsic, 1824) supplies the basis of all the later work on the Tables anterior to that of Voigt. Schoell, in his *Legis XII Tab. reliquiae* (Berlin, 1866), made a valuable contribution to the literature of the subject from a philological point of view. His version has been adopted substantially by Bruns in his *Fontes juris romani antiqui*, p. 16 *sq.*, and Wordsworth, in his *Fragments and Specimens of Early Latin* (Oxford, 1874), p. 253 *sq.* The latter, in a subsequent part of his volume (pp. 502-538), has added notes, historical, philological, and exegetical, which constitute a valuable commentary on the Tables as a whole. Voigt's two volumes, under the title of *Geschichte und System des Civil- und Criminal-Rechtes, wie-Processes, der XII Tafeln, nebst deren Fragmenten* (Leipsic, 1883), contain an exposition of the whole of the earlier *jus civile*, whether embodied in the Tables or not. The history of them occupies the first hundred pages or thereby of the first volume : his reconstruction of fragments and allusions—a good deal fuller than any earlier one, and supported by an imposing array of authorities, but not to be accepted without caution—is in the same volume, pp. 693-737. · The following is an outline of the arrangement generally adopted, with Voigt's variations :— I. Summons, and initial procedure in litigation before consul or prætor. II. Second stage of procedure,—before the centumviral court or one or more judges or arbiters, on remit from the consul or prætor. III. Execution by a judgment creditor against the body of his debtor. IV. Law of the family (Voigt—Law of the family and of succession). V. Succession and guardianship (Voigt—Acquisition of property and law of contractual obligations). VI. Acquisition and possession of property (Voigt—Guardianship of various sorts). VII. Rights pertaining to land (Voigt—Private delicts generally and their penalties). VIII. Delicts (Voigt—Relations between conterminous landowners and agrarian delinquencies). IX. Public law (Voigt—Public and criminal law). X. Regulation of funerals. XI. and XII. Miscellaneous supplementary provisions.

manum endo jacito."[1] "Aeris confessi rebusque jure judicatis XXX dies justi sunto. Post deinde manus injectio esto. In jus ducito."[2] "Si intestato moritur, cui suus heres nec escit, adgnatus proximus familiam habeto."[3] "Cum nexum faciet mancipiumque, uti lingua nuncupassit ita jus esto."[4] Here and there the rules they embodied were potestative, but for the most part they were peremptory, running on broad lines, surmounting instead of removing difficulties. Their application might cause hardship in individual instances, as when a man was held to the letter of what he had declared in a *nexum* or mancipation, even though he had done so under error or influenced by fraudulent misrepresentations; the decemvirs admitted no exceptions, preferring a hard and fast rule to any qualifications that might cause uncertainty.

The system as a whole is one of *jus* as distinguished from *fas* (§§ 6, 7); their respective spheres had by the beginning of the fourth century of Rome become much more clearly separated than in the reigns of the earlier kings. Not that the *fas* had ceased to influence the lives of the citizens even in their private relations; but it had become a power outside the law,—one may believe was purposely and carefully kept outside of it by the authors of the Tables, who were drafting a legislation that was to apply to a mixed community, holding somewhat diverse ideas of what religion enjoined and could enforce. The same feeling probably accounts for the disappearance of purely religious or sacral penalties for crimes and offences. In the royal laws execration (*sacratio capitis, sacer esto*) was not an uncommon sanction (p. 54); but in the Tables it occurs only once pure

---

[1] The words "si in jus vocat" were the initial words of the Tables (Cic., *De Leg.*, ii. 4, § 9). The rest of the provision is a composite of fragments from Porph. *in Hor. Sat.*, i. 9, 76; Festus, v. *Struere* (Bruns, pp. 17, 295); and Gai., *lib.* 4. *ad XII Tab.*, (*Dig.*, l. 16, 233 pr.)

[2] Aul. Gell., xx. 1, § 45.   [3] Ulp., xxvi. 1.

[4] Festus, v. *Nuncupata* (Bruns, pp. 23, 275).

and simple, and that with reference to an offence that could be committed only by a patrician,—material loss caused by a patron to his client (*patronus, si clienti fraudem faxit, sacer esto*).[5] In all other cases the idea that a crime was an offence against public order, for which the community was entitled in self-protection to inflict punishment on the criminal, is as prominent as the older one that it was a sin against the gods, to be expiated by dedication of the sinner to the divinity more especially outraged by his offence. Hanging and beheading, flogging to death, burning at the stake, throwing from the Tarpeian rock,—such are the secular penalties that are met with in the Tables; but often, though not invariably, the hanging and so forth is at the same time declared a tribute to some deity, to whom the goods of the criminal are forfeited (*consecratio bonorum*).

It is not unworthy of notice that traces remained in the Tables of the old system of self-help. The *manus injectio* of the third Table—the execution done by a creditor against his debtor—was essentially the same procedure as under the kings, but with the addition of some regulations intended to prevent its abuse. Against a thief taken in the act something of the same sort seems still to have been sanctioned;[6] while it was still lawful to kill him on the spot if the theft was nocturnal,[7] or even when committed during the day if he used arms in resisting his apprehension.[8] According to Cicero[9] there was a provision in these words—" si telum manu fugit magis quam jecit, arietem subicito:" this is just a re-enactment in illustrative language of the law attributed to

---

[5] Serv. *ad Aen.*, vi. 609. Comp. law of Romulus in Dion. Hal., ii. 10 (Bruns, p. 4). It is quite possible that Servius was in error in attributing this provision to the Tables.
[6] Gai., iii. 189.   [7] Aul. Gell., xx. 1, § 7.
[8] Gai., *lib.* 13. *ad ed. prov.*, (*Dig.*, xlvii. 2, fr. 54, § 2).
[9] Cic., *Top.*, 17, § 64 ; *p. Tull.*, 21, § 51. One cannot help suspecting that this is rather a figurative paraphrase of the enactment, which may have become proverbial, than its actual words.

Numa,[10] that for homicide by misadventure—"if the weapon have sped from the hand rather than been aimed"—a ram was to be tendered as a peace-offering to the kinsmen of him who had been slain. The original purpose must have been to stay the blood-revenge, and it may have been so with Numa (p. 52); but in the Tables it can only have been intended to stay the prosecution which it was incumbent on the kinsmen of a murdered man to institute. So with talionic penalties. "Si membrum rupit, ni cum eo pacit, talio esto,"[11]—such, according to Gellius, were the words of one of the laws of the Tables, that undoubtedly contain a reminiscence of a time when talion was recognised, "an eye for an eye, a tooth for a tooth;" but in the mouths of the decemvirs they were nothing more than a clumsy mode of enabling an injured man to exact the greatest money recompense he could, and to have it measured according to the position and fortune of the individual who had done him the injury.

[10] Serv. *in Virg. Bucol.*, iv. 43 (Bruns, p. 10).
[11] Aul. Gell., xx. 1, § 14.

CHAPTER THIRD.

THE PRIVATE LAW WITHIN AND BEYOND THE TABLES.

SECTION 25.—CITIZEN AND NON-CITIZEN.[1]

THE early law of Rome was essentially personal,—not territorial. A man enjoyed the benefit of its institutions and of its protection, not because he happened to be within Roman territory, but because he was a citizen,—one of those by whom and for whom its law was established. The theory of the early *jus gentium* was that a man sojourning within the bounds of a foreign state was at the mercy of the latter and its citizens; that he himself might be dealt with as a slave, and all that belonged to him appropriated by the first comer;[2] for he was outside the pale of the law. Without some sort of alliance with Rome a stranger—*hostis*, as he was called in those days—had no right to claim protection against maltreatment of his person or attempt to deprive him of his property; and even then, unless he belonged to a state entitled by treaty to the international judicial remedy of *recuperatio*, it was by an appeal to the good offices of the supreme magistrate, and not by means of any action of the *jus civile*.[3] So far did this go that, in the time of Gaius,

[1] See Müller-Jochmus, *Gesch. d. Völkerrechts im Alterthum* (Leipsic, 1848), p. 133 *sq.;* Voigt, *Das Jus Naturale d. Römer*, vol. ii. p. 8 *sq.;* Van Wetter, "La condition civile des étrangers d'après le droit romain," appended to Laurent's *Droit civil international*, vol. i. (Brussels, 1880), p. 667 *sq.;* Voigt, *XII Tafeln*, vol. i. §§ 24, 28.

[2] This doctrine is embalmed in the Digest as still the law of Rome in the time of Justinian (*Dig.*, xlix. 15, fr. 5, § 2).

[3] Some great authorities, such as Keller, Mommsen, and Van Wetter, hold that a stranger who enjoyed *commercium* was entitled, by some modifications

when *recuperatio* had become a thing of the far past, if a non-citizen had had a thing stolen from him, he could not maintain a civil *actio furti* against the thief without the aid in the pleadings of the prætorian device of a fiction ot citizenship;—a fiction which had in like manner to be employed if he was the thief and the action against him, the penalties being imposed by a statute that applied to none but citizens.[4] The domestic relations of a stranger were beyond the cognisance of the Roman tribunals; he might be husband and father, with rights over his wife and children according to the law of his own state, but on these a Roman court could not be called to adjudicate. He might claim to be heir under a testament or by intestacy according to the law of his own country; but on the validity of his claim no Roman magistrate or judge could be asked to express an opinion. Just as little would they listen to him if he claimed the rights the law of Rome accorded to a husband or father or heir; those rights were the heritage of the citizen, in which a stranger could have no participation.

Conubium, commercium, and *actio* were the three abstract terms in which were summed up the private rights[5] peculiar to a Roman citizen under the *jus civile*. *Conubium* was the capacity to enter into a marriage which would be productive of the *patria potestas* and agnation of Roman law, these in turn being the foundation of the intestate succession of *sui*

---

of their words of style or the intervention of a procurator, to the benefit of the *legis actiones*, as, for example, one *per sacramentum*. But against this view it is to be remembered (1) that modified actions (*actiones utiles* or *ficticiae*) were first introduced by the prætors, and that when the *legis actiones* were going out of use; (2) that procuratory was unknown under the system of the *legis actiones* (Gai., iv. 82); (3) that it was of the essence of the *judicia legitima*, of which the *legis actiones in personam* were the earliest forms, that parties and judge should all be citizens (Gai., iv. §§ 104, 109); and (4) that if the *legis actiones* had been competent *recuperatio* would have been unnecessary.

[4] Gai., iv. 37.

[5] *Testamenti factio* was a public right (Papinian, as in § 11, note 13). So was adrogation. From one point of view tutory was a public duty; but as a right it was private.

SECT. 25.] CONUBIUM, COMMERCIUM, ACTIO. 109

heredes and agnates, and of the tutories and curatories claimable by the agnates or the clansmen. *Commercium*[6] was the capacity for acquiring or alienating property by civil methods unconnected with *conubium*, such as mancipation, cession in court, or usucapion; and of becoming a party to an obligation by any civil contract, such as *nexum*, sponsion, and one at least of the forms of literal contract. *Actio* was the capacity for being a party to a *legis actio*,—an action clothed in the forms of the *jus civile*, and employed for the vindication, protection, or enforcement of a right either included in or flowing from *conubium* or *commercium*, or directly conferred by a statute that embraced only citizens in its purview.[7] Those three capacities were at common law enjoyed only by Roman citizens. A non-citizen—originally *hostis*, and afterwards usually called *peregrinus*[8]—in time

[6] Ulpian (*Frag.*, xix. 5) defines *commercium* as *emendi vendendique invicem ius*. The definition was probably traditional. But in the early law *emere vendere* did not mean to buy and sell, but, generally, to acquire and alienate; see authorities in Appendix, Note B. No. 1 of 2nd paragraph, and Pompon. in *Dig.*, xl. 7, fr. 29, § 1. The *invicem* in Ulpian's definition suggests a relative meaning. In fact, both *conubium* and *commercium* had abstract, concrete, and relative meanings. In the abstract they were prerogatives of Roman citizens generally. But though a citizen had *conubium* in the abstract, yet if he was under marrying age he was without it in the concrete; and though every citizen had *commercium* in the abstract, yet in the concrete he might be without it, as when he had been interdicted on account of prodigality (Paul., iii. 4a, 7). Relatively every citizen had both *conubium* and *commercium* with his fellow-citizens; but not with non-citizens, unless the latter enjoyed them by special concession.

[7] As, for example, the law of the XII Tables, and the Aquilian law of 467 U.C. giving an action of damages for culpable injury to property. Although the wrong for which a remedy was sought in an action upon the latter statute had about it nothing peculiar to the *jus civile*, yet Gaius says expressly (iv. 30) that such an action was competent to or against a *peregrinus* only under a fiction of citizenship.

[8] Neither "alien" nor "foreigner" is an adequate rendering of *peregrinus*. For *peregrini* included not only citizens of other states or colonies, independent or dependent, but also ἄπολιδες,—men who could not call themselves citizens (*cives*) at all; as, for example, the *dediticii*, whom Rome had vanquished and whose civic organisation she had destroyed, offenders sent into banishment, &c.; and until Caracalla's general grant of the franchise, the greater proportion of her provincial subjects were also spoken of as peregrins. This, though

came to be regarded as entitled to all the rights the *jus gentium* recognised as belonging to a freeman, and to take part as freely as a Roman in any transaction of the *jus gentium*; but that was not until Rome, through contact with other nations and the growth of trade and commerce, had found it necessary to modify her jurisprudence by the adoption of many new institutions of a more liberal and less exclusive character than those of the *jus civile*. From participation in the rights conferred by the latter the non-citizen was in theory excluded; he could enjoy them to a limited extent only indirectly as a friend or guest, or directly either as a citizen of an allied state or as an ἄπολις to whom they had more or less been specially conceded.

Amicitia and *hospitium*[9] in all probability were in observance before Rome was founded, and were adopted by her as institutions essential to the pacific intercourse of states. The first was a treaty or convention of friendship, formal or informal, guaranteeing the safe sojourn of members of the one state within the territory of the other. *Amici* were regarded as *in publica tutela* of the power within whose bounds they were temporarily resident, and entitled to protection in their persons and property through the direct intervention of king or other chief magistrate.[10] *Hospitium*, which might be either public or private, *i.e.*, accorded either to the citizens of another state generally or only to an individual, and which

---

linguistically objectionable, is a safer word than "non-citizen;" for the latter would include the Junian Latins of the early empire (§ 66), who, though not citizens, yet were not reckoned as *peregrini*.

[9] See Mommsen, "Das Röm. Gastrecht," in his *Röm. Forsch.*, vol. i. p. 319 *sq*.

[10] Justinian says (*Inst.*, iv. 10, pr.) that under the system of procedure *per legis actiones* procuratory in litigation was allowed only *pro populo, pro libertate*, or *pro tutela*; and it has been suggested that the latter may have included intervention for an *amicus* as *in tutela* of the whole Roman people. But this would have been to give to those who were *amici* and nothing more—as, for example, a Carthaginian under the treaty of 406 U.C.—a right of action in excess of that allowed to the much more intimately allied Latins, who had only *recuperatio*.

was usually hereditary, involved something like patronage; for the *hospes* was under the protection of some one *paterfamilias* in particular, who by the rules of *fas* was bound to see to his safety and honourable entreatment as he would to that of his client, with this difference, that, while the latter was a dependant, he was bound to treat a *hospes* as his equal. So urgent was a man's duty to a stranger who stood related to him as a guest, that, according to Sabinus, it came next that he owed to his children and his wards, and took precedence of that owing to his clients and his kinsmen.[11] But there is no reason to suppose that, in the earlier period of the republic at all events, it gave the guest any right beyond that of hospitality and protection through the medium of his patron. Anything further depended upon treaty in the case of foreign states, concession by Rome in the case of her dediticain subjects. The latter seem to have had conferred on them what was technically called *jus nexi mancipiique*,—the right of using Roman forms of contract and conveyance, and probably Roman actions for their protection; but we have no authentic details in regard to it.[12]

Rome's treaties with foreign states often assured reciprocally *commercium* and *recuperatio*, and sometimes even *conubium*. With the cities of the Latin League, for example,

---

[11] Gell., v. 13, § 5. Gellius himself, however, postpones the *hospes* to the client.

[12] Voigt (*XII Tafeln*, vol. i. 273) connects it with the mysterious provision in the Tables about the *forcti sanatesque* mentioned in a very defective passage in Festus, v. *Sanates* (Bruns, p. 290), and which he reconstructs as follows (vol. i. p. 733) :—" Nexum mancipiumque idem quod Quiritium forcti sanatisque supra infraque Urbem esto." " Nex . . . forcti sanati " are the only words of the provision legible in Festus; but he says the *sanates* were people who had fallen from their allegiance and soon returned to it, while the *forcti* had remained true. Might not "nexum mancipiumque forcti sanatisque idem esto " be sufficient ? See also Voigt's *Jus. nat.*, vol. iv. pp. 266-285 ; and for a different view, Hoffmann, *Das Gesetz d. XII Tafeln von den Forcten u. Sanaten*, Vienna, 1866.

Rome had all three;[13] so with the Hernicans; in certain cases with the Samnites; and with the Campanians under the treaty of 414 U.C.[14] More frequently her treaties conferred nothing more than *commercium* and *recuperatio*, and often were limited to *amicitia*, with trading privileges on an international footing. But *conubium* in such cases meant nothing more than right of intermarriage. It empowered a Roman citizen to marry a foreign woman, and *vice versa*, so that in each country the union was regarded as *justae nuptiae*. But it gave the husband no *manus* over his wife; she did not become a Roman because he was one; on the contrary, she remained *peregrina*, and was only naturally, not civilly, a member of her husband's family. His children by her, however, were in his *potestas;* that was the *ipso jure* consequence of the marriage; whereas *manus* resulted from confarreation or coemption, and with a *peregrina* these were impossible.[15] Had *manus*, which was dissoluble only by diffareation or remancipation, been an accompaniment of marriage between a Roman and a peregrin, it would have been impossible to accept the story told by Dionysius, that in 257 U.C., before their war with the Latins which ended in the victory of Lake Regillus, the Roman senate ordained that all mixed marriages should be held dissolved, so that all Latin women married to Roman citizens should be free to go back to their own country, while all Roman women married to Latins were required to return home.[16] Com-

---

[13] The moment Rome became associated with the Latin cities, there was *conubium* as a matter of course; an express concession by convention was unnecessary; which accounts for the absence of any mention of it in the Cassian treaty of the year 261.

[14] Voigt, *Jus. nat.*, vol. ii. pp. 147-154.

[15] As coemption was a purely civil transaction *per aes et libram*, and *commercium* (which included capacity for mancipation) always ran with *conubium*, it may be that *manus* could be acquired by coemption with a *peregrina;* but the authorities seem adverse to this view.

[16] Dion., v. 1. His further statement, that, of the issue of such dissolved marriages, sons were to go with their fathers and daughters with their mothers, is not so credible.

mercium conferred by treaty gave the citizens of the one state the right of trafficking within the bounds of the other, according to the forms of conveyance and contract peculiar to the latter. The only question of difficulty connected with it is whether or not it included a right in favour of the citizens of one of the allied states to hold land and other immovable estate within the territory of the other. The fact that in time Latins did settle in Rome, and acquired a limited vote in the comitia of the tribes, is not necessarily to be attributed to their possession of *commercium;* but opinions vary on the subject. The third element in the triad, *recuperatio*, often in treaties called *actio*, was the right to have the benefit of judicial procedure in an international form, and will be referred to in a subsequent section (§ 38).

SECTION 26.—THE GENS OR CLAN.

That the gentile relations should be affected by the decemviral code, one of whose main purposes was to give all the citizens equal rights [1] whether they happened to be members of a gentile association or not, was inevitable. Some of the clan customs and prerogatives no doubt did not require to be disturbed—those, namely, whose exercise could give no occasion for collision with the common law (*lex publica*). So far as they did not conflict with this last, any lawful association or incorporation (*sodalitas*) was entitled to make such rules for its own government as it thought fit, and enforce them amongst its members; [2] and the same liberty could not be refused to the patrician clans. They retained, therefore, their right of making statutes, their peculiar *sacra*, their lands and other property, their disciplinary jurisdiction over their members, their right to refuse their consent to the withdrawal of a family from their ranks in order to found a new *gens*, their power to sanction

[1] " Duodecim tabulae finis aequi juris" (Tac., *Annal.*, iii. 27).
[2] Gai., *lib.* 4. *ad XII Tab.*, (*Dig.*, xlvii. 22, 4).

H

or forbid the marriage of a female member, who had not the *gentis enuptio* as a personal privilege, with a man belonging to another gentile house:[3] the exercise of such privileges as these, which affected patricians alone, could not possibly conflict with the common law, whose provisions affected patrician and plebeian alike. But it was different with matters which, though previously regulated within the *gens* by gentile custom or statute, were now brought within the domain of the common law, and made the subject of general regulation. The *gens* in times past had claimed a right of succession to any of its members dying without a testament and without heirs of his body or heirs by adrogation (§ 11); but a new order of intestate succession was introduced by the Tables (§ 32), and to have allowed gentile statute or custom to have set it aside would have been inconsistent with the idea of *aequum jus*. So with tutory and curatory; the *gens* had provided for the guardianship of its pupil, female, and imbecile members, and charged itself with the superintendence of their guardians (§ 9); but the Tables dealt with the whole matter in the interests of non-gentile as well as gentile citizens, and any gentile rules, therefore, in reference to it were for the future subordinated to those of the common law. It was the same with the interdiction of a spendthrift (p. 32); the right to ordain it now passed to the consuls and afterwards to the prætor. And as regards clients, the jurisdiction formerly exercised over them by the *gens* passed to the ordinary civil magistrate, except in questions between them and their patrons not falling within the purview of the Tables; for now they were citizens, entitled to equal rights with their fellows; and not the least of these was the right to sue and be sued in the ordinary tribunals, and to be judged according to the new *jus scriptum*.

[3] Mommsen, *Röm. Forsch.*, vol. i. p. 10. It is not certain that the sanction of the *gens* was necessary in the case of a *filiafamilias* passing in *manum mariti*, for her marriage could not defeat any gentile chance of succession; but the reason of it is obvious in the case of a woman *sui juris*.

SECTION 27.—THE FAMILY RELATIONS PROPER.

1. So far as appears, no serious inroad was made by the Tables on the law of husband and wife, unless in the recognition of the legality of marriage entered into without any solemnity, and not involving that subjection of the wife to the husband (*manus*) which was a necessary consequence of the patrician confarreation (p. 26) and plebeian coemption (p. 65). These were left untouched. But it seems to have become a practice with some of the plebeians to tie the marriage bond rather loosely in the first instance; possibly —as became quite general at a later period—in consequence of objection by the women to renounce their independence and right to retain their own property and earnings; more probably because taking a woman to be merely the mother of their children (*matrimonium*) had been forced upon them before coemption had been introduced as a means of making her a lawful wife, and so they had become in a manner habituated to it. But there seems also to have been an idea that, as a man might acquire the ownership of a thing to which his legal title was defective by prolonged possession of it, so he might acquire *manus*, with all its consequences, over the woman with whom he had thus informally united himself, by prolonged cohabitation with her as his wife. This had become customary law. The Tables accepted it; all that was needed was to define the conditions under which *manus* should be held to have been superinduced, and the wife converted from a doubtful *uxor* into a lawful *materfamilias*.[1] Hence the provision that if a woman, married neither by

[1] "Genus est uxor, ejus duae formae: una matrumfamilias, eae sunt quae in manum convenerunt; altera earum, quae tantummodo uxores habentur" (Cic., *Top.*, 3, § 14). Boethius, commenting on the passage, says that the word *materfamilias* was applied only to wives who had passed *in manum* by coemption. His error may be due to the fact that he derived his information from some author who wrote after *manus* by cohabitation had gone out of date, and after confarreation had been declared by statute to be no longer productive of it except *quoad sacra* (Gai., i. §§ 111, 136).

confarreation nor coemption, desired to retain her independence, she must periodically absent herself for three nights from her husband's house; twelve months' uninterrupted cohabitation being required to give him that power over her which would have been created instantly had the marriage been accompanied by either of the recognised solemnities.[2]

Amongst the fragments of the Tables so industriously collected there is none that refers to a wife's marriage provision (*dos*); but it is hardly conceivable that it was as yet unknown. Justinian says that in ancient times it was regarded as a donation to the husband with his wife,[3] rather than as a separate estate that was to be used by him while the marriage lasted, but to revert to her or her representatives on its dissolution. And it is easy to see that where there was *manus*, the wife becoming a member of her husband's family and everything of hers becoming his, such must originally have been its character. But even then, when a man gave his daughter (*filiafamilias*)— who could have nothing of her own—in marriage, and promised her husband a portion with her, there must have been some process of law for compelling him to pay it; and Voigt's conjecture that an *actio dictae dotis* was employed for the purpose has much in its favour.[4]

As regards divorce, Cicero alludes vaguely to a provision in the Tables about a man depriving his wife of the housekeys and turning her out of doors, with some such words

---

[2] Gai., i. 111; Macrob., *Sat.*, i. 3, § 9.   [3] *Cod. Just.*, v. 3, 20.
[4] Voigt, *XII Tafeln*, vol. ii. p. 486. The *dotis dictio* of the time of the classical jurists, and described by Gaius (iii. 96) and Ulpian (*Frag.*, vi. §§ 1, 2), was of a different character; for it presumed the absence of *manus* and possibility of the wife herself being debtor for it. *Dictio* by a parent in the older law must have been regarded as something more than a *nudum pactum*, and therefore actionable on the strength of the confarreation or coemption of which it was an accompaniment; just as a man's *dicta* about the qualities of land he was selling were actionable because made part of the conveyance *per aes et libram* (*infra*, p. 139).

as "Take what is thine and get thee gone."[5] A procedure so summary and simple can hardly have applied where marriage had been contracted by confarreation or coemption. We are told that divorce, except for grave misconduct on the part of a wife, though lawful, was in practice unknown until the sixth century of the city; and that, until the same date, any man who turned his wife away, however serious the ground, without the cognition of the family council (*consilium domesticum*), was liable to penalties at the hands of the censors. Moreover, a confarreate marriage could be dissolved *inter vivos* only by diffareation,[6] and a coemptionate one only by remancipation.[7] It is, therefore, in the highest degree probable that the provision to which Cicero alludes had reference to the loose and informal plebeian marriage in which the wife was at most *uxor* only and not *materfamilias*; and that its purpose was to ensure the use before witnesses of a prescribed but simple act, with corresponding words, which should serve as proof positive that the relation had been put an end to.

2. In connection with the law of parent and child, and with a view probably to settle possible questions about the right of an infant born after a man's death to succeed to him as one of the heirs of his body, the Tables declared that the birth must be within ten months of the alleged father's death, that being the longest possible period of gestation.[8] Two or three other fragments relate to the

[5] Cic., *Phil.*, ii. 28, § 69. See also Cic., *De orat.*, i. 40, § 183; Gai. *ad ed. prov.*, in *Dig.*, xxiv. 2, fr. 2, § 1.

[6] Paul. Diac., v. *Diffarcatio* (Bruns, p. 266).

[7] In the time of Gaius (i. 137a) a coemptionate marriage might be dissolved *quoad* the matrimonial relationship by simple repudiation; remancipation was necessary only for the purpose of extinguishing the *manus*. But this is obviously the doctrine of a much later period than the Tables, and introduced after *manus* had come to be regarded as a relation capable of existing apart from marriage (see Gai., i. 114).

[8] Gell., iii. 16, § 12. At a later period it became not uncommon for a testator, in providing for posthumous issue, to make birth within ten months after his decease an express condition of his succession.

patria potestas (p. 27). This power of the family head over his children was assumed to be so well established by customary law as to need no statutory sanction or definition. The only question of principle one would not have been surprised to find dealt with is whether *potestas* resulted from an informal marriage that had not been followed by a year's uninterrupted cohabitation. The patricians, in the debate on the Canuleian law a few years later (pp. 34, 86), could find no language opprobrious enough to depict such unions; yet the silence of the Tables on this head, so far as can be judged from the fragments we possess, seems to indicate that, although the position of the wife was an inferior one until a year's uninterrupted cohabitation had been completed, that of the children was the same, so far as the *potestas* was concerned,[9] as if they had been born of a confarreate or coemptionate marriage.[10] This limitation is said by Cicero to have been put by the Tables on the father's power (though Dionysius attributes it to Romulus),[11]—that, while he might expose a new-born infant that was grievously deformed, he was not allowed to kill it;[12] but this, of course, did not affect his general right of life and death, which was an adjunct of his domestic jurisdiction.

Another interesting point of detail in connection with the *patria potestas* was dealt with in a law which runs— " si paterfamilias ter filium venum duit, a patre filius liber esto."[13] This came to be construed by the jurists as mean-

[9] Confarreate birth was a necessary qualification for the higher priesthoods (Gai., i. 112).

[10] Karlowa (*Röm. Ehe*, p. 71) expresses the opinion that the issue of a formless marriage, not cured before their birth by a year's *usus*, were not *in potestate*, and could not be their father's *sui heredes*. But *potestas* depended on *justae nuptiae*, *i.e.*, the existence of *conubium*,—not on a marriage ceremony; and the fact is notorious that marriage in the later jurisprudence was purely consensual, and the issue *in potestate* notwithstanding.

[11] Dion. Hal., ii. 15; *supra*, p. 28.

[12] Cic., *De leg.*, iii. 8, § 19.

[13] Gai., i. 132; Ulp. x. 1. This also is attributed by Dionysius (ii. 15) to Romulus.

ing that so powerful was the bond of the *potestas* that it could not definitively be loosed until the father had three times gone through the process of fictitious sale by which emancipation was effected. But the conception of the law seems to indicate that its original purpose was to confer a benefit on a son *in potestate*, by declaring him *ipso jure* free from it on a certain event, rather than to place difficulties in the way of his emancipation. " If a house-father have thrice sold his son, the latter shall be free from his father." It reads as if the intention were to rescue the son from what, by its frequent repetition, was suggestive of a total absence of parental affection rather than reluctant obedience to overwhelming necessity. May not its object have been to restrain the practice, which prevailed to a late period in the empire, of men giving their children to their creditors in security for their loans,[14]—a process that, at the time of the Tables, could be effected only by an actual transfer of the child *per aes et libram* as a free bondman (*mancipii causa*), under condition of reconveyance when the loan was repaid ?

So far as appears, there was not a word in the Tables about adrogation of a *paterfamilias* or adoption of a *filius-familias* as a means of recruiting a family when natural issue failed. The inference as regards the first is that, being competent only in the comitia of the curies, to which the plebeians as yet had no access, it was still an exclusively patrician institution. The second was an adaptation of the conveyance *per acs et libram* (§ 13). The natural parent mancipated his child to a friend for a nominal price (the process being twice repeated in the case of a son), and the friend then remancipated to the parent. In the latter's hands the child was no longer *in potestate*, but *in mancipio;*

[14] Paul. in *Dig.*, xx. 3, 5, says that a creditor knowingly taking a *filius-familias* from his debtor as a security was liable to banishment. But the practice still continued ; for it was again prohibited by Diocletian in *Cod.* viii. 17, 6, and iv. 43, 1, and by Justinian in *Nov.* 134, c. 7.

he was now in a position in which he could be transferred to the adopter. This was effected by *in jure cessio*,—a friendly suit in which the adopter averred that the child was his *filiusfamilias*, and in which judgment was at once given in his favour on the natural parent's admission or tacit acquiescence.[15]

3. The nature of the relation between master and slave, like that of *manus* and *patria potestas*, seems also to have been too notorious to require exposition in the Tables. We have record of no more than two references to it, one dealing with the case of a slave who had a conditional testamentary gift of freedom (*statu liber*),[16] the other with noxal surrender (*noxae deditio*).[17] The first is interesting as showing the advance that had already been made in testamentary disposition,—that a testator might not only by his last will enfranchise a slave, but that he might annex a condition, such as payment of a certain sum by the slave to the heir. The enactment of the Tables was that the condition was not to be defeated by the heir's alienation of the slave; his conditional status was to run with him, and payment to any one acquiring him from the heir to be as effectual as if made to the latter himself. The provision about noxal surrender in all probability was not limited to a slave, but was to the effect that if a member of a man's family (*familiaris*), *i.e.*, a son or a daughter *in potestate* or a slave, committed a theft from or did mischief to property belonging to a third party, or a domestic animal belonging to one man did harm to another, the father of the delinquent child, or the owner of the slave or animal, should either surrender him or it to the person injured or make reparation in damages. In course of time the surrender came to be regarded as a means of avoiding the primary obligation of making reparation. But comparative jurisprudence recognises in the enactment of

---

[15] Gai., i. 134. [16] Ulp., *Frag.*, ii. 4; Modest. in *Dig.*, xl. 7, 25.
[17] Gai., iv. 76; Just., *Inst.*, iv. 9, pr.

the Tables a modified survival of the ancient right of an injured party to have the delinquent *corpus*,—man, beast, or thing,—given up to him to wreak his revenge upon it privately;[18] the modification consisting in the alternative of reparation offered to the owner. This noxal surrender, failing reparation, had gone out of use in the case of daughters *in potestate* before the time of Gaius, and in the case of sons before that of Justinian; but the law remained unchanged so far as slaves and domestic animals were concerned even in that emperor's legislation.

SECTION 28.—GUARDIANSHIP AND INTRODUCTION OF THE
ORDER OF AGNATES.

So long as Rome was patrician the *gens* charged itself with seeing to the guardianship of a clansman's orphaned pupil children and his widow and unmarried daughters above pupillarity after his decease (*tutela*), as well as with that of male members of his family who were *sui juris* but above the age of pupillarity, when they chanced to be lunatic, imbecile, prodigal, or helplessly infirm (*cura, curatio, curatela*). That was on the supposition, as regarded children, widow, and unmarried daughters above pupillarity, that no testamentary appointment of tutors by their deceased parent had displaced the *gens*, (though whether testamentary nominations were then held competent it is impossible to say). The *gens* in council, in all probability, appointed one of its members to act as tutor or curator as the case might be, itself prescribed his duties, and itself called him to account for any failure in his administration. His office was regarded as of a most sacred character, at least when his wards were pupils; Gellius and others speak repeatedly of

[18] Dirksen, *Civilistische Abhandlungen* (Berlin, 1820), vol. i. p. 104; Holmes, *Lectures on the Common Law* (Boston, 1882), p. 9.

the grave nature of the trust that was held to be reposed in tutors and of the heinousness of unfaithfulness to it.[1]

But as this old gentile tutory could not be extended to the plebeians, among whom some law of guardianship was as much required as among their fellow-citizens of the higher order, the decemvirs found it expedient to devise a new one of universal application. The Tables contained no express authority for testamentary nomination of tutors to the widow of the testator, or to his pupil children and grown-up unmarried daughters; but such appointment, if unknown previously, was soon held to be justified by a liberal interpretation of the very inclusive provision—" uti legassit suae rei, ita jus esto."[2] In the absence of testamentary appointment the nearest male agnates of lawful age were to be tutors. This tutory of agnates was an invention of the decemvirs, just as was the agnates' right of succession on intestacy (p. 172). The plebeians had no *gentes*, at least until a much later period; so, to make the law equal for all, it was necessary to introduce a new order of heirs and tutors. " Tutores . . . ex lege XII Tabularum introducuntur . . . agnati" is the very notable language of Ulpian.[3] And his words are very similar in speaking of their right of succession; for while he says of testamentary inheritances no more than that they were *confirmed* by the XII Tables,[4] he explains that the *legitimae hereditates* of agnates and patrons were *derived* from them.[5] The phrases

[1] " Ex moribus populi Romani primum juxta parentes locum tenere pupillos debere, fidei tutelaeque nostrae creditos. . . . M. Cato . . . ita scripsit : quod majores sanctius habuere defendi pupillos quam clientem non fallere " (Gell., v. 13, §§ 2, 4).

[2] So the law is given by Gaius, ii. 24. The words " super pecunia tutelave," interjected by Ulpian (*Frag.*, xi. 24) and other authors after " legassit," savour of a gloss by the interpreters.

[3] Ulp., *Frag.*, xi. 3 ; see note 7.

[4] Ulp. *ad leg. Jul.*, in *Dig.*, l. 16, 130,—" lege duodecim Tabularum testamentariae hereditates confirmantur."

[5] Ulp., *Frag.*, xxvii. 5,—" legitimae hereditatis jus . . . ex lege duodecim Tabularum descendit." This derivation of agnatic inheritance from the Twelve

legitima cognatio,[6] *legitima hereditas, legitimi heredes, tutela legitima, tutores legitimi*, themselves proclaim the origin of agnation, agnatic inheritance, and agnatic tutory; for though the word *legitimus* might be applied to any institution based on statute, yet in the ordinary case it indicated one introduced by the XII Tables,[7] the law of laws.

A man's agnates were those of his kinsmen who were subject to the same *patria potestas* as himself, or would have been had the common ancestor been still alive.[8] A man's sons and daughters *in potestate*, therefore, whether the relationship was by birth or adoption, and his wife *in manu* (being *filiae loco*),[9] were each other's agnates;[10] but a wife not *in manu* was not her children's agnate, nor were children who had been emancipated or otherwise *capite minuti* (§ 29) the agnates of either their brothers and sisters or their mother *in manu*. A man was an agnate of his brother's children, assuming always that there had been no *capitis deminutio* on either side; but he was not an agnate of his sister's

---

Tables was specially noticed by Danz in his *Gesch. d. R. R.*, vol. ii. p. 95, but is generally overlooked.

[6] "Vocantur autem agnati qui legitima cognatione juncti sunt" (Gai., iii. 10). Prior to the Tables kinship and kinsmen were always spoken of as *cognatio* and *cognati*; it was only after it that these words came to have a narrower signification, and to be limited to kinsmen other than agnates.

[7] "Legitimi tutores sunt, qui ex lege aliqua descendunt: per eminentiam autem legitimi dicuntur, qui ex lege XII Tabularum introducuntur" (Ulp. xi. 3).

[8] This definition is simpler than those given by Gaius (i. 156), and Justinian (*Inst.*, i. 15, § 1, and iii. 3, § 1). That of Ulpian (*Frag.*, xxvi. 1), which seems to deny that any female except a sister could stand related to a man as an agnate, is influenced by the restrictive interpretation put on the word *adgnatus* in connection with the law of succession by the jurists of the latter half of the republic, and inconsistent with the meaning borne by it in the Tables, (see *Inst.*, iii. 3, § 3a).

[9] Gai., §§ 115b, 136, ii. 139.

[10] Although a husband and his wife *in manu*, a *paterfamilias* and his children *in potestate*, were in some sense agnates, yet, for obvious reasons, they were not usually so called. In everyday language, agnation was a collateral relationship. By some jurists—*e.g.*, Ulpian (*Frag.*, xxvi. 1)—brothers and sisters by the same father were in preference called *consanguinei*. (Of course they could not be agnates unless they had the same father.)

children, for they were not *ejusdem familiae* ;[11] they were agnates of their father's family, not of their mother's. In like manner, and again assuming the absence of *minutio capitis*, the children of brothers were each other's agnates, but not the children of a brother and sister or of two sisters. Brothers and sisters were agnates of the second degree; a man and his brother's children were of the third, the children of two brothers (*consobrini*) of the fourth, and so on; it being a condition, however, that the kinship should always result either from lawful marriage or adoption in one or other of its forms.

When, therefore, a man died leaving pupil male descendants, or unmarried female descendants, who by his death became *sui juris*,[12] they got their brothers of lawful age as their tutors; if he was survived by his wife, and she had been *in manu*, her sons, or it might be stepsons, acted for her in the same capacity; in either case they took office as the nearest qualified male agnates. If the widow had no sons or stepsons of full age, and the children consequently no brothers, the tutory devolved on the agnates next in order,—*i.e.*, the brothers-german and consanguinean of the deceased husband and father, for they were agnates of the third degree. And so with agnates of the fourth and remoter degrees.[13] Failing agnates who could demonstrate their propinquity, the tutory probably passed to the *gens* when the ward happened to belong to one. This is nowhere expressly stated; but Cicero gives what he represents to be

---

[11] Ulp., *Frag.*, xxvi. 1.

[12] It was persons *sui juris* that alone needed or could have tutors. A grandson *in potestate*, if his father was alive and had not undergone *capitis deminutio*, passed into the latter's *potestas* on his grandfather's death, and did not become *sui juris*.

[13] To determine the degree of propinquity between two persons, it was necessary to count the generations upwards from the first to the common ancestor, and downwards from him to the second. Consequently brothers were related in the second degree, uncle and nephew in the third, first cousins in the fourth, and so on : " tot gradus quot generationes."

an enactment of the Tables, making the fellow-gentiles of a lunatic his guardians on failure of agnates;[14] and analogy seems to justify the extension of the same rule to the case of sane pupil and female wards.[15]

It is natural to suppose that in introducing an institution that to the plebeians at least was new, the Tables must have given some indication of the nature of the powers, duties, and responsibilities of tutors. They could not be very minute; for tutory was an *officium*, to be fulfilled not according to any hard and fast lines, but according to the dictates of *fides*,—an honest and conscientious regard for the interests of the ward. All we know with certainty is, that, if a tutor converted anything of his pupil ward's to his own use, he was liable in an action *ex delicto* —a variety of the *actio furti*—for double its value;[16] and that if his administration was suspicious, any one might raise an action in the pupil's interest to have him removed.[17] There was, no doubt, liability to account in every case when the tutory of a male pupil (at least) came to an end, but it does not appear how originally it was enforced; the ordinary *actio tutelae*, though spoken of by Cicero as if of some antiquity, seems to have proceeded on lines that did not become familiar until the sixth century at soonest.

The curatory of minors above pupillarity was of much later date than the Tables. The only curatories they sanctioned were those of lunatics and spendthrifts. A lunatic

---

[14] Cic., *De inv.*, ii. 50, § 149. Comp. Paul. in *Dig.*, l. 16, 53.

[15] The *gens* succeeded *ab intestato* on failure of agnates; and Gaius (i. 165) says it was a general principle that tutory and succession should run together. But it ought to be observed that the succession of the *gens* had ample justification in the rule which denied it to agnates of a remoter degree if any of a nearer one existed when it opened (Gai., iii. §§ 12, 22); whereas no such rule was recognised in devolution of a tutory (Just., *Inst.*, iii. 2, 7). The passage in which it is supposed Gaius spoke of the right of the *gens* in the matter of tutory (*i.e.*, between §§ 164 and 165 of his first book) is unfortunately illegible.

[16] Tryph. in *Dig.*, xxvi. 7, 55, § 1.

[17] Ulp. in *Dig.*, xxvi. 10, 1, § 2; Just., *Inst.*, 1, 26, pr.

(*furiosus*) was committed to the care of his agnates, and, failing them, of his fellow-gentiles;[18] and a few words in Festus seem to suggest that arrangements had to be made for his safe custody.[19] Beyond this we know nothing of the decemviral curatory of lunatics, nor to whom his guardians were responsible. The curatory of a spendthrift (*prodigus*) probably followed upon his interdiction. In earlier times this was a matter for the interference of his *gens*. But by the Tables the cognisance of the prodigal misconduct of a man who was squandering his patrimony (*bona paterna avitaque*), and reducing his children to poverty, seems to have been transferred to the consul;[20] and the fact of his interdiction seems to have entitled his agnates—or rather, as he was prohibited from any longer managing his own affairs, to have rendered it necessary for them—to assume the position of his guardians.[21]

SECTION 29.—CAPITIS DEMINUTIO.[1]

Whatever may have been the original signification of *caput*, it came to mean primarily a person whom the law regarded as capable of having rights, and derivatively his personality or jural capacity, passive and active, in public and private life. The measure of that capacity depended, according to Roman notions, on three considerations,—(1) whether he was free or slave, (2) whether, being free, he was citizen or non-citizen, and (3) what, being a citizen, was his position with regard to family. If a man was not free he had no rights at all, according to the theory alike of

[18] Cic., *De inv.*, ii. 50, § 148.
[19] "Ast ei custos nec escit" (Festus, v. *Nec;* Müll., p. 162).
[20] Paul., *Sent.*, iii. 4a, 7 ; Ulp. in *Dig.*, xxvii. 10, 1.
[21] Ulp., *Frag.*, xii. 2.
[1] Savigny, *System*, vol. ii. §§ 68–74, and Beilage vi.; Puchta, *Inst.*, vol. ii. §§ 219, 220 ; Rattigan, *The Roman Law of Persons* (London, 1873), p. 58 *sq.;* Pernice, *Labeo*, vol. i. p. 172 *sq.;* Kuntze, *Excurse*, p. 428 ; Moyle, *Inst.*, vol. i. p. 172 *sq.*

the *jus civile* and the *jus gentium*;[2] it was not until the doctrines of the *jus naturale* began to gain ground that he was reckoned as anything more than a chattel, spoken of as a *persona*, or taken directly under the protection of the law. Being free, the extent of his capacity varied according as he was or was not a citizen; in the latter case it was only exceptionally that he could enjoy any of the public rights of a citizen, while his private ones included only those he enjoyed under the *jus gentium* and such civil ones as had been specially conceded to him. It was only among citizens that the supremacy of the *paterfamilias* and the subjection of those *in manu, potestate,* or *mancipio* was recognised,— only among them therefore that the position of an individual in the family was of moment. While in public life a man's supremacy or subjection in the family was immaterial, in private life it was the *paterfamilias* alone that enjoyed full jural capacity; those subject to him had a more limited personality;[3] and, so far as capacity to take part in transactions of the *jus civile* was concerned, it was not inherent in them but derived from their *paterfamilias*,—they were the agents of his will, representatives of his *persona*, in every act whereby a right was acquired by them for the family to which they belonged.

Consistently with this view, when a man lost either freedom or citizenship, or changed his family, he was said to have undergone *capitis deminutio*,—*i.e.,* loss or diminution of his jural capacity. The first, loss of freedom, was *maxima capitis deminutio;* the second, loss of citizenship, as when he went into exile or joined a Latin colony, was *media capitis deminutio;* the third, *familiae mutatio* or *commutatio,* was *minima capitis deminutio*. That the two first must have had a serious and very prejudicial effect upon a man's

[2] "Servile caput nullum jus habet" (Paul. in *Dig.,* iv. 5, fr. 3, § 1).

[3] I leave out of view, as not affecting the general principle, some qualifications of a later period, as, for example, that a *filiusfamilias* in dealings with his *castrense peculium* was regarded as a *paterfamilias*, and the like.

capacity is too obvious to require explanation. They manifestly involved a diminution of that capacity. But it is by no means so clear at first sight that a mere change of family could reasonably be spoken of as a *deminutio capitis*. There were three categories under one or other of which every such change necessarily fell,—either (1) a person *sui juris* became *alieni juris*, or (2) a person *alieni juris* became *sui juris*, or (3) a person *alieni juris* passed from one *jus* into another. We have examples of the first in the transit by adrogation of a *paterfamilias* into the *potestas* of another person who became his adoptive parent, and in that of a woman *sui juris* by confarreation or coemption into the *manus* of a husband; in both of these there was unquestionably *capitis deminutio*,— a change of family for the worse. We have examples of the second in the case of children *in potestate* becoming *sui juris* by the death of their *paterfamilias*, a *filiusfamilias* being consecrated as a flamen, a *filiafamilias* being taken as a vestal, a child being emancipated from the *patria potestas*, or a wife *in manu* being freed from it by remancipation. In all of these the change was of the same character,—from dependence to independence. But their effects in law were very different. Children who became *sui juris* by their parents' death did not change their family; the change was not in them but in the disappearance of the family head; therefore they were not regarded as *capite minuti*. Neither were vestals nor flamens; for though they changed their family, yet it was by passing from a human into a divine one. But emancipated children and a remancipated wife were held to have undergone *capitis deminutio*, although they distinctly improved their position.

Some jurists, founding on an observation of Paul's, attempt to account for the apparent contradiction by reference to the fact that, in the process of emancipation or remancipation, the person eventually acquiring independence had to descend temporarily into a quasi-servile position, and was thus for the moment degraded and really and truly *capite minutus*. This explanation proceeds on the notion that *capitis deminutio minima* necessarily involved descent in the family scale. But such a notion is erroneous. It was immaterial whether the change was from a higher family position to a lower, or from a lower to a higher, or to the same position in the new family that had been held in the old; for it was the change of family, not the change of family position, that constituted the *capitis deminutio*. Although an emancipated son (say) himself became a *paterfamilias*, and in that character was the founder of a new family and acquired a new and independent capacity, yet he had lost the birthrights as well as the derivative capacity he had previously enjoyed as a member of the family he had quitted, and therefore was *capite minutus* in so far as that family was concerned. His relation to it was at an end; his old *persona* or personality was extinguished, although by the same act a new one was created. The same was the case when a person *alieni juris* passed from one *jus* into another, as when a *filiusfamilias* was transferred by his father into the *potestas* of an adopter, or when the *filiifamilias* of a person giving himself in adrogation passed with him into the *potestas* of the adrogator. There was no change in the genus of the children's *persona* by either of those events; they were *filiifamilias* both before and after them. But the species was changed; for, from being subject-members of family A, they became subject-members of family B. There was consequently and necessarily a *capitis deminutio*; for, however much they might gain in the long run by translation into their new family, they had lost the position they had hitherto enjoyed in their old one, with all its attendant rights and privileges.

The most important consequence of *minima capitis deminutio* (or *mutatio familiae*) was that it not only extinguished *patria potestas* where it existed, but severed the

I

bond of agnation between the *capite minutus* and all those who had previously been related to him as agnates.[4] There was no longer any right of succession between him and them on intestacy (p. 174); their reciprocal prospective rights of tutory were defeated, and the *minutio* of either tutor or ward put an end to a subsisting guardianship, assuming always that it was a *tutela legitima* or agnatic *cura furiosi*. There were various other consequences that are said to have resulted from the *familiae mutatio* of a person *sui juris*, for which there was no room if he were *alieni juris;* some of them, however, seem only indirectly attributable to the *capitis minutio*. It is said, for example, that if a *paterfamilias*, after executing a testament, gave himself in adrogation, his testament was thereby nullified;[5] but that was due not so much to the *capitis minutio* as to the rule of the civil law which required that a testator's testamentary capacity should continue uninterruptedly from the moment of making his will until his death. It is said also that certain patrimonial rights enjoyed by a man, such as usufructs, sworn services due by him as a freedman, and one or two others, were extinguished by his *capitis minutio ;*[6] but the more accurate way of stating it is that *all* his patrimonial rights were extinguished so far as his old *persona* was concerned, but passed simultaneously, claims against debtors of his included, to his new *paterfamilias* by universal acquisition, with the exception of two or three that for special reasons were regarded as intransmissible. More directly attributable to the *minutio* was the rule that a copartnery of which the *minutus* was a member was thereby dissolved;

[4] This was true even as regarded a *paterfamilias* and his children *in potestate* passing together into a new family by adrogation; their old agnation ceased, and a new one, of which the adoptive parent was the connecting link, came into existence. In the case of direct transfer of a *filiusfamilias*, however, by his natural parent to an adoptive one, the rule in the text was modified by the legislation of the later empire (see Just., *Inst.*, i. 11, 2).

[5] Relaxed by the prætorian jurisprudence (Gai., ii. 145).

[6] Gai., iii. 83.

Gaius assigning as the reason that *capitis deminutio* in the estimation of the *jus civile* was equivalent to death.[7] Parties might of consent go on as before; but it was really a new copartnery, with a *filiusfamilias* as a member of it instead of a *paterfamilias* as formerly. Very remarkable, yet quite logical, was the doctrine that the *minutio* extinguished the claims of creditors of the *minutus*;[8] their debtor, the person with whom they had contracted, was civilly dead, and dead without an heir; and therefore there was no one against whom an action of the *jus civile* could be directed in order to enforce payment. This cannot but have opened a door to fraud, a *paterfamilias* giving himself in adrogation, or a *materfamilias* passing in *manum*, in order to defeat the claims of creditors. But equity eventually provided a remedy, by giving the creditors a prætorian action in which the *minutio* was held as rescinded, and which the new *paterfamilias* was bound to defend on pain of having to give up to them all the estate he had acquired through the adrogation or *in manum conventio*.[9]

SECTION 30.—MANCIPATION AND THE LAW OF PROPERTY.

In the early law there was no technical word for ownership of things; it was an element of the house-father's *manus*. In time, although it is impossible to say when, the word *dominium* came into use; but, so far as can be discovered, it did not occur in the Tables, and must have been of later introduction. In those days, when a man asserted ownership of a thing, he was content to say,—"It is mine," or "It is mine according to the law of the Quirites." The distinction, as already explained in § 10, was this,—that while

[7] Gai., iii. 153. [8] Gai., iii. 84, iv. 38.
[9] Gai., iii. 84, iv. §§ 38, 80. Those passages are not quite consistent; for while in the two first the action is said to have been against the *minutus* or *minuta*, in the last it is said that the *paterfamilias* had to defend it.

the first was sufficient to entitle a man *de facto* holding a thing as his own to protection against a thief or any one forcibly attempting to dispossess him, the second was necessary when he appealed to a court of law to declare the legality of his title and his right to oust an individual who had obtained possession neither theftuously nor by force. It is maintained by some jurists of eminence that under the law of the Tables what afterwards came to be called "dominium ex jure Quiritium" was competent only in the case of *res mancipi* (p. 63),—of a man's house and farm, and the slaves and animals with which he worked them;[1] in other words, that under the Tables there could be no formal *vindicatio* of a right of property in *res nec mancipi*. Speculatively there is something to be said for this contention; but it is incidentally contradicted by such authorities as Paul and Ulpian, who tell us that by an enactment of the decemvirs vindication of building materials, vine-stakes, and the like (*tigna juncta*) was sometimes exceptionally excluded.[2] But such things were unquestionably *res nec mancipi*; and so there can be little room for doubt that these, as well as *res mancipi*, were already at the time of the publication of the Tables regarded as objects of quiritarian ownership-right, and ordinarily susceptible of vindication in the usual form.[3]

[1] *E.g.*, Ihering, *Geist*, vol. iii. § 55, note 262, and *Zweck*, vol. i. p. 275, note; Karlowa, *Röm. CP.*, pp. 34, 38; Voigt, *XII Tafeln*, vol. ii. p. 88. Ihering has not yet developed his view, reserving it for a subsequent volume of the *Geist*.

[2] Paul., in *Dig.*, xlvi. 3, fr. 98, § 8; Ulp., in *Dig.*, xlvii. 3, 2; *infra*, note 64.

[3] Cicero (*Top.*, 4, 23) says that while, by the Twelve Tables, lands might be acquired by two years' possession, *all* other things (*ceterae res omnes*) might be usucapted in one year. There is no doubt that usucapion was not an invention of the Tables; they only defined the period, hitherto uncertain, for which possession (*usus*) as owner had to be continued in order to create a property title. There is just as little doubt that the title created by usucapion was a quiritarian one,—the right one of *dominium ex jure Quiritium*. A *res nec mancipi*, therefore, that had been possessed for a year by a person who had not come by it theftuously, was clearly his in quiritarian right. But once

The modes in which those two classes of things might be acquired in property were very various. But there was this important difference,—that while a natural mode of acquisition sufficed in the case of *res nec mancipi*, some civil one was necessary for the derivative acquisition, at all events, of *res mancipi*. The most important were mancipation, surrender in court, usucapion, and bequest as singular modes; inheritance, *in manum conventio*, adrogation, and purchase of a confiscated estate as universal ones. All of these, with the exception of mancipation, applied equally to *res nec mancipi*. But the commonest of all the modes of transferring things of this class was simple tradition. If the transfer was by the owner, with the intention of passing the property, then the simple delivery of possession was enough, unless it was in virtue of a sale ; in such a case, and because a vendor had as yet no action for the price, the Tables provided that the ownership should remain with him, notwithstanding the change of possession, until the price was paid or security given for it.[4]

The origin of the distinction between mancipable and non-mancipable things, and of the form of conveyance by mancipation applicable to the first, has already been explained in connection with the reforms of Servius Tullius (§ 13).[5] As Servius introduced it, mancipation (then called

this was admitted, a step farther was inevitable. If a man could competently aver that a *res nec mancipi* was his in quiritary right the day after he had completed a year's possession of it, it would not be long before it would be allowed that his right to it was of exactly the same character even before the year had expired, provided he was able to establish ownership independently of the usucapion.

[4] Just., *Inst.*, ii. 1, 41. Some writers are of opinion that the provision in the Tables to which Justinian alludes, (and which, strangely enough, is not mentioned in the remains of any earlier authority), can have applied only to mancipations of *res mancipi*. But there seems no sufficient reason for thus limiting its application ; for though an informal contract of sale had not yet been recognised as creative of legally enforceable obligations, yet sale without mancipation was an ordinary transaction of daily life,—acquisition of a specific article in exchange for a certain amount of metal or (afterwards) money.

[5] Literature : Leist, *Mancipation und Eigenthumstradition*, Jena, 1865 ;

mancipium) was not the imaginary sale that Gaius speaks of,[6] but as real a sale as could well be conceived,—the weighing in scales, held by an official, of the raw metal that was to be the consideration for the transfer of a *res mancipi*, and the handing of it by the transferee to the transferrer, with the declaration that thereby and therewith the thing in question became his in quiritary right; and all this in words of style, and in the presence of certain witnesses who represented the people and thus fortified the conveyance with a public sanction. There is some reason to believe that, when large quantities of metal had to be weighed, the practice crept in of having this done before the witnesses had assembled; and in the formal act only a single pound was weighed as representing the whole amount.[7] This paved the way for the greater change that resulted from the introduction by the decemvirs of coined money. From that moment weighing became unnecessary. The price was counted out before the ceremony, and sometimes left to be done afterwards; and though, in that spirit of conservatism that was so marked in the adhesion to time-honoured forms after their *raison d'être* was gone, the scale-bearer and the scales were still retained as indispensable elements of the mancipation, yet the latter were simply touched by the purchaser with a single coin, in order that he might be able to recite the old formula—" I say that this slave is mine in quiritary right, and that by purchase with these scales and this bit of copper." And that one coin, says Gaius, was then handed by the transferee to the transferrer, as if it were in fact the price of the purchase (*quasi pretii loco*). Thus transformed, the mancipation was undoubtedly nothing more

---

Ihering, *Geist. d. R. R.*, vol. ii. § 46; Bechmann, *Geschichte des Kaufs im Röm. Recht*, (Erlangen, 1876), pp. 47-299; Voigt, *XII Tafeln*, vol. i. § 22, vol. ii. §§ 84-88.

[6] Gai., i. 119.

[7] See this more fully explained in § 13, and the justification of the conjecture in note 16 to that section.

than an imaginary sale; for the real price might have been paid weeks or months before, or might not be paid until weeks or months afterwards. The actual sale might be, and probably usually was, contemporaneous; but the mancipation itself had become nothing more than a conveyance, and in this form it continued down to the end of the third century of the empire to be the appropriate mode of transfer of a *res mancipi*, or at least of conferring on the transferee of such a thing a complete legal title (*dominium ex jure Quiritium*). After that, however, it seems gradually to have gone into disuse, being inapplicable to lands out of Italy that did not enjoy the privilege known as *jus Italicum*;[8] and long before the time of Justinian it had entirely disappeared.[9]

The effects of a mancipation, provided the price had been paid or security given for it,[10] were that the property passed instantly to the purchaser, and that the transferrer was held to warrant the transferee against eviction from the moment the price was received. In the absence of either payment or sureties for it, the title still remained with the vendor; so that it was in his power, by means of a real action, to get back what had been mancipated, even though it had passed into the possession of the vendee. With the change from weighed metal to coined money, payment of the price or sureties for it also became a condition of the vendor's liability to the vendee in the event of eviction.[11] This liability

---

[8] Gai., ii. 15. See § 52, note 3.

[9] The latest mention of it as a still subsisting institution is in an enactment of the year 355 (*Theod. Cod.*, viii. 12, 7).

[10] What sort of security the Tables required we are not informed. We know from Gellius (xvi. 10, 8) that there was a provision in them about sureties who got the name of *vades*; that may have dealt with the matter. See Voigt, "Ueber das Vadimonium," in *Abhandl. d. phil. hist. Classe d. Königl. Sächs. Gesellsch. d. Wissensch.*, vol. viii. p. 299 *sq*. According to him, if the *vades* failed to pay the price for which they had become sureties, they might be convened in an "actio vadimonii deserti." See also his *XII Tafeln*, vol. ii. p. 490.

[11] Paul., *Sent.*, ii. 17, §§ 1, 3.

is usually supposed to have arisen *ipso jure*,[12] that is to say, without anything expressly said about it; the acceptance by the transferrer of the coin with which the scales had been struck was held to have imposed upon him an obligation to maintain the transferee in possession, under a penalty of double the amount of the price, recoverable by the latter by what is usually called an *actio auctoritatis*.[13] But this *ipso jure* obligation did not arise when the mancipation was either really or fictitiously gratuitous; really, in the case of donations, &c.,[14] fictitiously, when, on purpose to exclude the warranty, the recital of the transferee was that the price was a single sesterce.[15]

That so serious a consequence for the vendor should have arisen without anything said by him to bind himself, seems a little inconsistent with the general principle of the law of contractual obligation in the fourth century of Rome, and with the importance ascribed by Cicero to the words spoken by a contracting party as the test and measure of his liability.[16] Referring especially to the position of the transferrer in a mancipation, Cicero speaks of him as having obliged himself—*qui se nexu obligavit*;[17] and this, it has been said, suggests something more on his part than the simple acceptance of the *raudusculum*. It has also been a matter of observation that a man transferring a *res mancipi* by surrender in court (*in jure cessio*) incurred no such obligation;[18] an

---

[12] The authorities for this are mostly from Plautus; they are collected in Voigt, *XII Tafeln*, vol. ii. p. 190.

[13] See a paper on "L'action auctoritatis," by P. F. Girard, in the *Nouv. Rev. Hist.*, vol. vii. (1882), p. 180. Latterly it was called "actio pro evictione."

[14] Examples in Leist, *Mancipation*, p. 169.

[15] It appears from an *instrumentum fiduciae*, discovered in Spain in 1876 (Bruns, p. 200), that this practice must have been common in the early empire; for the creditor bargains that in selling by mancipation any of the lands or slaves included in his mortgage he should not be bound to do so for more than a single sesterce, *i.e.*, he should not be held to warrant them to a purchaser. The single sesterce (silver) was quite distinct from the *raudusculum*, which was of copper.

[16] Cic., *De Off.*, iii. 16, § 65.   [17] Cic., *Pro Mur.*, 2, § 3.

[18] Voigt, *XII Tafeln*, vol. ii. p. 189, note 2. The reason was that it was

immunity usually (but wrongly) ascribed to the fact that he said nothing that could even be construed into warranty. Two theories [19] have been propounded to obviate the difficulty. According to one,[20] the warranty was express, and was therefore obligatory under the provision of the XII Tables that what was publicly declared by word of mouth in the course of a mancipation should be held as law.[21] If so, the liability could have been avoided by omitting any such declaration; whereas a variety of passages in the lay writers prove that onerous mancipation without warranty was a thing unknown.[22] The other theory is that the liability did arise *ipso jure;* not, however, in consequence of the words spoken by the transferee, or of the *raudusculum* or coin accepted by the transferrer, but because of words spoken by the latter, which were substantially an echo of those spoken by the former. This is Voigt's view,[23] quite novel, and somewhat specious. He stands upon the broad ground that it is inconsistent with the supremacy of the word spoken, and the fruitlessness of the unexpressed *voluntas* in the fourth and fifth centuries of Rome, to suppose either that property could pass from A to B simply because B said so without contradiction from A, or that A could be laid under obligation to warrant the possession to B without a syllable spoken by him. He contends that there must have been a declaration by the vendor, following that of the vendee,—

not the cedent, but the magistrate by his decree (*addictio*), that gave the thing to the cessionary.

[19] A third view is that of Ihering (*Geist*, vol. ii. p. 528, note 716),—that the *actio auctoritatis* was really an action of theft, on the ground that the vendor had swindled the vendee out of his money. But it is refuted by the fact that the *duplum* was exigible even though the vendor had manifestly acted in perfect good faith.

[20] See Eck, *Die Verpflichtung des Verkäufers zur Gewährung d. Eigenthums* (Halle, 1874), p. 2. With him concur Rudorff and Karlowa as quoted by him.

[21] " Cum nexum faciet mancipiumque, uti lingua nuncupassit ita jus esto " (Fest., v. *Nuncupata*, Bruns, p. 275).

[22] See note 12.

[23] Voigt, *XII Tafeln*, vol. i. p. 217, vol. ii. p. 137.

"I say that the slave is thine in quiritary right, acquired by thee by purchase with those copper scales and this copper coin;" and that the vendor as well as the vendee appealed to the witnesses for their testimony. An appeal to the witnesses was certainly made in some cases by the vendor; for that was the position held by the testator in a testament-mancipation, and both Gaius and Ulpian narrate his nuncupatory declaration and request for testimony.[24] An "aio tuum ese," &c., however, is vouched by no authority, either lay or professional. Yet it is quite conceivable; for though *aio* ordinarily introduced an averment of the existence of a right in the person of the speaker, yet it seems to be generally admitted that it was used by the defendant in a *legis actio sacramenti in personam* when expressly admitting the plaintiff's claim.[25]

The right of a vendee to sue an *actio auctoritatis* arose only when eviction resulted from a decree in a regular judicial process at the instance of a third party disputing his title; and was conditional on his having done all that was necessary on his part to bring his vendor (*auctor*) into the field to defend his own interests (§ 34, n. 10). And the duration of the *auctoritas* was limited by statute to two years in the case of lands and houses, one year in that of other things.[26] As possession for those periods was sufficient to cure any defect in the vendee's title, it was but reasonable that with their expiry the vendor's liability on his warranty should be at an end.

By the provision of the Twelve Tables in reference to the *verba nuncupata* that accompanied a mancipation,[27] its

---

[24] Gai., ii. 104; Ulp., xx. 9. It to some extent supports Voigt's view that Justinian (*Inst.*, ii. 10, 1, 2) speaks of a testament *per aes et libram* as made *emancipatione*, i.e., by an act of the testator's putting his estate *out of* his *manus*.

[25] On the authority of the note in Valer. Prob. § 4, No. 3 (*Collect. libror. jur. antejust.*, vol. ii. p. 144),—Q.N.Q.A.N.Q.N. = "Quando neque ais neque negas."

[26] Cic., *Pro Caec.*, 19, § 54; *Top.*, 4, § 23.   [27] See *supra*, note 21.

importance was immensely increased; for any sort of qualification germane to the transaction might be superinduced upon it, and the range of its application thus greatly extended. Such qualifications were spoken of as *leges mancipii*,[28]—self-imposed terms, conditions, or qualifications of the conveyance, which, as integral parts of the transaction *per aes et libram*, partook of its binding character and were law between the parties. The matter of oral declaration might be the acreage of lands, their freedom from burdens or right to easements, reservation of a usufruct, limitation of their mode of use, undertaking to reconvey on a certain event, or what not; the result was just so many obligations created *per aes et libram*, whose contravention or denial was punished with a twofold penalty.[29] But the words spoken in the hearing of the witnesses were the beginning and the end of the liability; it was enough that they were literally complied with, however much the other party might be injured by something inconsistent with their spirit, or which he had not taken the precaution to require should be made matter of declaration. What had not been clothed in words could not be enforced as a *lex mancipii*. What had been intended could not be inquired into; the rule was—" according as a man has spoken, so shall be law;" interpretative equity had no place as yet in the *jus civile*, unless, perhaps, in the case of a *lex fiduciae*.

Among the declarations, restrictions, limitations, burdens, conditions, and so forth (*dicta et promissa*) that might be incorporated with a mancipation as *leges mancipii*,[30] and which imposed obligations sometimes on one party, sometimes on the other, none was more important, and from some points of view remarkable, than this so-called *lex fiduciae*, or often, for brevity's sake, simply *fiducia*.[31] It was

---
[28] See § 7, note 7.   [29] Cic., *De Off.*, iii. 16, § 65.

[30] See illustrations of a great variety of them in Voigt, *XII Tafeln*, vol. ii. pp. 149-165. Several of them, however, are of questionable authority.

[31] The subject of *fiducia* has latterly been much discussed in connection

introduced when it was the intention of parties that the mancipatory transference, although in form absolute, should in reality be only provisional; the transferee was therefore taken bound to reconvey either to the transferrer or to a third party, or to manumit a slave he had received, or to denude himself of the thing in any other way that might be embodied in the engagement. According to some jurists, such a qualification of the vendee's right might be introduced as an ordinary *lex mancipii*, without any fiduciary words; in that case the obligation was *stricti juris*, and the vendor, if he failed to comply, was inevitably condemned in the twofold penalty which followed breach of the *verba nuncupata*. But it was usually deemed expedient—although the practice can hardly have been introduced until considerably later than the XII Tables—to free alike the right of the vendor and the obligation of the vendee from the hard-and-fast lines of the *jus strictum*, and subordinate them to the principles of *bona fides*. This was done by importing fiduciary words into the mancipatory formula,—" Hunc ego hominem fidei fiduciae causa ex jure Quiritium meum esse aio,"—" I say that this slave is mine in quiritary right, committed to my honour, for a fiduciary purpose, and that he is mine by purchase for a single sesterce,[32] with this copper and these scales, in order that I may remancipate him to you," or what not, according to the nature of the transaction.[33]

with the Spanish *mancipatio fiduciae causa*, referred to in note 15. See Gide, in *Rev. de Législat.*, vol. i. (1870), p. 74 *sq.*; Degenkolb, in *Z. f. RG.*, vol. ix. (1870), pp. 117 *sq.*, 407 *sq.*; Krüger, *Krit. Versuche im Röm. Rechte* (Berlin, 1870), pp. 41-58; Rudorff, in *Z. f. RG.*, vol. xi. (1873), pp. 52 *sq.*

[32] As the sesterce was first coined in 485, the formula must have been somewhat different before then; but we know it only from the Spanish inscription, which was of the early empire. May not the *fidei fiduciae* (which occur in it) have been one single word, like *jurisjurandi*?

[33] Ihering (*Geist*, vol. ii. p. 515) holds that the *fiducia* was not embodied in the *nuncupatio* of the mancipation, but was a subsequent agreement in which *fides* was pledged, and which therefore gave rise only to a *bonae fidei* action. The strongest reason against regarding it as a *lex mancipii* is that it might be

[SECT. 30.] PURPOSES OF FIDUCIA. 141

Gaius[34] speaks of *fiducia* contracted either with a friend or with a creditor: with a friend, for safe custody of the thing transferred to him during the absence of the transferrer; with a creditor, for the purpose of giving him security for a debt incurred or contemplated, and which might be coupled with special agreements defining his powers of dealing with it. He mentions also in another place[35] that, in emancipating his child, a *paterfamilias*, if he desired to be his tutor and have the right of succession to him on his death, usually bargained fiduciarily with the transferee for remancipation, so that he (the father) should become the child's manumitter from the state of free bondage in which for the moment he was placed. This case, however, as well as that of the fiduciary coemption devised by the jurists of the sixth century,[36] was by no means of the same importance as those with friends and creditors just referred to. In them the transferee was vested with the legal right of property in the thing transferred to him, and in law entitled to deal with it as owner, in so far as not restrained by special agreements; but at the same time he was a trustee (*fiduciarius*), bound so to deal with it as not unduly to prejudice the interests of the transferrer. The latter had for his protection an action (*a. fiduciae*) which differed from that for enforcement of an ordinary *lex mancipii* in this very important respect,—that it proceeded, not upon in-

an adjunct of a transfer by surrender in court (*in jure cessio*), as well as of a mancipation (Gai., ii. 59); but that only amounts to this,—that it might take the form of a *lex in jure cessionis* as well as of a *lex mancipii*. The truth appears to be that in course of time it became the practice to follow up the mancipation and its fiduciary clause with a separate agreement setting forth details.

[34] Gai., ii. 60.
[35] Gai., i. 132, 133 (which are defective in the Verona MS.), compared with *Gaii Epit.*, i. 6, 3, and Just., *Inst.*, iii. 2, 8.
[36] To enable a woman *sui juris* to substitute for her legal tutors others of her own selection who were bound to do her bidding, or to enable her to make a testament, or to enable her to get rid of the *sacra* (*infra*, p. 179) that had devolved on her along with an inheritance. See Cic., *Pro Mur.*, 12, § 27; Gai., i. §§ 114, 115. See also *supra*, § 11, note 6.

flexible rules of law, but on considerations of what was reasonable and fair in view of the whole circumstances of the case—*uti inter bonos bene agier oportet*.[37] With this action a considerable latitude was given to the judge. True, if the *fiduciarius* deliberately failed to reconvey when it was his duty to do so, or had by his doleful actings rendered reconveyance impossible, he not only was condemned in the usual double penalty,[38] but became infamous on account of the breach of his expressly and publicly pledged faith.[39] If, on the other hand, his inability to reconvey was attributable to no fault of his, he was entitled to judgment in his favour; while there might be anything intermediate between double condemnation and full acquittal according to the view taken by the judge of the circumstances as a whole.

Another advantage of the *fiducia* was this,—that as the radical right still remained in him who had given the object of it in mancipation, he could reacquire the legal title without reconveyance by continuing in possession for a year;[40] the usucapion in that case was called *usurcceptio*, and one year's possession instead of two held sufficient even for immovables, upon the pretext that what was usucapted was a *fiducia*, and therefore included amongst the "other things" of the Twelve Tables.[41] This one year's usureception was competent at all times where the fiduciary mancipation had been to a

---

[37] Cic., *De Off.*, iii. 15, § 61; 17, § 70; *Top.*, 17, § 66.

[38] Paul. (*Sent.*, ii. 12, § 11) says that under the XII Tables there was an *actio in duplum* in the case of deposit. As deposit, as an independent contract, was unknown until long after the Tables, Paul's words possibly refer to the *fiducia cum amico depositi causa;* although it is also probable that breach of trust by a depositary, when no mancipation had intervened, was treated as theft, and visited with the same twofold penalty.

[39] Cic., *Pro Caec.*, 3, § 7. [40] Gai., ii. 59.

[41] "Lex XII tabularum soli quidem res biennio usucapi jussit, ceteras res vero anno" (Gai., ii. 54). It was on the same somewhat sophistical construction of the law that *usucapio pro herede* (*infra*, p. 179) was held to be completed in a year, even though the bulk of the hereditary estate might consist of immovables (*res soli*).

friend, and probably was the ordinary method of extinguishing the fiduciary right. Where, however, the mancipation had been to a creditor in security of his claim, there was this qualification,—that while the usureception might proceed on any *causa possessionis* after the debt secured had been paid, it was competent before payment only when the debtor's possession was not directly derived from the creditor either by lease or precatory grant during pleasure ; in either of those cases, according to the general principles of possession, he was holding for the creditor rather than himself.[42]

It is very generally, if not universally, maintained that mancipation was not only inappropriate but inapplicable to *res nec mancipi*,—that mancipation of a thing of this sort was ineffectual as a conveyance. There does not seem to be any distinct authority for such a statement.[43] In the ordinary case parties would rarely dream of resorting to so cumbrous a procedure if nothing was to be gained by it; but it is conceivable that it might be employed for some ulterior purpose, such as getting the benefit of a *lex mancipii* or a *fiducia*, whose efficacy depended on the transaction *per aes et libram* to which it was annexed.[44] If tradition actually accompanied the mancipation of a movable *res nec mancipi*, then it is difficult to conceive that the superinduction of the civil ceremonial could deprive it of its power to pass the property of the thing delivered. That surrender

---

[42] Gai., ii. 60.

[43] A passage in the *Vatican Fragments* (No. 313)—an enactment of Diocletian's—runs : "Donatio praedii ... traditione atque mancipatione perficitur ; ejus vero, quod nec mancipi est, traditione sola." But the two last words do not mean that donation of a non-mancipable could be perfected only by tradition ; they are to be read—"is perfect by tradition alone," *i.e.*, without the necessity of mancipation.

[44] There is no express mention of such a thing in the text ; but as only movables could be objects of deposit, and most were *nec mancipi*, one would think that they must have figured in the "fiducia cum amico depositi causa" of which Gaius speaks, before deposit had been recognised as an independent real contract imposing obligations upon a depositary apart from any mancipation.

in court (*in jure cessio*), adjudication, and usucapion applied both to mancipables and non-mancipables is indisputable.

Surrender in court,[45] which was apparently of later introduction than mancipation,[46] was simply a *rei vindicatio* (or action to have a right of property declared) arrested in its initial stage (p. 189). The parties, cedent and cessionary, having previously arranged the terms of transfer,—sale, exchange, donation, or what not,—appeared before the magistrate; the cessionary, taking the position of plaintiff, declared the thing his in quiritary right; the cedent, as defendant, was asked what he had to say in answer; and, on his admission or silence, the magistrate at once pronounced a decree (*addictio*),[47] which completed the transfer, but might be subject to a condition or other limitation, or even to a fiduciary reservation.[48] It was probably more resorted to for the constitution of servitudes, both real and personal, and transfer of such rights as *patria potestas*, tutory-at-law of a woman, or an inheritance that had already vested,[49] than for conveyance of property. For it was not only inconvenient, inasmuch as it required the parties to appear before the supreme magistrate in Rome, and could not be carried through by a slave on his owner's behalf (as mancipation might), but it had these serious disadvantages, —that it did not *ipso jure* imply any warranty of title by the cedent, or afford the cessionary any action against him in the event of eviction. The reason was that in form the right of the cessionary flowed from the magisterial decree,— " Since you say the thing is yours, and the cedent does not say it is his, I declare it yours,"—and not from any act or word of the cedent's, who was passive in the matter.

[45] Ihering, *Geist*, vol. ii. § 46; Voigt, *XII Tafeln*, vol. ii. § 83.
[46] But earlier than the XII Tables, because confirmed by them (Paul. in *Vat. Frag.*, No. 50).
[47] Gai., ii. 22, 24; Ulp., *Frag.*, xix. 9, 10.
[48] Gai., ii. 59; Paul., in *Vat. Frag.*, No. 50.
[49] None of these could be transferred by mancipation, as manifestly they could not by tradition.

Adjudication was the decree of a judge in a divisory action, such as one for partition of an inheritance amongst co-heirs; it conferred upon each of them a separate and independent right in a part of what as a whole had previously been joint property.[50]

Usucapion,[51] regulated by the XII Tables, but not improbably recognised previously in a vague and uncertain way, converted uninterrupted possession (*usus*) into quiritary property by efflux of time. The provision in the Tables was to this effect—"usus auctoritas fundi biennium esto, ceterarum rerum annuus esto."[52] The relation in which the words *usus* and *auctoritas* stand to each other has been a subject of much discussion; the prevailing opinion amongst modern civilians is that the first alone refers to usucapion and the second to the warranty of title incumbent on the vendor in a mancipation, and that both were limited to two years in the case of lands (and, by extensive interpretation, houses), and to one year in the case of anything else. In the later jurisprudence the possession—" use " was the technical term in the earlier law—required to be based on a sufficient title, and the possessor to be in good faith.[53] But the decemviral code, as is now generally admitted, contained no such requirements; any citizen [54] occupying immovables or holding movables as his own, provided they were usucaptible [55] and

[50] Ulp., *Frag.*, xix. 16.
[51] Literature: Stintzing, *Das Wesen von bona fides und titulus in d. Röm. Usucapionslehre*, Heidelberg, 1852; Schirmer, *Die Grundidee d. Usucapion im Röm. Recht*, Berlin, 1855; Pernice, *Labeo*, vol. ii. pp. 152 *sq.*; Voigt, *XII Tafeln*, vol. ii. § 91; Esmein, "Sur l'histoire de l'usucapion," in the *Nouv. Rev. Hist.*, &c., vol. ix. (1885), p. 261 *sq.*
[52] Cic., *Top.*, 4, § 23; *Pro Caec.*, 19, § 54; Gai., ii. §§ 42, 54, 204.
[53] Just., *Inst.*, ii. 6, pr.
[54] Usucapion was peculiar to citizens—"jus proprium est Romanorum" (Gai., ii. 65). The provision in the XII Tables, "Adversus hostem aeterna auctoritas" (Cic., *De Off.*, i. 12, § 37), which has been the subject of a somewhat voluminous literature, is sometimes adduced as proof of statutory declaration to the same effect.
[55] What belonged to the state or to religion was of course excluded from usucapion; so were the *res mancipi* of a woman in tutelage of her agnates or

K

that he had not taken them theftuously,[56] acquired a quiritary right in two years or one as the case might be, merely on the strength of his possession. Originally, therefore, it was simply the conversion of *de facto* possession, no matter how acquired, so long as not by theft, into legal ownership, when prolonged for the statutory period,—too often the maintenance of might at the cost of right. But in time it came to be regarded rather as a remedy for some defect of title, arising either from irregularity of conveyance or incapacity of the party from whom a transfer had been taken; and with the progress of jurisprudence developed into the carefully regulated positive prescription which has found a place in every modern system.

The Twelve Tables contained a variety of provisions regulating the relations between conterminous proprietors,[57] and imposed penalties of considerable severity for offences against property. For example, any one intentionally setting fire to another man's house, or to straw or such-like in its immediate vicinity, was to be flogged and burned at the stake.[58] The malicious driving of cattle by night to graze upon another man's young corn, was punished with hanging of the offender and forfeiture of his goods to Ceres.[59] Bewitching another person's hanging fruit, or spiriting away a crop from his field, was also punished with death.[60] Cutting a tree belonging to another entailed a penalty of twenty-five *asses*,[61]

---

patron, if alienated by her without their authority (Gai., ii. 47), the five feet of free space between two properties (Cic., *De Leg.*, i. 21, § 55), and a few other things.

[56] Gai., ii. 45.
[57] See fragments 1-10 in the seventh table of the arrangement in Bruns, p. 24.
[58] Gai., *lib.* 4. *ad XII Tab.*, in *Dig.*, xlvii. 9, 9.
[59] Plin., *H.N.*, xviii. 3, 12.
[60] Sen., *Nat. Quaest.*, iv. 7, 3; Plin., *H.N.*, xxviii. 2, 17; Serv. *in Virg. Ecl.*, viii. 99; Aug., *De Civ. Dei*, viii. 19. The penalty was probably death by burning; at least that was the punishment of sorcerers in the classical jurisprudence (Paul., *Sent.*, v. 23, § 17). See Voigt, *XII Tafeln*, vol. ii. p. 800.
[61] Plin., *H.N.*, xvii. 1, 7.

—the same as was imposed for an affront offered to a freeman, or an assault upon him that did not end in breaking bones.[62] The culpable killing or hurting of a slave or four-footed animal gave its owner a right to claim amends, but it does not appear in what form. Theft was envisaged from a great many points of view.. If a thief was caught plying his vocation by night, he might be slain on the spot; it was not lawful, however, to kill him by day, unless he used arms in resisting apprehension, (which was always the act of private parties, there being as yet no city watch or police establishment). A thief taken in the act (*fur manifestus*), if he was a freeman, was scourged and given over by the magistrate (*addictus*) to the person whose goods he had stolen; if a slave, he was flogged and thrown from the Tarpeian rock. A thief who was not taken at the time suffered only a pecuniary penalty,—twofold the value of the stolen goods. Very remarkable provisions were made to prevent third parties receiving and concealing stolen property. Thus the occupant of a house in which it was alleged that stolen property was concealed was bound to submit to a search for it, on pain of being held guilty of what was called *furtum prohibitum*, and punished as if he were a manifest thief; but the searcher was required to go through the house with nothing on him but a cloth round his loins, and carrying a platter in his hands, obviously to exclude all suspicion of foul play. If the result of the search was the discovery of the stolen property (*furtum linteo et lance conceptum*), the occupant was liable to the owner in threefold its value, however innocent and ignorant he might have been of its presence within his premises ; but he had relief against the person who had smuggled it into his house by what was called an *actio furti oblati*.[63]

---

[62] Gai., iii. 223.

[63] All those varieties of theft and *actiones furti* are described by Gaius (iii. 183-193), but not without some confusion. Krüger, in an article in the

The *actio de rationibus distrahendis* against a tutor who had embezzled property of his ward's was just a variety of the *actio furti*. So originally was the *actio de tigno juncto*,— an action competent to the owner of building materials against him who had theftuously incorporated them in his house. Their owner's property in them was suspended during their incorporation; he was not allowed to insist on their removal, for the public interest was of greater moment than his; but he was entitled by this action to double their value, and when the house came down he might again revindicate them.[64]

The abstract conception of a real right in (or over) the property of another person (what was called *jus in re aliena*) is not to be looked for at so early a period in the history of the law as that now under consideration. The rural servitudes of way and water were no doubt very early recognised; for they ranked as *res mancipi*, and the Twelve Tables contained various regulations in reference to the former. Usufruct, too, was probably not unknown; but the urban prædial servitudes bear the impress of a somewhat later jurisprudence. Emphyteutic and superficial rights were of still later origin. Pignorate and hypothecary rights were equally unknown as rights protected by action at the time now being dealt with.[65] Between private parties, the only thing legally recognised of the nature of a real security was the *fiducia* already described. Approaching more nearly to

Z. d. Sav. Stift., vol. v. (1884), R. A., p. 219 sq., has given a somewhat different explanation of them. See also Gulli in the Arch. Giurid., vol. xxxiii. (1884), p. 107 sq.

[64] Gai. in *Dig.*, xli. 1, 7, § 10 ; Ulp. in *Dig.*, xlvii. 3, 1, § 1. The later law did not allow eventual vindication if there had been no *mala fides* in the appropriation, and the double value had already been paid.

[65] Hypothecary rights were certainly unknown until near the end of the republic. But Festus (v. *Nancitor*, Bruns, p. 274) speaks of a provision in the Cassian league between Rome and the Latin states of the year 262 U.C.—"Si quid pignoris nasciscitur, sibi habeto "—which makes it difficult to believe that the Romans were altogether unacquainted in *de facto* practice with impignoration of movables.

the modern idea of a mortgage was the security *praedibus praediisque* required by the state from those indebted to it in assurance of their obligations. Here there was the double guarantee of sureties (*praedes*) and mortgaged lands of theirs (*praedia subsignata*); but how they were dealt with when the debtor made default is by no means clear.[66]

SECTION 31.—NEXUM AND THE LAW OF OBLIGATIONS.

The jurists of the classical period attribute obligation either to contract, delict, or miscellaneous causes (*variae causarum figurae*); and those arising from contract fill a place in the later jurisprudence vastly greater than those arising from delict. In the Twelve Tables it is very different. In them delicts are much more prominent than contracts,—wrongs entitling the sufferer to demand the imposition of penalties upon the wrong-doer, that in most cases covered both reparation and punishment. The disproportion in the formulated provisions in reference to the two sources of obligation, however, is not surprising. For, first of all, the purpose of the decemviral code was to remove uncertainties and leave as little as possible to the arbitrariness of the magistrates. In nothing was there more scope for it than in the imposition of penalties; and as different offences required to be differently treated, the provisions in reference to them were necessarily multiplied. In the next place, the intercourse that evokes contract was as yet very limited. Agriculture was the occupation of the great majority; trade and commerce were more backward than in the later years of the regal period; coined money was just beginning to be used as a circulating medium. Lastly, the safeguards of engagement lay to a great extent in the sworn oath or the plighted faith; of which the law

[66] For note of the literature on the subject, see Baron, *Gesch. d. R. R.*, vol. i. p. 169.

indeed did not yet take cognisance, but which found a protection quite as potent in the religious and moral sentiments that had so firm a hold of the people.

It was a principle of the law of Rome through the whole of its history, though in course of time subject to an increasing number of exceptions, that mere agreement between two persons did not give him in whose favour it was conceived a right to demand its enforcement. To entitle a man to claim the intervention of the civil tribunals to compel implement of an engagement undertaken by another, it was necessary either that it should be clothed in some form the law prescribed or recognised, or that it should be accompanied or followed by some relative act which rendered it something more than a mere interchange of consent. Under the jurisprudence of the XII Tables the formalities required to elevate an agreement to the rank of contract and make it civilly obligatory sometimes combined ceremonial act and words of style, sometimes did not go beyond words of style, but in all cases before witnesses. *Dotis dictio,* the undertaking of a parent to provide a dowry with his daughter whom he was giving in marriage, and *vadimonium,* the guarantee of a surety for the due fulfilment of the undertaking either of a party to a contract or a party to a litigation, probably required nothing more than words of style before persons who could if necessary bear witness to them; whereas an engagement incident to a mancipation, or an undertaking to repay borrowed money, required in addition a ceremony with the copper and the scales. The historical reason for the employment of the scales has already been explained. They became as time progressed mere matter of form or ceremonial; but originally they were matter of substance. In early days neither sale nor loan was possible without them; for both the price in the one case, and the copper that was being lent in the other, had to be weighed. It was the spirit of conservatism, so manifest in all departments of the law, that induced their retention as formalities after they had ceased to be of moment substantially; had they had no practical significance in the first instance, it is not likely they would ever have been resorted to. There were many formal observances in Roman law that seemed to have not much bearing upon the proceeding of which they formed part; but there was hardly one of them that had not its historical explanation. They were often retained, more or less modified, simply because they had been always associated with some particular transaction, and sometimes long after they had ceased to be of any substantial significance; but it was not the practice to introduce merely for the sake of form a ceremonial that at the time of its introduction had no utilitarian value. If all that was wanted was deliberation in contracting, certainty as to the nature and terms of the contract, publicity and trustworthy testimony, words of style, spoken in presence of witnesses, as in the *vadimonium* and *dotis dictio*, were sufficient for the purpose.

The opinion is very generally entertained that the only proper contracts recognised by the XII Tables were those annexed to a mancipation or surrender in court and embodied in a *lex mancipii* or *in jure cessionis*, and the *nexum*,[1] the *vadimonium*, and the *dotis dictio*. Some reckon amongst them the verbal contract by stipulation, which in time came to be the most important and inclusive form of contract known to the law; but it is impossible to discover even the most remote allusion to it in any extant fragment of the Tables, and the better opinion seems to be that it was of later introduction.

[1] The literature on the subject of the *nexum* is very abundant, and the views taken of it very discordant. Danz (*Gesch. d. R. R.*, vol. iii. § 146) gives a list of the more important writings about it, and a *résumé* of the principal theories. To his list, which comes down to 1870, may be added Vainberg, *Le nexum . . . en droit Romain*, Paris, 1874; Brinz, "Der Begriff *obligatio*," in *Grünhut's ZSchr.*, vol. i. (1874) p. 11 *sq.;* and Voigt, *XII Tafeln*, vol. i. §§ 63-65.

The condition of the *nexi* (as debtors who had been bound by nexal contract were called) during the first two centuries of the republic, and the commotions to which their grievances again and again gave rise, have been alluded to in a previous section (§ 20). Although much has been written on the subject, opinions differ not a little as to who exactly those *nexi* were, how they became so, and what was their status in law. In this, however, there seems to be a general agreement,—that the first step towards their reaching the miserable condition which Livy and Dionysius have so graphically, though perhaps not always with strict accuracy, depicted, was a loan transaction, real or fictitious,[2] which was technically called *nexum* or *nexi datio*.[3] The practice of lending *per libram* was doubtless of great antiquity,—indeed the intervention of the scales was a necessity when money or what passed for it had to be weighed instead of counted; and not improbably old custom conceded to a lender who had thus made an advance in the presence of witnesses some very summary and stringent remedy against a borrower who failed in repayment. How Servius subjected it to much the same formalities as he appointed for mancipation,—the state scales, the official *libripens*, the five witnesses representing the nation,—has been shown already (p. 68). With the introduction of a coinage the transaction, instead of being *per libram* simply, became one *per aes et libram;* the scales were touched with a single piece, representing the money

[2] The opinion is entertained by some writers that, after the introduction of coined money, and when touching the scales with a single *as* took the place of the weighing of so many pounds of metal as part of the ceremonial, the *nexi datio* upon pretence of a loan might be, and was, employed to create a bond for payment of a definite sum, no matter what the real ground of indebtedness. It is extremely probable. The sale in a mancipation was in many cases only simulated, and the payment in *nexi liberatio* did not need to be real; arguing from analogy, therefore, there is no reason why a man may not have become *nexus* as if for borrowed money, when in fact the ground of debt was something different.

[3] See Appendix, Note C.

which had already been or was about to be paid, a formula recited whereby the obligation of repayment was imposed on the borrower, and an appeal made to the witnesses for their testimony. Unfortunately this formula is nowhere preserved. Huschke[4] and Giraud,[5] assuming that the lender was the only speaker, formulate it thus,—" Quod ego tibi mille libras hoc aere aeneaque libra nexas dedi, eas tu mihi post annum jure nexi dare damnas esto "—" Whereas, with this coin and these copper scales, I have given thee a thousand asses, be thou therefore bound *jure nexi* to repay them to me a year hence."[6] The phrase *damnas esto*, like the rest of the formula, is unsupported by any conclusive authority; but as it was that most frequently employed during the republic for imposing, by a public act, liability to pay a fixed and definite sum,[7] it may not be wide of the mark.[8]

What was the effect of this procedure? The question is one not easily answered. Brinz has expressed the opinion

[4] Huschke, *Ueber das Recht des nexum* (Leipsic, 1846), p. 50.

[5] Giraud, *Des nexi, ou de la condition des débiteurs chez les Romains* (Paris, 1847), p. 67.

[6] If the loan was to bear interest, the words *cum impendio unciario*, or equivalents, would be incorporated.

[7] See Huschke, *l.c.* He renders *damnas esto* (p. 51), " Du sollst ein zu geben Verfluchter sein." There has been much speculation as to the derivation and original meaning of the words *damnum, damnare, damnas*. See the more important suggestions in Voigt, *Bedeutungswechsel*, p. 142 *sq.*

[8] Voigt, who holds that the *nexi datio* was at once a mode of transferring the property of the money or other ponderable from the lender to the borrower, and of imposing upon the latter an obligation to repay it, proposes a different formula (*XII Tafeln*, vol. ii. p. 483), which has the merit of coming nearer that of the *nexi liberatio* than Huschke's : " Haec ego octingenta aeris ex jure Quiritium tua esse aio ea lege, uti tantundem cum impendio unciario proximis kalendis Martiis recte solvas liberasque aenea libra. Hanc tibi libram primam postremam adpendo, lege jure obligatus ; " and this he holds to have been echoed by the borrower, in accordance with his theory that in every transaction *per aes et libram* there must have been *nuncupatio* on both sides. He rejects the words *damnas esto*, because of another theory of his own,—that there was nothing peculiar in the obligation created *nexo, i.e.*, that it did not impose any immediate liability on the borrower which the lender could enforce without judicial intervention, but that the latter required to proceed against the former in ordinary course, by what he calls an *actio pecuniae nuncupatae*.

that the creditor was entitled in virtue of the *nexum* to take his debtor into custody at any time when he considered such a course necessary for his own protection, even before the conventional term of repayment,—that the debtor was in bonds, virtually a pledge, from the very first, and the tightness or looseness of them a matter in the discretion of his creditor.[9] Voigt holds that the *nexum* did not give the creditor any peculiar hold over his debtor; and that, on the latter's failure to repay, an ordinary action was necessary, to be followed by the usual proceedings in execution if judgment was in favour of the former.[10] These views may be said to be the two extremes, and between them lie a good many others more or less divergent. The difficulty of arriving at a conclusion is caused to some extent by the ambiguity of the words *nexus* and *nexum*. The transaction itself was called *nexum*; the money advanced was *nexum aes* (hence *nexi*, *i.e. aeris, datio*); the bond was *nexus* (of the fourth declension); and the debtor on whom the bond was laid was also *nexus* (of the second). All this is simple enough. But we find the same word *nexus* employed by the historians as almost synonymous with *vinctus*,—to denote the condition of a debtor put in fetters by his creditor. That might be the condition either of a nexal borrower or of an ordinary judgment-debtor (§ 36). The former in such a case was doubly *nexus*; he was at once in the bonds of legal obligation and in those of physical constraint. In many passages in which Livy and others speak of the *nexi* it is extremely difficult, sometimes impossible, to be sure in which meaning they use the word. It is therefore not sur-

---

[9] Brinz, *Grünhut's ZSchr.*, vol. i. p. 22. He likens the position of the *nexus* to that of a thing, land say, mortgaged to a creditor in security of a claim. Such a security is constantly spoken of by the Roman jurists as *res obligata* or *res nexa*. As Brinz observes, the thing was *obligata* from the first, and continued so as long as the debt it secured was unpaid, even though the creditor found it unnecessary to reduce it into possession or interfere with it in any way.

[10] See reference in note 8.

prising that there should be considerable diversity of opinion on the subject, and such frequent identification of the legal status of a nexal debtor (*nexus*) with that of a judgment debtor (*judicatus, addictus*). Consideration of the texts inclines me to the conclusion that, although *de facto* a creditor may have made little or no difference in his treatment of his *nexi* and *addicti*, yet *de jure* their positions were quite distinct both before and after the legislation of the Tables.[11] The right of a nexal creditor whose debtor was in default was, at his own hand, and without any judgment affirming the existence of the debt, to apprehend him, and detain him, and put him to service until the loan was repaid.[12] Its parallel is to be met with amongst all ancient nations,—Jews, Greeks, Scandinavians, Germans, &c.[13] And it was not altogether unreasonable. If a borrower had already exhausted all available means of raising money, had sold or mortgaged everything he possessed of any value, what other recourse was open to him in his necessity than to impledge himself?[14] For this was substantially what he did in entering

[11] Dionysius (viii. 83), speaking of the events that gave rise to the first secession of the plebeians and the measures proposed for remedying their grievances, pointedly distinguishes between borrowers whose bodies had been taken by their creditors because they had failed to repay their loans at the proper period, and debtors who had magisterially been given up to their creditors because they had failed to implement judgments obtained against them.

[12] This meets the definition of Varro (*De L. L.*, vii. 105, Bruns, p. 308)— " Liber qui suas operas in servitutem pro pecunia quam debet dat, dum solveret nexus vocatur "—" a freeman who gives his services as a slave in return for money that he owes is called *nexus* so long as it is unpaid."

[13] See authorities in Bruns' paper in *Grünhut's ZSchr.*, vol. i. p. 25. The Greek phrase was 'ἐπὶ σώματι δανείζειν. There is a curious style in Marculfus (*Form.*, ii. 27), in which a borrower engages that, until he shall have repaid his loan, his creditor shall have right to his services so many days a week, and shall have power to inflict corporal punishment if there be dilatoriness in rendering them. Kohler, in his *Shakespeare vor dem Forum der Jurisprudenz* (Würzburg, 1884), p. 7 *sq.*, gives scores of illustrations from the early (and in some cases present) laws and customs of all parts of the world of the powers of creditors over the bodies of their debtors, which form a most instructive study in comparative jurisprudence. See *infra*, Appendix, Note F.

[14] " He told them how he had been obliged to borrow money, because, when

into the nexal contract;[15] not in so many words, but by
necessary implication.[16] That the creditor should have
been entitled to realise the right he had thus acquired
without the judgment on it of a court of law is equally
intelligible. The nexal contract was a public act, carried
out in the presence of the representatives of the people,
who were witnesses alike of the acknowledgement of indebtedness and the tacit engagement of the debtor. The
only valid objection that could be stated against the creditor's apprehension of his debtor in execution was that the
indebtedness no longer existed,—that the loan had been
repaid. But a nexal debt could be legally discharged only
by *nexi liberatio;* which also was a solemn procedure *per
aes et libram* in the presence of five citizen witnesses.[17]

he had been away fighting against the Sabines, his farm had remained un-
cropped, his house had been burned, his cattle driven off, everything plun-
dered, and at the same time, unhappily for him, a tribute imposed ; how first
his ancestral lands had gone, then his other property, and at last, like a
wasting disease, it had come to his body ; how his creditor, instead of putting
him to work (*in servitium*), had thrown him into a dungeon and a torture-
chamber " (Liv., ii. 23).

[15] It is often argued, in opposition to this view of the matter, that a Roman
citizen could neither sell himself as a slave nor place himself *in causa mancipii*.
This is true. But it is irrelevant. The *nexus* was neither a slave nor *in
causa mancipii.* His creditor's right was to detain him and use his services ;
protected possibly by a real action, but certainly by an action of theft 'against
any third party maliciously carrying him off. In these respects the relation
of the *nexus* to his creditor was analogous to that of an *auctoratus* to his
lanista (Gai., iii. 199) ; yet the *auctoratus* was undoubtedly a freeman, and the
relation the result of contract.

[16] Some jurists hold that a debtor's giving himself as *nexus* was something
distinct from the engagement to repay, and might be either contemporaneous
with it or of later date. In the former case they assume that there was a
separate agreement or *lex nexi* annexed to the main contract. For the latter
they call in evidence the historians, who once or twice speak of men having
yielded themselves as *nexi* in respect of loans they themselves had not contracted. But in such instances it was invariably a son that gave himself up
in respect of money borrowed by his deceased father,—the heir fulfilling, as
the law compelled him to do, the obligation of his predecessor.

[17] Gai., iii. 174. The formula of *nexi liberatio* is instructive as showing the
actual relation in which the debtor stood to his creditor—" me a te solvo
liberoque hoc aere aeneaque libra "—" I unbind and free *myself* from thee,"
&c. ,

What need for a judicial inquiry in the presence of facts so notorious? A creditor would rarely be daring enough to proceed to *manus injectio* if his loan had been repaid; if he did, the testimony of the witnesses to the discharge would at once procure the release of his alleged debtor. It was probably to give opportunity for such proof, if there was room for it, that the XII Tables required that a creditor who had apprehended a nexal debtor should bring him into court before carrying him off into detention.

The provisions of the Tables on the subject of *manus injectio*,[18] there seems good reason to believe, applied for the most part only to judgment-debtors. There are some, however, who hold they had no application at all to mere *nexi*;[19] while others again are of opinion that they applied to them in their integrity as much as to *judicati*.[20] As described by Gellius they commenced thus: " Aeris confessi rebusque jure judicatis triginta dies justi sunto. Post deinde manus injectio esto: in jus ducito. Ni judicatum facit," &c., *i.e.*, " for acknowledged money debts and judgments obtained by regular process of law the days of grace shall be thirty. Then the creditor may apprehend his debtor, but must bring him before the prætor. If the judgment-debtor still fail to implement the judgment," and so on. That the words " aeris confessi . . . triginta dies justi sunto "[21] referred to a nexal debtor, and not, as is generally assumed, to a defendant who had formally admitted his liability in the initial stage of an ordinary action, will be shown more conveniently in a subsequent section (§ 36). He was to have thirty days' grace after the maturity of his

[18] Gell., xx. i. 45.
[19] *E.g.*, Voigt, *XII Tafeln*, vol. i. p. 629 *sq.*
[20] *E.g.*, Huschke, who is of opinion (*Nexum*, p. 95) that the Tables must have contained a provision that a *nexus* was to be dealt with in the same way as a *judicatus*.
[21] There is no good objection to the phrase "dies aeris confessi;" for "dies pecuniae" occurs in Cic., *Ad Att.*, x. 5, and "dies pecuniarum" in Colum., *De R. R.*, i. 7, 2.

debt; and then his creditor might apprehend him, presenting him, however, to the magistrate before carrying him home (*domum ductio*), in order, no doubt, that the one might prove the nexal contract, and the other have an opportunity, if the fact justified it, of proving by the mouths of the witnesses of the *nexi liberatio* that the loan had been repaid. All that follows in Gellius of the provisions of the Tables on the subject of *manus injectio* seems to refer solely to the case of a judgment-debtor. The possible intervention of a *vindex*, the two months' provisional detention of the debtor, his periodical production in the market-place, his formal overgiving to his creditor (*addictio*) on the expiry of the sixty days, the *capite poenas datio*, the sale beyond Tiber, the *partis secare*,—all these (§ 36) refer solely to the *judicatus*. There was no room for a *vindex* or champion in the case of a nexal debtor; for there was no judgment whose regularity the former could impugn. Nor was there any room for a magisterial *addictio* of the debtor to his creditor; for the latter's right was founded on a publicly vouched contract, and needed no decree to strengthen it. He was entitled at once, after apprehension of his debtor and production of him in court in terms of the statute, to carry him home, take such steps as were necessary to ensure his safe custody, and employ his services in profitable industry. But that he could kill him or sell him, as some suppose, is a proposition that is unsupported by any distinct authority.

Equally untenable is the notion that the *nexus* became a slave, or that, while retaining his freedom, his wife, children, and belongings fell with him into the hands of his creditor. He certainly was not in a worse position than an *addictus*,—a judgment-debtor given over to his creditor by magisterial decree on failure to make an arrangement; yet Quintilian states distinctly that an *addictus* did not become a slave,—that he still retained his position in the census and in his tribe.[22] Many a time, when the exigencies of the state required it, were the *nexi* temporarily released in order to obey a call to arms,—to fulfil the duty incumbent on them as citizens. In fact, a nexal debtor suffered no *capitis deminutio* at all because of his detention. If he was a house-father, he still retained his *manus* over his wife and *potestas* over his children. But they did not share his quasi-servitude.[23] Their earnings legally belonged to him; but were no doubt retained by them with his consent for their own support. They certainly did not fall to his creditor. We may well believe that in the ordinary case a *nexus*, when he fell into that condition, had not much to call his own; but to assume that all that he then had, and all that he subsequently acquired by inheritance or otherwise, passed *ipso jure* to his creditor, would be to set at naught the statement of Varro—"dum solveret nexus vocatur." How could he pay his debt and thus obtain his release if all that he had to pay with already belonged to his creditor? And what, on such assumption, of the provision of the Poetilian law, which made *bonam copiam jurare* a condition of the release of the *nexi* then in bondage?[24] Whatever these words may mean—and it is matter of controversy[25]— they undoubtedly imply that a *nexus*, even when confined

[22] Quint., *Decl.*, 311.
[23] If they had done so as a matter of course, there would have been no occasion for a son to yield himself as *nexus* for his father's debt on the latter's death, as we are told sometimes happened (see note 16). A passage in Livy (ii. 24) seems at first sight to partially contradict what is stated above : " Servilius . . . edixit ne quis civem Romanum vinctum aut clausum teneret, quo minus edendi apud consules potestas fieret, neu quis militis, donec in castris esset, bona possideret aut venderet, liberos nepotesve ejus moraretur." But this edict bore no special reference to *nexi*. It was a general prohibition of the appropriation of the goods or detention of the children of a citizen while on service, no matter on what pretext. Besides, it was nearly fifty years earlier than the XII Tables, and before there was any definite law to protect the plebeians against the high-handed oppression of their patrician fellow-citizens.
[24] Varro, *De L. L.*, vii. 105 (Bruns, p. 308).
[25] See *infra*, note 35.

in his creditor's prison-house, might still have means of his own. It was the body of his debtor that the creditor was entitled to, and too often he wreaked his vengeance on it by way of punishment; there was as yet no machinery for attaching the debtor's goods in substantial reparation for the loss caused by his breach of contract.

The abuses to which the system gave rise alike in the case of nexal and of judgment-debtors have already more than once been alluded to. Their detaining creditors, instead of being content to employ them in productive industry, and resorting to no more restraint or punishment than was necessary for safe custody or in the exercise of discipline, often confined them in dungeons, put them in chains, starved them and flogged them, and subjected them to the grossest indignities. In the year 428 [26] a more than ordinarily flagrant outrage committed by a creditor upon one of his young *nexi*, who, Livy says, had given himself up as responsible for a loan contracted by his deceased father, roused the populace to such a pitch of indignation as to necessitate instant remedial legislation. The result was the famous Poetilian law (*lex Poetilia Papiria*).[27] It has often been summarily described as a law abolishing imprisonment for debt, and substituting real for personal execution. Its scope, however, was by no means so extensive. The imprisonment of a judgment-debtor was still competent under the legislation of Justinian,[28] although by the Julian law of *cessio bonorum* it might be avoided or put an end to by the unreserved surrender of his goods to his creditor;[29] while execution against a debtor's estate independently of his person was first made

[26] According to Livy. Dionysius puts it in 462.
[27] Cic., *De Rep.*, ii. 34, § 59; Liv., viii. 28; Dion. Hal., *Frag.*, xvi. 9 (Reiske, vol. iv. p. 2338); Varro, *De L. L.*, vii. 105 (Bruns, p. 303).
[28] See references to it as a subsisting institution in *Dig.*, xlii. 1, 34, and *Cod.*, vii. 71, 1.
[29] Severus Alexander in *Cod.*, vii. 71, 1.

matter of general regulation by an edict of Pub. Rutilius Rufus,[30] who was prætor in 647 U.C.[31]

So far as can be gathered from the meagre accounts of it we possess, the Poetilian law contained at least these three provisions: (1) that fetters and neck, arm, or foot blocks should in future be applied only to persons undergoing imprisonment for crime or delict; (2) that no one should ever again be the *nexus* of his creditor in respect of borrowed money; and (3) that all existing *nexi qui bonam copiam jurarent* should be released. The first was intended to prevent unnecessary restraint upon judgment-debtors formally given over (*addicti*) to their creditors. Bonds were not altogether forbidden; on the contrary, the charter of foundation of one of Cæsar's colonies, in authorising *manus injectio* upon a judgment, expressly empowered the creditor to incarcerate his debtor, and put him in bonds such as were allowed by the *jus civile*.[32] It is not improbable that in addition the statute contained this positive provision in reference to the *addictus*,—that he should work for his creditor until his debt was paid; at least Quintilian more than once mentions an anonymous statute in which he says it was so laid down.[33] The second provision above referred

[30] Gai., iii. 78, iv. 35. This edict was really a bankruptcy law, to preserve an insolvent debtor's estate and regulate its division among his creditors. But there is no reason for doubting that long before its date the prætor may have interfered in the same direction on special application in regard to each case as it arose.

[31] What, no doubt, has given rise to the notion that the Poetilian law was meant to substitute real for personal execution, is the phrase in Livy's account of it,—" Pecuniae creditae bona debitoris non corpus obnoxium esset." But this is clearly comment and nothing more; the Romans did not express their enactments in language so abstract and so vague. All that Livy meant, probably, was that it was the goods of a debtor (including the produce of his labour), and not his body as such, that ought to be made responsible for money borrowed by him.

[32] *Lex coloniae Juliae Genetivae* (710 A.U.C.), cap. 61 (Bruns, p. 110),—" Judicati jure manus injectio esto. . . . Secum ducito. Jure civili vinctum habeto."

[33] " Quid enim lex dicit? 'Addictus, donec solverit, serviat'" (*Decl.*, 311). See also *Inst. Or.*, vii. 3, 26.

L

to did not necessarily abolish the contract of loan *per aes et libram*, but only what had hitherto been an *ipso jure* consequence of it,—the creditor's right to incarcerate his debtor without either the judgment of a court or the warrant of a magistrate. For the future, execution was to be done against a borrower only as a judgment-debtor formally made over to his creditor by magisterial decree, and under the restrictions and limitations imposed by the Poetilian law itself. This very soon led to the disuse of nexal obligation; once it was deprived of its distinctive processual advantages it rapidly gave place to the simpler engagement by stipulation enforcible *per condictionem* (§ 39). As for the release of the then existing *nexi*, Cicero, Livy, and Dionysius say nothing of any condition annexed to the boon the statute conferred upon them; it is only Varro that limits it to those *qui bonam copiam jurarunt*,—those apparently who were able to declare on oath that they had done their best, and could do no more to meet their creditors' claims.[34] Such a limitation can hardly be called unreasonable, even were we to assume—as probably we ought to do—that the release spoken of was only from the bonds of physical restraint, not from those of legal obligation.[35] It might be proper enough to liberate those whose inability it was, and not their will, that prevented them fulfilling their engagements; but to have done the same with those who, being able to do so, fraudulently refused to pay their debts, would have been an

---

[34] The same words occur in the *Lex Julia Municipalis* (line 113, Bruns, p. 101) as descriptive of a class of persons thereby disqualified for holding office in a municipality. They must therefore have implied insolvency rather than solvency. Comp. Marezoll, *Frag. legis Rom. in tab. Heracleensis parte* (Göttingen, 1816), p. 142 *sq.*; Dirksen, *Ad tab. Heracl. part. alteram* (Berlin, 1817), p. 105 *sq.* Cic., *Ad Fam.*, ix. 16, has *bonam copiam ejurare*. Paul. Diac. (Bruns, p. 266) defines *ejuratio* as "id, quod desideretur, non posse praestare."

[35] Livy's phrase is "ita nexi soluti;" and "nexi soluti" he employs elsewhere in opposition to "nexi vincti," thus distinguishing between *nexi* in bonds and *nexi* at large. In ii. 23, § 8, he has "nexi vincti solutique."

injustice to their creditors that even the abuses that gave occasion for the statute could hardly have excused.

It is obvious that the contract of *nexum* and the contractual or quasi-contractual relations arising from a *lex mancipii*, a *vadimonium*, or a *dotis dictio*, must have been far from sufficient to meet the requirements even of an agricultural population such as that of Rome in the fourth century of her history. If a man purchased sheep or store cattle, a plough, a toga, a jar of wine or oil, had he no action to compel delivery, the vendor no action for payment of the price? Did the hire of a horse or the loan of a bullock create no obligation? Was partnership unknown, and deposit, and pledge, and suretyship in any other form than that of *vadimonium*? One can have no hesitation in answering that, as transactions of daily life, they must all have been more or less familiar. It does not follow, however, that they were already regulated by law and protected by the ordinary tribunals. The historical jurists are pretty well agreed that not only the real contracts of loan (*mutuum* and *commodatum*), deposit, and pledge, but also the consensual ones of sale, location, partnership, and mandate, and the verbal one of suretyship, were as yet very barely recognised by law. Sale was the offspring of barter,—of instant exchange of one thing for another. With such instant exchange there was no room for obligation to deliver on either side, even when the ware (*merx*) given by one of the parties was so much rough copper weighed in the scales. The substitution of coined money for the raw metal can hardly have operated any radical change; the ordinary practice of those early times must still have been ready-money transaction,—an instant exchange of ware against price; and it can only have been when, for some reason or other, the arrangement was exceptionally for delivery or payment at a future date, say next market-day, that obligation was held to have been created. Was that obligation enforceable by the civil tribunals? Some jurists hold that it was,—that at no time were the *juris gentium* contracts outside the protection of judicial remedies, although by a simpler procedure than that resorted to for enforcement of the contracts of the *jus civile*. But a couple of provisions in the XII Tables seem to prove very clearly that it was not. The first is that already referred to as recorded by Justinian,[36]—that where a thing was sold and delivered, the property, nevertheless, should not pass until the price had been paid or sureties (*vades*) for it accepted by the vendor. Far from being a recognition of the obligatory nature of the transaction, this provision is really a recognition of the inability of the law to enforce payment of the price by the vendee; it is a declaration that on the latter's failure to pay, the vendor, unprotected by any personal action, should be entitled to recover the thing sold as still his own, no matter in whose hands he found it. The second related to the case of a person who had bought a victim for sacrifice, but had failed to pay for it. A real action for its revindication by the seller after it had been consumed on the altar was out of the question; so he was authorised by the Tables,[37] by the process of *pignoris capio* (§ 37), at his own hand to appropriate in satisfaction a sufficient equivalent out of the belongings of the purchaser, against whom he had no personal action.[38]

It would seem, therefore, that in the earlier centuries of the history of the law *juris gentium* conventional obligation was cognisable by the civil courts only to a very limited extent. But it has already been pointed out in dealing with the regal period (p. 50) that if the party in whose favour

---

[36] See § 30, note 4.   [37] Gai., iv. 28.

[38] Gaius (*l.c.*) records an analogous provision in reference to location: if A gave one of his draught cattle in location to B, as a means of raising money for a sacrifice, and B failed to pay the hire, A might recoup himself by *pignoris capio*. Here again the exceptional procedure was in the interests of religion; but it would have been unnecessary had there been a personal action on the contract.

such an obligation was conceived took the precaution of having it corroborated either by a solemn oath (*iusjurandum*) or an invocation of Fides, then a breach of it fell within the cognisance of the ministers of religion, or of the magistrate invested for the time being with the *regimen morum*. There were various transactions and relations, moreover, that were held to be peculiarly under the protection of Fides, even although there might have been no actual invocation; and in some of them breach of the engagement involved, when accompanied by substantial injury to another, entitled the latter to institute proceedings against the defaulter. A guardian, for example, who had converted the funds or property of his ward to his own use, was liable in double their value. A depositary who was unfaithful to the trust reposed in him was also liable to an action for double the value of what he had failed to restore, one-half in reparation and the other half by way of penalty.[39] And it is quite possible, although we have no record of it, that the same rule applied to the borrower of some specific article (*commodatarius*), when by his own malfeasance he was unable to return what had been lent him.[40]

Those were cases of breach of conventional or quasi-conventional obligation which, because of the grossness of the perfidy involved in them, were punished as if they were delicts. Of delicts proper—offences against life, limb, reputation, and property, independent of any breach of special duty incumbent on the offender—the Tables, as there has been occasion to notice from time to time, contained a goodly list. But contract and delict were not the only sources of obligation under their *régime* any more than at a later period. There were some that arose from facts and circumstances,— events that placed one person in the position of debtor to

[39] Paul., *Sent.*, ii. 12, § 11. See *supra*, § 30, note 38.
[40] That deposit and commodate stood in some respects on the same footing appears from Gai., iv. 47.

another (*ex re*). To this class belonged the *depensum* (or *depensio*) more than once mentioned by Gaius.[41] He speaks of it in connection with a *lex Publilia*, which authorised sureties (*sponsores*), who had paid debts for their principals, to proceed against them by *manus injectio* if the *depensum* was not repaid within six months. He does not say, however, that the notion of obligation in respect of such outlay was new, or that an *actio depensi* was for the first time introduced by the Publilian law. And it can hardly have been so. The *vindex* and the *vas* of the Twelve Tables, it may reasonably be assumed, must have had an action of relief against the party for whom they had been required to make payment; and there seems ground for the opinion that this must have been the *actio depensi*, carried out by the summary process of *manus injectio* (§ 36).[42] To the class of obligations *ex re* may also be assigned those arising between co-heirs from the fact of their co-inheritance, and which were adjusted by means of the decemviral *actio familiae erciscundae*.[43] There may have been one or two others of the same sort; but the materials at command do not enable us to speak of them with certainty.

SECTION 32.—THE LAW OF SUCCESSION.

Patrician Rome had two varieties of testament,—that made at stated periods in the comitia of the curies, under advice of the college of pontiffs, and that made by soldiers in the hearing of a few comrades on the eve of battle, and which probably was originally nothing more than an apportionment of the testator's belongings amongst his proper heirs. Both still remained in use in the early republic; but were in course of time displaced by the general adoption of that executed with the copper and scales (*testa-*

---

[41] Gai., iii. 127, iv. 22.   [42] See Voigt, *XII Tafeln*, vol. ii. p. 495.
[43] Gai. *ad ed. prov.*, in *Dig.*, x. 2, fr. 1, pr.

mentum per aes et libram). It seems to be the general opinion that it was to the first two alone that the words applied which stood in the forefront of the provisions of the XII Tables about inheritance,—" uti legassit suae rei ita jus esto."[1] Whether resort was to the comitia or to the army, the testator's own will in the matter was henceforth to be supreme. There was to be no more reference to the pontiffs as to the expediency of the testament in view of the interests of the family *sacra* and of creditors of the testator's; from legislators, sanctioning a departure from the ordinary rules of succession, the assembled Quirites became merely witnesses,—recipients of the oral declaration of the testator's will in regard to his inheritance.

The testament with the copper and the scales is depicted by Gaius as a written instrument. But he presents it in what was apparently the third stage of its history. Its probable origin has already been explained (p. 66) in describing the result of the Servian reforms upon the private law. It was not a testament but only a makeshift for one. A plebeian was not qualified in the regal period to make a testament in the comitia; so, instead, he transferred his estate to a friend on whom he could rely,—the transferee was called *familiae emptor*, because the conveyance was in form a mancipation for a nominal price,—with instructions how to distribute it on his death.[2] It is not at all unlikely that the same device may occasionally have been resorted to by a patrician who had neglected to make a regular testament and was seized with mortal illness before he had an opportunity of appealing to the curies. But such a

---

[1] Gai., ii. 224; Just., *Inst.*, ii. 22, pr. Ulpian and others interpolate "super pecunia tutelave" before "suae rei." But this has the appearance of a gloss by the interpreters of the republic; the Tables, in dealing with intestate succession, speak not of *pecunia* but of *familia*. *Legare* does not mean "bequeath," but is equivalent to *legem dicere* (see *supra*, § 7, note 7; § 11, note 8). *Suae rei* refers to what is often called the *res familiaris*, or more briefly *familia*.

[2] Gai., ii. 103.

disposition was not a testament, and may not have been so called. A testament was the nomination of a person as the testator's heir,—sometimes the substitution of an individual of the testator's choice for the heir assigned to him by law, sometimes the acceptance of the latter in the character of testamentary heir, so that the testator might be able to impose upon him what burdens he pleased as the tacit condition of heirship. It made the person instituted as fully the representative of the testator after his death as his heir-at-law would have been had he died intestate. The *mortis causa* mancipation, however, that opened the way for the testament *per aes et libram*, conferred upon the *familiae emptor* no such character. Gaius says that he stood in place of an heir (*heredis loco*), inasmuch as he had such of an heir's rights and duties as the *familiae venditor* had it in his power to confer and impose; but the transaction was but a conveyance of estate, with a limitation of the right of the grantee.

It has been argued that, as the law did not recognise conditional mancipation, the conveyance must have operated a complete and immediate divestiture of the grantee. But this does not follow. For it was quite competent for a man, in transferring property by mancipation, to reserve to himself a life interest;[3] and apparently it was equally competent for him to postpone delivery of possession,[4] without infringing the rule that the mancipation itself could not be *ex certo tempore*. So far as one can see, therefore, there was nothing to prevent the grantee of the conveyance (or quasi-testator) bargaining that he was to retain the possession till his death; and as the *familia* was an aggregate of estate (*universitas rerum*), which retained its identity notwithstanding any change in its component elements, he must in such case have been as free to operate on it while he survived as if he had never conveyed it by mancipation. But

[3] Gai., ii. 33.   [4] Gai., iv. 131a.

on his death how did it stand affected by the claims of creditors? Fraudulent alienations to defeat their rights were set aside by prætorian law; but we have no reason to believe that any such process was competent in the third century of the city. It would almost appear as if creditors must have been as much at the mercy of the *familiae emptor* as were those among whom he had been directed to distribute the estate. These, certainly, had nothing to depend on but his sense of honour; they had no action against him, because he was not the deceased's heir, neither between them and him was there any bond of contract. He was a trustee and nothing more; and it was not until early in the empire that the law undertook to enforce a *mortis causa* trust.[5] Probably, however, in those early times the risk was not so great as it might have been at a later period; the *Romana fides* held men to fulfilment of their engagements quite as effectually as the most elaborate machinery of the law.

Cicero incidentally remarks[6]—what indeed the nature of the business of itself very distinctly suggests—that the true testament with the copper and scales had its statutory warrant not in the *uti legassit suae rei* of the XII Tables, but in that other equally famous provision,—" cum nexum faciet mancipiumque, uti lingua nuncupassit ita jus esto" (p. 139). Reflection on the import and comprehensiveness of these words led the interpreters to the conclusion that there was nothing in them to prevent the direct institution of an heir in the course of the *verba nuncupata* annexed to a mancipation. From the moment this view was adopted and put in practice, the *familiae mancipatio* ceased to be a transfer of the testator's estate to the *familiae emptor;* the latter's purchase was now for form's sake only, though still an indispensable form, since it was it alone that, according to the letter of the statute, imparted efficacy to the *nun-*

[5] Just., *Inst.*, ii. 23, 1.   [6] Cic., *De Orat.*, i. 57, § 245.

cupatio. But it was the *nuncupatio*—the oral declaration addressed to the witnesses—that really contained the testamentary disposition, *i.e.*, the institution of an heir, with such other provisions as the testator thought fit to embody in it. This was the second stage in the history of the testament *per aes et libram*. The third was marked by the introduction of tablets in which the testamentary provisions were set out in writing, and which the testator displayed to the witnesses, folded and tied up in the usual manner, declaring that they contained the record of his last will. Gaius narrates the words spoken by the *familiae emptor* as follows :—" Your estate and belongings (*familia pecuniaque tua*), be they mine by purchase with this bit of copper and these copper scales, subject to your instructions but in my keeping, that so you may lawfully make your testament according to the statute (*quo tu jure testamentum facere possis secundum legem publicam*)."[7] The meaning of the words "in my keeping" (*endo custodelam meam*) is not quite obvious; they may have been remnants of an older style. Certain it is that they no more imported a real custody than a real property in the *familiae emptor*; for the testator remained so entirely master of his estate that the very next day if he pleased he might mancipate it anew to a different purchaser, and nuncupate fresh testamentary writings. The nuncupation was in these terms : " As is written in these tablets, so do I give, so do I legate, so do I declare my will; therefore, Quirites, grant me your testimony;" and, adds Gaius, " whatever the testator had set down in detail in his testamentary tablets he was regarded as declaring and confirming by this general statement." To the appeal of the testator the witnesses responded by giving their testimony[8] in words which unfortunately are not preserved; and then the testament was sealed by testator, officials, and witnesses,[9] the

---

[7] Gai., ii. 104. [8] Paul., *Sent.*, iii. 4a, § 4.
[9] Bachofen, *Ausgewählte Lehren d. röm. Civilrechts* (Bonn, 1848), p. 256.

seals being on the outside, and over the cord with which the tablets were tied.

Although this testament with the copper and the scales was justified in the first instance by the provision of the XII Tables as to the effect of nuncupative words annexed to a mancipation, yet one cannot fail to perceive that in course of time it came to be subordinated to that other one which dealt directly with testamentary dispositions,—*uti legassit suae rei ita jus esto*.[10] Upon the words *uti legassit* the widest possible meaning was put by the interpreters: not only was a testator held entitled on the strength of them to appoint tutors to wife and children, to enfranchise slaves, and make bequests to legatees, but he might even disinherit his proper heir (*suus heres*) in favour of a stranger, so long as he did so in express terms. Institution of a stranger without mention of the proper heir, however, was fatal, at least if the latter was a son; for without express disherison (*exheredatio*) his father could not deprive him of the interest he had in the family property, as in a manner one of its joint owners. It can hardly be supposed that disherison was contemplated by the compilers of the Tables,—it was altogether foreign to the traditional conception of the family and the family estate; but it was a right whose concession could not be resisted when claimed as embraced in the *uti legassit*, although generally discountenanced, and as far as possible restrained by the strictness of the rules imposed on its exercise. The potency of the innate right of the *suus heres* made itself manifest in yet another direction,—namely, in the effect exercised upon a testament by his attaining the position after its execution. A testator had to provide, either by institution or disherison, not only for *sui heredes* in life at the date of his will, but also for any that might emerge subsequently; if he neglected that precaution, the result of the birth of another child was to invalidate the testament.

[10] See *supra*, § 11, note 8.

It was a deed disposing of the family estate. But in that the newly-born child had an interest as a joint owner, which could not be defeated except by his institution or exheredation.

In the absence of a testament, or on its failure from any cause, the succession opened to the heirs *ab intestato*. So notoriously were the *sui heredes* entitled to the first place— and that not so much in the character of heirs as of persons now entering upon the active exercise of rights hitherto existing, though in a manner dormant [11]—that the compilers of the XII Tables thought it superfluous expressly to declare it. "If a man die intestate, leaving no *suus heres*, his nearest agnate shall have his estate.[12] If the agnate also fail, his gentiles shall have it."[13] It has been pointed out in dealing with the tutory of agnates (p. 122) that the notion of agnation,[14] as a bond distinct from that which connected the gentile members of a clan, was due to the decemvirs.[15] They had to devise a law of intestate succession suitable alike to the patricians who had *gentes* and the plebeians who had none. To put the latter in exactly the same position as the former was beyond their power; for the fact had to be faced that the plebeians had no gentile institutions, and to create them was impossible. The difficulty was overcome by accepting the principle of agnation upon which the patrician *gens* was constructed, and establishing an agnatic circle of kinsmen within the sixth degree, to which the *gens* as a corporation should be postponed in the

[11] See Huschke, *Studien*, pp. 241, 242.

[12] "Si intestato moritur, cui suus heres nec escit, adgnatus proximus familiam habeto" (Ulp., *Frag.*, xxvi. 1).

[13] "Si adgnatus nec escit, gentiles familiam habento" (Ulp., *lib. regul.*, in the *Collatio*, xvi. 4, 2).

[14] For a definition of "agnation" reference is made to p. 123, and to notes 8 and 10 thereon.

[15] This view is expressed by Danz, *Gesch.*, vol. ii. p. 95, and Hölder, *Zur Geschichte d. röm. Erbrechts* (Erlangen, 1881), p. 56, note. But the latter seems to go too far in also attributing the right of the gentiles of a deceased intestate to the Tables. It was much earlier.

case of patricians, and which should come in place of it in the case of plebeians. It was not perfect equalisation, but the nearest approach to it that the circumstances permitted. The difference was that, when the agnates of a plebeian intestate failed, his inheritance was vacant; whereas, on failure of those of a patrician, there was devolution to his *gens* in its collective capacity. An interpretation put upon the statute, probably in the interest of the gentile houses, and which one can hardly suppose was in the minds of the decemvirs, made vacancy in the one case and devolution in the other more frequent than it would otherwise have been, viz., the limitation of the right of succession to the nearest agnates of the deceased; if brothers (say) survived him, and they declined the inheritance, an uncle or other remoter agnate was not allowed to take it, for he was not the nearest of degree in existence;[16] the succession passed to the *gens* if the deceased had been a patrician, and was vacant if he had been a plebeian. Another interpretation, probably of later date, curtailed the right of female agnates, by denying the succession to any kinswoman of a deceased intestate more remotely related to him than a sister;[17] the avowed object being to keep estates as much as possible within the family to which the intestate belonged, and prevent them being dispersed through marriages. The non-admission of representation, *e.g.*, the exclusion of children of a brother who had predeceased from participation along with surviving brothers and sisters of the intestate, was an inevitable result of the language of the Tables;[18] the inheritance went to the nearest agnates, to the exclusion of all remoter ones; and the division, therefore, when several heirs concurred, was invariably *per capita* and not *per stirpes*.[19]

The order of intestate succession thus established by the XII Tables, and which prevailed until amended by the

[16] Gai., iii. 12; Ulp., xxvi. 5.   [17] Gai., iii. 14; Ulp., xxvi. 6.
[18] Gai., iii. 15.   [19] Gai., iii. 16; Ulp., xxvi. 4.

prætors, probably in the eighth century of the city, was first to the *sui heredes* of the deceased, next to his nearest agnate or agnates, and finally, if the deceased was a patrician, to his *gens*. His *sui heredes* included those of his descendants in his *potestas* when he died, who by that event (or even after it, but before his intestacy became manifest)[20] became *sui juris*, together with his wife *in manu* (who, as regarded his succession, was reckoned as a daughter); but did not include children whom he had emancipated, or daughters who had passed *in manum* of husbands. Emancipated children did not even come in as agnates on failure of *sui*; for emancipation severed the tie of agnation as well as that of *potestas*. For the same reason no kinsman who had been emancipated, and so cut off from the family tree, could claim as an agnate; for those only were agnates who were subject to the same *patria potestas*, or would have been had the common family head been still alive.

The opening of the succession (technically *delatio hereditatis*) in favour of *sui heredes*, whether in virtue of a testamentary institution or by operation of law on intestacy, at once invested them with the character, rights, and responsibilities of heirs. No acceptance was requisite, nor, according to the rules of the *jus civile*, was any declinature competent. They had been all along in a manner joint owners with their parent of the family estate, which by his death had become, nominally at least, an inheritance; and as he had not thought fit to terminate their interest in it by emancipating or disinheriting them, they were not now allowed to disown it.[21] Hence they were spoken of as necessary heirs (*heredes sui et necessarii*). A slave, too, whom his owner had instituted in his testament, was a necessary heir; he could not decline; and was invested with the character of heir the moment the testator died.[22]

[20] Just., *Inst.*, iii. 1, 7.   [21] Gai., ii. 157.
[22] Gai., ii. 153; Ulp., xxii. 24.

Not so with stranger institutes or agnates taking on intestacy; they were free to take or reject the inheritance as they saw fit; consequently an act of acceptance (*aditio*) was required on their part to make them heirs. This was originally a formal declaration before witnesses, which got the name of *cretio;* but in course of time informal acceptance, or even behaviour as heir, was in some cases sufficient.[23] It was not unusual for a testator, in instituting an heir, to require that he should make his formal declaration of acceptance within a limited time, failing which his right should pass to a substitute, who in turn was required to enter within a certain time; and so on with any number of substitutes,[24] the series ending with one of his slaves, who became heir without entry, and thus saved the testator from the disgrace of *post-mortem* bankruptcy in the event of the inheritance proving insolvent.[25]

The *uti legassit* of the Tables, as already remarked, conferred upon a testator very great latitude of testamentary disposition, even to the extent of disherison of *sui heredes*. This was a course, however, that it can well be assumed was rarely resorted to unless when a child had been guilty of gross ingratitude, or when the parent had reason to believe his estate was insolvent, and desired to protect his children from the responsibilities of inheritance. Usually his *sui*, if he had any, would be his institutes; and the purpose of the testament either to apportion the estate amongst them as he thought expedient, or to give him an opportunity of appointing tutors, bequeathing legacies, or enfranchising slaves. On intestacy the *sui* took equally, but *per stirpes;* that is to say, that grandchildren by a son who had predeceased or been emancipated, but who themselves had been retained in their grandfather's *potestas*, took amongst them the share to which their father would otherwise have been entitled, instead of taking equal shares with

[23] Gai., ii. 164-173.   [24] Gai., ii. 174-177.   [25] Gai., i. 21.

their surviving uncles.[26] It was by no means unusual, when the whole inheritance descended to sons, for them to hold it in common for many years as partners (*consortes*); indeed this seems to have been the earliest partnership known to the law; and some of the rules affecting the relationship of partners in the later jurisprudence bear the impress of their derivation from this early form of it.[27] But any one of them was entitled at any moment to claim a partition; which was effected judicially, by an arbitral procedure introduced by the XII Tables, and termed a *judicium* (sometimes *arbitrium*) *familiae erciscundae*.[28] Where two or more strangers were instituted testamentarily, whether to equal or unequal shares, if one of them failed, either by predecease or declinature, his share accrued *ipso jure* to the others; for it was a rule that very early became proverbial that a man could not die partly testate and partly intestate.[29] There was the same accrual amongst agnates on intestacy;[30] and both they and stranger testamentary institutes had the same action for division of the inheritance that was made use of by *sui heredes*.

Inheritance was by far the most frequent form of what in the texts is sometimes called universal acquisition, sometimes universal succession. But it was by no means the only one; for, not to speak of some of later introduction, the law was early familiar with the universal succession resulting alike from adrogation (pp. 29, 119), and in *manum conventio* (p. 27). An adrogator acquired in mass (*per universitatem*) all the property and patrimonial rights (with a few exceptions) of the *paterfamilias* he had adopted, and a husband acquired all those of a woman *sui juris* passing into his *manus* on marriage.[31] So did an heir, or a group of heirs, acquire all the property and patrimonial rights of the

[26] Gai., iii. 7, 8; Ulp., xxvi. 2. [27] See *supra*, § 11, note 7.
[28] Gai., ii. 219; and *ad ed. prov.*, in *Dig.*, x. 2, 1, pr.
[29] *Dig.*, l. 17, 7.   [30] Ulp., xxvi. 5.   [31] Gai., iii. 82, 83.

testator by whom they had been instituted, or of the person whose inheritance had come to them by devolution of law. But while an heir was liable for the debts of the person to whom he had succeeded, an adrogator and a husband were not.[32] It is obvious, therefore, that liability for debts was not inherent in the idea of universal succession. How account for the liability of an heir? The brocard *heres eadem persona cum defuncto* rather formulates a rule than explains the reason of it. So far as a *suus heres* was concerned, the reason may not be difficult to discover; as he had in his parent's lifetime been a member of the *familia*, and in a manner joint owner of the family estate, so it may be argued that he had been joint debtor with him in his engagements. But the stranger instituted in a testament and the agnate taking on intestacy were by no means in the same position. There was no room to pretend that either of them had in any sense been joint debtor with the testator or intestate; and if, as Gaius says, the *capitis deminutio* (which was civil death)[33] of a debtor extinguished his debts, it is a little difficult to comprehend how his actual death without leaving *sui heredes* could have failed to produce the same result. It would rather appear that the liability of heirs who were not *sui* arose from statutory enactment. Diocletian in one of his constitutions attributes it to the XII Tables;[34] and there are other passages in the texts which state that these contained a provision to the effect that, where there was a plurality of heirs, each should be liable for a share of the hereditary debts corresponding to the share of the inheritance to which he had been instituted or to which he had succeeded *ab intestato*.[35] Claims against debtors of the testator or intestate were apportioned

[22] Gai., iii. 83, iv. 38.
[32] Gai., iii. 153.
[34] *Cod.*, iv. 16, 7.
[35] Paul. *ad ed.*, in *Dig.*, x. 2, 25, § 13; Diocl., in *Cod.*, ii. 3, 26; Sever. and Car., in *Cod.*, iv. 2, 1.

on the same principle; they did not require to be dealt with in an *actio familiae erciscundae*.[36]

As an heir was burdened with the defunct's debts, so was he also with his family *sacra*,—the sacrifices and other religious services that had periodically to be performed for the repose of the souls of the deceased and his ancestors. Whether the XII Tables contained any provision in reference to this matter is uncertain; it may be that it rested from the first on consuetude and pontifical regulation. The rule of the *jus civile* in reference to it was a very simple one,—that the heir was responsible for their maintenance. But in time this presented difficulties, especially when there was no heir, or when, although there was one, the substantial benefits of the inheritance went to third parties. Cicero[37] comments on two celebrated pontifical edicts amending the law on the subject, one published by Tib. Coruncanius, the first plebeian chief pontiff, who held that office in the year 502 of the city, and the other by P. Mucius Scævola, chief pontiff in the year 631. Without going into the details of their arrangements, it may be enough to observe that the leading idea of both edicts was that the burden of the *sacra* should run with the *pecunia*, that is to say, should lie on him or those who had taken the greatest beneficial interest in the estate of the deceased, but without receding from the old principle that in the ordinary case the heirs were the proper parties on whom to impose it,— *heredum causa justissima est*. In time, as religious sentiment declined, the responsibility came really to be regarded as a burden, and an inheritance unaffected by it (*hereditas sine sacris*) to be hailed as a matter for rejoicing; and Cicero

---

[36] Gordian, in *Cod.*, iii. 36, 6.
[37] Cic., *De Leg.*, ii. 19, § 45, ii. 20, § 53. See on the subject generally, Savigny, *Verm. Schrift.*, vol. i. p. 153 *sq.*; Heimbach, *De sacror. privator. mortui continuandor. apud Romanos necessitate*, Jena, 1827; Leist, *Bonor. Possessio*, vol. i. p. 10 *sq.*, 41 *sq.*; Leist-Glück, vol. i. p. 164 *sq.*; Hölder, *Erbrecht*, p. 137 *sq.*

tells of the fiduciary coemption the jurists devised as a means of enabling women to rid an inheritance to which they had succeeded of an encumbrance which to them was often peculiarly inconvenient.[38]

According to Gaius, it was as a stimulus to heirs to enter as soon as possible on an inheritance that had opened to them, and thus make early provision alike for satisfying the claims of creditors of the deceased and attending to his family *sacra*, that the law came to recognise the somewhat remarkable institution of usucapion or prescriptive acquisition of the inheritance in the character of heir (*usucapio pro herede*).[39] Such usucapion was impossible—there was no room for it—if the deceased had left *sui heredes*; for the inheritance vested in them the moment he died.[40] But if there were no *sui heredes*, then any person, by taking possession of the effects that had belonged to the deceased, and holding them for twelve months without interruption, thereby acquired them as if he were heir,—in fact, according to the views then held, he acquired the inheritance itself. Gaius characterises it as a dishonest acquisition, inasmuch as the usucapient knew that what he had taken possession of was not his. But, as already explained, the usucapion of the XII Tables did not require *bona fides* on the part of the usucapient; he might acquire ownership by prolonged possession of what he knew did not belong to him, so long as he did not appropriate it theftuously, *i.e.*, knowing that it belonged to another. But an inheritance unappropriated by an heir who had nothing more than a right to claim it, in strictness belonged to no one; and there was no theft, therefore, when a person took possession of it with a view to

---

[38] Cic., *Pro Mur.*, 12, § 27. See *supra*, § 30, note 36.

[39] Gai., ii. 52-55. The probable origin of *usucapio pro herede* is adverted to *supra*, § 11, *in fine*. On the subject generally, see Huschke, in the *Z. f. gesch. RW.*, vol. xiv. p. 145 *sq.*; Leist·Glück, vol. i. p. 208 *sq.*; Hölder, *Erbrecht*, p. 129 *sq.*; Ihering, *Scherz u. Ernst*, pp. 137-171.

[40] Gai., ii. 58, iii. 201.

usucapion in the character of heir. There can be little doubt that on the completion of his possession he was regarded as heir just as fully as if he had taken under a testament or as heir-at-law on intestacy,—that is to say, that he was held responsible to creditors of the deceased, and required to charge himself with the family *sacra*. Gaius does not say as much, but both the Coruncanian and Mucian edicts imposed the latter burden upon him who had usucapted by possession the greater part of a deceased person's estate; and it is but reasonable to suppose that the burden of debts must in like manner have fallen on the usucapient or usucapients in proportion to the shares they had taken of the deceased's property.[41]

[41] See Leist-Glück, vol. i. p. 173.

CHAPTER FOURTH.

JUDICIAL PROCEDURE UNDER THE DECEMVIRAL SYSTEM.

SECTION 33.—THE LEGIS ACTIONES GENERALLY.[1]

WE owe to Gaius the only connected account we possess of the *legis actiones*, as the system of judicial procedure was called which prevailed in Rome until the substitution of that *per formulas* (§ 71) by the Æbutian and Julian laws. It is a slight account at the best; and unfortunately, owing to the condition of the Verona MS., has reached us very defectively. Moreover, it is not implicitly to be relied on; it was matter of history with which Gaius was dealing, his information probably imperfect, and his ideas certainly on some points confused. He says that the *legis actiones* were so called " either because they had been introduced by statute (*leges*), or because the very words of the enactments on which they proceeded were embodied in them, so that in style they became as immutable as those enactments themselves;" and

---

[1] The literature on the subject is very voluminous, great part of it in periodicals. Amongst the leading works are those of Keller, *Der röm. Civilprocess u. die Actionen* (1st ed. 1852, 6th ed. by Wach, Leipsic, 1883), §§ 12–21; Bethmann-Hollweg, *Der röm. Civilprocess in seiner geschichtl. Entwickelung* (3 vols., Bonn, 1864-66), the first volume of which is devoted to the *legis actiones*; Buonamici, *Delle Legis Actiones nell' antico diritto romano*, Pisa, 1868; Bekker, *Die Aktionen d. röm. Privatrechts* (2 vols., Berlin, 1871-73), particularly vol. i. pp. 18-74; Karlowa, *Der röm. Civilprozess zur Zeit d. Legisactionen*, Berlin, 1872; Padeletti, " Le Legis Actiones," in *Arch. Giurid.*, vol. xvii. (1875), p. 321 *sq.*; Buonamici, *La Storia della Procedura Romana*, vol. i- (Pisa, 1886), pp. 15-86. Schultze, *Privatrecht u. Process in ihrer Wechselbeziehung*, vol. i. (Freiburg, 1883, vol. ii. not yet published), in pp. 439-532, presents some novel and not unimportant views.

he proceeds to illustrate this latter view by narrating the case of a man suing another for penalties for maliciously cutting his vines, whose action was thrown out of court because he complained of injury to his vines instead of to his trees (*arbores*), this last being the word used in the provision of the XII Tables on which he was founding.[2] Here there is a manifest confusion of *legis actiones* as generic modes of procedure, and *legis actiones* as specific actions falling under one or other of those modes. Even as regards such specific actions it is clear that in many of them no statute was founded on at all, as when a man was claiming a thing as his property; and it is difficult to believe that those which had a statutory foundation were so stereotyped as Gaius represents, or to suppose that those who from time to time made and published collections of them always literally reproduced the styles recommended by their predecessors.[3] As generic modes of procedure (*genera agendi*), there can be no doubt that they underwent modification as time progressed; both Rudorff and Bekker have called attention to a variety of instances in which we know for certain that some new feature was added or some old one discarded or amended.[4] This is a difficulty that besets the subject, as it does so many other branches of Roman law,—the operation of changes which must necessarily, though sometimes all but imperceptibly, have been wrought on an institution in the lapse of centuries.

As *genera agendi*[5] Gaius tells us that the *legis actiones* were five in number, each taking its name from its special characteristic feature, viz., (1) the *legis actio per sacramentum*, (2) that *per judicis postulationem*, (3) that *per condictionem*, (4) that *per manus injectionem*, and (5) that *per pignoris capionem*. The third was unknown in the decemviral period,

---

[2] Gai., iv. 112. [3] Bekker, *Aktionen*, vol. i. p. 95.
[4] Rudorff, *Röm. RG.*, vol. i. p. 105; Bekker, *l.c.*
[5] So they are called by Pomponius, in *Dig.*, i. 2, fr. 2, § 7.

and will be dealt with subsequently (§ 41). The other four were all more or less regulated by the XII Tables, but must in some form have been anterior to them. It is utterly impossible, however, to say of any one of them at what time it was introduced, or what was the statute (*lex*) by which it was sanctioned; indeed it may well be that they were not of statutory introduction at all, but called *legis actiones* simply because recognised and indirectly confirmed by the Tables.[6] In character and purpose they were very different. The first two were directly employed for determining a question of right or liability, which, if persistently disputed, inevitably resulted in a judicial inquiry; the fourth and fifth might possibly result in judicial intervention, but primarily were proceedings in execution, in which the party moving in them worked out his own remedy. Which of them was of greatest antiquity is naturally a matter of controversy. There is much to be said for the view of Ihering and Bekker that *manus injectio*, as essentially nothing more than regulated self-help, must have been the earliest,—that the *legis actio sacramento* and the *judicis postulatio* must have been introduced in aid of it, and to prevent too hasty resort to it where there was room for doubt upon question either of fact or law.

Before any step could be taken in either of the judicial *legis actiones* a preliminary procedure was necessary for bringing the respondent into court. The duty was not committed to any officers of the law; there was no writ of

[6] Bekker (*Aktionen*, vol. i. p. 83, note) says that *lege agere* meant to proceed according to statute (*nach dem Gesetz verfahren*),—the view generally adopted. "To proceed as prescribed by statute" seems to be the idea in his mind. "To proceed in the way recognised by statute," *i.e.*, by the XII Tables, appears more accurate. *In jure cessio* (surrender before a magistrate) was a *legis actio* (Gai., ii. 24), whether employed to effectuate an adoption, an emancipation, a manumission, or a conveyance of property; but there is no reason to believe that it was a statutory invention; all that we are told of its history is that it was confirmed by the XII Tables (Paul., *lib. i. manual.*, in *Vat. Frag.*, § 50); and, as regards the *leg. act. per pignoris capionem*, Gaius says expressly that in some cases its employment was sanctioned not by statute but by custom.

summons of any sort; the party moving in the contemplated litigation had himself to do what was needed. How it was to be gone about was explained in the very commencement of the XII Tables. " If a man summon another to court, the latter must go. If he go not, witnesses must be called. Then let the summoner apprehend him. If he hang back or try to take to his heels, then there may be *manus injectio*.[7] Should illness or old age be an obstacle, the summoner must provide a conveyance, but need not furnish a litter unless he likes," and so on.[8] Once before the magistrate (king, consul, or prætor), the plaintiff stated his contention in a few formal words. If admitted unqualifiedly by the defendant, the magistrate at once pronounced his decree, leaving the plaintiff to work out his remedy as the law prescribed. But if the case presented was met either with a denial or a qualified defence, and appeared to the magistrate to be one proper for trial, he remitted it for that purpose either to a collegiate tribunal or to one or more private citizens as judges or arbiters. The act of remit was technically *litis contestatio* or *ordinatio judicii;* the first so named because originally the parties called upon those present to be witnesses to the issue that was being sent for trial.[9] This was the ordinary practice both under the system of the *legis actiones* and that of the *formulae*, and prevailed until the time of Diocletian.

In the first stage the proceedings were said to be *in jure*, and the duties of the magistrate in reference to them made up his *jurisdictio;* in the second they were said to be *in judicio*, those presiding in it being styled *judices*. The similarity of the terms used to denote those two distinct functions is remarkable. *Judex* is the same as *jus dicens;*

---

[7] A party who would not do what was necessary to the trial of a cause was regarded as declining the defence, and dealt with as *judicatus*. See Unger, *Z. f. RG.*, vol. vii. p. 206.

[8] See Bruns, p. 16, and compare Voigt, *XII Tafeln*, vol. i. p. 693.

[9] Paul. Diac., v. *Contestari* (Bruns, p. 265).

yet the magistrate was also said *jus dicere*.[10] The most likely explanation is that given by Cicero and Dionysius,— that originally the judicial office was not thus partitioned, but that in ordinary litigation the king not only decided whether there was a relevant case averred, but himself heard and considered the merits and pronounced a final judgment.[11] As the duties and avocations of the supreme magistrate became more onerous, it was found necessary to delegate to others part of his judicial functions. In some cases the delegation seems to have been to the pontiffs, in others to lay senators, and at last to have been definitely regulated by Servius Tullius, to whom there seems reason to attribute alike the creation of the centumviral court and the institution of the single judge (*unus judex*).[12] After that it became the rule that the magistrate, in the exercise of his *jurisdictio*, if the matter could not be settled at once by admission on the part of the defendant (*confessio in jure*), did no more than determine whether the plaintiff was entitled to an issue, remitting it if granted either to the centumvirs or a single judge to pass judgment on the question involved. This was all the judge, whether sole or collegiate, had to do. He was " right-declarer " only, not " right-enforcer." If his judgment was for the plaintiff, the latter, if he failed in obtaining an amicable settlement, had himself to make it operative by subsequent proceedings by *manus injectio*, and that under the eye of the magistrate, not of the judge.

From an enumeration in Cicero of a variety of causes proper to the centumviral court, the conclusion seems warranted that it was its peculiar province to decide questions of quiritary right in the strictest acceptation of the words.[13]

[10] The consuls were sometimes officially styled *judices* (Varro, *De L. L.*, vi. 88, Bruns, p. 306).
[11] Cic., *De Rep.*, v. 2, 3 (as in § 15, note 4); Dion. Hal., x. 1.
[12] See *supra*, § 15, and notes 8–15.
[13] "In quibus usucapionum, tutelarum, gentilitatum, agnationum, allu-

They were all apparently real actions (*vindicationes*);[14]— claims of property in land or of servitudes over it, of right as heir under a testament or in opposition to it, of rights of tutory and succession *ab intestato* as agnate or gentile, and so forth. In all of these it was a numerous court of Quirites, advised in the early republic by a pontiff, that determined by its vote the question of quiritary right submitted to it. Many such questions in course of time, possibly at first of express consent of parties, came to be referred to a single judge; but some, and notably claims of inheritance under or in opposition to a testament, were still remitted to the centumviral court in the classical period. Personal actions, however, do not appear ever to have fallen within its cognisance: these were usually sent to a single judge—a private citizen— selected by the parties, but appointed by the magistrate, and to whom the latter administered an oath of office. But in a few cases in which an action involved not so much a disputed question of right as the exercise of skill and discretion in determining the nature and extent of a right that in the abstract was not denied, the remit was to a plurality of private judges or arbiters, usually three.

SECTION 34.—THE LEGIS ACTIO SACRAMENTO.[1]

The characteristic feature of the *legis actio sacramento* (or

vionum, circumluvionum, nexorum, mancipiorum, parietum, luminum, stillicidiorum, testamentorum ruptorum aut ratorum, ceterarumque rerum innumerabilium jura versentur" (Cic., *De Or.*, i. 38, § 173).

[14] The "*nexorum* .. *jura*" in the passage quoted in last note does not refer to the obligationary *nexum* described in a previous section (§ 31), and which was abolished by the Poetilian law of 428, but to one of the titles (*fiducia*) on which real property might be held. The word occurs frequently in Cicero in this sense; *e.g.*, *De harusp. resp.*, 7, § 14—" Multae sunt domus in hac urbe . . . jure hereditario, jure auctoritatis (usucapion ?), jure mancipi, jure nexi."

[1] To the literature in § 33, note 1, may be added Asverus, *Die legis actio sacramenti*, Leipsic, 1837; Huschke (rev. Asverus), Richter's *Krit. JB.*, vol. iii. (1839), p. 665 *sq.*; Stintzing, *Verhältniss d. l. a. sacramento zum Verfahren durch sponsio praejudicialis*, Heidelberg, 1853; Danz, *Sacrale Schutz*, pp. 151-

THE LEGIS ACTIO SACRAMENTO.

actio sacramenti) as described by Gaius,[2] and that from which it derived its name, was that the parties, after a somewhat dramatic performance before the consul or prætor, each challenged the other to stake a certain sum, whose amount was fixed by statute, and which was to abide the issue of the inquiry by the court or judge to whom the cause was eventually remitted. This stake Gaius refers to indifferently as *sacramentum, summa sacramenti*, and *poena sacramenti*. The formal question the court had to determine was,—whose stake had been justified, whose had not (*cujus sacramentum justum, cujus injustum*); the first was returned to the staker, the second forfeited originally to sacred and afterwards to public uses. But the decision on this formal question necessarily involved a judgment on the matter actually in dispute; and, if it was for the plaintiff, entitled him, failing an amicable arrangement, to take ulterior steps for making it effectual. The procedure was still employed in the time of Gaius in the few cases that continued to be referred to the centumviral court, but otherwise had been long in disuse.

Gaius explains that it was resorted to both in real and personal actions. Unfortunately the MS. of his Institutes is defective in the passage in which he described its application to the latter. We possess the greater part of his account of the *actio in rem* as employed to raise and determine a question of ownership; but the illustration he adduces is that of vindication of a slave,—not so interesting or instructive as the proceedings for vindication of land. These, however,

---

221; Maine, *Anc. Law*, p. 375 *sq.*; Danz, "Die l. a. sacram. u. d. lex Papiria," in *Z. f. RG.*, vol. vi. (1867), p. 339 *sq.*; Huschke, *Die multa u. d. sacramentum*, Leipsic, 1874; Lotmar, *Zur l. a. sacramento in rem*, Munich, 1876; Brinz (crit. Lotmar), "Zur Contravindication in d. l. a. sacr.," in the *Festgabe zu Spengel's Doctor-jubiläum* (Munich, 1877), pp. 95-146; Münderloh, "Ueber Schein u. Wirklichkeit an d. l. a. sacramenti," in the *Z. f. RG.*, vol. xiii. (1878), p. 445 *sq.*; E. Roth, in the *Z. d. Sav. Stift.*, vol. iii. (1882), *R. A.*, p. 121 *sq.*; Fioretti, *Legis actio sacramento*, Naples, 1883; Ihering, "Reich u. Arm im altröm. Civilprozess," in his *Scherz u. Ernst*, p. 175 *sq.*

[2] Gai., iv. 13-17.

can be reconstructed with tolerable certainty with the aids derivable from other sources.[3]

The parties appeared before the magistrate, each armed with a rod (*festuca*) representing his spear (*quir* or *hasta*), the symbol, as Gaius says, of ownership in law.[4] The first word was spoken by the raiser of the action, and addressed to his opponent:[5] " I say that the land in question [describing it sufficiently for identification] is mine in quiritary right (*meum esse ex jure Quiritium*); wherefore I require you to go there and join issue with me in presence of the magistrate (*in jure manum conserere*)." Thereupon, according to the earliest practice, the magistrate and the parties, accompanied by their friends and backers (or, as one might say, their seconds), proceeded to the ground for the purpose,— the court was transferred from the forum to the land itself. As distances increased, however, and the engagements of the consuls multiplied, this became inconvenient. Instead of it this course was adopted,—that the parties went to the spot without the magistrate but on his command, and joined issue in the presence of their backers, who had been ordered to accompany them, and who may have made a report on their return of the due observance of formalities. Still later the procedure was further simplified by having a turf brought from the place beforehand—probably as time advanced there would be no very particular inquiry as to where it had been obtained—and deposited a few yards from the magistrate's chair; and when he ordered the parties to go to the ground and join issue, they merely brought forward the turf and set it before him, and proceeded to make their formal vin-

---

[3] Principally Cic. *Pro. Mur.*, 12, § 26, and Aul. Gell., xx. 10.

[4] Gai., iv. 16.

[5] In a sacramental litigation about a question of property the parties were not exactly plaintiff and defendant; for he against whom action was taken had to maintain his own right, and not merely deny that of his opponent. Hence Gaius does not speak of them as *actor* and *reus* (plaintiff and defendant), but as adversaries (*adversarii*). One vindicated; the other counter-vindicated.

dications upon it as representative of the whole land in dispute.[6]

The ritual was as follows. The raiser of the action, addressing his adversary, again affirmed his ownership,[7] but this time with the significant addition—" As I have asserted my right by word of mouth, look you, so do I now with my *vindicta;*"[8] and therewith he touched the turf with his rod, (which was called *vindicta* when employed for this purpose). The word was then taken up by the magistrate in the shape of a question to the other party whether he meant to counter-vindicate. If he replied in the negative, or made no response, there was instant decree (*addictio*) in favour of the first party, and the proceedings were at an end.[9] If, however, he counter-vindicated, it was by repeating the same words and re-enacting the same play as his adversary: —" I say that the land is mine in quiritary right, and I too lay my *vindicta* upon it." The verbal and symbolical

[6] Joinder of issue on the spot in presence of the magistrate was technically IN *jure manum conserere;* before witnesses, but outwith his presence, it was EX *jure manum conserere;* on the turf before him it was again IN *jure manum conserere.* Some editors read *manus conserere* instead of *manum conserere.* But this destroys the idea. It was not that the parties lifted or pretended to lift their hands against each other; it was that they asserted and counter-asserted ownership under the old name of *manus.* This is evident from the language of Gellius in xx. 10, § 8—*correptio manus,* not *manibus;* and xx. 10, § 9—*ad conserendam manum,* not *conserendas manus.*

[7] The words in Gaius (iv. 16) are—" meum esse aio secundum suam causam." The "secundum suam causam" is generally printed as part of the formula recited by the vindicant, and supposed to have occurred in all vindications. But it rather seems to be parenthetical. Gaius is giving the ritual appropriate in vindication of an individual (*homo*); and in such a case it was often necessary to explain in what character he was claimed,—as a *filiusfamilias,* pupil ward, free bondman, or what not. All he means, therefore, by the words "secundum suam causam" is that the vindicant should be careful to make the necessary explanation. There was often no occasion for it in vindication of land, as in the example in the text.

[8] This is a free paraphrase of the words of Gaius—" sicut dixi, ecce tibi, vindictam imposui."

[9] By arrangement between transferrer and transferree, the procedure down to this point was often employed as a mode of conveyance, the transferree taking the position of vindicant; it constituted the surrender in court (*in jure cessio*) referred to in previous sections (see p. 144).

vindication and counter-vindication completed what was technically the *manus consertio*. The parties were now in this position,—that each had asserted his ownership, and had figuratively had recourse to arms in maintenance of his contention.. But the matter was to be settled judicially; so the magistrate once more intervened, and ordered both to withdraw from the land. The dialogue was then resumed, the vindicant demanding to know from his opponent upon what pretence (*causa*) he had counter-vindicated. In the illustration in Gaius he avoided the question, and pleaded the general issue,—" I have done as is my right in laying my *vindicta* on the land." [10]

The proceedings had now reached the stage at which the sacrament came into play. The first challenge came from the vindicant,—" Since you have vindicated unrightfully, I challenge you with a sacrament of 500 *asses;*" to which the counter-vindicant responded,—" And I you." This was technically the *sacramento provocatio*. The magistrate thereupon remitted the matter for trial to the centumviral court, or possibly, in certain cases, to a single judge; [11] and in the

[10] There can be little doubt, however, that in certain circumstances the counter-vindicant would deem it expedient to disclose his title. This was very necessary where he attributed his right to a conveyance upon which two years' possession had not yet followed; in such a case he had to name his author (*auctorem laudare*) if he desired to preserve recourse against the latter on the warranty implied in the mancipation. That probably entailed a suspension of the proceedings, to allow of the author's citation for his interest; and on their resumption, if he appeared and admitted his *auctoritas*, he was formally made a party to the action. Valerius Probus, iv. 7 (*Coll. lib. jur. antejustiniani*, vol. ii. p. 144), has preserved the interrogatory addressed to him by the vindicant—" Quando in jure te conspicio, postulo, anne far (fias?) auctor?" Cicero (*Pro Mur.*, 12, § 26) quotes the first five words. On the subject of *laudatio auctoris* generally see Voigt, *XII Tafeln*, vol. ii. p. 195 *sq.*

[11] In what remains of his description of the *actio sacramento in personam* Gaius says that, in terms of a *lex Pinaria* (which Huschke, Rudorff, and Mommsen attribute to the year 282, and Voigt to 322), the prætor required the parties to attend on the thirtieth day after the *sacramento provocatio* for the appointment of a judge; and because, in speaking of the action *in rem*, he says that after provocation the same procedure followed as in the personal

presence of witnesses called by the parties (*litis contestatio*) declared what exactly was the question put in issue, and which court or judge was to decide. At the same time, according to Gaius's account of the procedure, he required sureties from the parties for the eventual payment by him who was unsuccessful of the sacrament he had offered to stake, and which became a forfeit to the exchequer. (The original practice was that the stake was deposited by both parties in the hands of the pontiffs before they were heard by the centumviral court; after judgment that of the gainer was reclaimed by him, while that of the loser was retained for religious uses.[12]) The magistrate also made arrangements for the interim possession of the land by one or other of the litigants, taking security from him that, if he was eventually unsuccessful, it should be returned to his opponent, along with all the fruits and profits drawn in the interval. At the trial, as both parties were vindicants, there must have been a certain burden of proof upon both sides. The vindicant, one may believe, must have been required to establish in the first instance that the thing he claimed had at some time been his; and then, but probably not till then, the counter-vindicant would have to prove a later title in his person, sufficient to exclude that of his opponent. The judgment, as already observed, necessarily involved a finding on the main question; but in form it was a declaration as to the sacrament,—that of the party who prevailed was declared to be just, and that of his unsuccessful opponent unjust.[13]

Looking at this ritual as a whole, the conviction is irresistible that it could not have been so devised by one brain.

one (*eadem sequebantur quae cum in personam ageretur*), most writers assume that here too there was a remit after thirty days to a single judge. Probably in time, with certain exceptions, this became common enough; but originally, as has been shown in a previous section, and possibly for a couple of centuries, the remit in real actions was usually to the centumviral court.

[12] See Appendix, Note D.   [13] Cic., *Pro Cacc.*, 33, § 97.

It reveals and combines three distinct stages in the history of procedure,—appeal to arms and self-help, appeal to the gods and the spiritual power,[14] appeal to the civil magistrate and his judicial office. As Gellius says, the real and substantial fight for might, that in olden days had been maintained at the point of the spear, had given place to a civil and festucarian combat in which words were the weapons, and which was to be settled by the interposition of the prætor.[15] But this does not explain the *sacramentum*. Very various are the theories that have been proposed to account for it. According to Gaius, it was nothing more than the sum of money staked by each of the parties, and which was forfeited originally to sacred and afterwards to public uses by him who was unsuccessful, as a penalty for his rashly running into litigation; and substantially the same explanation is given by Festus in one of his definitions of the word.[16] But this is far from satisfactory; for it involves the absurdity of declaring that a penalty imposed by law could be unjust (*injustum*) in any case, and the still greater absurdity of declaring it just in the case of the party who was in the right, and unjust in the case of him who was in the wrong. There is another definition in Festus [17]—" a thing is said to be done *sacramento* when the sanction of an oath is interposed"—that lends support to the opinion of Danz, Huschke, E. Roth, and one or two others, that there was a time when parties to a question of right were required to take an oath to the verity of their respective assertions; that they were also required concurrently to deposit five bullocks or five sheep, according to the nature or value of

---

[14] It must not be lost sight of that in the regal period the king was also chief pontiff,—that he was the embodiment of the spiritual as well as of the secular power.

[15] Aul. Gell., xx. 10, § 10. *Vindicare* is just *vim dicare*, to proclaim a mightful right.

[16] Fest., v. *Sacramentum* (Bruns, p. 289).

[17] Fest., v. *Sacramento* (Bruns, p. 289).

the thing in dispute, to abide the issue of the inquiry;[18] that the question for determination was whose oath was just and whose unjust; and that he who was found to have sworn unjustly forfeited his cattle or sheep as a *piamentum*, —a peace-offering to the outraged deity,—while the other party reclaimed his from the repository in which they had been detained in the interval.[19].

The authors referred to are far from unanimous as to details, which is not surprising considering how meagre are the materials upon which their theories are constructed. But there seems to be enough to render it more than probable that, at an intermediate stage between the *vera solida vis* of the ancient times and the *vis civilis et festucaria* which Gellius and Gaius depict, there was a procedure by appeal to the gods through means of oaths of verity sworn by the parties, in the manner and with the consequences that have been indicated. Whether that was still the practice at the time of the decemviral legislation there is no means of judging. That in time it should have dropped out of the ritual is quite in the order of things. Its tendency was to become a mere form, imposing no real restraint on reckless litigation. The restraint was rather in the dread of forfeiture of the sacramental cattle, sheep, or money that would follow a verdict that an oath had been unjust. And it must have been felt besides that it was unfair to brand a man as a false-swearer, needing to expiate his offence by an offering to the gods, whose oath had been perfectly honest. That he should suffer a penalty for his

[18] It was the *Lex Aternia Tarpeia* of the year 300 U.C. that commuted the five bullocks and five sheep into 500 and 50 lbs. of copper respectively (Cic., *De Rep.*, ii. 35, § 60, where the words usually printed "de multae sacramento" should read "de multa et sacramento"); Fest., v. *Peculatus* (Bruns, p. 279). For the pounds' weight of raw metal the XII Tables substituted the same number of *asses*; declaring that 500 should be the *summa sacramenti* when the cause of action was worth 1000 *asses* or more, 50 when worth less, or the question one of freedom or slavery (Gai., iv. 14).

[19] See Appendix, Note E.

imprudence in not having taken more care to ascertain his position, and for thus causing needless annoyance to others, was reasonable, but did not justify his being dealt with as one who had knowingly outraged the deity to whom he had appealed. So the oath—the original *sacramentum*—disappeared, the name passing by a natural enough process to the money which had been wont to be deposited before it was sworn; but which now ceased to be an offering in expiation by a false-swearer, and became a mere penalty of rash litigation (*poena temere litigantis*).[20] The incongruity was in the retention in the mouth of the *judex* of the old formula— "The sacrament of A is just, that of N unjust;" to be explained only by that spirit of conservatism which pervaded the Roman jurisprudence, and which forbade the abandonment of old forms on merely theoretical considerations, so long as they could be adapted in practice to altered conditions.

It may well be assumed that in most cases the finding of the court as to the justness or unjustness of the respective sacraments of the parties was the end of the case,—that it was at once accepted and loyally given effect to. If in favour of the party to whom interim possession had been awarded by the magistrate, there could be no difficulty; he retained the object of dispute, with the fruits and profits he had drawn in the interval between litiscontestation and judgment. If, however, the finding was for the other party, and amicable arrangement was delayed, it is by no means quite clear what course was followed. Gaius says that in awarding interim possession (*vindicias dicere*) the prætor required the grantee to give security by sureties (*praedes*) to his adversary for restitution to the latter in the event of his success;[21] while Festus preserves a law of the XII Tables which, according to Mommsen's rendering, declared that when it turned out that interim possession had

[20] Rubr. tit. *Inst.*, iv. 16.   [21] Gai., iv. 16.

been awarded to the wrong party, it was to be in the latter's power to demand the appointment of three arbiters, who should ascertain the value of the object of vindication and its fruits, and assess the damages due for non-restitution at double the amount.[22] This provision seems to have been intended to afford the wrongful interim possessor, who was not in a position to make specific restitution to his successful opponent, a means of avoiding the apprehension and imprisonment which were the statutory consequences of failure to implement a judgment (§ 36).[23] It is probable that in time this duplicated money payment came to be regarded as the satisfaction to which the successful party in a vindication was entitled in every case in which, no matter for what reason, he was unable to obtain the thing itself and its fruits from their interim possessor; that consequently an *arbitrium litis aestimandae*, or reference to arbiters to assess their value, resulted in every such case; and that it was to assure its payment that the prætor required the party to whom the interim possession was awarded to give to his opponent the sureties (*praedes litis et vindiciarum*) to whom Gaius alludes.

Such was the *legis actio sacramento in rem* when the ownership of lands was the matter of controversy. But every sort of *manus* which a man could pretend to have over persons or things might be vindicated by the same process, although necessarily with variations, more or less important, in the ritual. If his right over a woman whom

---

[22] "Si vindiciam falsam tulit, si velit is, praetor arbitros tris dato. Eorum arbitrio rei fructus duplione damnum decidito:" Fest., v. *Vindiciae* (Bruns, p. 300); Mommsen, *Fest. cod. quatern. XVI.* (Berlin, 1864), p. 84. This law was in one of the supplementary Tables of the year 304; which suggests that it was intended to qualify the rigour of the provisions about *manus injectio* in Table iii. See Voigt, *Jus. nat.*, vol. iii. pp. 702-716.

[23] Voigt (*Jus. nat.*, vol. iii. p. 705 *sq.*; *XII Tafeln*, vol. ii. p. 656, note 14) holds, contrary to the view generally entertained, that the provisions of the Tables in reference to execution upon *res jure judicatae* were not confined to judgments for money.

he alleged to be his wife was disputed, or over a person who he averred was his *filiusfamilias*, or his free bondman *in mancipio*, or his slave, an *actio sacramenti in rem* was the appropriate remedy. So it was when he claimed an inheritance as heir; and so it was when he claimed an easement or right of servitude over another person's land, or desired to have it established that his own was free from such a burden. If a man detained by another as a slave alleged that he was really a freeman, it was by the same process that he obtained a judgment, suing by a third party who got the name of *adsertor libertatis*; in this case the XII Tables limited the sacramental penalty to fifty *asses*, and prescribed that during the dependence of the process the party whose status was in dispute should enjoy that of a freeman. It has even been suggested, though somewhat tentatively, by so circumspect an authority as Brinz,[24] that it is possible that the *actio sacramento in personam* (described by Gaius in a page of which unfortunately not more than half-a-dozen words are legible in the Verona MS.) was originally nothing but a *vindicatio*. Entertaining, as he does, the opinion that in the old law a debtor was practically subject to the *manus* of his creditor, who might reduce him into quasi-slavery on his failure to meet his engagements, he asks—Was the personal action at first anything else than a dispute as to the bondage or freedom of the debtor,—an action *in rem*, in which a *vindex* (p. 206) took the place of an *adsertor libertatis*? The suggestion is novel, and worthy of further consideration.

The ordinarily received opinion, but which rests on slender foundations, is that from the first the parties to a personal action met on equal terms; that if it was a case of money debt, the creditor commenced the proceedings with the averment that the defendant owed him the sum in question,

[24] In his paper "On the idea involved in the word *obligatio*" (*Grünhut's ZSchr.*, vol. i. p. 23 *sq.*)

—"I say that you ought to pay me (*dare oportere*) 1000 *asses;*" that this was met with a denial; and that a sacramental challenge followed on either side.[25] All are agreed that the remit was to a single *judex*, after an interval of thirty days from the proceedings *in jure;* that where the claim was for a definite sum the plaintiff had to establish his case to the letter; and that his sacrament was necessarily declared unjust if he failed to prove his claim by a single penny. But there is considerable diversity of opinion as to whether by this form of process a claim of uncertain amount could be insisted on,—as, for example, one for damages for breach of a warranty (by *lex mancipii*) of acreage of lands sold, or of their freedom from burdens. If it could, then probably the question raised and dealt with *sacramento* was the abstract one of liability,—was the warranty given, and has it failed? the sum due in respect of the breach being left to be dealt with in a subsequent arbitral process (*arbitrium litis aestimandae*).

SECTION 35.—THE LEGIS ACTIO PER JUDICIS POSTULATIONEM.[1]

The defects of the Verona MS. have deprived us of Gaius's account of the *legis actio per judicis postulationem*. There is little elsewhere that can with any certainty be said to bear upon it. The most important is a note of Valerius Probus—*T.PR.I.A.V.P.V.D.*, which is generally interpreted

---

[25] Valer. Prob., iv., Nos. 1 and 2, has these *formulae*—"aio te mihi dare oportere," and "quando negas, te sacramento quingenario provoco." The latter has all the appearance of having belonged to the sacramental procedure; but the former may quite as well have belonged to the *legis actio per condictionem* (*infra*, § 41).

[1] To the literature in note 1 to § 33 add—Baron, "Zur leg. act. per judicis arbitrive postulationem," in the *Festgabe für Aug. W. Heffter* (Berlin, 1873), p. 29 *sq.;* Huschke, *Multa*, &c., p. 394 *sq.;* Adolf Schmidt, "Ueber die l. a. per jud. post.," in the *Z. d. Sav. Stift.*, vol. ii. (1881), *R. A.*, p. 145 *sq.;* Voigt, *XII Tafeln*, vol. i. § 61.

—*te, praetor, judicem arbitrumve postulo uti des.*[2] This petition to the magistrate—king, consul, praetor—to appoint a judge, arbiter, or arbiters (as the case might be), in all probability was part of the procedure in the action, and that from which it derived its distinctive name. Beyond this all is conjecture alike as to the nature and form of the action and the cases to which it was applicable. Gaius says of the *legis actio sacramento* that it was general, and that it was the procedure that was to be resorted to where no other was prescribed by statute. The extant fragments of the XII Tables contain no such indications as this would lead us to expect; there is not a trace in them of an express instruction that proceedings in any particular case were to be *per judicis postulationem*. There are amongst them, however, two or three provisions about *arbitria*,[3]—references of questions to arbiters, which were to be determined by them, not necessarily by an affirmance or negation of the respective pretensions of parties, but according to their conviction of what was right in the circumstances, although it might fall short of what was claimed on the one side or be in excess of what was conceded on the other. The number of those *arbitria* may have increased subsequently to the decemviral legislation; indeed, Cicero applies the name to all those actions which gave rise to what are more familiarly termed *bonae fidei judicia* (p. 360); and some of them may have been initiated by proceedings *per judicis postulationem* so long as the *legis actiones* were in general use.

An incidental observation of Gaius's, however, about another matter,[4] leaves little doubt that the *judicis postulatio*

[2] Valer. Prob., iv. 8 (*Coll. libror. jur. antejust.*, vol. ii. p. 144).
[3] *E.g.*, "arbitrium falsae vindiciae," Fest., v. *Vindiciae* (Bruns, p. 300); "arbitrium familiae erciscundae," Cic., *P. Caec.*, 7, § 19, Gai. in *Dig.*, x. 2. 1, pr.; "arbitrium finium regundorum," Cic., *De Leg.*, i. 21, § 55.
[4] Gai., iv. 20. He is speaking of the *leg. act. per condictionem* (*infra*, § 41), introduced by the Silian and Calpurnian laws. That action was for obtaining a judgment upon a claim for a definite sum of money or some other *res certa*. He says the necessity for it was far from obvious, seeing that such claims could

was also employed to initiate *stricti juris judicia*,—actions in which the judge had no latitude, but was bound to find for the defendant unless the plaintiff established his claim to the very letter of it. What were they? When one looks into the matter, it is apparent that under the arrangements of the XII Tables sacramental procedure must often have been out of the question.[5] A man would hardly think of raising in that form a vindication of property of less value than the minimum sacramental penalty, or of claiming by it (say) a fine of five-and-twenty *asses* for an assault, or of the same sum for the loss of a tree of his cut down maliciously.[6] As the *condictio* was of later introduction, the conclusion is all but inevitable that his remedy must have been *per judicis postulationem*. Many jurists, however, are of opinion that its employment was not limited to cases whose trifling pecuniary importance rendered sacramental procedure inappropriate. Huschke seems inclined to hold that in most personal actions the plaintiff had it in his option to proceed in either form he pleased. Karlowa maintains the doctrine that outside the XII Tables there was a great variety of rights whose sanction was *jus*,—consuetudinary, not statute law; that actions for their protection were *jurgia*, not *lites;* and that *judicis postulatio* was the procedure by which such *jurgia* were dealt with.[7] Voigt discovers ample scope for the employment of this form of procedure within the Tables themselves. He finds in them the matter of not less than fifty-two actions; and, undaunted by Gaius's remark about the generality of the *actio sacramento*, does not hesitate to assign to each of them its appropriate procedure. No fewer

quite well have been insisted in *sacramento* or *per judicis postulationem*. Yet the *judicia* to which those statutes gave rise were in the first instance essentially *stricti juris*.

[5] Bekker (*Aktionen*, vol. i. pp. 65–67) points out a considerable number of the remedies of the XII Tables which it would have been very difficult to make operative *sacramento*.

[6] Such was the penalty imposed by the Tables for the offences referred to.

[7] Karlowa, *Röm. CP.*, pp. 47 *sq.*, 122 *sq.*

than thirty-five of them must, in his view, have been initiated by *judicis arbitrive postulatio*, of which nine resulted in *arbitria* and the remainder in *judicia*.[8] His reasoning is ingenious, but, in the almost entire absence of direct authority to support it, can hardly be called convincing.

While it is impossible with certainty to trace the history of this procedure to its first beginnings, yet the impression is general that it must have originated in the regal period. There were three different positions in which an appeal for aid might be made to a court of justice,—(1) when it was a question of civil right that had to be decided in terms directly affirmative or directly negative of the contention of the raiser of the action, and in which questions both of law and fact were involved; (2) when it was only a question of fact that had to be ascertained, the legal result of the fact, if established, being known beforehand; (3) when facts had to be set against facts, and a result arrived at that in the judgment of those who had to balance them was fair and reasonable in the circumstances. In the first case, as when the contention was *meum esse* or *dari oportere* (otherwise than under an obligationary *nexum*), the procedure was *sacramento*, and the reference originally (in all probability) to the pontiffs, although afterwards to the centumviral court or to a *judex*; in the second, as when the question was— had or had not the defendant assaulted the plaintiff, and so incurred the fixed and invariable statutory penalty?—it was probably to a *judex* without the intervention of a sacrament; in the third, as when the matter in hand was the partitioning of an inheritance amongst co-heirs, or the determining whether operations of the defendant were interfering with the natural drainage of the plaintiff's land and how the mischief was to be abated, or the assessment of damages for injury to property, or of the sum sufficient to relieve

[8] Voigt, *XII Tafeln*, vol. i. pp. 586-589. See also Ihering (as in § 34, note 1), p. 203 *sq.*

from talion or the statutory penalty of theft, the reference was to an arbiter or arbiters. In the procedure *sacramento* the pleadings opened directly with an averment of right— " I say that this is mine," " I say that the defendant is bound to pay me so much;" but in that *per judicis arbitrive postulatio* there is reason to surmise that they commenced with an averment of fact, followed by the resulting demand of the plaintiff. The details, however, are quite uncertain; with this exception, that in some *arbitria* the plaintiff expressly threw himself upon the discretion of the arbiters—*quantum aequius melius est ob eam rem mihi dari.*

SECTION 36.—THE LEGIS ACTIO PER MANUS INJECTIONEM.[1]

In one of his most interesting chapters, and in the shape of a dialogue between Sex. Cæc. Africanus the jurist and Favorinus the philosopher, while they and a few others were waiting in the quadrangle of the palace to pay their court to the emperor, Aulus Gellius introduces an account, put into the mouth of Africanus, of some of the provisions of the XII Tables, and in particular those regulative of *manus injectio*.[2] Africanus is made to say that, according to his belief (*opinor*) the words of the statute were these : " Aeris confessi rebusque jure judicatis triginta dies justi sunto. Post deinde manus injectio esto. In jus ducito. Ni judicatum facit, aut quis endo eom jure vindicit, secum

[1] To the literature in § 33, note 1, may be added Huschke, *Nexum* (1846), p. 79 *sq.*; Savigny, "Das alt-röm. Schuldrecht," in his *Verm. Schrift.*, vol. ii. (1850), p. 369 *sq.*; Hoffmann, *Die Forcten u. Sanaten, nebst Anhang über d. altröm. Schuldrecht* (Vienna, 1866), p. 54 *sq.*; Unger, in the *Z. f. RG.*, vol. vii. (1868), p. 192 *sq.*, Vainberg, *Le nexum et la contrainte par corps en droit Rom.* (Paris, 1874), p. 36 *sq.*; Bruns, in the *Z. f. RG.*, vol. xii. (1876), p. 128 *sq.*; Exner, in the *Z. f. RG.*, vol. xiii. (1878), p. 392 *sq.*; Voigt, "Ueber d. Gesch. d. röm. Executionsrechtes," in the *Berichte d. K. Sächs. Gesellsch. d. Wissenschaften, phil.-hist. Cl.*, vol. xxxiv. (1882), p. 76 *sq.*; Voigt, *XII Tafeln*, vol. i. §§ 63-65; Ihering, (as in § 34, note 1,) pp. 196 *sq.*, 232 *sq.*

[2] Gell., *Noct. Att.*, xx. 1, §§ 41-51.

ducito: vincito aut nervo aut compedibus. Quindecim pondo, ne majore, aut si volet minore, vincito.³ Si volet suo vivito. Ni suo vivit, qui eom vinctum habebit, libras farris endo dies dato. Si volet plus dato." Africanus continues *narrativé:* "There was still room for the parties to come to terms; but if they did not, the debtor was kept in chains for sixty days. Towards the end of them he was brought before the prætor in the comitium on three consecutive market-days, and the amount of the judgment-debt proclaimed. After the third *capite poenas dabat,* or else he was sent across Tiber to be sold to a foreigner. And this capital penalty, sanctioned in the hope of deterring men from unfaithfulness to their engagements, was one to be dreaded because of its atrocity, and of the new terrors with which the decemvirs thought right to invest it. For if it was to more creditors than one that the debtor had been adjudged, they might, if they pleased, cut up and divide his body. Here are the words of the statute,—'Tertiis nundinis partis secanto. Si plus minusve secuerunt, se fraude esto.'"

Such is Gellius's account of the provisions of the XII Tables in reference to this *legis actio.* I have preferred giving the statutory words in the original; because in some points there is considerable dubiety as to their meaning. But it is to be borne in mind that Gellius does not vouch for their accuracy; the Tables were already in his time matter of antiquity, and even the jurists knew nothing of them beyond what was still in observance.⁴ That he has reproduced them only partially seems almost beyond question; for in another chapter he himself quotes a couple of sentences that are to all appearance from the same context, —" Adsiduo vindex adsiduus esto. Proletario jam civi, quis

---

³ The MSS. have "ne minore aut si volet majore." Puchta (*Inst.*, vol. i. § 179, note *i*), Lange (*Röm. Alt.*, vol. i. p. 155), and Hoffmann (*l.c.*, p. 68) support this reading; but most authors concur in altering it as above.

⁴ Gell., xvi. 10, §§ 2-8.

volet vindex esto "—"The *vindex* for a freeholder must himself be a freeholder; but any one who likes may be *vindex* for a proletarian."[5] We have to face, therefore, the extreme probability that the record is incomplete, and the possibility besides that it is not literally accurate. There is room for error, consequently, in two directions; but the nature and effect of the procedure in its main features may be gathered from the texts as they stand with reasonable certainty.

It was a procedure in execution; but against whom? The answer depends on the interpretation of the words, "Aeris confessi rebusque jure judicatis." The natural reading is—"For acknowledged money debts and judgments obtained by regular process of law (*jure*) there shall be thirty days' grace." The general opinion is that the *aeris confessi* referred to formal admission by a defendant in an action for money due, when he first appeared before the magistrate, of the incontrovertibility of the plaintiff's claim, —what in the later jurisprudence was called *confessio in jure*; and that the *rebus jure judicatis* referred to judgments by *judices* on remit from the magistrate in cases of disputed litigation.[6] But this view of the matter is open to the objection that it excludes *manus injectio* on a party's acknowledgement or confession where the cause of action was any-

[5] Gell., xvi. 10, § 5. These two sentences are usually imported into the first Table, which regulates *in jus vocatio;* but comparison with chap. lxi. of the *L. colon. Jul. Genetivae* (Bruns, p. 111) shows that they related to *manus injectio.*

[6] Most modern civilians hold that a judgment required to be for a certain sum of money in order to warrant *manus injectio.* But,' if the generally accepted reading of Gaius, iv. 48, be right, namely, that under the system of the *legis actiones* a judicial condemnation was in the *ipsa res* and not in a pecuniary equivalent, there does not seem to be any authority for such an opinion. (This view of Gaius's statement, however—which, it is admitted on all hands, requires some correction—has been vigorously combated by Brini, "Della condanna nelle leg. act.," in the *Arch. Giurid.*, vol. xxi. (1878), p. 213 *sq.*, and Montagnon, *Sur la nature des condemnations civiles* (Lyons, 1883), p. 6 *sq.* They hold that what Gaius really said was that from the first condemnations were always in a sum of money.)

thing else than money resting-owing.[7] The more probable explanation is that every acknowledgement before the magistrate in the initial stage of a litigation was regarded in the decemviral period as *res jure judicata* ;[8] for, although it is nowhere so stated, it is impossible to suppose that an admission or non-negation of a plaintiff's claim by the defendant was not followed by a magisterial finding or declaration, which was as much a judgment as the decision of the centumvirs or a *judex* on the justness or unjustness of a sacrament. From this point of view the *aeris confessi* of the Tables must have had reference to something else than *confessio in jure* ; and this, as has already been observed, can only have been nexal indebtedness (p. 157). If, as some think, this was created not simply by a lender imposing obligation on a borrower by the words *dare damnas esto*, but by the latter acknowledging its existence in the words *dare damnas˙ sum*, it would be difficult to conceive a more perfect illustration of *aes confessum*. But even without the debtor's verbal acknowledgement, his acceptance of the loan on the terms recited by his creditor in presence of the representatives of the people was a public recognition of indebtedness to which the epithet was hardly less appropriate. Gaius, in explaining the way in which an obligation was discharged by the copper and the scales,[9] says it was the proper course to be followed when the debt had arisen either *per aes et libram* or *ex causa judicati* ; in the former case, he says, the debtor was called *damnatus*, in the latter *judicatus* or *condemnatus*. In his brief description of *manus injectio*,[10] he limits its application to the same two

---

[7] There was, of course, no room for *manus injectio* on confession, or rather non-counter-vindication, in an *actio sacramento in rem* in reference to a movable at any time, or to land when the procedure was on the spot ; for the vindicant had simply then and there to appropriate it.

[8] What else was the meaning of the brocard—" Confessus pro judicato habetur ? "

[9] Gai., iii. 173-175. [10] Gai., iv. 21.

classes, the *judicati* and the *damnati*. There is not a word in either passage about the (*in jure*) *confessus*. No other explanation of the omission is possible but this,—that such an one was regarded as *judicatus*. The *acris confessi* of the Tables, therefore, must have referred to the case of the debtor whom Gaius calls *damnatus*,—him who had been laid under obligation *per aes et libram* and *dare damnas esto ;* in other words, the *nexus* or nexal debtor.[11]

The *legis actio* was competent, then, against either a *nexus* or a judgment-debtor, (the latter including an *in jure confessus*); but only after thirty days from maturity of the debt in the one case, or of the judgment (or admission) in the other. It was apprehension of the debtor by the creditor himself; in its first stage, at least, an act of pure self-help. What accompanied and followed it in times anterior to the XII Tables it is impossible to say; probably there was an indefiniteness and uncertainty about the whole procedure which the new provisions were intended to abate. According to Gaius[12] the cause of the arrest had to be stated by the creditor then and there,—for example, that the arrestee was due so much on a judgment, but had not paid, and that the *manus injectio* was in respect of the debt referred to. Whether nexal or judgment debtor, he had at once to be brought before the magistrate. But the purpose was not the same in both cases. In that of the nexal debtor, as has been explained in a previous section (p. 158), it was to give him an opportunity of proving by the mouths of the five witnesses of the *nexi liberatio* that his loan had been repaid, or he at any rate formally released by the lender ; if he did not avail himself of it, the procedure, so far as he

---

[11] Gaius includes amongst the *damnati* the heir whom a testator had burdened with a legacy by the words "dare damnas esto" (termed "legatum per damnationem," Gai, ii. 201). But this was unknown at the time of the enactment of the Tables; and the *acris confessi*, therefore, can have referred only to the case of the *nexus*. See Appendix, Note F.

[12] Gai., iv. 21.

was concerned, was at an end, and the creditor at once and at his own hand carried him off in the exercise of his contractual right of detention.[13] With a judgment-debtor it was different. He also was brought before the magistrate; but the object was that his creditor might obtain authority to carry him away and provisionally confine him in the domestic lock-up (*domum ducere*). Such a course, however, was avoided either (1) by instant payment or other implement of the judgment (*ni judicatum facit*), or (2) by the intervention of a *vindex* or champion.[14] The position taken by the latter was not exactly that either of a surety or of an attorney for the *judicatus* demanding a rehearing of the case; he appeared rather as a controverter in his own name of the right of the creditor to proceed further with his execution, on the ground that the judgment was invalid. This necessitated a new action between the creditor and the *vindex*, but to which the debtor was not a party. If it failed, then the *vindex* was liable for double the amount of the original debt,[15] as a penalty on him for having improperly interfered with the course of justice; but on payment he had relief against the original debtor, who had been liberated through his intervention.[16] Failing a *vindex* and

---

[13] Our only authority is Gellius; and, so far as his description goes, the proceedings subsequent to the first bringing of the arrestee before the magistrate (*in jus ducito*) are limited to the case of a judgment-debtor (*judicatus*). As pointed out on p. 158, some of them would have had no meaning in that of a nexal debtor arrested in respect of *aes confessum*.

[14] *Vindex* = " qui in eo vim dicit," *i.e.*, "in eo vim monstrat" (Schoell, *XII Tab. reliquiae*, p. 91). In the *Lex col. Juliae Genetivae*, cap. 61 (Bruns, p. 111), the corresponding phrase is "in eo vim facit."

[15] Unger (*l.c.*, note 1) holds that the *vindex*, if he failed in his action with the creditor, lost his *sacramentum*, but was not liable any further; that the creditor might then proceed with his execution against his arrestee, and that it was against the latter that the amount of the debt was duplicated, as the penalty of *his* denial (involved in his putting forward the *vindex*) of the validity of the judgment.

[16] He probably operated his relief by *manus injectio pro judicato* on his own account, on the ground of his payment for the debtor, technically *depensum*; for though Gaius (iv. 24) appears to attribute the introduction of that pro-

failing payment, the creditor took his debtor home and put him, or at least was entitled to put him, in chains, whose weight was limited by the statute to fifteen pounds. The prisoner might live at his own cost if he pleased; but otherwise his creditor had to give him daily at least a pound of spelt. This provisional confinement was to continue for sixty days, to allow opportunity for arrangement; and during the last month the creditor had to produce his debtor in the comitium on three consecutive market-days, proclaiming aloud the amount for which he was detained, on the chance that some compassionate citizen might offer a ransom. If the third market-day passed without payment or compromise, there was a formal *addictio* or magisterial decree awarding the debtor to his creditor.[17] The debtor, says Gellius, *capite poenas dabat*, or was sold across the frontier as a slave; and if the judgment on which he had been incarcerated had been obtained by a plurality of creditors, they might cut his body in pieces and divide it, but without prejudice if any one had more or less than his fair share.

Such, says Gellius, was the law of the XII Tables; and so also says Quintilian fifty years earlier, and Tertullian fifty years later,[18] although there is not a hint of it in Cicero, Livy, or Dionysius,[19] or in the pages of any of the jurists. While there are still some very eminent authorities[20] who,

cedure to a *Lex Publilia*, yet there is reason to think that that statute merely extended to a *sponsor* what had previously been the practice in the case of a *vas*, a *praes*, and a *vindex*. Comp. Bekker, *Aktionen*, vol. i. p. 41, and see *supra*, p. 166.

[17] Gellius (xx. 1, § 44) speaks of the magistrate's warrant to the creditor to carry home and incarcerate his debtor as the *addictio*. But as Livy constantly refers to *judicati* and *addicti* as distinct classes, the better opinion seems to be that the *addictio* was the final magisterial decree, when the provisional detention of the *judicatus* had failed to elicit a satisfactory arrangement.

[18] Quint., *Inst. Or.*, iii. 6, 84; Tertull., *Apolog.*, 4. Their language is vague. Neither professes acquaintance with the words of the statute; and both admit that a *sectio corporis* had never been known in history.

[19] It is mentioned, however, by Dio Cassius, writing a quarter of a century after Tertullian. See the fragments in Mai, *Coll. script. vet.*, vol. ii. p. 144.

[20] Kohler, who applies the provisions of the Tables to the *nexus* as well as

like Gibbon, "prefer the literal sense of antiquity to the refinements of modern criticism," yet latterly the majority alike of jurists and historians seem to be of opinion that Gellius has put on the words of the Tables an interpretation they were never meant to bear. It is a little remarkable, however, that though they resent the idea of an actual section and partition of the debtor's body, very few of them find any difficulty in accepting the notion that his creditor or creditors might put him to death. Yet it is one that cannot well stand examination; the results to which it leads are too extravagant. For example: the punishment the XII Tables imposed upon manifest theft was slavery,—the thief became the slave of the individual whose goods he had stolen.[21] That of non-manifest theft was a pecuniary penalty,—twofold the value of the thing that had been abstracted.[22] But if it had been the case that every *judicatus* who failed within three months to satisfy his creditor might be put to death, then the non-manifest thief, against whom a judgment had been obtained, must often in the end have suffered a penalty more serious than that which overtook him whose theft had been manifest,—slavery for the graver offence, death for the lighter.[23] *Capite poenas dabat*, therefore, cannot have meant death. But it is just as impossible that it can have meant slavery.[24] Indeed there is abundant

the *judicatus* and *confessus*, is one of them; see his *Shakespeare*, &c., p. 8. There is no denying that, with the aid of the comparative jurisprudence in which he is so profoundly versed, he makes out a strong case for the realistic interpretation he puts upon them. The results of his researches are summed up in a few sentences in his tractate *Das Recht als Culturerscheinung* (Würzburg, 1885), p. 17, quoted *infra*, Appendix, Note G.

[21] Gell., xi. 18, § 8, xx. 1, § 7; Gai., iii. 189.
[22] Gai., iii. 190.
[23] Even the man sentenced to twenty-five *asses* for a petty assault, and who could not pay it, might in this view have had to suffer death as the alternative!
[24] *Capitis poena*, capital punishment, meant death, slavery, or deprivation of citizenship; and this no doubt accounts for the all but universally prevalent idea that by *capite poenas dabat* the Tables must have meant one or other of them.

evidence that the *addictus*, even when his two months of provisional detention were ended, was not only still *de jure* free, but was not *capite minutus* even as regarded citizenship or family rights, and that any property he had still remained his own.[25] The only other explanation is that " he paid the penalty [26] with his person," [27] in contradistinction to " his means." [28] *Caput* is used in opposition to *bona*. Under the law of the Tables, unless when the debtor was sold beyond Tiber and thus made the slave of his foreign purchaser, the extent of the creditor's right was to detain him in free bondage, making what use he could of his services, and exercising discipline over him as if he were a slave. But for the mistaken notion that a creditor was entitled after the expiry of the three months to put his debtor to death,—of which there is not a single instance on record,—it is unlikely that so many would have thought of imputing to the *partis secanto* such an inhuman meaning as that a plurality of creditors might cut the body of their *addictus* in pieces and each take a share.

Those who hold that *capite poenas dabat* meant death can hardly avoid this interpretation of the *partis secanto*; but console themselves, like Gellius, with the conviction that it was never meant to be enforced. Those, again, who hold

[25] It is true that Dionysius (vi. 36) speaks of a creditor incarcerating not only his debtor but also the latter's two sons, and that he once or twice indicates that the debtor's goods were likewise seized. But those instances were anterior to the law of the Tables, and before the power of creditors exercising their right of self-redress had been made matter of statutory regulation. The *servitium* to which an *addictus* was subjected was essentially a punishment. But it was a principle of Roman law that punishment affected only the wrongdoer. A man's wife and children were not sent into exile, or banishment, or slavery with him on account of his offence; and there is no authority for holding that they were treated differently when the punishment was bondage without loss of either freedom or citizenship.

[26] More accurately, " made amends " (Curtius, *Gr. Etym.*, No. 373).

[27] A very familiar signification of *caput*, as in the old definition of *tutela* in *Inst.*, i. 13, 1,—" Vis ac potestas in capite libero," &c.

[28] "Fama et corpore judicati atque addicti creditoribus satisfaciebant, poenaque in vicem fidei cesserat " (Liv., vi. 34, § 2).

that the former of those phrases implied slavery, assume that the second meant joint ownership of the slave or distribution of the price obtained for him; while some, who are of opinion that *addictio* involved the passing of the debtor's *familia* to his creditor, hold that this also fell within the *sectio*. There is no objection to the employment of the word *secare* in the sense of "distribute;" for he who had bought a confiscated estate in mass, and afterwards resold it in lots, was called *bonorum sector*; and both Cicero and Varro speak of *sectio personae* when meaning nothing more than dispersal of his estate.[29] But the application of the phrase simply to the case of the detention of a debtor as a free bondman does not seem altogether appropriate, and renders the "si plus minusve secuerunt se fraude esto" harder than ever to explain.[30] The difficulty disappears at once if we make a slight rearrangement of the provisions brought under our notice by Gellius, and accept the suggestion that the plurality of creditors he speaks of can have referred only to the case of co-heirs taking proceedings against a debtor of their predecessor's.[31] Rearrangement is quite legitimate,—some rearrangement indeed is imperative if the words of the Tables are to be

---

[29] Cic., *Philipp.*, ii. 26, § 65, xiii. 14, § 30; Varro, *De R. R.*, 10, 4 (Bruns, p. 311). In like manner the "praedes vendere jus potestasque esto" of the *Lex Malacitana* (*temp.* Domitian, § 64; Bruns, p. 139) can have meant no more than sale of the estates of the defaulting sureties.

[30] One of the first to condemn the Gellian interpretation of *partis secanto* was Dr. Taylor, in his *Commentarius ad l. decemviralem de inope debitore in partis dissecando*, (Cambridge, 1742). He himself understands it thus (p. 15): "Qui uni debet, uni addictus serviat; qui pluribus, ejus addicti partis, *i.e.*, operas, servitia, ministeria communes illi foeneratores communiter dividunto; communis sit servus eorum qui quidem adfuerint; et sine fraude esto, si ceteri toties procitati suas quoque partis in debitore non vindicaverint."

[31] The suggestion is Voigt's (*XII Tafeln*, vol. ii. p. 361). He puts it that once a debtor was *domum ductus* it was impossible for any other creditor to proceed with *manus injectio*. Co-heirs were on a different footing; for, by a law of the Tables, each was entitled to proceed against a hereditary debtor only for so much of the debt as corresponded to his share of the inheritance. But Voigt holds—wrongly, as I think—that what they divided was the debtor himself, the members of his family, and his goods.

reconstructed.[32] On consideration of the whole matter, the explanation that most commends itself to me is this,—that where there was but one creditor concerned, and the two months of provisional detention expired without payment, intervention of a *vindex*, or compromise of some sort, the debtor definitively became his creditor's free bondman in virtue of the magisterial *addictio*;[33] but that where co-heirs were concerned, as bondage and service to all of them would have been inconvenient if not impossible when they were not to continue to possess the inheritance in common, the debtor was sent over Tiber and sold as a slave, and the price got for him divided amongst them. If one or other got more than his fair share, no harm was done; for the disproportion would eventually be redressed in an action of partition (*actio familiae erciscundae*).[34]

The abuses to which *manus injectio* gave rise, particularly in the case of nexal debtors, have already been referred to (§§ 20, 31). The *nexi* were probably much more numerous than the *judicati* (or more properly *addicti*); and, being in great part the victims of innocent misfortune, it was the sufferings they endured at the hands of relentless creditors that so often roused the sympathies and indignation of the

[32] Gellius quotes the law as "Tertiis nundinis partis secanto;" whereas immediately after the "Tertiis nundinis" must have come the provision as to what was to be done with the debtor when there was only one arresting creditor. That he explains *narrativé*.

[33] There is room for speculation as to what were the actual words of the statute. Quintilian (*Inst. Or.*, vii. 3, 26) says: "Addictus, quem lex servire, donec solverit, jubet;" and in *Decl.*, 311: "Quid enim lex dicit? addictus, donec solverit, serviat." Voigt (*Execution*, p. 88) supposes Quintilian to refer to the Poetilian law. May it not have been to the XII Tables?

[34] Reconstructions are always hazardous; and Krüger and Ihering have recently used their pens in sympathetic warning. But, on the footing above explained, the provision of the Tables may have been something like this: "Tertiis nundinis addicitor. Capite poenas dato. Si plures sunt, trans Tiberim peregre venum danto: partis secanto. Si plus minusve secuerunt, se fraude esto"—" On the third market-day there shall be decree of addiction. The *addictus* shall then pay the penalty with his person. If there be several creditors to whom he is awarded, let them sell him beyond Tiber and divide the price. If any of them have got more or less than his fair share, this shall not prejudice them."

populace, and more than once brought the republic to the verge of dissolution. But the judgment-debtors had suffered along with them; and some of the provisions of the Poetilian law (p. 161) were meant to protect them against the needless and unjustifiable severity that had characterised their treatment by their detaining creditors. The *manus injectio* itself was not abolished, nor the possible intervention of a *vindex;* neither were the *domum ductio* that followed, and the provisional imprisonment, with the light chains authorised by the Tables while it lasted; nor was the formal *addictio* of the debtor to his creditor when the sixty days had expired without arrangement.[35] But after addiction, if it was for nothing more than civil debt, there were to be no more dungeons and stripes, fetters and footblocks; the creditor was to treat his debtor and his industry as a source of profit that would in time diminish and possibly extinguish his indebtedness, rather than as an object upon which he might perpetrate any cruelty by way of punishment. Although the edict of P. Rutilius of 647 U.C. provided a creditor with machinery for attacking the estate of his debtor, yet he had still the alternative of incarceration. This, as already shown (pp. 96, 160), might be avoided under the Julian law of *cessio* by the debtor's making a complete surrender of his goods to his creditor; but, failing such surrender, incarceration continued to be resorted to even under the legislation of Justinian.[36] Latterly, however, it was not by *manus injectio* that the incarceration was effected; for it went out of use with the definitive establishment of the formular system of procedure.[37]

---

[35] Proof abounds in Plautus and Terence, Cicero, Seneca, Quintilian, and Gellius; as also in the *Lex col. Juliae Genetivae* of 710 U.C., cap. 61 (Bruns, p. 111). The latter enactment contains the provision—"jure civili vinctum habeto."

[36] See § 31, note 28.

[37] Gaius (iv. 30) attributes the establishment of the formular system (§ 71) to the Æbutian law in the beginning of the sixth century, and the Julian judiciary laws in the time of Augustus; but it is clear (note 35) that it could not have been till after 710 U.C. that *manus injectio* disappeared.

It was as directed against nexal and judgment debtors that *manus injectio* was of most importance, and chiefly made its mark in history. But there were other cases in which it was resorted to under special statutory authority, where a remedy seemed advisable more sharp and summary than that by ordinary action. In some of these it was spoken of as *manus injectio pro judicato* (*i.e.*, as if upon a judgment); in others as simple *manus injectio* (*manus injectio pura*). In the first the arrestee was not allowed to dispute his alleged indebtedness in person; he could do so only through a *vindex;* and if no one intervened for him in that character, he was carried off and dealt with by his arresting creditor as if a judgment had been obtained against him. A person who, having by *sponsio* become surety for another, had been required to pay for him, was entitled by a Publilian law of uncertain date to deal in this way with the principal debtor if he did not within six months refund what had been paid (*depensum*) on his account; but this was probably nothing more than an extension to a *sponsor* of the remedy previously competent to the *vas*, the *praes*, and the *vindex* (p. 166). Gaius states that the same procedure was sanctioned by statute in a variety of other cases; and there is reason for thinking that it was employed by a legatee against an heir delaying to pay a legacy bequeathed in the words " heres dare damnas esto." [38] In simple *manus injectio* the arrestee was not required to find a *vindex*, but might himself dispute the verity of the charge made against him, under penalty, however, of a duplication of his liability if he failed in his defence; as, for example, when proceedings were instituted against a usurer (under the Marcian law) to compel him to repay interest taken by him beyond the legal rate, or against a legatee (under the Furian law) to compel him to refund what he had taken by way of legacy in excess of what that law allowed. By a certain *Lex Vallia*,

[38] Gai., ii. 201, compared with iii. 175 and iv. 21.

probably in the latter half of the sixth century of the City, this *manus injectio pura* was substituted for that *pro judicato* in all cases in which the ground of arrest was neither judgment nor *depensum*.[39]

SECTION 37.—THE LEGIS ACTIO PER PIGNORIS CAPIONEM.[1]

In the ritual of the *actio sacramenti*, as described in a previous section (§ 34), the *vis civilis et festucaria* was a reminiscence of the *vera solida vis* with which men settled their disputes about property in the earliest infancy of the commonwealth. *Manus injectio* was a survival from times when the wronged was held entitled to lay hands upon the wrongdoer, and himself subject him to punishment; custom and legislation intervened merely to regulate the conditions and mode of exercise of what essentially was still self-help. In *pignoris capio* self-help was likewise the dominant idea. It may be fairly enough described by the single word "distress,"—the taking by one man of property belonging to another, in satisfaction of or in security for a debt due by the latter, but which he had failed to pay. The taking did not proceed upon any judgment, nor did it require the warrant of a magistrate; it might be resorted to even in the absence of the debtor; but it required to be accompanied by certain words of style, spoken probably in the presence of witnesses.[2]

The remedy, however, was not competent to creditors generally, but limited to a few special cases. Gaius says of it that by customary law a soldier might distrain upon his

---

[39] On *manus injectio pro judicato* and *pura*, see Gai., iv. 22-25, and note 16 above. *Manus injectio* upon nexal debt had been abolished long before the Vallian law.

[1] To the literature in § 33, note 1, may be added Degenkolb, *Die lex Hieronica* (Berlin, 1861), p. 95 *sq.*; Ihering, *Geist*, vol. i. § 11c; Voigt, *XII Tafeln*, vol. i. p. 502 *sq.*

[2] Gai., iv. 29.

paymaster for his pay,[3] and a knight for the sum allowed him for the purchase of a charger or for his forage money.[4] By the XII Tables distress was authorised at the instance of the vendor of an animal for sacrifice against the vendee who failed to pay for it; and so it was at the instance of a husbandman against a neighbour for the hire of a plough-ox given in location on purpose thereby to raise money for a periodical offering to Jupiter Dapalis.[5] The farmers of the revenue (*publicani*) were also empowered by the contracts entered into by them with the censors to make use of the same remedy against persons whose rates or taxes (*vectigalia*) were in arrear.[6] Whether this exhausted the list of cases in which it was competent it is of course impossible to say.[7]

Quite as difficult is it to determine what was the effect

---

[3] It was not until the year 348 U.C. that soldiers were paid from the public purse (Liv., iv. 59).

[4] Gai., iv. 27.

[5] Gai., iv. 28; Cato, *De R. R.*, §§ 50, 131, 132; Paul. Diac., v. *Daps* (Müll. p. 68).

[6] Gai., iv. 28.

[7] Bethmann-Hollweg (*Röm. CP.*, vol. i. p. 204, note 13) and Karlowa (*Röm. CP.*, p. 216) are of opinion that it was resorted to in the case of *damnum infectum*, *i.e.*, that, when a man had reason to apprehend damage from (say) the ruinous state of his neighbour's house, he might if necessary at his own hand enter into possession of it and make the requisite repairs. This view is combated by Bekker (*Aktionen*, vol. i. p. 45) and by Burckhard (*Die cautio damni infecti*, Glück-Burckhard, vol. ii. p. 73 *sq.*); but receives some countenance from the words of Gaius (iv. 31), who, after saying that it was still competent to proceed by *legis actio* on account of *damnum infectum*, adds that no one any longer cared to do so, "sed potius stipulatione, quae in edicto proposita est, obligat adversarium suum; itaque et commodius jus et plenius est [quam] per pignoris [capionem]." (The word "quam" is not in the MS.; "pignoris" is the last word in the page, and the whole of that which follows is illegible. Most editors regard "est" as the last word of the sentence, and make "per pignoris capionem" the commencement of a new paragraph. But, as the matter of *pignoris capio* is apparently exhausted in §§ 26-29, and one would naturally expect an indication of the particular procedure which was surpassed in convenience and amplitude by the prætorian stipulation, it seems more reasonable to assume that the transcriber accidentally omitted the letter "q" —the ordinary contraction for "quam," and that the passage should read as printed above.)

of the distress. An observation of Gaius's,[8] in speaking of the action which, under the formular system of procedure, was granted to a revenue collector in place of the *legis actio per pignoris capionem*, favours the assumption that the debtor had the right, within a limited period, to redeem his property from the distrainer; and the time is by some supposed to have been two months, the term of redemption of the later *pignus in causa judicati captum*.[9] If indebtedness was admitted, one can understand that the debtor might either abandon the thing distrained to his creditor if it did not greatly exceed in value the amount of the debt, or claim its redemption on payment of what was due, with possibly a small addition as a fine. At the same time it is obvious that prolongation of this power of redemption even for two months would in some cases have defeated the purpose of the distress; for example, the farmer who had to make his offering to Jupiter Dapalis could not postpone it, and delay in converting his *pignus* into money must often have been extremely inconvenient to a soldier. It is by no means improbable, therefore, that, even when the debt was not disputed, the power of redemption was in some cases more circumscribed than in others. But what if the existence of the debt was either wholly or partially denied? It cannot be doubted that in such a case the legitimacy of the distress might be called in question in a judicial process; otherwise *pignoris capio* might have become a cloak for robbery. We are very much in the dark, however, as to the course of procedure. Ihering, founding on some expressions of Cicero's,[10] conjectures that, whether the debt was disputed or not, the distrainer could neither sell nor definitively appropriate his *pignus* without magisterial authority,—that in every case he was bound to institute proceedings in justification of his caption, and to take in them the position of

[8] Gai., iv. 32.   [9] *Dig.*, xlii. 1, fr. 31.
[10] Cic., *In Verr. II.*, iii. 11, § 27.

plaintiff. The idea is ingenious, and puts the *pignoris capio* in a new and interesting light. It makes it, like the *sacramentum* and (in many cases) the *manus injectio*, a summary means of raising a question of right, for whose judicial arbitrament no other process of law was open; with this additional advantage,—that it secured instant satisfaction to the raiser of it in the event of the question being determined in his favour. If against him, the inevitable result, in substance at least, must have been a judgment that he had no right to retain his pledge, with probably a finding that he was further liable to its owner in the value of it, as a punishment for his precipitancy.[11]

SECTION 38.—JUDICIAL OR QUASI-JUDICIAL PROCEDURE OUTSIDE THE LEGIS ACTIONES.

Whatever may have been the extent of the field covered by the actions of the law, it is very manifest that they did not altogether exclude other judicial or quasi-judicial agencies. The supreme magistrate every now and then was called upon to intervene in matters brought under his cognisance by petition or complaint, and in which his aid was sought not so much to protect a vested right of property or claim as to maintain public order, or prevent the occurrence or continuance of a state of matters that might prove prejudicial to family or individual interests. The party whose conduct was complained of was not brought into court (*in jus vocatus*)

---

[11] This was according to the spirit of the early system, which endeavoured to check reckless or dishonest litigation by penalties; *e.g.*, forfeiture of the *summa sacramenti* and duplication of the value of unrestored property and profits in the sacramental procedure; duplication of the value of the cause when judgment was against the defendant in an action upon an engagement embodied in a *lex mancipii* or *lex nexi;* duplication against a *vindex* who interfered ineffectually in *manus injectio* against a judgment-debtor; duplication against an heir who refused without judicial compulsitor to pay a legacy bequeathed *per damnationem* (Gai., ii. 282); the addition of one-third more by way of penalty against a debtor found liable in an *actio certae creditae pecuniae* (Gai., iv. 171), &c.

by the complainer, but usually cited by the magistrate if the complaint seemed to him relevant. The process was not an action, with its stages *in jure* and *in judicio*, but an inquiry (*cognitio*) conducted from first to last by the magistrate himself; and his finding, unless it was a dismissal of the complaint or petition, was embodied in an order (*decretum*, *interdictum*), which it was for him to enforce by such means as he thought fit,—*manu militari*, or by fine or imprisonment.

Some jurists are disposed to give a very wide range to this magisterial intervention. One of its most important manifestations was in connection with disputes about the occupancy of the public domain lands. These did not belong in property to their occupants (p. 90); so that an action founded on ownership was out of the question. But as the occupancy was not only recognised but sanctioned by the state, it was right, indeed necessary in the interest of public order, that it should be protected against disturbance. In the measures resorted to for its protection Niebuhr recognised the origin of the famous possessory interdict *uti possidetis*; and although opinions differ as to whether protection of the better right or prevention of a breach of the peace was what primarily influenced the magistrate's intervention, there is a pretty general accord in accepting this view. It may well be that originally the procedure was simpler than that described by Gaius;[1] but it can hardly be doubted that it commenced with a prohibition of the disturbance of the *status quo*, and was followed when necessary by an inquiry and finding as to which of the disputants was really in possession, and which of them therefore, by persisting in his pretensions, was contravening the interdict. Another illustration of this magisterial intervention is to be found in the interdiction of a spendthrift (p. 126),—a decree depriving of his power of administration a man who was squandering his

[1] Gai., iv. §§ 160, 166–170; *infra*, p. 370.

family estate, and reducing his children to penury;[2] a third presents itself in the removal of a tutor from office on the ground of negligence or maladministration, brought under the notice of the magistrate by any third party in what was called *postulatio suspecti tutoris* (p. 125); and a fourth in the putting of a creditor in possession of the goods of an insolvent debtor, which must have been common enough even before the general bankruptcy regulations of the Rutilian edict (p. 161). These are to be taken merely as examples of this magisterial intervention, which manifested itself in very various directions; indeed it does not seem to be going too far to assume that, although the classification belongs to a later period, the interdicts already in use were not confined to the prohibitory, but included many that were either exhibitory or restitutory,—that is to say, in which the party complained of was ordered to produce or restore something in which the complainer had an interest.[3] It is easy to see how largely such procedure might be utilised for remedying the grievances of persons who, from defect of complete legal title, want of statutory authority, or otherwise, were not in a position to avail themselves of the ordinary " actions of the law."

In one of the Valerio-Horatian laws consequent on the second secession of the plebeians there was mention of ten judges (*judices decemviri*), whose persons were declared as inviolable as those of the tribunes of the people and the plebeian ædiles. It has already been explained (pp. 76, 85) that those were a body of judges elected to officiate on remit from a tribune or ædile acting as *jus dicens* in questions

---

[2] Ulpian (in *Dig.*, xxvii. 10, fr. 1, pr.) says that this interdiction was authorised by the XII Tables; Paulus (*Sent.*, iii. 4a, § 7) attributes it to custom (*mores*). But both probably are right. The practice was customary before the Tables; these confirmed it, with this new feature (Ulp., *Frag.*, xii. 2), that the interdicted spendthrift was to be in the guardianship of his agnates.
[3] Gai., iv. §§ 140, 142.

arising between members of the plebeian body.[4] We are without details as to the institution of this plebeian judicatory, the questions that fell under its cognisance, the forms of process employed, the law administered by it, and the effect of its judgments. The tribunes were not invested with the jurisdictional any more than the military *imperium*, and manifestly were not magistrates qualified to superintend and direct the course of a *legis actio*. One can understand that, prior to the enactment of the XII Tables, but after the constitutional recognition of the *plebs* as a quasi-corporation with its own officials and its own council, they may have thought it expedient, because of the uncertainty of the law, and the scant justice their members got from patrician magistrates and judges, to invest their presidents with jurisdictional powers, and elect some of their own number to act under them as *judices*, and in this way to some extent mitigate one of their grievances, the tribunes being fettered by no strict rules in formulating the question at issue, and the judges —who probably acted singly and not collegiately—determining it with equal freedom, untrammelled by statutory practice. But after the promulgation of the Tables, establishing a written law that was to apply to all the citizens alike, the reason for the maintenance of this plebeian tribunal is far from obvious. Did its members still act under a reference from a tribune or aedile? Or did they continue to be elected annually as a body independent of the tribunes and aediles, but from which the supreme magistrate (consul or praetor) was required to select a *judex* when both the parties were plebeians and formulated a demand to that effect? Whichever view may deserve preference, it may reasonably be inferred from the absence of further allusion to it in the pages of the historians, that the institution did not long

---

[4] See Schwegler, *Röm. Gesch.*, vol. ii. p. 270; Hartmann, *Der Ordo jud. privator.* (Göttingen, 1859), p. 87 *sq.*; Huschke, *Das alte röm. Jahr*, p. 301, note 206; Voigt, *XII Tafeln*, vol. i. p. 634 *sq.*

survive; the equalisation of the orders in matters social and political deprived it of its *raison d'être*.[5] As all in a manner exercising judicial or quasi-judicial functions must also be mentioned the pontiffs, the consuls and afterwards the censors as *magistri morum*, the chiefs of the *gentes* within the gentile corporations, and heads of families within their households. While it may be the fact that with the enactment of the XII Tables the jurisdiction of the pontiffs[6] was materially narrowed, yet it certainly did not disappear; witness the famous case in which Cicero made before them the oration of which he was so proud *pro domo sua*. In the time of the kings, with a variety of laws whose contravention entailed *consecratio capitis*, and with the sacramental procedure in their hands, the judicial duties of the pontiffs must have been somewhat onerous. But even after these had devolved on secular judges, and the *sacer esto* had all but disappeared from the sanctions of penal statutes, there were still not a few matters in which their judicial functions could not be dispensed with. It was the *pontifex maximus* that alone exercised jurisdiction and discipline over vestals and flamens. It may be that, with the positive declaration of the Tables, *uti legassit . . . ita jus esto*, he and his colleagues were no longer called upon to decide and report to the comitia whether or not a citizen's testamentary intentions were such as religion and law could

---

[5] Hartmann (*Ordo*, p. 109) attributes the decadence of this plebeian tribunal to the fact that the *Lex Hortensia* of 468 made the *nundinae* lawful court days (*dies fasti*), and so made it possible for the country folks coming to the city to market to carry on their processes before the prætor. As observed in a previous section (p. 76), there is no sufficient ground for identifying the plebeian *judices decemviri* with the *decemviri litibus judicandis* who, Pomponius says (*Dig.*, i. 2, fr. 2, § 29), were made presidents of the centumviral court early in the sixth century of the City.

[6] Comp. Hüllmann, *Jus pontificium der Römer* (Bonn, 1837); Cauvet, *Le droit pontifical chez les anciens Romains* (Caen, 1869); Bouché-Leclerq, *Les Pontifes de l'ancienne Rome* (Paris, 1871); Marquardt, *Röm. Staatsverwalt.*, vol. iii. p. 290 *sq*.

sanction; but their assistance long continued to be indispensable in an adrogation,—the ceremony could not proceed until they had investigated the circumstances (*cognitio*), embodied their finding in a judgment (*decretum*), and dissociated the *adrogatus* from the cult of his father's house (*alienatio sacrorum*). It was the pontiffs that determined what were impediments to marriage, that were judges in contraventions of the *annus luctus*, that not only performed the ceremony of diffareation but were judges of its legality. They alone could determine whether land or buildings or movables were excluded from commerce on the ground of their being sacred or religious. It has been maintained that, as charged with the cognisance of perjury and disregard of an oath, they really exercised jurisdiction in questions of breach of contract or engagement. It is extremely probable that at one time it was within their province to impose a penalty for violation of a promissory oath; but during the earlier republic the action of the consuls and censors as guardians of public morals,[7] and the social and political disqualifications and pecuniary penalties with which they visited persons who had been guilty of perjury or gross perfidy, did more than any intervention of the pontiffs to foster fidelity to engagements. Through the same agency the exercise of a variety of rights was controlled and kept within bounds whose abuse could not be made matter of action,—the husband's power over his wife, the father's over his children. It was not on light grounds, indeed, that the majesty of the *paterfamilias* within the household could be called in question; but only when he forgot that in the exercise of serious discipline within his family he was bound to act judicially. For he also was a judge,—*judex domesticus*, as he is sometimes called;[8] required,

---

[7] See Jarcke, *Darstellung des censorischen Strafrechts d. Römer* (Bonn, 1824); Karlowa, *Röm. RG.*, p. 236 *sq.*

[8] See § 9, note 23.

however, in all cases of gravity to invoke the advice of his kinsfolk as a family council.[9] On him lay the duty of controlling his family; if he failed to do so he was himself in danger of censorial animadversion. That his *gens* also, if he were a patrician, had some supervision and power of calling him to account is extremely probable; every corporation had it more or less over its members; but neither historians nor jurists give us any definite information.[10]

Between citizens and foreigners, with whom Rome was in alliance by a treaty conferring reciprocal right of action (*actio*), the proceedings took the form known as *recuperatio*.[11] A foreigner could not be a party to a *legis actio*, nor could a Roman citizen in foreign territory claim the benefit of the laws and civil procedure there prevailing. Yet, where *commercium* (p. 111) had been established between them, matters of dispute must occasionally have arisen in connection with their trading and other transactions, demanding the intervention of a tribunal for their settlement. It was therefore usually provided in the treaty conceding reciprocal *commercium* that *recuperatio* should run along with it. This was an international process, modelled to some extent upon and deriving some of its technical terms from the fetial *clarigatio*. In the Cassian treaty of 262 U.C.—and no doubt it was the universal practice whether expressed or not—it was provided that it should be instituted in the *forum con-*

---

[9] In 447 U.C. the censors removed L. Annius from the senate because he had divorced his wife without laying the matter before the *consilium* (Val. Max., ii. 9, 2). There is no recorded instance of the interference of the censors on account of abuse of the *patria potestas*; but it can hardly be doubted that the interests of children would no more be neglected by them than those of a wife.

[10] Livy (vi. 20, §§ 13, 14) speaks of a *nota gentilicia*; but he is in fact referring to a decree of the Manlian *gens*, forbidding that any member of it should afterwards be called Marcus. See Voigt, *XII Tafeln*, vol. ii. § 170.

[11] See *supra*, § 25, and Festus, v. *Reciperatio* (Bruns, p. 286). Comp. Collman, *de Romanor. jud. recuperatorio*, Berlin, 1835; Carl Sell, *Die recuperatio der Römer*, Brunswick, 1837; Huschke (rev. Sell), in Richter's *Krit. Jqhrb.*, vol. i. (1837), pp. 868-911; Voigt, *Jus nat.*, &c., vol. ii. §§ 28-32; Karlowa, *Röm. CP.*, pp. 218-230.

tractus. The generally accepted opinion is that it commenced with what was called a *condictio*,—a formal and public requisition by the plaintiff to the defendant to attend on the thirtieth day thereafter, before a competent magistrate of the state in which the process was raised, in order that, if there was no settlement in the interval, the matter of dispute might be formulated and sent to recuperators for trial. The adjustment of the issue on the thirtieth day (*condictus dies*) was the work of the magistrate; he heard what parties had to say in plaint and defence, and then put in simple shape the points of fact and law arising on them, authorising the recuperators to find for plaintiff or defendant according to circumstances. The recuperators were sometimes three, sometimes five, sometimes still more numerous, but always in odd number; whether the nationality of both parties required to be represented does not appear. The day appointed for further procedure before them, usually the third, was called *status dies*. So imperative was it that parties should appear at both stages that in Rome *status condictusve dies cum hoste* was a valid excuse for a man's absence from proceedings in a *legis actio*, and relieved a soldier from joining the ranks.[12] Expedition being in most cases a matter of importance, the recuperators were required to give judgment within ten days. How execution proceeded upon it, if it were for the plaintiff, does not clearly appear; Voigt,[13] founding on a few words in Festus,[14] concludes it must have

---

[12] From the order in which the two words occur in various passages in the lay writers, Karlowa is of opinion—contrary to the ordinary interpretation of the definitions of *status dies* in Festus, v. *Status* (Bruns, p. 295), and Macrob., i. 16, § 14—that this was the first term of appearance before the magistrate; that the *condictio* was given in his presence; that the *condictus dies* was not the thirtieth day after the *condictio*, but, if circumstances justified it, might even be the next; and that the proceedings before the *recuperatores* might be at any time convenient for all parties, so long as they were finished within ten days from the remit to them.

[13] *Jus nat.*, &c., vol. ii. p. 195.

[14] Festus, v. *Nancitor* (Bruns, p. 274): "In foedere Latino, 'Si quid pignoris nasciscitur, sibi habeto.'"

been by something like the *pignoris capio* explained in last section.

This recuperatory procedure in time came to be resorted to in some cases even where both parties were citizens. There are numerous instances of it in Cicero; and it is remarkable that in most of the purely prætorian actions *ex delicto* the remit was not to a *judex* but to recuperators. The explanation may be in the comparative summariness of the remedy.

CHAPTER FIFTH.

THE STIPULATION AND THE LEGIS ACTIO PER CONDICTIONEM.

SECTION 39.—INTRODUCTION OF THE STIPULATION.[1]

FEW events in the history of the private law were followed by more far-reaching consequences than the introduction of the stipulation. It exercised an enormous influence on the law of contract; for by means of it there was created a unilateral obligation that in time became adaptable to almost every conceivable undertaking by one man in favour of another. By the use of certain words of style in the form of question and answer, any lawful agreement could thereby be made not only morally but legally binding; so that much which previously had no other guarantee than a man's sense of honour now passed directly under the protection of the tribunals. Stipulations became the complement of engagements which without them rested simply on good faith; as when a vendor gave his stipulatory promise to his vendee to guarantee peaceable possession of the thing sold or its freedom from faults, and the vendee in turn gave his promise for payment of the price. The question and answer

---

[1] Literature: Liebe, *Die Stipulation u. das einfache Versprechen* (Brunswick, 1840); Schmidt (rev. Liebe), in Richter's *Krit. Jahrb.*, vol. v. pp. 869 *sq.*, 961 *sq.*; Gneist, *Die formellen Verträge d. Röm. Rechts* (Berlin, 1845), p. 113 *sq.*; Heimbach, *Die Lehre vom Creditum*, Leipsic, 1849; Danz, *Der sacrale Schutz im Röm. Rechte* (Jena, 1857), pp. 102-142, 236 *sq.*; Schlesinger, *Zur Lehre von den Formalcontracten* (Leipsic, 1858), § 2; Voigt, *Jus nat., &c., d. Röm.*, vol. ii. § 33, vol. iv., Beilage xix.; Girtanner, *Die Stipulation*, Kiel, 1859; Bekker, *Aktionen*, vol. i. pp. 382-401; Karsten, *Die Stipulation*, Rostock, 1878.

in the form prescribed by law made the engagement fast and sure. Hence the generic name of the contract; for Paul's derivation of it from *stipulum*, "firm," is much to be preferred to the earlier and more fanciful ones from *stips* or *stipula*.[2] It was round the stipulation that the jurists grouped most of their disquisitions upon the general doctrines of the law of contract,—capacity of parties, requisites of consent, consequences of fraud, error, and intimidation, effects of conditions and specifications of time, and so forth. It may well be said, therefore, that its introduction marked an epoch in the history of the law.

And yet there is no certainty either as to the time or as to the manner of its introduction. So far as appears, it was unknown at the time of the compilation of the XII Tables, at least in private life; and one of the first unmistakable allusions to it is in the Aquilian law of 476 U.C.[3] The mention of it in that enactment, however, is with regard to a phase of it which cannot have been reached for some years after it had come into use; and the probability is that it originated before the middle of the fifth century. In its earliest days it bore the name not of *stipulatio* but of *sponsio;* for the reason that the interrogatory of the party becoming creditor was invariably formulated with the word *spondes*—*e.g., centum dare spondes?*—while the answer was simply *spondeo*. There has been much speculation as to the significance of the word.[4] Modern criticism has three theories,—(1) that it was the verbal remnant of the *nexum*, after the business with the copper and the scales had gone into disuse; (2) that it was evolved out of the oath of covenant at the great altar of Hercules or the appeal to Fides

---

[2] *Stipulum,*—Paul., *Sent.*, v. 7, 1, Just., *Inst.* iii. 15, pr. ; *Stips,*—Fest., v. *Stipem* (Bruns, p. 295), Varro, *De L. L.*, v. 182 (Bruns, p. 303); *Stipula,*— Isidore, *Orig.*, v. 24, § 30 (Bruns, p. 327).

[3] Gai., iii. 215.

[4] See Festus, v. *Spondere* (Bruns, p. 295); Varro, *De L. L.*, vi. 69-72 (Bruns, pp. 304, 305).

(p. 50); (3) that it was imported from Latium, which it had reached from some of the Greek settlements farther south. The latter is the most probable. Verrius Flaccus, as quoted by Festus, connects it with the Greek σπένδειν and σπονδή; and Gaius incidentally observes that the word was said to be of Greek origin.[5] A libation (σπονδή) is frequently referred to by Homer and Herodotus as an accompaniment of treaties and other solemn covenants,— a common offering by the parties to the gods, which imparted sanctity to the transaction. Leist[6] is of opinion that the practice passed into Sicily and Lower Italy, but that gradually the libation and other religious features were dropped, although the word σπονδή was retained in the sense of an engagement that bound parties just as if the old ritual had been observed; and that it travelled northward into Latium and thence to Rome under the name of *sponsio*, being used in the first instance in public life for the conclusion of treaties, and afterwards in private life for the conclusion of contracts. The meaning of *spondes* as a question by a creditor to his debtor (although latterly, we may well believe, unknown to them) thus came to be—"Do you engage as solemnly as if the old ceremonial had been gone through between us?" There are many parallels for such simplification of terms; none more familiar than when a man says, "I give you my oath upon it," without either himself or the individual addressed thinking it necessary to go through the form.

It is not a little remarkable that, although the idea was derived from abroad, the use of the words *spondes* and *spondeo* in making a contract, down at least to the time of Gaius, were confined in Rome to Roman citizens.[7] The

[5] Gai., iii. 93.
[6] *Graeco-ital. Rechtsgesch.*, pp. 465-470. Upon the *sponsionis vinculum* internationally, see Liv. ix. 9.
[7] Gai., iii. §§ 93, 119, 179. It is sometimes said (on the authority of Gaius, iii. 120, iv. 113) that the heir of a *sponsor* (as the debtor was called) was not

sponsio as a form of contract was essentially *juris civilis*. So at first were the later and less solemn forms of stipulation,—*promittisne? promitto, dabisne? dabo*, and the like. Gaius speaks of these as *juris gentium*, *i.e.*, binding even between Romans and peregrins. Such they became eventually; but not until towards the end of the republic. Yet, although *juris civilis*, both the *sponsio* and the later forms were from the first free from many of the impediments of the earlier *actus legitimi*. No witnesses were required to assist at them; and they were always susceptible of qualification by conditions and terms. It was very long, however, before parties had much latitude in their choice of language; *spondeo* was so peculiarly solemn that no equivalent could be admitted; and even the later styles may be said to have remained stereotyped until well on in the empire. And it was the use of the words of style that made the contract. It was formal, not material; that is to say, action lay upon the promise the words embodied, apart from any consideration whether or not value had been given for it. In time this serious disadvantage was abated: first by the introduction in certain cases of words that excluded action in presence of fraud, antecedent or subsequent, on the part of the creditor (*clausula doli*); and afterwards by prætorian exceptions, such as a plea of "no value," or by having the contract set aside on the motion of the nominal debtor before proceedings had been taken upon it by the creditor.

SECTION 40.—THE SILIAN AND CALPURNIAN LAWS.

Bekker seems to be the only authority of note who holds that stipulations were in use before the XII Tables, and enforcible by an *actio sacramenti*.[1] Most writers agree that,

liable under the latter's engagement. Was this universal in the time of Gaius? or was it only when the *sponsor* was a surety, and because of the nature rather than the form of his obligation?

[1] *Aktionen*, vol. i. pp. 146, 147.

whether in use earlier or not, they first became actionable, and therefore effectual in law, in virtue of a *lex Silia*. Gaius speaks of it as the enactment that introduced the *legis actio per condictionem* for enforcing payment of a definite sum of money.[2] Its date is matter of controversy;[3] and Gaius remarks that the purpose of it was far from obvious, as there was no difficulty in recovering money either by a sacramental action or by one *per judicis postulationem*. He overlooks the fact that money due under a nexal contract was recoverable by neither of those processes, but by the much more summary one of *manus injectio* (§ 31). By the Poetilian law of 428 this was declared unlawful. I am disposed to regard the *lex Silia* and the new procedure it authorised as a result of the change. To have put off a creditor for money lent either with a sacramental action or one *per judicis postulationem*, would have been to deprive him of the advantages of *manus injectio* to a greater extent than was called for. It was right and proper in the interests of humanity that a creditor should no longer have the power of reducing his debtor to a condition of *de facto* slavery; but there was no good reason why the debtor should be allowed to dispute his obligation without incurring any penalty if unsuccessful.[4] So it was provided by the Silian law that when a man disputed his liability for what was called *pecunia certa credita*, and forced his creditor to litigation, the latter was entitled to require from him an engagement to pay one-third more than the sum claimed by way of penalty in the event of judgment being against him; while the *soi-disant* creditor had to give an engagement to

[2] Gai., iv. 19.

[3] Voigt places it between the years 325 and 329 U.C.; Ihering ascribes it to the first half of the fifth century; Huschke and Rudorff to the beginning of the sixth. But the fact that stipulation is referred to in the Aquilian law of 476 as a contract already well developed seems to put the sixth century out of the question.

[4] The *sacramentum* was a penalty in one sense; but the successful litigant gained nothing by it, as it was forfeited to public uses (p. 187).

pay as penalty the same amount in case of judgment in favour of the alleged debtor.[5]

Those engagements (*sponsio et restipulatio tertiae partis*) were not allowed in every case in which a definite sum of money was claimed *per condictionem*, but only when it was technically *pecunia credita*. In Cicero's time *creditum* might arise either from loan, stipulation, or literal contract (*expensilatio*, p. 275);[6] but the last dated at soonest from the beginning of the sixth century, and stipulation was a result of the Silian law itself; so that the *pecunia credita* of this enactment can have referred only to borrowed money. The same phrase, according to Livy, was employed in the Poetilian law; it was thereby enacted, he says, that for *pecunia credita* the goods, not the body of the debtor, ought to be taken in execution.[7] A connection, therefore, between the Poetilian law and abolition of the *nexum* on the one hand, and the Silian law and introduction of the *legis actio per condictionem* on the other, can hardly be ignored; and raises more than a probability that the latter statute was a consequence of the former, and must have been passed immediately or soon after the year 428. And we are entitled to regard it not merely as the enactment introducing a new action, applicable (though with different limitations) to suits alike for re-payment of loans and for payment of money debts of definite amount, no matter how arising, but as that which gave legal sanction to the *sponsio* or stipulation. The *sponsio tertiae partis* was its first exemplification. But once recognised as a binding contract, its manifest convenience must very soon have given it a greater range in money obligations, especially in agreements for interest upon loans.

There was a sort of loan, however, which was very common, whose repayment nevertheless could not be enforced by a condiction under the Silian law, namely, a loan of seed corn,

---

[5] Gai., iv. §§ 13, 171, 172, 180.
[6] Cic., *Pro Rosc. com.*, 4, § 13; 5, § 14.   [7] Liv., viii. 28, § 9.

to be repaid after harvest, with a certain addition by way of interest. The reason was that the Silian condiction was limited to actions for current money. A later statute, the *lex Calpurnia*, extended the remedy, which was much simpler than that by sacrament, to every personal claim for a thing or quantity of things, other than money, that was definite and certain (*omnis certa res*);[8] and the action authorised by it got the name of *condictio triticaria*,[9] from the material (*triticum*) in reference to which the need for it was first experienced.

In course of time the stipulation came to be employed in engagements that were from the first indefinite. But this seems to have been due to the intervention of the prætors, and to have originated after the system of the *legis actiones* had begun to give place to that *per formulas* (§ 71). The remedy in such a case was not spoken of as a condiction, but as an *actio ex stipulatu*.[10]

SECTION 41.—THE LEGIS ACTIO PER CONDICTIONEM.[1]

Little is known of the procedure in the *legis actio* introduced by the Silian and Calpurnian laws; for, in consequence of the loss of a leaf in the Verona MS., we are deprived of part of Gaius's account of it. It got its distinctive name, he says, from the *condictio* or requisition made by the plaintiff on the defendant, whom he had brought into court in the usual way, to attend again on the expiry of thirty days to

[8] Gai., iv. 19.
[9] Fr. 1 *Dig. De condictione triticaria* (xiii. 3). The action was so called at any rate under the formular system; and it is more than probable that popularly it was so known under that of the *legis actiones*.
[10] Gai., iv. 136; Just., *Inst.*, iii. 15 pr.
[1] To the literature in § 33, note 1, add—Asverus, *Die Denunciation der Römer* (Leipsic, 1843), p. 129 *sq.;* Mommsen (rev. Asverus), in Richter's *Krit. Jahrb.*, vol. ix. (1845) p. 875 *sq.;* Bekker, *Aktionen*, vol. i. cap. 4-7; Voigt, *Jus nat.*, vol. iii. §§ 98, 99, vol. iv. Beilage xix. Nos. 1, 2, 7; Baron (as in § 35 note 1), p. 40 *sq.;* Baron, *Die Condictionen* (Berlin, 1881), §§ 15, 16.

have a judge appointed. Exception has been taken to this explanation by many jurists, on the ground that a requisition or invitation by one only of the parties hardly corresponds to the idea of *condictio*, which seems to imply common action; but it is a matter of detail of pure form and comparatively little importance. That the requisition was made in presence of the prætor, and in consequence of the denial by the defendant of the plaintiff's claim,[2] is more than probable; for it was the *condictio* that was the essential feature of the *legis actio*; and we have for it the testimony of Gaius that, except in *pignoris capio*, what was characteristic of the *legis actiones* was done *in jure*.[3] The procedure on the reappearance of parties on the thirtieth day (provided a settlement had not been arrived at in the interval) must have varied according as the action was (1) for a definite sum of money that fell under the category of *pecunia credita*, (2) for any other definite sum of money, or (3) for a definite thing or quantity of things other than money. It was in the first case alone that there intervened promise and re-promise of a third part of the sum claimed by way of penalty (*sponsio et restipulatio tertiae partis*); and it is probable that, if either party refused on the prætor's command so to oblige himself towards the other, judgment was at once pronounced in favour of the latter without any remit to a *judex*.

How the issue was adjusted when the sponsion and restipulation were duly given we are not informed; but, judging by analogy from the procedure in an action for breach of interdict under the formular system,[4] and on the broader ground that there must have been machinery for a condem-

---

[2] In the edict which regulated the formular *actio certae creditae pecuniae* (which came in place of the *legis actio*), the prætor declared that, if the plaintiff referred the matter to the oath of the defendant, he (the praetor) would compel the latter either to swear that he was not resting owing or to pay,—"solvere aut jurare cogam" (*Dig.*, xii. 2, fr. 34, § 6). Some jurists think this must originally have been a provision of the Silian law. If so, it would greatly enhance the value of the remedy.

[3] Gai., iv. 29.   [4] Gai., iv. 165, and *infra*, § 73.

nation of the plaintiff on his restipulation in the event of his being found in the wrong,[5] it may reasonably be concluded that there were in fact three concurrent issues sent to the same *judex*,—the first on the main question, the second on the defendant's sponsion, and the third on the plaintiff's restipulation. The first issue was an echo of the averment with which the plaintiff had originally come into court,— "If it appear that the defendant ought to pay (*si paret dare oportere*) the plaintiff the sum of 1000 *asses* of *credita pecunia*, in that the judge will condemn him; should it not so appear, he will acquit him." Where a sum of money other than *pecunia credita* was sued for, the issue was substantially the same, those two words being omitted; but subsidiary issues were unnecessary, as there was neither sponsion nor restipulation.

As Baron has demonstrated, it was not the usual practice to introduce any words explanatory of the ground of indebtedness when the action was either for money (other than *pecunia credita*) or for a thing or quantity of things. It might be loan, or bequest, or sale, or purchase, or delict, or unjustifiable enrichment, or any of a score of *causae*; it would have to be condescended on of course before the judge; but in the initial stage before the prætor and in the issue all that was necessary was the averment that the defendant was owing such a sum of money or such a thing. It was for the judge to determine whether or not the averment was established, and, in certain cases, that non-delivery was due to the fault of the defendant; the plaintiff, however, being bound to make his averment good to the letter of his claim. Proof of 900 resting owing where 1000 had been claimed necessarily involved a judgment for the defendant; unless the plaintiff proved all, he got nothing; for the procedure was pre-eminently *stricti juris*. In the event of the plaintiff

[5] "Restipulationis poena omnimodo damnatur actor si vincere non potuerit" (Gai., iv. 180).

being successful in an action for *certa pecunia*, but delay made by the defendant in satisfying the judgment, execution followed in ordinary form. How the matter was arranged in an action on the Calpurnian law for a *certa res* is not so obvious. What the plaintiff wanted was specific delivery or damages, and by some the opinion is entertained that he formulated his claim alternatively. Of this there is no evidence; and Gaius's statement that under the system of the *legis actiones* condemnation was always in the *ipsa res*, *i.e.*, the specific thing sued for,[6] leads to the assumption that a judgment for the plaintiff, on which specific implement failed, must have been followed by an *arbitrium litis aestimandae* for assessment of the damages in money, and that execution proceeded thereon as if the judgment had been for a sum of money in the first instance. The general opinion, however, is that the judge to whom the issue was remitted assessed the damages himself and as a matter of course,—that the instruction to him was *quanti res erit, tantam pecuniam condemnato*.

[6] Gai., iv. 48. But see *supra*, § 36, note 6.

PART III.
THE JUS GENTIUM AND JUS HONORARIUM.
Latter Half of the Republic.

PART III.
THE JUS GENTIUM AND JUS HONORARIUM.

Latter Half of the Republic.

CHAPTER FIRST.
INFLUENCES THAT OPERATED ON THE LAW.

SECTION 42.—GROWTH OF COMMERCE AND INFLUX OF FOREIGNERS.

WHILE it may be admitted that commerce was beginning to take root in Rome in the fifth century, yet it was not until the sixth that it really became of importance. The campaigns in which Rome was engaged until the end of the First Punic War absorbed all her energies. But after it the influx of strangers, and their settlement in the city for purposes of trade, became very rapid,—first Latins and other allies, and afterwards Greeks, Carthaginians, and Asiatics. For them and the regulation of their affairs the *jus civile*—the law peculiar to Rome and her citizens [1]—was applicable only if they were members of allied states to which *commercium* and *recuperatio* were guaranteed by treaty (p. 111). But multitudes were not in this favoured position; and even those who were, soon found the range of Roman modes of acquiring property and contracting obligations too narrow for their requirements. So

[1] Just., *Inst.*, i. 2, 1.

there gradually developed a *jus gentium*² which very early in its history drove treaty covenants for *recuperatio* out of use; whose application may for a time have been limited to transactions between non-citizens, or between citizens and non-citizens, but which was eventually accepted in the dealings of citizens *inter se*, and became part and parcel of the *jus Romanorum*. Gaius and Justinian speak of it as "the common law of mankind," "the law in use among all nations."³ But the language must not be taken too literally. The Roman *jus gentium* was not built up by the adoption of one doctrine or institution after another that was found to be generally current elsewhere. In the earliest stages of its recognition it was "an independent international private law, which, as such, regulated intercourse between peregrins, or between peregrins and citizens, on the basis of their common *libertas*;"⁴ which during the republic was purely empirical and free from the influence of scientific theory, but whose extensions in the early empire were a creation of the jurists,—a combination of comparative jurisprudence and rational speculation.⁵ To say that it was *de facto* in observance everywhere is inaccurate; on the contrary, it was Roman law, built up by Roman jurists, though called into existence through the necessities of intercourse with and among non-Romans.

It was in matters of contract that there was the greatest scope for the development of the new system; and to it may be attributed the relaxation of the stipulation and the recognition of the so-called real and consensual contracts as creative of obligation apart from any formalities of word or

---

² On the Roman *jus gentium*, see Voigt, *Das jus naturale, aequum et bonum, und jus gentium d. Römer*, 4 vols., Leipsic, 1856-75: Nettleship, in the *Journal of Philology*, vol. xiii. (1885), p. 169 *sq*.

³ Gai., i. 1; Just., *Inst.*, i. 2, 1.

⁴ Voigt, *Jus nat.*, vol. ii. 661. He distinguishes the *jus civile*, *jus gentium*, and *jus naturale* as the systems which applied respectively to the citizen, the freeman, and the man. Comp. Cic., *De Orat.*, i. 13, § 56.

⁵ Voigt, vol. i. pp. 399, 400.

deed. But it was not without its influence in other departments of the law. It is questionable whether, as sometimes said, the great reform worked on the law of property by the Publician edict,—the recognition, namely, of an inferior sort of ownership of *res mancipi*, the beneficial interest without the quiritary title (§ 52), can be regarded as one of its manifestations; for what Theophilus calls *dominium bonitarium* proceeded upon a fiction of usucapion, and this, down at least to the time of Gaius, was competent only to citizens and non-citizens enjoying *commercium*.[6] It made its mark, however, both on the law of the family and on that of succession. This indeed was inevitable. Marriages between Roman citizens and women of peregrin birth with whom they had no *conubium* became not uncommon. They were not *justae nuptiae*, and so did not make the wife *justa uxor* or give the husband *potestas* over his children. To have altogether ignored such a union, however, would have been disastrous; so it was treated as *juris gentium* marriage. The wife consequently was allowed an action for her dowry when the union was dissolved,[7] and the husband an *accusatio adulterii* when his wife proved unfaithful.[8] His children, although they were held to be peregrins like their mother,[9] and were not in his *potestas*, yet were in a sense his lawful children (*justi liberi patris*),[10] so that he was bound to aliment them, entitled to plead his paternity as an excuse from undertaking a tutory,[11] and so forth; and Theophilus states expressly that it was on their account that testamentary trusts (*fideicommissa*) were originally introduced, their want of citizenship preventing them from taking their father's succession *ab intestato*, and him from either instituting them as his testamentary heirs or leaving them direct bequests.[12]

[6] Gai., ii. 65.　　　[7] Cic., *Top.*, 4, § 20.
[8] Ulp., *lib.* 2 *de adult.*, in *Dig.*, xlviii. 5, fr. 13, § 1.
[9] Gai., i. 67.　　　[10] Gai., i. 77.
[11] Papin., *lib.* 5 *quaestion.*, in *Vat. Frag.*, 194.
[12] Theoph., *Paraphr.*, ii. 23, § 1.

Q

It may be a little difficult for a modern jurist to say with perfect precision what were the doctrines and institutions of the *jus gentium* as distinguished from the *jus civile*. But the distinction must have been very familiar to the Romans; otherwise we should not have had the statement of Marcian in reference to the ἀπόλιδες,—that they enjoyed all the rights competent to a man under the former, but none of those competent to him under the latter.[13]

SECTION 43.—THE INSTITUTION OF THE PEREGRIN PRÆTORSHIP.

The prætorship[1] was an outcome of the Licinian laws of the year 387 U.C. (p. 88). The object of its institution was that the administration of justice might be retained in the hands of patricians, although the consulate had been thrown open to the lower order. " Qui jus in urbe diceret " are the words in which Livy describes the principal function of the new official.[2] In dignity he was on a footing of almost perfect equality with the consuls, and in their absence from the city he was qualified in some matters to act as their substitute; in fact, he had the same *imperium* as they in all but military command. In course of time the office, which, like the consulate, was an annual one, was opened to plebeians as well as patricians; but nothing was changed in its duties; down to the end of the fifth century the prætor superintended single-handed the administration of justice, alike between citizens and foreigners. But with the altered conditions of things in the beginning of the sixth century, and the influx of strangers which has already been alluded to, the work seems to have been found too onerous for a single magistrate, and a second

[13] *Dig.*, xlviii. 19, fr. 17, § 1.
[1] See Labatut, *Histoire de la Préture* (Paris, 1868); Mommsen, *Röm. Staatsrecht*, vol. ii. p. 176 *sq.*; Faure, *Essai historique sur le Préteur Romain*, Paris, 1878; Karlowa, *Röm. RG.*, vol. i. p. 217 *sq.*
[2] Liv., vi. 42, § 11.

prætor was appointed. The date is not absolutely certain, though generally assumed to have been about the year 512 U.C.;[3] but Pomponius[4] says distinctly that the creation of the new office was rendered necessary by the increase of the peregrin population of Rome, and that the new magistrate got the name of *praetor peregrinus* because his principal duty was to dispense justice to this foreign element.[5] After the submission of Sicily and Sardinia the number of the prætors was increased to four, and after the conquest of Spain to six; Sulla raised the number to eight, and Cæsar eventually to sixteen. But all the later creations were for special purposes; the ordinary administration of justice within the city was left with the representatives for the time of the two earliest, who came to be distinguished as *praetor urbanus* (*qui jus inter cives dicit*) and *praetor peregrinus*.

Although material fails for instituting a comparison between the edicts[6] of those two magistrates, and estimating the extent to which each may be credited with influencing the development of the *jus gentium*, yet it is but reasonable to assume that, in many directions at least, the greater impetus must have been given to it by the peregrin prætor, moulding and modifying the *jus civile* to suit peregrin requirements where that was possible, and where it failed introducing a *jus honorarium*. It would be going too far to speak of him as the principal author of the *jus gentium*; for a large proportion of the actions for enforcing *juris gentium* rights were civil, not honorary,—a fact which proves that the rights they were meant to protect and enforce had

[3] Lydus (*De Magistr.*, i. 38, 45) says it was in the year 507, which corresponds to 510 of the Varronian era. Livy (*Epit.*, 19) says it was in 512.
[4] Pompon., in *Dig.*, i. 2, fr. 2, § 28.
[5] In the extant remains of later republican legislation and in inscriptions he is alluded to sometimes as "prætor qui inter peregrinos jus dicit," sometimes as "prætor qui inter cives et peregrinos jus dicit," and sometimes simply as "prætor peregrinus."
[6] Gaius (i. 6) speaks of the edicts of the peregrin prætor as equally a source of the *jus honorarium* with those of his urban colleague.

their origin in the *jus civile*, although moulded to meet new requirements by tacit consuetude and the agency of the jurists. But even in this view the peregrin prætor must have had a powerful influence in giving shape and consistency to the rising jurisprudence, through means of the *formulae* he adjusted for giving it practical effect.

SECTION 44.—SIMPLIFICATION OF PROCEDURE AND INTRODUCTION OF NEW REMEDIES UNDER THE AEBUTIAN LAW.

The *lex Aebutia* is only twice mentioned by ancient writers,[1] and we know neither its precise date nor its specific provisions. And yet, to judge by its effects, it must have been one of the most important pieces of comitial legislation in the latter half of the republic; for Gellius speaks of it as having given their death-blow to many of the institutions of the XII Tables, and Gaius couples it with two Julian laws as the statutory instruments whereby the formular system of procedure (§ 71) was substituted for that *per legis actiones*. The probability is that it was enacted immediately or soon after the institution of the peregrin prætorship.[2] Its purpose, whatever may have been its terms, seems to have been to authorise the prætors to simplify the existing forms of process or substitute new ones in actions on the *jus civile*. It can hardly be that it authorised the prætors to publish and enforce edicts, for that had from time immemorial been a prerogative of all magistrates invested with the *imperium*. Nor can it be that it authorised them to give the character of rights and wrongs to what had not previously been so regarded, by supporting the one with actions and visiting the other with punishment; for not only would that have been to empower the prætors *jus facere* (which they always

[1] Gell., xvi. 10, 8 ; Gai., iv. 30.
[2] It has sometimes been put as late as the beginning of the seventh century. For some of the dates assigned to it, and the reasons for them, see Padeletti, *Storia del diritto romano* (Florence, 1878), p. 251 *sq.*

disclaimed), but it would have made it incomprehensible why prætorian actions could be raised only within the year of office of the prætor who had promised to grant them, while actions of the *jus civile*, though appearing for the first time in their new shape on the prætor's album, were perpetual. It seems rather to have been intended to empower them to adapt existing remedies to altered circumstances, and to fashion new actions on the *jus civile* for the use of the peregrins to whom the procedure of the *legis actiones* was incompetent; while it may possibly at the same time have expressly authorised the insertion in the styles to be devised by them of clauses that would give protection when required against claims that in law were well founded but in fact inequitable. But whatever may have been the actual provisions of the statute, the result was the introduction of a procedure which gradually supplanted that by the " actions of the law; " which was much more pliant than the latter; and whose characteristic was this,—that instead of the issue being declared by word of mouth by the parties, and requiring in many cases to embody with perfect accuracy the statutory provision upon which it was based, it was now formulated in writing by the prætor, in the shape of an instruction to the judge to inquire and consider, with power to condemn or acquit according to his finding (§ 71).

SECTION 45.—PROVINCIAL CONQUESTS.

The growth of commerce and the enormous increase of wealth, which made great capitalists and enabled them through the agency of freedmen and slaves to carry on trade on a scale hitherto unknown, and which thus helped to foster the *jus gentium*, was no doubt due to a large extent to provincial conquests. But these operated also in other directions. The authorities who proceeded to the conquered provinces as governors found themselves face to face with laws and institutions in many respects differing from those of Rome. Political considerations dictated how far these were to be respected, how far subverted. In some provinces, more especially the eastern ones, it was thought unnecessary to do more than supplement the existing system by the importation of doctrines of the *jus gentium* and the procedure of the prætor's edicts; while in others, in which it was deemed expedient to destroy as rapidly as possible all national feeling and every national rallying-point, a romanising of all their institutions was resorted to, even to the extent of introducing some of the formal transactions which previously had been confined to citizens. But in either case there was a reflex action. The native institution had to be studied, its advantages and disadvantages balanced, the means considered of adapting it to the prætorian procedure, and the new ideas so presented as to make them harmonise as far as possible with the old. All this was a training of no small value for those who, on their return to Rome, were to exercise an influence on legislation and the administration of the law. They brought back with them not merely an experience they could not have obtained at home, but sometimes a familiarity with foreign institutions that they were very willing to acclimatise in Italy. Roman law was thus enriched from her provinces, deriving from them her emphyteutic tenure of land, her hypothec, her Rhodian law of general average, and a variety of other features that were altogether novel. Some of them were sanctioned by tacit recognition, others by edicts of the prætors; but, in whatever way received, they were indirectly fruits of provincial conquest.

SECTION 46.—SPREAD OF LITERATURE AND PHILOSOPHY.

The effect on Roman civilisation of the addiction of educated men in the later republic to literature and philosophy is a matter for consideration in connection with Rome's general history. It is not proposed to consider here the question how far specific doctrines of Roman law bear the impress of the influence of the schools, especially that of the Stoics; it is a subject much too large to be disposed of in a few lines.[1] The matter is mentioned simply for the sake of noting that the spirit of critical inquiry, aroused and fostered by literary and philosophical study seriously and conscientiously undertaken, contributed greatly to promote a new departure in jurisprudence that became very marked in the time of Cicero,—the desire to subordinate form to substance, the word spoken to the will it was meant to manifest, the abstract rule to the individual case to which it was proposed to apply it. This was the first effort of what then was called equity to temper and keep within bounds the rigour of the *jus strictum*. The prætors, the judges, and the jurisconsults all had their share in it. Although modern jurists are prone to speak of prætorian equity as if it were a thing apart, yet the same spirit was leavening the law in all directions and in the hands of all who had to deal with it; the difference being that the form and publicity of the Edict gave to its applications by the prætors a more prominent and enduring record than was found in the decisions of private *judices* or the opinions of counselling jurisconsults.

[1] It is one that was discussed with much greater fervour a century ago than it is now. Of the later literature may be mentioned—Van Vollenhoven, *De exigua vi, quam philosophia graeca habuit in efformanda jurisprudentia romana*, Amsterdam, 1834; Ratjen, *Hat die Stoische Phil. bedeutenden Einfluss gehabt*, &c., Kiel, 1839; Voigt, *Jus nat.*, &c., vol. i. §§ 49-51; Laferrière, *De l'influence du Stoicisme sur la doctrine des jurisconsultes romains*, Paris, 1860; Hildenbrand, *Gesch. u. System d. Rechts- und Staatsphilosophie*, Leipsic, 1860, vol. i. §§ 141, 142. For the earlier literature, see Hildenbrand, *l.c.*, p. 593.

SECTION 47.—DECLINE OF RELIGION AND MORALS.

It would be equally out of place to enlarge here on the causes and manifestations of that decline in religious sentiment and public and private virtue which were fraught with such disastrous results in the later days of the republic. The private law was influenced by it to a considerable extent, alike in those branches of it which regulated the domestic relations and those which dealt with property and contract.

The ever-increasing disregard of the sanctity of the marriage tie is one of those features in the history of the period which strikes even the most unobservant. While from the first the law had denounced causeless separation and visited it with penalties, yet in principle it maintained the perfect freedom of divorce,—that it was improper to force persons to continue in the bonds of matrimony between whom matrimonial affection no longer existed. With the simple and frugal habits of the first five centuries of Rome and the surveillance of the *consilium domesticum*, the recognition of this principle produced no evil results; family misunderstandings were easily smoothed over, and divorces were of rare occurrence. But from the time of the enactment of the Mænian law in 586 [1] there seems to have been a change for the worse. It *inter alia* displaced the family council as a divorce court, and transferred its functions in that matter

[1] See Voigt, *Die Lex Maenia de dote* (Weimar, 1866), and criticism by Arndts in the *Z. f. RG.*, vol. vii. (1866), p. 1 *sq*. Gellius relates (iv. 3) that in 523—in another place he says 519, while Dion. Hal. and Valer. Max. say 520—Sp. Carvilius Ruga, with approval of the domestic council (xvii. 21, § 44), put away the wife he fondly loved because she was barren, and he consequently unable with a safe conscience to assure the censors that he had a wife who would bear him children. There seems to have been a difficulty about her dowry; for Gellius observes, on the authority of Servius Sulpicius, that thenceforth it was thought proper to have a dotal settlement providing for such a contingency. The Mænian law appears to have been, in part at least, a statutory regulation of the matter.

to a *judicium de moribus*,—a court of inquiry nominated by the prætor, and whose duty it was to decide to what extent there should be forfeiture of the nuptial provisions in case of separation or repudiation. The motives of the statute may have been of the best, but its tendency was injurious; for not only did it indirectly facilitate divorce, but it rendered the idea of it familiar, and overthrew that respect for the domestic council which had hitherto been a check upon it.

This looseness of the marriage bond, as was naturally to be expected, had its effect on the other family relations. The obligation of a father to provide for his children began to be lightly esteemed. The law—possibly only the interpretation put upon the *uti legassit* of the XII Tables—had empowered him testamentarily to disinherit them, or in instituting them to limit their right to a mere fraction of the inheritance (p. 171); but it was assumed that this power would be exercised with discretion and only when justified by circumstances. But in the latter days of the republic, amid the slackened ties of domestic life, paternal as well as conjugal duty seems to have often been lost sight of, and children disinherited, or cut off with a nominal share of the inheritance, in order that a stranger might be enriched. This led to the introduction by the centumviral court, without any legislative enactment or prætor's edict to warrant it, of what was called the *querela inofficiosi testamenti*,—challenge of a testament by a child whose natural claims had been capriciously and causelessly disregarded.[2] While

[2] The mention by Cicero (*In Verr. II.*, i. 42, § 107) of a "testamentum non improbum, non inofficiosum, non inhumanum," has led most writers to the conclusion that the remedy in question was already known in his time, although there are some who postpone it to the Augustine period. Valerius Maximus, however, refers to it (vii. 7, 4) in connection with Calpurnius Piso, the urban prætor, whom Drumann (*Gesch. Roms*, vol. ii. p. 92 *sq.*) takes to have been the same who held that office in the year of Verres's prosecution. It is extremely probable that the practice of the court in regard to it was at first irregular, perhaps spasmodic; and that, though commenced during the republic, it did not become settled until early in the empire.

the practice may for a time have been hesitating and uncertain, yet before long, through means of this *querela*, the rule came to be established that every child was entitled, notwithstanding the terms of his father's testament, to at least a fourth (*portio legitima, quarta legitima*, the legitim of the law of Scotland and various Continental countries)[3] of what would have come to him had his parent died intestate, unless it appeared that the latter had had adequate grounds for excluding him or limiting him to a smaller share.[4] A parent might in like manner challenge an undutiful testament made by his child to his prejudice; and in certain cases so might brothers and sisters *inter se*.

The decline of morals had an equally marked effect on the transactions of daily life, calling for precautions and remedies that had not been found requisite in the heyday of the πίστις τῶν 'Ρωμαίων. Men no longer cared to rely on each other's good faith unless backed by stipulations, cautions (*cautiones*), and guarantees of one sort and another. The Rutilian bankruptcy arrangements,[5] and the *actio Pauliana* for setting aside alienations in fraud of creditors,[6] indicate a laxity in mercantile dealings that was perhaps an inevitable consequence of the growth of trade and commerce. But that such remedies as, for example, the *exceptio rei venditae et traditae* or the *exceptio non numeratae pecuniae* should have been found necessary,—the one an answer to a vendor (with the price in his pocket) who attempted to dispossess his vendee simply because some of

[3] It was called *portio legitima*, statutory share, because the "fourth" was borrowed from the *Lex Falcidia* (*infra*, p. 288), which declared that every testamentary heir should be entitled to have that proportion of the succession free from bequests to legatees. Justinian (*Nov.* 18) raised the legitim to one-third in any case, and to one-half where more than four children had to participate (*infra*, p. 425).

[4] Justinian, by his 115th Novel, remodelled the details of the practice, fixing statutorily what should in future be regarded as sufficient grounds of disherison, and requiring them to be expressly narrated in the testament (*infra*, p. 424).

[5] Gai, iii. §§ 77-81.   [6] Cic., *Ad Att.*, i. 1, § 3 ; Just., *Inst.*, iv. 6, 6.

the formalities of conveyance had been neglected, the other an answer to an action on a bond for repayment of money that by some accident had never been advanced,—proves that the law had now to encounter fraud in all directions, and that *graeca fides* had to a great extent displaced the old Roman probity.

CHAPTER SECOND.

FACTORS OF THE LAW.

SECTION 48.—LEGISLATION.

IT cannot be said that during the period of nearly two centuries and a half embraced within the present chapter the private law owed much to legislation. The vast majority of the enactments of the time referred to by the historians dealt with constitutional questions, municipal and colonial government, agrarian arrangements, fiscal policy, sumptuary prohibitions, criminal and police regulations, and other matters that affected the public law rather than the private. Those of the latter class mentioned by Gaius and Ulpian in their institutional works barely exceed a score in number; and of these not above half a dozen can be said to have exercised a permanent influence on the principles (as distinguished from the details) of the law. Most of them were enactments of the *concilium plebis*[1] or of the comitia of the tribes, to which ordinary legislation had passed as more readily convened and more easily worked than the comitia of the centuries.[2]

---

[1] Gellius (x. 20, 9) observes that enactments that were strictly speaking *plebiscita* were nevertheless usually spoken of as *leges*.

[2] Among them may be mentioned the *Lex Aebutia* (*supra*, p. 244) that directly or indirectly introduced the formular procedure; a Cornelian law of 687, requiring the prætors to adhere to the law they had published in their edicts on accession to office; the *Lex Cincia de donis* of 550, which exercised a considerable influence on the law of donation, but was primarily enacted for a political purpose,—to restrain lavish gifts to public men and pleaders, as really often a vehicle of corruption; the Atilian and Julia-Titian laws, empowering magistrates in Italy and the provinces respectively to appoint

SECTION 49.—EDICTS OF THE MAGISTRATES.[1]

The practice of propounding edicts was very ancient, and had been followed by kings and consuls long before the institution of the prætorship. It was one of the most obvious ways of exercising the *imperium* with which the supreme magistrate was invested,—to lay an injunction upon a citizen and enforce his obedience, or to confer upon him some advantage and maintain him in its enjoyment. It was one of the ways in which public order was protected where there had been no invasion of what the law regarded as a right, and where, consequently, there was no remedy by action. That the earlier edicts of the prætors were of this character—issued, that is to say, with reference to particular cases, and what afterwards came to be called *edicta repentina* or *prout res incidit posita*—there is little reason to doubt. In time a new class of edicts appeared which got the name of *edicta perpetua* (or *perpetuae jurisdictionis causa proposita*),—announcements by the prætor, published

tutors to pupils and grown women, failing testamentary appointees and tutors-at-law; the *Lex Plaetoria*, for the protection of minors beyond the age of pupillarity; the *Lex Atinia*, prohibiting the usucapion of stolen goods even by innocent third parties; the *Lex Aquilia* of 467, giving a remedy for culpable damage to property; the Apuleian, Furian, Cicereian, and Cornelian laws for alleviating the position of sureties; the *Lex Voconia* of 585, imposing disabilities upon women in the matter of succession, and forbidding legatees to take more than a certain amount under a testament; and the Falcidian law of 714, empowering a testamentary heir to retain one-fourth of the inheritance even though more than three-fourths had been given away in legacies. In Rudorff (*Röm. RG.*, vol. i. §§ 10-44) will be found a classified and descriptive list of all the *leges* and *plebiscita* mentioned either in law-books or elsewhere, including those of the early empire. The *Index Legum*, in the third part of Orelli's *Onomasticon Tullianum*, contains an account of those mentioned in Cicero, Livy, Vell. Paterculus, and Aul. Gellius. There is also a classified list, with references to the books in which fuller accounts may be found, in Rivier, *Introd.*, §§ 40-49.

[1] See Lenel, *Beiträge zur Kunde des praetorischen Edicts* (Stuttgart, 1878), and the introductory chapters in his great book, *Das Edictum Perpetuum* (Leipsic, 1883); Karlowa, *Röm. RG.*, § 60. The attempts made from time to time to reconstruct the Edict are referred to *infra*, § 58, in connection with the Julian consolidation.

on his album (as the white boards displayed for the purpose in the forum were called), of the relief he would be prepared to grant on the application of any one alleging that the state of facts contemplated had arisen. The conjecture lies near at hand that this may have been done in the first instance by some prætor who had experience of frequently recurring applications similar in nature and purpose; and who, judging that the remedy he offered was needed and appreciated, thought it wise to certiorate the lieges generally of his readiness to grant it. The next year's prætor was free to adopt the edicts of his predecessor or not; but it was usual for him to do so if they had been found beneficial in practice, he adding to them new provisions suggested by demands made upon past prætors for *edicta repentina* (which they had not seen fit to generalise), or even proposing for acceptance some remedy entirely of his own devising. As each new prætor entered upon office he announced his jurisdictional programme,—his *lex annua*, as it was called from this particular point of view;[2] by far the greater part of it *tralaticium*, *i.e.*, transmitted from his predecessors, and only a few paragraphs, diminishing in number as time progressed, representing his own contribution. And so it went on in the first years of the empire, until the prætorian function was eclipsed by the imperial; and at last, after having, by instruction of Hadrian, been subjected to revision, and consolidated with the edicts of the peregrin prætors and provincial governors, it was sanctioned as statute law for the empire through the medium of a senatusconsult (p. 308).

There is some reason for supposing that the Edict attained considerable proportions in the time of Cicero; for he mentions that, whereas in his youth the XII Tables had been taught to the boys in school, in his later years these were neglected, and young men directed instead to the prætor's

[2] Cic., *In Verr. II.*, i. 42, § 109.

edicts for their first lessons in law.³ Of a few of them the date and authorship are known with tolerable precision; but of the history of the majority, including some of the most important, such as those introducing *restitutio in integrum* on the ground of lesion through error, absence, minority, and the like, and those revolutionising the law of succession, we are to a great extent in the dark. It is not necessary to assume either that the Julian consolidation exhibits all the provisions that from first to last appeared on the album, or that those preserved in it were originally in the shape in which they are there presented. It is much more likely that we have in it only those that had stood the test of generations, and that many of them are the result of the combined wisdom and experience of a series of prætors. It was one of the great advantages the edicts had over legislative enactments that they might be dropped, resumed, or amended by a new prætor according to his judgment of public requirements. For the Edict was *viva vox juris civilis*,⁴ —intended to aid, supplement, and correct it in accordance with the ever-changing estimate of public necessities;⁵ and this would have been impossible had its provisions from the first been as stereotyped as they became by its consolidation in the time of Hadrian.

The Edict seems to have contained two parts; the first what may be called the edict or edicts proper, and the second an appendix of styles of actions, &c., whether derived from the *jus civile* or from the *jus praetorium*. The contents of the Edict proper were in detail very various, but all devoted to an exposition of the ways in which the prætor meant to

³ Cic., *De Leg.*, i. 5, § 15, ii. 23, § 59. Yet in a passage which he is supposed to have written before he had reached his twenty-fifth year (*De Invent.*, ii. 22, § 67) he speaks of some portions of the edict as having become fixed and certain on account of their long observance (*propter vetustatem*).

⁴ Marcian, in *Dig.*, i. 1, fr. 8.

⁵ "Quod praetores introduxerunt adjuvandi, vel supplendi, vel corrigendi juris civilis gratia, propter utilitatem publicam" (Papinian, in *Dig.*, i., 1, fr. 7, § 1).

explicate his jurisdiction during his year of office. They were not didactic or dogmatic formulations of law, but rather announcements or advertisements of what remedy he would grant in such and such circumstances, or direct orders to do or prohibitions against doing certain things. " I will hold it (an agreement) valid," "I will not sustain it," " I will give him an action," "I will give him an exception," "I will reinstate him in his former position," " I will ordain him to give security," " I will put him in possession of the estate he claims," "I will give him time to deliberate " (about acceptance of an inheritance), " I will require him either to deny the debt on oath or to pay it,"—these are examples of the operative words of edicts of the first class; while " He must restore it," " He must exhibit it," " He must not do it," "I forbid the employment of forcible means " (say to alter the state of possession), may be taken as examples of the second. A party claiming an action or whatever else it might be under any of them, did so not of right, as he would have done had his claim had a statutory or customary foundation, but of grace,—on the strength of the prætor's promise to grant him what he claimed [6] and make the grant effectual. That was why originally such an action had to be raised and concluded within the particular prætor's year of office; a rule which in time, by abuse, was converted into this somewhat different one,—that a purely prætorian action (*i.e.*, not originally of the *jus civile*) had to be raised within a year of the occurrence to which it referred.

As already observed, the prætors' edicts proceeded to a greater extent than the earlier legislation of the comitia upon lines of equity; that is to say, they set themselves against the strictness and formalism of the jurisprudence of the XII Tables. Such may be said to have been the general tendency of the prætorian edicts as a whole. But it was the tendency of

---

[6] Gaius frequently speaks of *bonorum possessiones* which *praetor pollicetur* or *promittit* (see ii. §§ 119, 135).

the whole jurisprudence of the time, and by no means peculiar to the prætorian creation. Nowhere in the texts are the prætors spoken of as the special mouthpieces of equity as distinguished from law. Such a distinction recurs frequently in Cicero; he identifies *aequitas* with the spirit of a law or agreement, and *jus* with its letter; but it is in order to sing the praises, not of the prætors, but of the pleaders who maintained the former as against the latter, and of the judges who were persuaded by their arguments. Much of what was contained in the Edict might quite as well have been embodied in statute, and we know that in time statute came to its aid; witness a very remarkable provision of it,—" I will give *bonorum possessio* as may be enjoined by statute, whether comitial enactment or senatusconsult."[7]

Of the edicts of the peregrin prætor and their relation to those of his urban colleague little is known. That they differed in some respects there can be no doubt; for in the *Lex Rubria* (of 706 ?) for settling the government of Cisalpine Gaul,[8] the magistrates were directed, with reference to a certain action, to formulate it in the way prescribed in the edict of the peregrin prætor. The latter, therefore, must to some extent have been in advance of that of the urban prætor; probably in this respect,—that, being prepared primarily for the regulation of questions affecting non-citizens, it more thoroughly than the other avoided formalities that were competent only to citizens, and thus to a greater extent simplified procedure. In the edict of the urban prætor there were provisions that could benefit none but citizens; for example, the Publician action introducing the tenure *in bonis* of *res mancipi*, which proceeded upon a fiction of completed usucapion, and therefore, even well into the empire, was not available to a peregrin. In that of the peregrin prætor, on the other hand, we are entitled to believe that such a remedy

[7] Ulp., *lib.* 49 *ad edict.*, in *Dig.*, xxxviii. 14, 1, pr.
[8] *Lex Rubria*, cap. 20 (Bruns, p. 92).

could have had no place, and that its provisions must have throughout been such as would apply indifferently to citizens and non-citizens. The edicts of the provincial governors must have varied according to circumstances; being in all cases composites of provisions, more or less numerous, borrowed from the edicts of the prætors, and additions suggested by the peculiar wants of the different provinces for which they were framed (*provinciale genus edicendi*). Among these may have been regulations for protection of quasi-property in land and quasi-real rights; for land in the provinces in theory belonged to the state, its occupants having no more than a transmissible and inheritable right of usufruct.[9] As for the edicts of the curule ædiles, who, amongst other duties, were charged with the supervision of markets, their range was very limited; their most important provisions having reference to open sales of slaves, horses, and cattle, and containing regulations about the duties of vendors exposing them, and their responsibility for faults and vices.[10]

SECTION 50.—CONSUETUDE, PROFESSIONAL JURISPRUDENCE, AND RES JUDICATAE.

Great as may be the difficulty experienced by philosophical jurists in defining the ground of the authority of consuetudinary law, there is no room to dispute the importance of its contributions to every system of jurisprudence, ancient or modern. The men who first drew, accepted, and endorsed a bill of exchange did as much for the law as any lawgiver has ever accomplished. They may or may not have acted on the advice of jurists; but, whether or not, they began a practice which grew into custom, and as such was recognised by the tribunals as a law-creating one,—one conferring rights and imposing obligations. There is much of this—

[9] Gai., ii. 7.
[10] See tit. *Dig.* " De aedilitio edicto et' redhibitione et quanti minoris " (xxi. 1), and tit. *Cod.* "De aedilitiis actionibus " (iv. 58).

far more probably than is commonly imagined—in the history of every system of law.

In Rome the process was sometimes wonderfully expeditious; witness what Justinian narrates of the introduction and recognition of testamentary trusts and codicils to last wills, both in the time of Augustus.[1] It can hardly be doubted that the literal contract *per expensilationem* (p. 275 *sq.*) originated in the same way, probably in the end of the fifth or beginning of the sixth century. The keeping of domestic account-books may have been enjoined and enforced by the censors; but it was custom, and neither statute nor prætor's edict, that made an entry in them to another person's debit creative of a claim against the latter for *certa pecunia credita*, that might be made effectual by an action under the Silian law (§ 40). It must have been in exactly the same way that *mutuum*, formless loan of money, came to be regarded as the third variety of *certa credita pecunia*, and to be held recoverable by the same sort of action. True, this could not have been attained without the co-operation of the courts. But then those courts were composed each of a single private citizen, whose office ended with his judgment in the particular case remitted to him, and who was untrammelled by the authority of any *series rerum judicatarum*.[2] He had simply to decide whether in his view expensilation or formless loan created such an obligation as was covered by the words *pecuniam dari oportere*. There may for a time have been a divergent practice, contradictory findings, as Cicero says there were in his day upon the question whether *aequitas* or *jus strictum* was to be applied to the determination of certain matters; but the gradual ascendency and

[1] Just., *Inst.*, ii. 23, 1, ii. 25, pr.
[2] It was not until the empire that a "series rerum perpetuo similiter judicatarum," a uniform series of precedents, was held to be law. During the republic a judge was much freer, and not only entitled but bound to decide according to his own notion of what was right, taking the risk of consequences if his judgment was knowingly contrary to law.

eventual unanimity of judicial opinion in the affirmative was but the expression of the general sentiment of the citizens of whom the *judices* were the representatives.

These are but examples of the way in which consuetudinary law was constructed. It required the combined action of the laity and the *judices*, both at times acting under professional advice. In some cases even that of the prætors was necessary. It would have been impossible, for instance, to have introduced the consensual contracts into the Roman system, and determined what were the obligations they imposed on either side, without magisterial co-operation in framing the *formulae* that were to be submitted to the judges. Taking the action on sale as an illustration, the formula substantially was this:—" It being averred that the defendant sold such or such a thing to the plaintiff, whatever, Judge, it shall appear that the defendant ought in good faith to give to or do for the plaintiff in respect thereof, in that (or rather its equivalent in money) condemn the defendant; otherwise, acquit him." It is very manifest that the free hand here given to the judge must immensely have facilitated the reception of customary doctrine into the law. The judge was to a great extent the spokesman of the forum; his judgment was formed in accordance with current public opinion, which he had ample opportunity of gauging; it was the reflection of that general sentiment of right, which, phrase it how we may, is the real basis of all customary law. And so in an action for establishing a right of property in a *res nec mancipi*. The formula was very simple:—" If it appear that such or such a thing belongs to the plaintiff in quiritary right, should the defendant refuse to restore it on your order, then, Judge, whatever be its value for the plaintiff, in that condemn the defendant; should it appear otherwise, acquit him." The primary duty of a judge on such a remit was to determine whether the title on which the plaintiff founded his pretensions gave him a right that came up to property; and it can hardly be disputed that it was by the decisions of a series of judges, in a series of such actions, that the long list of natural modes of acquiring property given by Justinian under technical names was gradually brought into view. Those decisions, whether upon the obligations of a vendor, direct or indirect, or upon the sufficiency of a title founded on by a party averring a right of property by natural acquisition, may in many cases have been arrived at under professional advice, and were in all cases embodied in judgments. But that does not in the least deprive the doctrine deduced from them of its character of customary law. It was not until the empire that the opinions of the jurists submitted to a judge (*responsa prudentium*, see § 59) were invested with quasi-legislative authority. During the republic, if a judge deferred to them, it was simply because he regarded them as in consonance with well-qualified public opinion; and what a series of consistent judgments *of this sort* built up was in the strictest sense a law based on consuetude.[3]

As regards the professional jurists in particular,[4] it has already (p. 75) been observed that, according to the testimony of the historians, the law was a monopoly of the patricians down at least to the middle of the fifth century of the city. Livy goes so far as to speak of it as *in penctralibus pontificum repositum*,—among the secrets of the pontifical college.[5] It undoubtedly was so to a very great extent in the regal period. But after the publication of the

---

[3] The doctrines of the classical jurists as to the necessity of *longa, inveterata consuetudo*, and so forth, had no application to the formative jurisprudence of the republic, and in fact refer not to general consuetude but to particular custom when founded on in derogation of the common law.

[4] Rudorff, *Röm. RG.*, vol. i. §§ 62-65; Sanio, *Zur Geschichte der Röm. Rechtswissenschaft*, Königsberg, 1858; Grellet-Dumazeau, *Études sur le barreau Romain*, 2d ed., Paris, 1858; Danz, *Gesch. d. Röm. Rechts*, vol. i. § 49; Karlowa, *Röm. RG.*, § 61.

[5] Liv., ix. 46, 5.

Twelve Tables, with the letter of the law displayed before the eyes of the citizens in black and white, those words of his were true only in a qualified sense. Pomponius explains that no sooner was the decemviral legislation published than the necessity was felt for its interpretation, and for the preparation by skilled hands of styles of actions whereby its provisions might be made effectual.[6] Both of those duties fell to the pontiffs as the only persons who, in the state of civilisation of the period, were qualified to give the assistance required; and Pomponius adds that the college annually appointed one of its members to be the adviser of private parties and of the *judices* in those matters. The *interpretatio*, commenced by the pontiffs and continued by the jurists during the republic, and which, Pomponius says, was regarded as part of the *jus civile*, was not confined to explanation of the words of the statute, but was in some cases their expansion, in others their limitation, and in many the deduction of new doctrines out of the actual *jus scriptum*, and their development and exposition.[7]

An event that did much to diminish the influence of the pontiffs in connection with the law was the divulgement in the year 450 by Cn. Flavius, secretary of Appius Claudius Cæcus, and probably at his instigation, of a formulary of actions and calendar of lawful and unlawful days, which got the name of *Jus Flavianum*.[8] The practice adopted in the beginning of the sixth century by Tiberius Coruncanius, the first plebeian chief pontiff, of giving advice in law in public,[9] had a still greater effect in popularising it; and the *Jus Aelianum*, some fifty years later, made it as much the heritage of the laity as of the pontifical college.[10] From this

---

[6] Pomp., in *Dig.*, i. 2, fr. 2, §§ 5, 6. On the functions of the pontiffs in settling styles of actions upon the Tables, see Bekker, *Aktionen*, vol. i. p. 63.
[7] For illustrations, see Voigt, *Jus. nat.*, &c., vol. iii. pp. 287-294.
[8] Liv., ix. 46; Gell., vii. 9; Pomp., *l.c.*, § 7.
[9] Cic., *De Orat.*, iii. 33, § 134; Pomp., *l.c.*, §§ 35, 38.
[10] This was a compilation by Sext. Ælius Pætus, consul 556, censor 560,

time onwards there was a series of jurists (*prudentes*), gradually increasing in number and eminence, of whom a list is given by Pomponius, and many of whom are signalised by Cicero, particularly in his *Orator* and *Brutus*.[11] They occupied themselves in giving advice to clients, teaching,[12] pleading at the bar, framing styles of contracts, testaments, and various other deeds of a legal character, or writing commentaries or shorter treatises on different branches of the law. Among them may be mentioned the two Catos,— M. Porcius Cato Censorius, who wrote some commentaries on the *jus civile*, and his son, M. Porcius Cato Licinianus, the author of a famous doctrine in the law of legacies known as the *regula Catoniana*;[13] M. Junius Brutus, who wrote seven books *de jure civili*; M. Manilius, whose styles of contracts of sale are celebrated by Cicero, Varro, and Gellius; the three Scævolas,[14]—Quintius Mucius, the augur, who in his old age gave Cicero and his friend Atticus their first lessons in law, Publius Mucius, his cousin, and, greatest of

containing the XII Tables, the *interpretatio* down to date, and styles adapted to the *legis actiones* (which, the Aebutian law notwithstanding, were still largely in use); it seems also to have borne the name of *Tripertita*, from its threefold contents. See Pomp., *l.c.*, §§ 7, 38; Voigt, *Ueber das Aelius- und Sabinus-System*, Leipsic, 1875.

[11] It is remarkable that Cicero himself is not mentioned by Pomponius except for his oratory (*l.c.*, § 43), which does not say much for the estimation in which he was held as a jurist by his successors of the empire. Yet Gellius (i. 22, § 7) says he was the author of a book on the scientific treatment of the law—*De jure civili in artem redigendo*, (on which see Dirksen, *Hinterlassene Schriften*, Leipsic, 1871, vol. i. p. 1 *sq.*)

[12] Until about the middle of the seventh century the instruction a young man got in law after leaving school seems usually to have been acquired by attending the daily consultations of patrons of repute, by whom a great gathering of *auditores* as well as clients was regarded as an honourable distinction (Cic., *Orator*, 42, § 143). But after that some of the jurists seem to have been in the regular practice of devoting part of their time to more direct teaching,— either *institutio* in the general princples of the law, or *instructio* in its details. Pomponius (*l.c.*, § 43) says of Servius Sulpicius that, while he heard (*audiit*) several lawyers of eminence—*i.e.*, attended their consultations, he was *instituted* by Lucilius Balbus and *instructed* by Aquilius Gallus.

[13] Tit. *Dig. de regula Catoniana*, xxxiv. 7.

[14] See Schneider, *Die drei Scaevola Ciceros*, Munich, 1871.

the three, Quintus Mucius, the son of Publius, who, Pomponius says, first wrote systematically on the *jus civile*, arranging it in eighteen books,[15] from which a few extracts are incorporated in Justinian's Digest; P. Rutilius Rufus, the author of the bankruptcy procedure described by Gaius;[16] P. Aquilius Gallus, who devised the *actio* and *exceptio de dolo*, and the Aquilian stipulation;[17] Servius Sulpicius Rufus, frequently mentioned by Gaius and Justinian, regarded by his contemporaries as the greatest jurist of his time, and after Cicero the greatest orator;[18] Aulus Ofilius, a scholar of Servius's, and intimate friend of Cæsar's, who wrote at some length on the prætor's edict;[19] Alfenus Varus, also a scholar of Servius's, whose works are largely quoted and cited in Justinian's Digest;[20] and C. Ælius Gallus, author of a treatise *De Verborum quae ad jus civile pertinent significatione*, which must have been very welcome when the Roman law was penetrating into provinces in which the Latin language was strange.[21]

[15] Pomp., *l.c.*, § 41.
[16] Gai., iii. 77-79.
[17] Cic., *De Off.*, iii. 14, § 60; *De nat. deor.*, iii. 30, § 74; Just., *Inst.*, iii. 29, 2.
[18] See Cic., *Brutus*, 40-42. Pomponius (*l.c.*, §§ 43, 44) says he was the author of nearly 180 books on different branches of the law, but only two very short ones on the Edict,—the first that were written on that subject.
[19] Pomp., *l.c.*, § 44. On his connection with Julius Cæsar's contemplated digest of the law, see Sanio, *Rechtshistorische Abhandl. u. Studien* (Königsberg, 1845), pp. 68-126.
[20] Many of the quotations and citations are from an epitome of the *Digesta* of Alfenus by Julius Paulus.
[21] On the writings of the jurists of the republic generally, see Sanio, *Zur Geschichte d. Röm. Rechtswissenschaft*, Königsberg, 1858; Roby, *Introduction*, chaps. vii. and viii.; Ferrini, *Fonti*, pp. 20 *sq.*

CHAPTER THIRD.

SUBSTANTIVE CHANGES IN THE LAW DURING THE PERIOD.

SECTION 51.—CITIZENS, LATINS, AND PEREGRINS.

As may be gathered from what has been said in preceding sections, the extension of the benefits of the law to non-citizens was one of the most prominent features of its progress during the latter half of the republic. Before the end of it the number of the citizens had been vastly augmented by the admission to the franchise of almost all the inhabitants of Italy. There were no longer any non-citizens who, as a class, enjoyed *conubium* and *commercium* with Rome, as the Latins and some others of her allies had done at an earlier period (p. 112). But there was now between citizenship and peregrinity an intermediate condition known as *latinitas* or *jus Latii*, which gave those who enjoyed it *commercium* but not *conubium*. It seems to have originated in connection with some of the Latin colonies, which, for political reasons, were not favoured to the full extent with the rights, public and private, previously enjoyed by the *nomen Latinum*. Some communities in Transpadan Gaul got this new *jus Latii* in 665, and retained it until they acquired full citizenship; certain Italian, and particularly Etruscan, municipia had it substituted for citizenship in 673; and Cæsar from time to time extended it to other communities in Transpadan Gaul, Spain, and Gallia Narbonnensis. By the end of the republic it had ceased to exist in Italy, but was pretty widely spread in the western provinces. One of the advantages it conferred on the inhabitants of municipia enjoying it (who still continued to be called *latini coloniarii*) was, that there were many ways in which, by their own act, they could attain the full dignity of Roman citizens. Non-latin peregrins could not do so; and they were in an inferior position to the *latini* in that they could take no part in a transaction with the copper and the scales, no matter for what purpose employed, nor be parties to a stipulation conceived in the solemn form of *sponsio*, or a literal contract in its strictest form. But these disadvantages were every day becoming of less and less moment; for the ordinary transactions of trade and commerce were being rapidly denuded of any peculiarities they had derived from the old *jus civile*, and remodelled in such a way as to make them available alike to citizen and non-citizen.

SECTION 52.—THE LAW OF PROPERTY AND THE PUBLICIAN EDICT.[1]

There were necessarily many changes during the period in the law both of property and minor real rights. A variety of natural grounds of ownership were recognised by the judges to whom the question was referred whether or not a *res nec mancipi* belonged to the party claiming it in a vindication. The favour shown to peregrins cannot have stopped short of allowing them a right of property at all events in movables, even though it may not have been *dominium ex jure Quiritium*.[2] Land in the provinces belonged to the state, its occupants having strictly no more than a right of

---

[1] See Ribéreau, *Théorie de l'in bonis habere ou de la propriété prétorienne*, Paris, 1867; Voigt, *Jus nat.*, &c., vol. iv. app. xxi. p. 470 *sq.*; Huschke, *Das Recht der Publicianischen Klage*, Stuttgart, 1874; Schulin (rev. Huschke), in *Krit. VJSchr.*, vol. xviii. (1876), p. 526 *sq.*; Lenel, *Beiträge*, p. 1 *sq.*; Appleton, "De la Publicienne et de l'utilis vindicatio," *Nouv. Rev. Hist.*, vol. ix. (1885), p. 481 *sq.*, vol. x. (1886), p. 276 *sq.*

[2] Arg. *Frag. Dositheï*, § 12, (in *Coll. libror. jur. antejust.*, vol. ii. p. 154).

usufruct or possession;[3] yet the tenure was popularly spoken of as *dominium*, and protected by what was called a vindication.[4] Usucapion was no longer the result of prolonged possession pure and simple (p. 145), but now subject to the condition that the usucapient had acquired in good faith on a sufficient title, though he had either unwittingly derived his right from one who was not owner or not in a position to alienate, or else had neglected the proper form of conveyance.[5] The list of prædial servitudes was greatly increased, as witness the enumeration in Cicero's list of the questions proper for the centumviral court;[6] and it was probably in the provinces, where the civil forms of constituting such rights were inapplicable, that the governors in their edicts first sanctioned their creation by pacts and stipulations,— agreements fortified with stipulatory penalties in the event of the granter or his heirs impeding the grantee or his successors in the exercise of the right conferred.[7] In the matter of real securities the *fiducia* (p. 141) was still extensively employed; but alongside it had been introduced the *pignus* or pledge,—informal delivery of a movable by or for a debtor to his creditor, to be held by the latter until the debt was paid, and the hypothec or mortgage by simple agreement

---

[3] Gai., ii. 7, 21. Under the empire certain favoured districts had a concession of what was called *jus Italicum*, which, *inter alia*, rendered immovables within them susceptible of *dominium ex jure Quiritium*, and of being acquired and transmitted by Roman modes of conveyance. On this subject see Savigny, *Verm. Schr.*, vol. i. p. 29 *sq.*; Beaudouin, in the *Nouv. Rev. Hist.*, vol. v. (1881), pp. 145 *sq.*, 592 *sq.*, vol. vi. (1882), p. 684 *sq.*; Heisterbergk, *Name u. Begriff d. Jus Italicum*, Tübingen, 1885.

[4] *Vat. Frag.*, 315, 316.

[5] There is no direct proof that this change took place during the republic; but it may be inferred from the requirements of the Publician action.

[6] Cic., *De Orat.*, i. 38, § 173.

[7] *Dig.*, xlv. 1, fr. 85, § 3. This mode of constituting a servitude looks as if it were the creation of nothing more than a personal obligation; but the resulting right was really regarded as a *jus in re*. The recognition of *usus et patientia* as a sufficient ground on which to maintain a servitude dates only from the second century of the empire, when the possibility was admitted of the quasi-tradition and quasi-possession of an incorporeal.

without possession,—imported from Greece and very alien to Roman first principles, but so manifestly convenient that, though originally limited to the conventional right of a landlord over the slaves, beasts, and implements of his farm tenant in security of the rent, it was soon extended to creditors generally, whatever the nature of their claims.

But the most important change in the law of property during the period was that effected by the Publician edict,[8] indirectly recognising the validity (1) of what Theophilus calls *dominium bonitarium* as an actual though inferior ownership of *res mancipi*, and (2) of what got the name of *bona fidei possessio* as a fictitious ownership of either *res mancipi* or *res nec mancipi*, valid against all the world except the true *dominus*. The accounts we possess of this edict are somewhat inconsistent and even contradictory; the explanation may be that it went through a process of amendment and expansion at the hands of successive prætors, and that eventually it may have had more than one section, without our always being able to say to which of them the criticism of a particular commentator is directed. But there is no doubt of its general tendency,—of the defects it was meant to correct and the way in which the correction was accomplished.

One of the defects was this,—that if a man had taken a transfer of a *res mancipi* from its rightful owner, but simply by tradition instead of mancipation or cession in court, he did not acquire *dominium ex jure Quiritium*, and the transferrer remained legally undivested. The result was that the latter was in law entitled to raise a *rei vindicatio* and oust the transferee, whose money he might have in his pocket; while if a third party had obtained possession of the thing, but

[8] There was a M. Publicius Malleolus prætor about 519, and a Q. Publicius prætor about 687. The latter was a colleague of Aquilius Gallus, who, Cicero says, invented the *formulae de dolo*. It is hardly credible that the Publician action should have preceded these by more than a century and a half. See Pernice, *Labeo*, vol. ii. p. 158, note 19.

in such a way as not to be amenable to an interdict, the transferee could have no effectual vindication against him, not being in a position to aver or prove *dominium ex jure Quiritium*. The first difficulty was overcome by the *exceptio rei venditae et traditae*, also a prætorian remedy, and probably older than the Publician;[9] to the transferrer's vindication on the strength of his unextinguished quiritary right, the transferee pleaded sale and delivery as an effectual prætorian defence. But when a third party was in possession, and the transferee by simple delivery had to take the initiative, the position was more complicated. Such third party might be in perfect good faith; he might even have acquired from the original transferrer, and fortified his acquisition with a formal conveyance. But that was no sufficient reason in equity why he should be allowed to defeat the prior right of the original transferee, who, if he had possessed for the requisite period of usucapion before the third party came upon the scene, would have cured the defect of the informal delivery and acquired an unassailable quiritary right. So the prætor announced in his edict that if a man came to him and represented that he had bought a *res mancipi* from its owner, and had had it delivered to him, but had lost possession within the period of usucapion, he (the prætor) would allow him a vindication embodying a fiction of usucapion, with which he might proceed either against the transferrer or any third party withholding the thing in question.

The instruction to the judge in such a case, instead of being in the simple and straightforward words—" If it appear that the thing in question belongs to the plaintiff in quiritarian right" (p. 260), ran thus: " Supposing the plaintiff to have possessed for the requisite period of usucapion the thing in question, which he says he bought and got

[9] It must have been older than the general *exceptio doli;* for if this had been in existence the special one would have been unnecessary.

delivery of,—if in that case it would appear to you that said thing belongs to the plaintiff in quiritary right," and so on.[10] The publication of such an edict and the formula of the action based upon it—which, though of prætorian origin, was in many respects dealt with as an *actio juris civilis* and just a variety of the *rei vindicatio*—had the same effect as if the legislature had directly enacted that in future delivery of a *res mancipi* in pursuance of a sale or other good cause[11] should straightway confer a right of ownership in it, even before usucapion had been completed. Till then, however, the transferee was not quiritary owner; the thing in question was only *in bonis*, " of his belongings;" the legal title, though a very empty one,—*nudum jus Quiritium*,[12]—remained in the transferrer;[13] it was only with the completion of the usucapion that it became the transferee's *pleno jure*.[14] The inevitable result of the recognition of this tenure *in bonis* was that mancipation came to be regarded in many cases as an unnecessary formality, and the marvel is that it continued to hold its ground at all. The explanation may be that it afforded a substratum for and gave force of law to the *leges nuncupatae* that accompanied the *negotium per aes et libram* (p. 139); and although many of these might quite well be thrown into the form of

---

[10] This is a free rendering of the formula as given by Gaius (iii. 46), in order to distinguish the matter of fiction from that which had to be established by proof,—the sale and delivery, the ownership of the seller, &c. It is noteworthy that Gaius says nothing of *bona fides* on the part of the plaintiff, although in his time it was undoubtedly required; from which Pernice (*Labeo*, vol. ii. p. 158 *sq.*) conjectures that it was not mentioned in the edict.

[11] While sale alone was mentioned in the edict, all other titles of ownership were brought within it by interpretation.

[12] Gai., i. 54, iii. 166.

[13] He ceased to have any beneficial interest in what he had transferred (Gai., ii. 88, iii. 166). But, under the rules of the early empire, it was only the quiritarian owner that could so effectually manumit a slave as to make him a citizen (Gai., i. 17; Ulp., i. 16); and it was he, and not the bonitarian manumitter, that became tutor of a non-citizen freedman who was a pupil, or a freedwoman of any age (Gai., i. 167; Ulp., xi. 19).

[14] Gai., ii. 41.

stipulations, yet there were others that it may have been thought safer to leave to take effect under the provisions of the earlier law.

The second case that was met by the Publician edict—whether as originally published or by an amendment of it cannot be determined—was that of the *bona fide* transferee of a thing by purchase or other sufficient title, who, having lost possession of it before usucapion, found to his cost that the transferrer had not been its owner, that no ownership therefore had been transmitted to him (the transferee), and that consequently he was not in a position to raise a vindication with its averment of *dominium ex jure Quiritium*.[15] As against the true owner, whose property had been disposed of by a stranger behind his back, there would have been no equity in giving him an action; but as against all the world except the true owner his "better right" was recognised by the prætor, who accorded to him also a vindication proceeding on a fiction of completed usucapion; for usucapion cured the defect of *his* title, just as it did that of the bonitarian owner. In this way the prætors introduced that *bonae fidei possessio* which was worked out with much skill by the jurists of the early empire, and which assumed very large proportions in the Justinianian law when the term of prescription had been greatly prolonged, and the difficulty of proving property (as distinguished from *bonae fidei* possession) consequently very much increased.

SECTION 53.—DEVELOPMENT OF THE LAW OF CONTRACT.[1]

It is impossible within reasonable limits in such a sketch as this to indicate a tithe of the amendments that were

---

[15] This case is the only one alluded to by Justinian (*Inst.*, iv. 6, 4). He had abolished the distinction between quiritarian and bonitarian property, and so it was unnecessary for him to mention the other.

[1] See Bekker, *Akt.*, vol. i. chaps. 5-8, and app. D, E, F, and vol. ii. chaps. 15, 16; Voigt, *Jus nat.*, &c., vol. iii. §§ 106-124, and vol. iv. app. xix., xxi.

272 DEVELOPMENT OF THE LAW OF OBLIGATION. [SECT. 53.

effected on the law of obligations during the period whose distinguishing features were the rise of a *jus gentium* and the construction of the prætor's edict. In every branch of it there was an advance not by steps but by strides; in that of obligations arising from contract, of those arising from delict, and of those arising from facts and circumstances, such as unjustifiable enrichment at another person's cost.[2] The law of suretyship, in its three forms of *sponsio*, *fidepromissio*, and *fidejussio*, received considerable attention, and formed the subject of a series of legislative enactments for limiting a surety's liability;[3] while that of agency, which was sparingly admitted in Rome, had a valuable contribution from the prætorian edict, in the recognition of a man's liability more or less qualified for the contractual debts of his *filiifamilias* and slaves, as also, and without qualification, for the debts properly contracted of persons, whether domestically subject to him or not, who were managing a business on his account, or whom he had placed in command of a ship belonging to him.[4] The development of the law in the matter of obligations generally was greatly facilitated by the prætorian simplification of procedure and introduction of new forms of actions; the instruction to a judge—" Whatever in respect thereof the defendant ought to give to or do for the plaintiff, in that condemn him," preceded by a statement of the cause of action, giving wide scope for the recognition of new sources of liability.

The origin of the verbal contract of stipulation[5] and its actionability under the Silian and Calpurnian laws have been treated of in previous sections (§§ 39–41). It was theoreti-

[2] Such obligations—usually imposing the duty of restitution of unjustifiable gains—filled a considerable space in the practice and doctrine of the period, and early gave rise to a variety of brocards, *e.g.*, " Nemo cum alterius damno lucrari debet," " Nemo damnum sentire debet per lucrum alterius," &c.
[3] See Gai., iii. §§ 118-127. [4] See Gai., iv. §§ 69-74.
[5] See the literature on Stipulation in § 39, note 1.

cally a formal contract, *i.e.*, creative of obligation on the strength of the formal question and answer interchanged by the parties, even though no substantial ground of debt might underlie it.[6] But in time it became the practice to introduce words—the single word *recte* was enough—excluding liability in case of malpractice (*clausula doli*); and finally even that became unnecessary when the prætors had introduced the general *exceptio doli*, pleadable as an equitable defence to any personal action. And it was essentially productive only of unilateral obligation, *i.e.*, the respondent in the interrogatory alone incurred liability; if mutual obligations were intended, it was necessary that each should promise for his own part, with the result that two contracts were executed which were perfectly independent. Originally the only words that could be employed were *spondes?* on the one side, *spondeo* on the other; and in this form the contract was *juris civilis* and competent only to citizens (and non-citizens enjoying *commercium?*).[7] In time the words *promittis? promitto*, came to be used alternatively. They were not new words in the law; for the expression *dicta et promissa* had long been familiar in reference to the assurances given by a party transferring a thing by mancipation.[8] They seem, eventually at least, to have been competent to peregrins as well as citizens; although that may not have been until the stipulation had become of daily use amongst

---

[6] *E.g.*, if A promised B (*spondes? spondeo*) a certain sum, B was entitled to action for it, although it might have been the price of a thing sold which B had not delivered. But as a stipulation might at all times be conditional or subject to a limitation of time, a purchaser in such a case as this could easily protect himself by making his promise conditional on delivery.

[7] It is said that this restriction of the *sponsio* to citizens must in time have been given up, as, though mentioned by Gaius (iii. §§ 93, 119, 179), it is not noticed by any of the later jurists. But Caracalla's extension of citizenship to all the free inhabitants of the empire is probably sufficient to explain the omission. A further peculiarity of the word *spondes* was that when used by a surety it did not bind his heir (Gai., iii. 120, iv. 113.

[8] See *supra*, p. 139. For the probable connection of the words with the *dextrae promissio* in an appeal to Fides, see *supra*, § 12, note 2.

S

the former in the still simpler phraseology *dabis? dabo, facies? faciam.*

Originally competent only for the creation of an obligation to pay a definite sum of money, and afterwards one for delivery of a specific thing other than money, the contract came in time, by the simplification of the words of interrogatory and response, the substitution of the condictions of the formular system for the *legis actiones* of the Silian and Calpurnian laws, and the introduction of the *actio ex stipulatu* to meet cases of indefinite promise, to be adaptable to any sort of unilateral engagement, whether initiated by it or only confirmed. No better illustration of its capabilities could be desired than the general stipulation formulated by Aquilius Gallus as the precursor of an equally general formal release by acceptilation : " Whatever on any ground you are, or will be, or ought to be bound to give to or do for me, now or at a future date; whatever I am or shall be in a position to claim from you by any sort of process ; whatever of mine you have, hold, or possess, or would be in possession of but for your fraud in parting with it,—of whatever may be the value of all these do you promise to pay me the amount in money ?"[9] It was of immense service too outside the ordinary range of contract in what were called necessary (in contradistinction to voluntary) stipulations. For example, if a man complained that the safety of his house was endangered by the ruinous condition of that of his neighbour, the latter was required under serious penalties to give his stipulatory undertaking that no damage should result; a tutor before entering on office had to give his *cautio* (as such a necessary stipulation was technically called) that his pupil's estate should not be diminished in his hands; an attorney appearing in a litigation could be required to give his *cautio* to the other side that his principal would ratify his procedure ; a usufructuary before entering on the enjoyment

[9] Just., *Inst.*, iii. 29, 2.

of his life-interest had in the same way to give security to the reversioner against waste, and so forth (p. 373).[10] In all directions advantage was taken of the stipulation to bind a man by formal contract either to do or refrain from doing what in many cases he might already be bound *ipso jure* to do or abstain from doing; and that because of the simplicity of the remedy—an action on his stipulation—that would lie against him in the event of his failure.

A second form of contract that came into use to a considerable extent in the latter half of the republic is what is commonly called the literal contract, or, as Gaius phrases it with greater accuracy, the *nomen transscripticium*.[11] Notwithstanding the prolific literature of which it has been the subject, it must be admitted that in many points our knowledge of it is incomplete and uncertain. The prevalent opinion, formed before the discovery of the Verona MS. had made known Gaius's description of it, and almost universally adhered to ever since, is that such contracts were created by entries in the account-books which the censors insisted that all citizens of any means should keep with scrupulous regularity. They are often alluded to by the lay writers; but the text principally relied on is what remains of Cicero's speech for the player Roscius. The latter had been sued by Fannius in an *actio certae creditae pecuniae* for 50,000 sesterces, with the usual one-third more by way of penalty.[12]

[10] See a variety of such stipulations, prætorian and judicial, in Just., *Inst.*, iii., tit. 18. Also *infra*, p. 372 *sq.*

[11] Literature: Savigny, "Ueber den Literalcontract der Römer" (originally 1816, with additions in 1849), in his *Verm. Schriften*, vol. i. p. 205 *sq.;* Keller, in Sell's *Jahrb. f. hist. u. dogm. Bearbeit. des Röm. Rechts*, vol. i. (1841), p. 93 *sq.;* Gneist, *Die formellen Verträge d. Röm. Rechts* (Berlin, 1845), p. 321 *sq.;* Heimbach, *Die Lehre vom Creditum* (Leipsic, 1849), p. 309 *sq.;* Pagenstecher, *De literar. obligatione*, &c., Heidelberg, 1851; Danz, *Gesch. d. Röm. Rechts*, vol. ii. p. 42 *sq.* (where there is a *résumé* of the earlier literature and principal theories); Gide, in *Rev. de Législat.*, vol. iii. (1873), p. 121 *sq.;* Buonamici, in *Arch. Giurid.*, vol. xvi. (1876), p. 3 *sq.;* Gide, *Études sur la Novation* (Paris, 1879), p. 185 *sq.;* Baron, *Die Condictionen* (Berlin, 1881), §§ 11, 12.

[12] Introduced by the Silian law with reference to the *legis actio per condic-*

Cicero's argument was that as *certa credita pecunia* could arise only from loan, stipulation, or expensilation (a popular name for literal contract), and neither of the two first was averred, the ground of action must have been the last. " But where," he proceeded, " is the evidence of it ? Fannius has produced his *adversaria* (journal, day-book, or memorandum-book), which are useless for such a purpose; but as for his *codices accepti et expensi* (records of receipt and expenditure), which might have been received as proof of debt due by Roscius, not a single entry has been posted in them for three years." On this, supplemented by various incidental remarks elsewhere, the conclusion has been formed that a citizen who made an entry in his *codex*—whether of the nature of a cash-book or a ledger is much disputed—to the debit of another, thereby made the latter his debtor for a sum recoverable by an *actio certae creditae pecuniae.*

Gaius in his description of the contract [13] does not mention the *codices;* but his account is not inconsistent with the notion that the entries (*nomina*) of which he speaks were made in them. He says that those entries were of two sorts, *nomina arcaria* and *nomina transscripticia*. The former were entries of advances in cash; and of them he observes that they did not create obligation, but only served as evidence of one already created by payment to and receipt of the money by the borrower. Of the latter he says there were two varieties,—the entry transcribed from thing to person, and that transcribed from one person to another; and that both of them were not probative merely but creative of obligation. The first was effected by a creditor (A) entering to the debit of his debtor (B) the liquidated amount of what the latter was already owing as the price of something purchased, the rent of a house leased, the value of work done, or the

---

tionem (supra, § 40), and continued by the praetors in the formular *actio certae creditae pecuniae* which was substituted for it (Gai, iv. 13).

[13] Gai., iii. 128–134.

like. The second was effected by A transcribing B's debt to the debit of a third party (C), hitherto a debtor of B's, and who consented to the transaction; A at the same time crediting B with the sum thus booked against C, and B in his books both crediting C with it (*acceptilatio*) and debiting A (*expensilatio*).

All this at first sight seems just a series of bookkeeping operations. But it was much more than that for the Roman citizens who first had recourse to it. There was a time when sale, and lease, and the like, so long as they stood on their own merits, created no obligation enforcible at law, however much they might be binding as a duty to Fides or (as moderns would say) in the forum of conscience; to found an action they required to be clothed in some form approved by the *jus civile*. The *nexum* (§ 31) may have been one of those forms, the vendee or tenant being fictitiously dealt with as borrower of the price or rent due under his purchase or lease; the stipulation was another, the obligation to pay the price or rent being made legally binding by its embodiment in formal question and answer. But stipulation was competent only between persons who were face to face (*inter praesentes*), whereas expensilation was competent also as between persons located at a distance from each other (*inter absentes*).[14] This

---

[14] Gai., iii. 138. Many jurists are of opinion that the booking of a debt arising out of an antecedent formless transaction created a literal obligation whether the debtor authorised it or not. But this is inconsistent with the idea of contract. Gaius says nothing about the assent required from the debtor. Theophilus, however, in his *Paraphr. Inst.*, iii. 2, 21,—the only professional account we have of the *literarum obligatio* except that of Gaius,—speaks of express authority given by him. Indeed he makes the *literarum obligatio* the act of the debtor himself; for he describes it as a writing at the request of the creditor, but under the hand of the debtor, whereby the latter bound himself afresh to pay a sum already due by him under a consensual, real, or verbal contract. It is quite possible that, under the empire and after the time of Gaius, such a document came to be spoken of as a *literarum obligatio;* but it does not follow that it was that of the republic and early empire, as to which the account of Gaius must be preferred. We may take from Theophilus, however, that the debtor had to be a consenting party. And it is not unreasonable to suppose that in early days, before sale, &c., were

of itself gave expensilation—which, originally at least, was as much a *negotium juris civilis* as the *sponsio*[15]—an advantage in some cases over stipulation. But it had also this further advantage, which was not affected by the subsequent recognition of the real and consensual contracts as productive of legal obligation on their own merits,—that it paved the way for subsequent transcription from one person to another. This latter must have been of infinite convenience in commerce, not only by enabling traders to dispense with a reserve of coin, but by obviating the risks attending the transit of money over long distances. It was this that led, as Theophilus says was the case, to the conversion even of stipulatory obligations into book-debts; it was not that thereby the creditor obtained a tighter hold over his debtor, but that an obligation was obtained from him which in a sense was negotiable and therefore more valuable.[16]

The evolution of the four purely consensual contracts— sale, location, partnership, and mandate—supplies matter for one of the most interesting chapters in the whole history of the law. They did not and could not all follow identically the same course; location ran most nearly parallel with sale; but partnership and mandate, from their nature, not only started at a different point from the other two, but reached the same goal with them—that of becoming productive of obligation simply on the strength of consent interchanged by the parties—by paths that were sometimes far apart. Nevertheless a sketch of the history of the rise of the independent contract of sale may be sufficient to indi-

actionable on their own merits, the thing sold would not be delivered, nor possession given of the house let, until authority to make the book-entry had been given.

[15] See Appendix, Note H.

[16] Delegation, the substitution by a debtor of a debtor of his own in his stead, was not necessarily associated with literal obligation; for it was quite common during the empire, after the practice of keeping household account-books had died out. But there is good reason for believing that originally it was always followed by relative entries in the books of all the parties.

cate generally some of the milestones that were successively passed by all four.[17]

Going back as far as history carries us, we meet with it under the names of *emptio* and *venditio;* but meaning no more than barter; for *emere* originally signified simply to take or acquire.[18] Sheep and cattle (*pecus*, hence *pecunia*) may for a time have been a very usual article of exchange on one side; and then came raw metal weighed in the scales. But it was still exchange; instant delivery of goods on one side against simultaneous delivery of so many pounds' weight of copper on the other. With the reforms of Servius Tullius came the distinction between *res mancipi* and *nec mancipi*, and with it a regulated mancipation for sale and conveyance of the former (§ 13). It was still barter; but along with it arose an obligation on the part of the transferrer of the *res mancipi* to warrant the transferee against eviction,—a warranty that was implied in the mancipation (p. 136). Whether this rule obtained from the first or was the growth of custom it is impossible to say; but it is in the highest degree probable that it was the XII Tables that fixed that the measure of the transferrer's liability to the transferee in the event of eviction should be double the amount of the price.[19] Equally impossible is it to say when the practice arose of embodying declarations, assurances, and so forth in the mancipation (*leges mancipii*), which were held binding on the strength of the *negotium juris civilis* in which they were clothed. They received statutory sanction

[17] The literature on the history of the contract of sale is profuse, but mostly scattered in periodicals, and much of it very fragmentary. It may be enough to refer to Bechmann, *Gesch. d. Kaufs im Röm. Recht*, Erlangen, 1876; three articles by Bréard, in the *Nouv. Rev. Hist.*, vol. vi. (1882), p. 180 *sq.*, vol. vii. (1883), p. 536 *sq.*, and vol. viii. (1884), p. 395 *sq.;* and Mommsen, "Die röm. Anfänge von Kauf u. Miethe," in the *Z. d. Sav. Stift.*, vol. vi. (1885), *R. A.*, p. 260 *sq.*

[18] Festus, v. *Redemptores* (Bruns, p. 286); Paul. Diac., vv. *Abemito* and *Emere* (Bruns, pp. 262, 267).

[19] Paul., *Sent.*, ii. 17, §§ 1, 3.

in the XII Tables, in the well-known words, "cum nexum faciet mancipiumque, uti lingua nuncupassit ita jus esto,"—substantially, "whatever shall by word of mouth be declared by the parties in the course of a transaction *per aes et libram* in definition of its terms shall be law as between them."

The substitution by the decemvirs of coined money that was to be counted for rough metal that had been weighed, converted the contribution on one side into price (*pretium*), as distinguished from article of purchase (*merx*) on the other; and sale thus became distinct from barter.[20] In contemplation of the separation of the mancipation and the price-paying, and the degeneration of the former into a merely imaginary sale,[21] they enacted that, mancipation notwithstanding, the property of what was sold should not pass to the purchaser until the price had been paid or security by sureties (*vades*)[22] given for it to the vendor; and it was probably by the interpretation of the pontiffs that this was added to the rule,—that until the price was paid no liability for eviction should attach to the tranferrer (or *auctor*). The reason of the provision in the XII Tables was that a vendor who, before receiving the price, had mancipated or delivered a thing sold by him, had no action to enforce payment of the former; and in such circumstances it was thought but right to give him the opportunity of getting back the thing itself by a real action. It might be, however, that the price had been paid, and yet the vendor refused to mancipate. It was long, apparently, before the purchaser could in such a case compel him to do so. But with the introduction of the *legis actio per condictionem* (§ 41) he (the purchaser) had undoubtedly the power to recover the money on the ground of the vendor's unjusti-

[20] Paul., in *Dig.*, xviii. 1, fr. 1, pr.
[21] *Imaginaria venditio* (Gai., i. 119).
[22] *Vadimonium*, as the engagement of *vades* was called, was one of the formal contracts of the XII Tables, but went out of use at a comparatively early date. See *supra*, p. 150, and Gellius, xvi. 10, 8.

fiable enrichment,—that the latter had got it for a consideration which had failed (*causa data causa non secuta*); and it is possible that before that he had a similar remedy *per judicis postulationem* (§ 35).

Down to this point, say the beginning of the sixth century, there were three several obligations consequent on sale of a *res mancipi*; but not one of them arose directly out of the sale itself, or could be enforced simply on the ground that it had taken place. The vendor was bound to support the purchaser in any action by a third party disputing his right, and to repay him the price twofold in the event of that third party's success; and he was bound, moreover, to make good to him any loss he had sustained through a deficiency of acreage he had guaranteed, non-existence of servitudes he had declared the lands enjoyed, existence of others from which he had stated they were free,[23] incapability of a slave for labour for which he was vouched fit, and so on. But these obligations were binding, not in virtue of the sale *per se*, but of the transaction *per aes et libram* superinduced upon it; and if the vendor had at any time to return the price on failure to mancipate what he had sold, it was not because he had committed a breach of contract, but because he had unjustly enriched himself at the purchaser's expense.

In sales of *res nec mancipi*, just as in those of *res mancipi*, a vendor who had been incautious enough to deliver his wares before he had been paid, or had got stipulatory security for the price, or had converted it into a book-debt, might recover them by a real action if payment was unduly delayed; while the purchaser who had paid in advance but failed to get delivery might also get back his money

[23] Cicero says (*De Off.*, iii. 16, § 65) that, though by the XII Tables it was enough if a vendor *per aes et libram* made good his positive assurances (*uti lingua nuncupassit ita jus esto*), the jurists held him responsible for reticence about burdens or defects he ought to have revealed, and liable in a *poena dupli* exactly as if he had guaranteed their non-existence.

from the vendor on the plea of unwarrantable enrichment. But as mancipation was unnecessary for carrying the property, —as some think, incompetent,—some other machinery had to be resorted to than that of the copper and the scales for imposing upon the vendor an obligation of warranty against eviction, defects, and so forth. It may be that, until trade began to assume considerable proportions, and when a transaction was between citizens, a purchaser was content to rely partly on the honesty of his vendor, partly on the latter's knowledge that he ran the risk of prosecution for theft if what he had sold belonged to another,[24] and partly on the maxim, common in all ages and climes, *caveat emptor*. When it was one between a citizen and a peregrin, a different set of rules may have come into play; for between them disputes were settled by recuperators (p. 223), whose decisions were arrived at very much on considerations of natural equity. It was the popularisation of the stipulation that facilitated a further advance, rendered all the more necessary by the expansion of intercourse with foreigners and the cessation of recuperation.

We read of a *satisdatio secundum mancipium*, a *stipulatio habere licere*, and a *stipulatio duplae*. The nature of the first is obscure; it seems to have been connected with mancipatory sales, and probably to have been the guarantee of a *sponsor* for the liabilities imposed upon the vendor by the transaction *per aes et libram* and the *verba nuncupata* that were covered by it. The stipulation *habere licere* occurs in Varro, in a collection of styles of sales of sheep, cattle, &c., some of which he says were abridgments of those of M. Manilius, who was consul in the year 605.[25] It was the guarantee of

---

[24] "In rebus mobilibus . . . qui alienam rem vendidit et tradidit furtum committit" (Gai., ii. 50).

[25] Varro, *De R. R.*, ii. 2, §§ 5, 6, ii. 5, § 11 (Bruns, p. 310). There are other styles in other parts of book ii. applicable to sales of swine, goats, donkeys, &c., which Bruns has not extracted; the two noted above refer to sales of sheep and oxen.

the vendor of a *res nec mancipi*, or even of a *res mancipi* sold without mancipation, that the purchaser should have peaceable enjoyment of what he had bought; it entitled him to reparation on eviction, measured not by any fixed standard but according to the loss he had sustained. It cannot have been introduced, therefore, until after the *lex Aebutia* and the formulation by the prætor of the *actio ex stipulatu* (p. 360). The idea of the *stipulatio duplae* may have been borrowed from the *duplum* incurred by a vendor on the eviction of a purchaser acquiring a thing by mancipation; for one of its earliest manifestations was in the edict of the curule ædiles (p. 258), who insisted on it from persons selling slaves,[26] probably because the dealers were for the most part foreigners, and therefore unable to complete their sales *per aes et libram*. Judging from Varro, it was a form of stipulation against eviction that in his time was used only in sales of slaves;[27] although he adds that by agreement of parties it might be limited to a *simplum*.

We learn from the same writer—what is also indicated in various passages of Plautus—that the vendor at the same time and in the body of the same stipulation guaranteed that the sheep or cattle he was selling were healthy and of a healthy stock and free from faults, and that the animals had not done any mischief for which their owner could be held liable in a noxal action; and similarly that a slave sold was healthy and not chargeable for any theft or other offence for which the purchaser might have to answer. If any of those guarantees turned out fallacious, the purchaser had an *actio ex stipulatu* against the vendor: " Whereas the plaintiff got from the defendant a stipulation that certain sheep he bought from him were healthy, &c. [repeating the words of guarantee], and that he, the plaintiff, should be free to hold them

[26] Ulp., in *Dig.*, xxi. 2, fr. 37, § 1.
[27] *De R. R.*, ii. 10, 5 (Bruns, p. 311), compared with his styles for sales of sheep and other animals.

(*habere licere*), whatever it shall appear that the defendant ought in respect thereof to give to or do for the plaintiff, in the value thereof, Judge, condemn him; otherwise, acquit him." It is an observation of Bekker's [28] that the *actio empti* in its original shape was just a simplification of the *actio ex stipulatu* on a vendor's guarantees; the stipulations to which allusion have been made had become such unfailing accompaniments of a sale as to be matters of legal presumption; the result being that the words "whereas the plaintiff *bought* from the defendant the sheep about which this action has arisen," were substituted in the *demonstratio* (as the introductory clause of the *formula* was called) for the detailed recital of what had been stipulated. Bekker justifies this by reference to the language of Varro,[29] who seems to include under the words *emptio venditio* not merely the agreement to buy and sell but also the stipulations that usually went with it.

The introduction of an *actio empti* in this shape, however, was far from the recognition of sale as a purely consensual contract. If the price was not paid at once, the purchaser gave his *promissio* for it, or got some one on whom the vendor placed more reliance to do so for him,[30] or else the vendor made a book-debt of it; and if it had to be sued for, it was in all those cases by a *condictio certi*, and not by an action on the sale. If the price was paid but the thing purchased not delivered, the only remedy open to the purchaser was to get back his money by the same condiction; unless, indeed, the guarantee *habere licere* was held to cover delivery, in which case the purchaser might obtain damages in an *actio ex stipulatu* under the name of *actio empti*. But this *actio empti*, whether insisted in on the ground of non-delivery, eviction, or breach of some other warranty, was really an action on the verbal contracts that had accompanied the sale,

[28] Bekker, *Aktionen*, vol. i. p. 158.   [29] See Bekker, *l.c.*, p. 157, note 72.
[30] Varro, ii. 2, § 5.

—a *stricti juris* action, in which the judge could not travel beyond the letter of the engagements of the purchaser. In the latter years of the republic, and probably from the time of Q. Mucius Scævola,[31] it was a *bonae fidei* action. How had the change come about? A single case of hardship may have been sufficient to induce it, such as the defeat of a claim for damages for eviction on the ground that the stipulatory guarantee had been accidentally overlooked. Says Ulpian,—" As the *stipulatio duplae* is a thing of universal observance, action on the ground of eviction will lie *ex empto* if perchance the vendor of a slave have failed to give his stipulatory guarantee; for everything that is of general custom and practice ought to be in view of the judge in a *bonae fidei judicium*."[32]

Very little was required to convert the *stricti juris actio empti*, really nothing more than an *actio ex stipulatu*, into a *bonae fidei* one,—simply the addition by the prætor of the words "on considerations of good faith" (*ex fide bona*) to the "whatever the defendant ought to give to or do for the plaintiff."[33] The effect, however, was immeasurable. Not that it did away with the practice of stipulatory guarantees; for Varro wrote after the time of Q. Mucius (who speaks of the action on sale as a *bonae fidei* one),[34] and references to them are abundant in the pages of the classical jurists.[35] But it rendered them in law unnecessary. It made sale a purely consensual contract, in which, in virtue of the simple agreement to buy and sell, all the obligations on either side that usually attended it were held embodied without express formulation or, still less, stipulatory or literal engagement.

[31] Cic., *De Off.*, iii. 17, § 70.
[32] Ulp., *lib.* 1. *ad ed. aedil.*, in *Dig.*, xxi. 1, fr. 31, § 20.
[33] Gai, iv. 47.   [34] See *supra*, note 30.
[35] Indeed one of the purposes for which a *bonae fidei actio empti* was sometimes employed was to compel a vendor to give a *stipulatio duplae* or *simplae* when it had by oversight been omitted, and the purchaser conceived it might be of service to him.

And in instructing the judges to decide in every case between buyer and seller suing *ex empto* or *ex vendito* on principles of good faith, it really empowered them to go far beyond "general custom and practice," and to take cognisance of everything that in fairness and equity and common sense ought to influence their judgment, so as to enable them freely to do justice between the parties in any and every question that might directly or indirectly arise out of their relation as seller and buyer.

The history of the four real contracts—*mutuum* (*i.e.*, loan of money or other things returnable generically), commodate (*i.e.*, loan of things that had to be returned specifically), deposit, and pledge—is more obscure than that of the consensual ones.[36] Down to the time of the Poetilian law, loan of money, corn, &c., was usually contracted *per aes et libram* (§ 31); and it is probable that atter the abolition of the *nexum* the obligation on a borrower to repay the money or corn advanced to him was made actionable, under the Silian and Calpurnian laws respectively, by a stipulation contemporaneous with the loan (§§ 39, 40). With the rise of the *jus gentium* loan became actionable on its own merits,—that is to say, the advance and receipt of money as a loan of itself laid the borrower under obligation to repay it, even though no stipulatory engagement had intervened; the *res* —in this case the giving and receiving *mutui causa*—completed the contract. The obligation that arose from it was purely unilateral, and enforcible, where the loan was of money, by the same action as stipulation and literal contract; and so strictly was it construed, that interest on the loan was not claimable along with it, the *res* given and received being the full measure of the obligation of repay-

---

[36] See Heimbach (as in note 11), pp. 498 *sq.*, 633 *sq.*; Bekker, *Loci Plautini de rebus creditis*, Greifswald, 1861; Demelius, in the *Z. f. RG.*, vol. ii. (1863), p. 217 *sq.*; Bekker, *Aktionen*, vol. i. p. 306 *sq.*; Ubbelohde, *Zur Gesch. d. benannten Realcontracte*, Marburg, 1870; Huschke, *Die Lehre vom Darlehn*, Leipsic, 1882.

ment.[37] The other three—commodate, deposit, and pledge—became independent real contracts very much later than *mutuum*, possibly not all at the same time, and none of them apparently until very late in the republic. All of them, of course, had been long known as transactions of daily life; the difficulty is to say when they first became actionable, and under what guise.

It is impossible here to criticise the various theories entertained of their vicissitudes, and which necessarily vary to some extent in regard to each. All that can be said is that eventually, and within the period now under consideration, they came to be recognised as independent real contracts, the *res* by which they were completed being the delivery of a thing by one person to another for a particular purpose, on the understanding that it was to be returned when that purpose was served. And this is to be noted,—that while *mutuum* transferred the property of the money lent, the borrower being bound to return not the identical coins but only an equal amount, in pledge it was only the possession that passed, while in commodate and deposit the lender or depositor retained both property and (legal) possession, the borrower or depositary having nothing more than the natural detention. In all but *mutuum*, therefore, there was trust; the holder was bound, to an extent varying according to circumstances, to care for what he held as if it were his own, and entitled to be reimbursed for outlay on its maintenance; bound to return it, yet excused if his failure to do so was due to a cause for which in fairness he could not be held responsible. Consequently the actions on those three contracts, differing from that on *mutuum*, were all *bonɑ fidei*, the judge being vested with full discretion to determine what was fair and equitable in each individual case.

[37] If interest was bargained for the agreement had to be clothed in a stipulation, which was really an independent contract separately enforcible.

SECTION 54.—AMENDMENTS ON THE LAW OF SUCCESSION.

The most important change in the law of succession during the latter half of the republic was due to the prætors. Not that either legislation, the interpretation of the jurists, or the practice of the centumviral court left it untouched. Of examples of the action of the first we have the Voconian law of 585, really the work of M. Cato,[1] imposing disabilities upon women in the matter of succession, and limiting the amount which legatees could take under a testament;[2] the Furian testamentary law of 571, also restricting legacies to a certain maximum;[3] and the Falcidian law of 714, securing heirs in at least one-fourth of the inheritance, however much might be bequeathed to legatees.[4] Of the action of the jurists we have an example in the denial of the right of intestate succession as agnates to all women except sisters; a restriction which Paul says was put upon the words of the XII Tables from the same motive that induced the Voconian law (*Voconiana ratione*),[5] and probably about the same time. Of the influence of the centumviral court we have an example in the challenge it allowed to children of the testament of a parent who had causelessly disinherited them or left them only a mere trifle in his testament (p. 249); a challenge, however, which, as it took the form of a reflection on the parent's sanity, was not allowed if any other remedy, civil or prætorian, was available.

But these changes were insignificant compared with those effected by the edicts of the prætors. They introduced, under the technical name of *bonorum possessio*,[6] what was really

[1] Cic., *De Sen.*, 5, § 14.
[2] Gai., ii. 26. See Giraud, *Du vrai caractère de la loi Voconia*, Paris, 1841; Bachofen, *Die L. Voconia*, Basle, 1843; Mommsen (rev. Bachofen) in Richter's *Krit. Jahrb.*,vol. ix. (1845) p. 1 *sq.*; Vangerow, *De lege Voconia*, Heidelberg, 1863.
[3] Gai., ii. 225, iv. §§ 23, 24.
[4] Gai., ii. 225; Just., *Inst.*, ii. tit. 22.
[5] Paul., *Sent.*, iv. 8, § 20; see also Gai., iii. 14.
[6] For a *résumé* of the principal theories (down to 1870) about the origin of

beneficial enjoyment of the estate of a deceased person without the legal title of inheritance. There is much to lead to the conclusion that the series of provisions in regard to it which we find in the Julian consolidation of the Edict were not devised by any single brain, but were the work of a succession of prætors, some of them probably not under the republic but under the empire; and we have proof that some amendments of considerable value were engrafted upon the institution by imperial enactments after the Edict was finally closed.[7] It will be convenient, however, to give here a general view of the subject as a whole, disregarding the consideration that some of its features may not have been given to it within the period that is now more particularly under review.

Justinian, speaking of the origin of *bonorum possessio*, observes that, in promising it to a petitioner, the prætors were not always actuated by the same motives; in some cases their object was to facilitate the application of the rules of the *jus civile*, in some to amend their application according to what they believed to be the spirit of the XII Tables, in others, again, to set these aside as inequitable.[8] Although there is a lack of positive evidence, it is not unreasonable to assume that it was with the purpose of aiding the *jus civile* that the first step was taken in what gradually became a momentous reform; and it is extremely probable that this first step was the announcement by some prætor that, where there was dispute as to an inheritance, and a testament was presented to him bearing not fewer seals than were required by law, he would give possession

---

bonorum possessio, see Danz, *Gesch. d. R. R.*, vol. ii. § 176. Of the later literature it is enough to mention Leist, in *Leist-Glück*, vols. i.-iv., Marburg, 1870-79, and Sohm, in his *Inst. d. R. R.*, p. 330 *sq.*, (where a novel and ingenious explanation of the institution is suggested).

[7] See instances in Gai., ii. §§ 120, 126; *Dig.*, xxviii. 3, 12, pr.

[8] *Inst.*, iii. 9, pr. and § 1, (*confirmandi, emendandi, impugnandi veteris juris gratia*).

T

of the goods of the defunct to the heir named in it.[9] In this as it stands there is nothing but a regulation of possession of the *bona* of the inheritance pending the question of legal right. Just as between two parties contending about the ownership of a specific thing in a *rei vindicatio* the prætor first settled the question of interim possession, so did he promise to do here when a question was about to be raised about the right to an inheritance (*si de hereditate ambigitur*). It was a provisional arrangement merely, and very necessary in view of the state of the law which permitted a third party, apart from any pretence of title, to step-in and complete a *usucapio pro herede* by a year's possession of the effects of the inheritance (p. 179). Even at the time when the Edict was closed it was not necessarily more than a provisional grant; for if heirs-at-law of the deceased appeared and proved that, although the testament bore on the outside the requisite number of seals, yet in fact some solemnity of execution, such as the *familiae venditio* or *testamenti nuncupatio* (p. 169), had been omitted, the grantee had to yield up to them the possession that had been given him pending inquiry.[10] It was only by a rescript of Marcus Aurelius's that it was declared that a plea by the heir-at-law of the invalidity of a testament on the ground of defect of formalities of execution might be defeated by an *exceptio doli*;[11] on the principle that it was contrary to good faith to set aside the wishes of a testator on a technical objection that was purely formal. Thus was the *bonorum possessio secundum tabulas*, i.e., in accordance with a testament, from being originally one in aid of the *jus*

[9] Cic., *In Verr. II.*, i. 45, § 117. He says (writing in 684) that an edict to that effect was already *tralaticium* (*supra*, § 49), *i.e.*, had been adopted year after year by a series of prætors. Gaius (ii. 119) speaks of seven at least as the requisite number of seals ; *i.e.*, those of the *libripens* and the five citizen witnesses (*supra*, p. 170), and of the *antestatus*, whose functions are not well understood, but whose official designation appended to his seal recurs so regularly as to leave no doubt that his was the seventh.

[10] Gai., ii. 119.   [11] Gai., ii. 120.

civile, in course of time converted into one in contradiction of it.

That the motives and purposes of the series of prætors who built up the law of *bonorum possessio* must have varied in progress of years is obvious; and once the machinery had been invented, nothing was easier than to apply it to new ideas. The prætor could not make a man heir,—that he always disclaimed;[12] but he could give a man, whether heir or not, the substantial advantages of inheritance, and protect him in their enjoyment by prætorian remedies. He gave him possession of the goods of the deceased, with summary remedies for ingathering them, so that, once in his hands, they would become his in quiritarian right on the expiry of the period of usucapion;[13] and, by interpolation into the *formula* of a fiction of heirship, he gave him effectual personal actions against debtors of the deceased, rendering him liable in the same way to the deceased's creditors.[14]

Another variety of the *bonorum possessio* was that *contra tabulas*,—in opposition to the terms of a testament. If a testator had neither instituted nor expressly disinherited a son who was one of his *sui heredes*, then his testament was a nullity, and the child passed over had no need of a prætorian remedy. Where *sui heredes* other than sons were passed over, the *jus civile* allowed them to participate with the instituted heirs by a sort of accrual.[15] But the Edict went further; for if the institute was a stranger, *i.e.*, not brother or sister of the child passed over, then, on the petition of the latter, the prætor gave him and the other *sui* concurring with him possession of the whole estate of the deceased, the institute being left with nothing more than the empty name of heir.[16] Another application of the

[12] Gai., iii. 32; *Inst.*, iii. 9, 2.   [13] Gai., iii. §§ 34, 80, iv. 144.
[14] Gai., ii. 81, iv. 34; Ulp., xxviii. 12.   [15] Gai., ii. 124.
[16] Gai., ii. 125.

bonorum possessio contra tabulas was to the case of emancipated children of the testator's. By the *jus civile* he was not required to institute or disinherit them; for by their emancipation they had ceased to be *sui heredes*, and had lost that interest in the family estate which was put forward as the reason why they had to be mentioned in the testament of their *paterfamilias* (p. 171). The prætors—although probably not until the empire, and when the doctrines of the *jus naturale* were being more freely recognised (§ 55)— put them on the same footing as unemancipated children, requiring that they also should be either instituted or disinherited, and giving them *bonorum possessio* if they were not.[17] It was *bonorum possessio contra tabulas* in this sense, —that it displaced the instituted heirs either wholly or partially; wholly when the institutes were not children of the deceased, partially when they were. In the latter case, at least when *sui* were affected by it, the grant of *bonorum possessio* was under this very equitable condition,—that the grantees should collate or bring into partition all their own acquisitions since their emancipation.[18] But for it those acquisitions would have belonged to the testator, and would have been included in his succession; it was but right that, if they claimed to share in it as if they had not been emancipated, they should throw into it what in that case would have formed part of it.

The third variety of *bonorum possessio* was that granted *ab intestato*. As has been shown in a previous section (§ 32), the rules of the *jus civile* in reference to succession on intestacy were extremely strict and artificial. They admitted neither emancipated children nor agnates who had undergone *capitis deminutio*; they admitted no female agnate except a sister; if the nearest agnate or agnates declined, the right did not pass to those of the next degree; mere cognates,—kinsmen of the deceased who were not

[17] Ulp., xxviii. 2.   [18] Ulp., xxviii. 4.

agnates, *e.g.*, grandchildren or others related to him through females, and agnates *capite minuti*, were not admitted at all; while a widow had no share unless she had been *in manu* of the deceased and therefore *filiae loco*. All these matters the prætors amended, and so far paved the way for the revolution in the law of intestate succession which was accomplished by Justinian.

The classes they established were these: (1.) Displacing the *sui heredes* of the *jus civile*, they gave the first place to descendants (*liberi*), including in the term all those whom the deceased would have been bound either by the *jus civile* or the Edict to institute or disinherit had he made a will, namely, his widow, if she had been in *manu* at his death, sons and daughters of his body, whether *in potestate* at his death or emancipated, the representatives of sons that had predeceased him,[19] and adopted children in his *potestas* when he died.[20] (2.) On failure of *liberi* the right to petition for *bonorum possessio* opened to the nearest collateral agnates of the intestate, under their old name of *legitimi heredes*.[21] (3.) Under the *jus civile*, on failure of agnates (and of the *gens* where there was one), the succession was vacant and fell to the fisc, unless perchance it was usucapted by a stranger possessing *pro herede*. The frequency of such vacancies was much diminished by the recognition by the prætors of the right of cognates to claim *bonorum possessio* in the third place. Who they had primarily in view under the name of "cognates" it is impossible to say. The epithet is most frequently applied by modern writers to kinsmen related through females; but in its widest sense it included all kinsmen without exception, and in a more limited sense all kinsmen not entitled to claim as agnates. There were included amongst them therefore—although it is very pro-

[19] Children of daughters were not admitted in this class until the later empire, being regarded as members of the family of their paternal, not of their maternal, grandfather.

[20] Gai., iii. §§ 26, 63; Ulp., xxviii. §§ 7, 8.   [21] Ulp., xxviii. 7.

bable that the list was not made up at once, but from time to time by the action of a series of prætors—not merely kinsmen related through females (who were not agnates), but also agnates of a remoter degree who were excluded as such because the nearest agnates in existence had declined, persons who had been agnates but by reason of *capitis minutio* had lost that character, female agnates more distantly related than sisters, and children of the intestate's who at the time of his death were in an adoptive family.[22] All these took according to proximity. (4.) Finally, the claim passed to the survivor of husband and wife,[23] assuming always that their marriage had not involved *manus*.[24] This list constituted the prætorian order of succession on intestacy.

All those *bonorum possessiones* had to be formally petitioned for. In that *ab intestato* descendants were allowed a year for doing so, while other persons were limited to a hundred days; the period for those entitled in the second place beginning when that of those entitled in the first had expired, and so forth. The grant was always made at the risk of the petitioner; nothing was assured him by it; it might turn out real and substantial (*cum re*) or merely nominal (*sine re*), according as the grantee could or could not maintain it against the heir of the *jus civile*. For the latter was entitled to stand on his statutory or testamentary right, without applying for *bonorum possessio;* although in fact he often did so for the sake of the summary remedies it afforded him for ingathering the effects of the deceased.

[22] See Gai., iii. §§ 27–31 ; Ulp., xxviii. §§ 7, 9.   [23] Ulp., xxviii. 7.

[24] The provisions of the edict, as of the *jus civile*, in reference to the succession of a patron to his freedman necessarily differed in many respects from those explained above and in § 32. They were very complicated, but need not here be entered on.

PART IV.

THE JUS NATURALE AND MATURITY OF ROMAN JURISPRUDENCE.

The Empire until the Time of Diocletian.

PART IV.

THE JUS NATURALE AND MATURITY OF ROMAN JURISPRUDENCE.

The Empire until the Time of Diocletian.

CHAPTER FIRST.

CHARACTERISTICS AND FORMATIVE AGENCIES OF THE LAW DURING THE PERIOD.

SECTION 55.—CHARACTERISTICS GENERALLY AND RECOGNITION OF A "JUS NATURALE" IN PARTICULAR.

THE first three centuries of the Empire witnessed the perfection of Roman jurisprudence and the commencement of its decline. During that time the history of the law presents no such great landmarks as the enactment of the XII Tables, the commencement of a prætor's edict, the recognition of simple consent as creative of a contractual bond, or the introduction of a new form of judicial procedure; the establishment of a class of patented jurists speaking as the mouthpieces of the prince, and the admission of all the free subjects of the empire to the privileges of citizenship, are about the only isolated events to which one can point as productive of great and lasting results. There were, indeed, some radical changes in particular institutions, such as the caduciary legislation of Augustus, intended to raise the tone of domestic morality and increase fruitful marriages, and the legislation of the same emperor and his immediate successor for regulation of the status of enfranchised slaves; but these, although of vast importance in themselves, and the first of them influencing the current of the law for centuries, yet left upon it no permanent impression. It was by much less imposing efforts that it attained the perfection to which it reached under the sovereigns of the Severan house, —a steady advance on the lines already marked out in the latter years of the republic. The sphere of the *jus Quiritium* became more and more circumscribed, and one after another of the formalities of the *jus civile* was abandoned. The *manus* of the husband practically disappeared; the *patria potestas* of the father lost much of its significance, by the recognition notwithstanding it of the possibility of a separate and independent estate in the child; slaves might be enfranchised by informal manumission; *res mancipi* constantly passed by simple tradition, the right of the transferee being secured by the Publician action; servitudes and other real rights informally constituted were maintained as effectual *tuitione praetoris;* an heir's acceptance of a succession could be accomplished by any indication of his intention, without observance of the formal *cretio* of the earlier law; and many of the bargains incident to consensual contract, but varying their natural import, that used to be embodied in words of stipulation, came to be enforcible on the strength of formless contemporaneous agreements.

The preference accorded by jurists and judges to the *jus gentium* over the *jus civile* is insufficient to account for these and many other changes in the same direction, as well as for the ever-increasing tendency evinced to subordinate word and deed to the *voluntas* from which they arose. They are rather to be attributed to the striving on the part of many after a higher ideal, to which they gave the name of *jus naturale*.[1] It is sometimes said that the notion of a *jus*

[1] See Voigt, *Das Jus naturale . . . der Römer*, particularly vol. i. §§ 52-64, 89-96; Maine, *Ancient Law*, chap. iii.

naturale as distinct from the *jus gentium* was peculiar to Ulpian, and that it found no acceptance with the Roman jurists generally. But this is inaccurate. Justinian, indeed, has excerpted in the Digest, and put in the forefront of his Institutes,[2] a passage from an elementary work of Ulpian's, in which he speaks of a *jus naturae* that is common to man and the lower animals, and which is substantially instinct. This is a law of nature of which it is quite true that we find no other jurist taking account. But many of them refer again and again to the *jus naturale;* and Gaius is the only one (Justinian following him) that occasionally makes it synonymous with the *jus gentium*. There can be no question that the latter was much more largely imbued with precepts of natural law than was the *jus civile*, but it is impossible to say they were identical; it is enough to cite but one illustration, pointed out again and again in the texts,—that while the one admitted the legality of slavery the other denied it. While the *jus civile* studied the interests only of citizens, and the *jus gentium* those of freemen irrespective of nationality, the law of nature had theoretically a wider range and took all mankind within its purview. We are assured that the doctrine of the *jus gentium* agreed with that of the *jus civile* in holding that a slave was nothing but a chattel; yet we find the latter, when tinctured with the *jus naturale*, recognising many rights as competent to a slave, and even conceding that he might be debtor or creditor in a contract,[3] although his obligation or claim could be given effect to only indirectly, since he could neither sue nor be sued.

Voigt thus summarises the characteristics of this speculative Roman *jus naturale:*—(1) its potential universal applicability to all men, (2) among all peoples, and (3) in all ages; and (4) its correspondence with the innate convic-

[2] *Dig.*, i. 1, fr. 1, § 3 ; *Inst.*, i. 2, pr.
[3] Ulp., in *Dig.*, xliv. 7, fr. 14: " Servi . . . ex contractibus civiliter non obligantur ; sed naturaliter et obligantur et obligant."

tion of right (*innere Rechtsüberzeugung*).[4] Its propositions, as gathered from the pages of the jurists of the period, he formulates thus :—(1) recognition of the claims of blood (*sanguinis vel cognationis ratio*); (2) duty of faithfulness to engagements,—*is natura debet . . . cujus fidem secuti sumus;*[5] (3) apportionment of advantage and disadvantage, gain and loss, according to the standard of equity; (4) supremacy of the *voluntatis ratio* over the words or form in which the will is manifested.[6] It was regard for the first that, probably pretty early in the principate, led the prætors to place emancipated children on a footing of equality with unemancipated in the matter of succession, and to admit collateral kindred through females alongside those related through males; and that, in the reigns of Hadrian and Marcus Aurelius respectively, induced the senate to give a mother a preferred right of succession to her children, and *vice versa*. It was respect for the second that led to the recognition of the validity of what was called a natural obligation,—one that, because of some defect of form or something peculiar in the position of the parties, was ignored by the *jus civile* and incapable of being made the ground of an action for its enforcement, yet might be given effect to indirectly by other equitable remedies. Regard for the third was nothing new in the jurisprudence of the period; the republic had already admitted it as a principle that a man was not to be unjustifiably enriched at another's cost; the jurists of the empire, however, gave it a wider application than before, and used it as a key to the solution of many a difficult question in the domain of the law of contract. As for the fourth, it was one that had to be applied with delicacy; for the *voluntas* could not in equity be preferred to its manifestation to the prejudice of other parties who in good faith

[4] Voigt, *l.c.*, p. 304. [5] Paul., in *Dig.*, l. 17, fr. 84, § 1.
[6] Voigt, *l.c.*, pp. 321–323.

had acted upon the latter. We have many evidences of the skilful way in which the matter was handled; speculative opinion being held in check by considerations of individual interest and general utility.

A remark of Voigt's on the subject is well worthy of being kept in view,—that the risks which arose from the setting up of the precepts of a speculative *jus naturale*, as derogating from the rules of the *jus civile*, was greatly diminished through the position held by the jurists of the early empire. Their *jus respondendi* (§ 59) made them legislative organs of the state; so that, in introducing principles of the *jus naturale* or of *aequum et bonum*, they at the same moment positivised them and gave them the force of law. They were, he says, "philosophers in the sphere of law, searchers after the ultimate truth; but while they—usually in reference to a concrete case—sought out the truth and applied what they had found, they combined with the freedom and untrammeledness of speculation the life-freshness of practice and the power of assuring the operativeness of their abstract propositions."[7]

There is another phrase of frequent occurrence in the writings of some of the jurists of the period, to which Voigt devotes special attention. According to Gaius and Paul, everything has a nature of its own,—the aggregate of what characterise its essential destination and its special properties and peculiarities. There is a nature of man, a nature of animals, a nature of every individual thing, a nature of every sort of contract, action, and so on. In each and all of those "natures" an ordinative energy and determinative rule are observable. These are its *naturalis ratio*. The product of such *rationes* is the *lex naturae*; and the substance of the *lex naturae* constitutes a *jus naturale*. "The philosophy of law of Gaius and Paul begins with the *naturalis ratio*."[8]

[7] Voigt, *l.c.*, p. 341.   [8] Voigt, *l.c.*, pp. 270–274.

SECTION 56.—INFLUENCE OF CONSTITUTIONAL CHANGES.

The changes in the constitution aided not a little the current of the law. Men of foreign descent reached the throne and peopled the senate; proud indeed of the history and traditions of Rome, yet in most cases free from prejudice in favour of institutions that had nothing to recommend them but their antiquity. Military life had not the same attractions as during the republic; there was no longer a tribunate to which men of ambition might aspire; the comitia soon ceased to afford an outlet for public eloquence; so that men of education and position had all the more inducement to devote themselves to the conscientious study and regular practice of the law. This was greatly encouraged by the action of Augustus in creating a class of licensed or patented jurists, privileged to give answers to questions submitted to them by the judges, and that *ex auctoritate principis* (§ 59); and still more so, perhaps, by Hadrian's reorganisation of the imperial privy council, wherein a large proportion of the seats were assigned to jurists of distinction. With several of the emperors lawyers were amongst their most intimate and trusted friends. Again and again the office of prætorian prefect, the highest next the throne, was filled by them; Papinian, Ulpian, and Paul all held it in the reigns of Septimius Severus and Alexander. Jurisprudence, therefore, was not merely an honourable and lucrative profession under the new arrangements, but a passport to places of eminence in the state; and till the death of Alexander the ranks of the jurists never failed to be recruited by men of position and accomplishment.

SECTION 57.—LEGISLATION OF COMITIA AND SENATE.

Augustus, clinging as much as possible to the form of republican institutions, thought it expedient not to break with the old practice of submitting his legislative proposals to the vote of the comitia of the tribes. Some of them were far from insignificant. Besides various measures for the amendment of the criminal law, three sets of enactments of great importance owe their authorship to him, the first to improve domestic morality and encourage fruitful marriage, the second to abate the evils that had arisen from the too lavish admission of liberated slaves to the privileges of citizenship, and the third to regulate procedure in public prosecutions and private litigations.

The first set included the *L. Julia de adulteriis coercendis* of 736 (urgently demanded by reason of the prevailing licentiousness, and whose title explains its tendency),[1] and the *Lex Julia et Pappia Poppaea*. This enactment—a voluminous matrimonial code—for two or three centuries exercised such an influence as to be regarded as one of the sources of Roman law almost quite as much as the XII Tables or Julian's consolidated Edict.[2] It originated in the *Lex Julia de maritandis ordinibus*, which was approved by the senate in the year 726, but met with such violent opposition that it was not until 736 that it passed the comitia. Finding by experience that its provisions were insufficient to attain its purpose, Augustus in the year 757 (4 A.D.) introduced an amended edition of it, which he only succeeded in carrying by allowing a three years' grace, afterwards extended to five, before it should come into operation. That postponed it till 762 (9 A.D.), in which year a supplement to it was carried through by the consuls M. Papius and

---

[1] For an account of its provisions, see Rudorff, *Röm. RG.*, vol. i. p. 88 *sq.* It was the subject of numerous commentaries by the Antoninian and Severan jurists.

[2] Restitutions have been attempted amongst others by Jac. Gothofredus, in his *Fontes IV jur. civ.*, Geneva, 1638; Heineccius, *Ad l. Jul. et Pap. Popp. comm.*, Amsterdam, 1731; Den Tex and Van Hall, *Font. III jur. civ.*, Amsterdam, 1840. For a view of its provisions, see Rudorff, *Röm. RG.*, vol. i. p. 64 *sq.*; and for an account of the writings of the jurists upon it, Karlowa, *Röm. RG.*, vol. i. p. 618 *sq.*

Q. Poppæus. The composite enactment got the name of *Lex Julia et Papia Poppaea*, but was often spoken of under other and simpler names, most frequently *lex Julia* or *lex caducaria*. Its leading provisions were intended to prevent misalliances,—marriages between men of rank and women of low degree or immoral character,[3] concubinage, however, being expressly sanctioned; to force men and women of a certain age to marry and have children, by declaring unmarried persons incapable (under certain qualifications) of taking anything of what they were entitled to under a testament, and married but childless persons incapable of taking more than a half, the lapsed provisions (*caduca*) falling to those other persons named in the testament who had fulfilled the requirements of the statute, and, failing them, to the fisc; to reward fruitful marriages by relieving women who had borne a certain number of children from the tutory of their agnates or patrons, and conceding various other privileges alike to fathers and mothers of children born in wedlock; and to regulate divorce by requiring express and formal repudiation, and fixing statutorily the consequences of it so far as the interests of the parties in the nuptial provisions were concerned. However well intended, the language of Juvenal and others raises doubts whether the law did not really do more harm than good. By the Christian emperors many of its provisions were repealed, while others fell into disuse; and in the Justinianian books hardly a trace is left of its distinctive features.

The second set of enactments referred to above included the Aelia-Sentian law of the year 4 A.D., the Fufia-Caninian one of the year 8, and the Junia-Norban one of the year 19,[4] —the latter really passed in the reign of Tiberius, but pro-

[3] This part of the statute was repealed by the Emperor Justin, at the instance of his nephew Justinian, who found it a bar to his marriage with Theodora.

[4] There has recently been considerable controversy as to the date of the Junia-Norban law and its relation to the Aelia-Sentian. See Romanet du

bably planned by Augustus; they will be alluded to in a subsequent section (§ 66). The third set included the two *Leges Juliae judiciariae*, of which we know but little. That regulating procedure in private litigations is the same that is mentioned by Gaius as having completed the work of the Aebutian law (p. 244), in substituting the formular system for that *per legis actiones*.[5] It must have been a somewhat comprehensive statute, as a passage in the Vatican Fragments refers to a provision of its 27th section.[6] Our ignorance of its contents, therefore, beyond one or two trifling details, is the more to be regretted.

The Junia-Norban law was about the last effort of comitial legislation; for although there are frequent references to a *Lex Claudia*, abolishing the tutory-at-law of women, there is some reason for thinking that it was really a senatusconsult.[7] It is true likewise that there exist in the Capitoline Museum the remains of a *Lex de imperio Vespasiani* of the year 70 A.D.;[8] but its language shows that it too must have been a senatusconsult, although it may subsequently have received the formal assent of the lictors, as representatives of the old comitia of the curies, whose prerogative it was to bestow the *imperium*. There are also the

Caillaud, *De la date de la loi Junia Norbana*, Paris, 1882; Cantarelli, "I latini Juniani," in *Arch. Giurid.*, vol. xxix. (1882), p. 3 *sq.*, vol. xxx. (1883), p. 41 *sq.*; Schneider, "Die lex Junia Norbana," in *Z. d. Sav. Stift.*, vol. v., *R.A.*, (1884), p. 225 *sq.*; Labbé, in app. to the 12th ed. of Ortolan, *Histoire de la législation romaine* (Paris, 1884), p. 791 *sq.*; Cantarelli, " La data della legge Jun. Norbana," in *Arch. Giurid.*, vol. xxxiv. (1885), p. 38 *sq.*; Hölder, "Zur gegenseitigen Verhältnisse d. lex Ael. Sent. und Jun. Norb.," in *Z. d. Sav. Stift.*, vol. vi., *R.A.*, (1885), p. 205 *sq.*

[5] Gai., iv. 30.   [6] *Vat. Frag.*, 197.

[7] In the index to Haenel's *Corpus legum ab imperatorib. Roman. ante Justinianum latarum*, (Leipsic, 1857), no fewer than fourteen senatusconsults of Claudius's are mentioned; and the reason is not obvious why in this particular instance a *lex* should have been resorted to. It is noticeable that Gaius, speaking in i. § 84, of one of those enactments of Claudius's as a senatusconsult, refers to it again in § 86 as *eadem lex*.

[8] Printed in Bruns, p. 128 *sq.* It seems probable that it was the application to Vespasian of the *Lex regia*, from which Gaius (i. 6) and Justinian (*Inst.*, i. 2, 6) say that the emperors derived their legislative authority.

Lex Malacitana and the *Lex Salpensana*, charters granted by Domitian to the municipalities of Malaga and Salpesa;[9] monuments of great interest historically, but no more comitial enactments than the *Lex metalli Vipascensis*,[10]—a concession of the right to work certain lead mines in Portugal. Laws of this sort were *leges datae*,—not *leges latae*.

From the time of Tiberius onwards it was the senate that did the work of legislation, for the simple reason that the comitia were no longer fit for it.[11] And very active it seems to have been. This may have been due to some extent to the fact that so many professional jurists, aware from their practice of the points in which the law required amendment, possessed seats in the imperial council, where the drafts of the senatusconsults were prepared. It was the senatusconsults that were the principal statutory factors of what was called by both emperors and jurists the *jus novum*,—law that departed often very widely from the principles of the old *jus civile*, that was much more in accordance with those of the Edict, and that to a great extent might have been introduced through its means had not the authority of the praetors been overshadowed by that of the prince. In the end of the second and the beginning of the third century the latter's supremacy in the senate became rather too pronounced, men quoting the *oratio* in which he had submitted to it a project of law, instead of the resolution which gave it legislative sanction. No doubt it must have been carefully considered beforehand in the

[9] Considerable portions of them were discovered in the year 1851 near Malaga. They are printed in Bruns, pp. 130-141. They have been commented by Berlanga, Mommsen, Laboulaye, Arndts, Giraud, Van Lier, Van Swinderen, &c. See note of literature in Bruns, p. 130. The most important contribution is that of Mommsen, *Die Stadtrechte d. latin. Gemeinden Salpensa u. Malaca*, Leipsic, 1855.

[10] Found at Aljustrel, the ancient Vipascum, in 1876. Probably of the second half of the first century after Christ. Printed in Bruns, pp. 141-145. Literature on p. 142; to which may be added Berlanga, *Los Bronces de Lascuta, de Bonanza, y de Aljustrel*, Malaga, 1881-84.

[11] Pomponius, in fr. 2, § 9, *Dig. De origine juris* (i. 1).

imperial council, and rarely stood in need of further discussion; but the ignoring of the formal act that followed it tended unduly to emphasise the share borne in it by the sovereign, and made it all the easier for the emperors after Alexander Severus to dispense altogether with the time-honoured practice.[12]

SECTION 58.—THE CONSOLIDATED EDICTUM PERPETUUM.[1]

The edicts of the prætors, which had attained very considerable proportions before the fall of the republic, certainly received some additions in the early empire. But those magistrates did not long enjoy the same independence as of old; there was a greater *imperium* than theirs in the state, before which they hesitated to lay hands on the law with the boldness of their predecessors. They continued as before to publish annually at entry on office the edicts that had been handed down to them through generations; but their own additions were soon limited to mere amendments rendered necessary by the provisions of some senatusconsult that affected the *jus honorarium*. They ceased to be that *viva vox juris civilis* which they had been in the time of Cicero; the emperor, if any one, was now entitled to the epithet; the annual edict had lost its *raison d'être*. Hadrian was of opinion that the time had come for writing its " explicit," and giving it another and a more enduring and authoritative shape,—for so fashioning and so sanctioning it that it might be received as law, and not merely as edict, throughout the length and breadth of the empire. He accordingly commissioned Salvius Julianus, urban prætor at

---

[12] In form a senatusconsult had nothing of the imperative of a *lex* about it. The presiding consuls or emperor submitted their proposal in simple language (*senatum consoluerunt, verba fecerunt*), and the senate approved (*censuerunt*). See examples in Bruns, pp. 145-164.

[1] See Karlowa, *Röm. RG.*, vol. i. § 82.

the time (p. 318), to revise it, with a view to its approval by the senate as part of the statute law. The revised version, like the XII Tables, is unfortunately no longer extant. It is only a very slight account we have of the revision,—a line or two in Eutropius and Aurelius Victor, and a few lines in two of Justinian's prefaces to the Digest.[2] We may assume, from what is said there, that there were both abridgment and rearrangement of the edicts of the urban prætor; but the question remains how far Julian consolidated with them those of the peregrin prætor and other magistrates who had contributed to the *jus honorarium*. Those of the curule ædiles, we are told, were included; Justinian says that they formed the last part of Julian's work,[3] and may have been a sort of appendix. There is reason to believe that so much of the edicts of the provincial governors as differed from those of the prætors were also incorporated in it; for Gaius wrote a commentary on the provincial edict;[4] and this can hardly have been anything else than the Julian version, seeing that before it there was no general provincial edict, but only a number of particular ones.[5] That the edicts of the peregrin prætors, in so far as they contained available matter not embodied in those of their urban colleagues or the provincial governors, were dealt with in the same way, seems more than likely. The consolidation got the name of *Edictum Perpetuum* in a sense somewhat different from that formerly imputed to *edicta perpetua* as distinguished from *edicta repentina* (p. 253); and, after approval by Hadrian, seems to have been formally sanctioned by senatusconsult. It was thus a closed chapter so far as the prætors were concerned;

---

[2] Const. Δέδωκεν (in front of the Digest), § 18, and Const. "Tanta" (*Cod.*, i. 17, 2), § 18.

[3] Const. Δέδωκεν, § 5.

[4] See the Florentine index, in Mommsen's greater edition of the Digest, vol. i. p. liii*.

[5] Mommsen, in *Z. f. RG.*, vol. ix. (1870), p. 96.

for, though it may have continued for a time to hold its place on their album, with its formularies of actions, they had no longer any power to alter or make additions to it. It had ceased to be a mere efflux of their *imperium* and had become matter of statute; and its interpretation and amendment were no longer in their hands but in those of the emperor.[6]

The Julian Edict does not seem to have been divided into books, but only into rubricated titles;[7] and the general impression is that the formularies of actions were split up and distributed in their appropriate places. The arrangement is not difficult to discover by comparison of the various commentaries upon it, particularly those of Ulpian and Paul, which each contained over eighty books. First came a series of titles dealing with the foundations and first steps of all legal procedure,—jurisdiction, summons, intervention of attorneys or procurators, &c.; secondly, ordinary process in virtue of the magistrate's *jurisdictio;* thirdly, extraordinary process, originally in virtue of his *imperium;* fourthly, execution against judgment-debtors, bankrupts, &c.; fifthly, interdicts, exceptions, and prætorian stipulations; and lastly, the ædilian remedies.[8] From the quotations from the Julian Edict embodied in the fragments of the writings of the commentators preserved by Justinian,[9] repeated attempts have been made to reproduce it. Most of them are nothing more than literal transcripts or attempted reconstructions of passages in the Digest that are supposed to have been borrowed from it, and are of comparatively little value. The only

---

[6] Julian, in *Dig.*, i. 3, fr. 11.

[7] Several of them are mentioned in the excerpts from commentaries on the Edict preserved in the Digest.

[8] See Lenel (as in note 10), pp. 23-38. This generally is the order of the Digest and the Code, which Justinian (*Cod.*, i. 17, 1, § 5) instructed his commissioners to model after the Edict.

[9] It is possible that we have the greater part of Ulpian's commentary; for nearly one-fifth of the Digest is taken from it.

really scientific and worthily critical efforts are those of Rudorff in 1869 and Lenel in 1883.[10]

SECTION 59.—RESPONSES OF PATENTED COUNSEL.[1]

The account given by Pomponius of the origin of the *jus respondendi ex auctoritate principis* (the right of giving opinions in law under imperial authority) seems on the first view a little contradictory, and to leave it in doubt whether Augustus or Tiberius is entitled to the credit of its introduction. Giving advice to clients in public was no new thing; for Pomponius himself attributes the commencement of the practice to Tiberius Coruncanius in the beginning of the sixth century of the City, and speaks of Scipio Nasica having a house in the *via sacra* presented to him at the public cost for greater convenience in counselling. During the last two centuries of the republic it was a matter of ambition to a patron to have daily a great levée of clients; they increased his importance and augmented his influence. When, therefore, Pomponius says that Sabinus was the first that enjoyed the privilege of responding in public, having had it conceded to him by Tiberius, he may possibly mean that he was the first that had permission to open one of those *stationes jus publice respondentium* of which mention is made by Gellius, and where, from his account, both practical and speculative questions of law were freely discussed.[2]

[10] Rudorff, *De jurisdictione edictum: edicti perpetui quae reliqua sunt*, Leipsic, 1869, and rev. by Brinz in the *Krit. VJS.*, vol. xi. (1870), p. 471 *sq.*; Lenel, *Das Edictum Perpetuum: ein Versuch zu dessen Wiederherstellung*, Leipsic, 1883. The last gained the "Savigny Foundation Prize" offered by the Munich Academy in 1882 for the best restitution of the *formulae* of Julian's Edict, but goes far beyond the limited subject prescribed; see Brinz's full report upon it to the Academy in the *Z. d. Sav. Stift.*, vol. iv., *R.A.* (1883), p. 164 *sq.*

[1] See Pompon., in *Dig.*, i. 2, fr. 2, § 47; Gai., i. 7; Just., *Inst.*, i. 2, § 8; Machélard, *Observations sur les responsa prudentium*, Paris, 1871.

[2] Gell., xiii. 13, 1. See Bremer, *Rechtslehrer u. Rechtsschulen im Röm. Kaiserreich* (Berlin, 1868), pp. 8-15.

The right of responding under imperial authority, first granted by Augustus and continued by his successors down to the time of Alexander Severus, was something quite different, and did not imply publicity. Neither did it imply any curtailment of the right of unpatented jurists to give advice to any one who chose to consult them. What it did was to give an authoritative character to a response, so that the judge who had asked for it and to whom it was presented —for the judges were but private citizens, most of them unlearned in the law—was bound to adopt it as if it had emanated from the emperor himself. It may be that Augustus was actuated by a political motive,—that he was desirous by this concession to attach lawyers of eminence to the new régime, and prevent the recurrence of the evils experienced during the republic from the too great influence of patrons. But whatever may have prompted his action in the matter, its beneficial consequences for the law can hardly be overrated. For the quasi-legislative powers with which they were invested enabled the patented counsel to influence current doctrine not speculatively merely but positively (*jura condere*),[3] and to so leaven their interpretations of the *jus civile* and *jus honorarium* with suggestions of natural law as to give a new complexion to the system (§ 55).

Instead of giving his opinion, like the unlicensed jurist, by word of mouth, either at the request of the judge or at the instance of one of the parties, the patented counsel, who did not require to give his reasons,[4] reduced it to writing and sent it to the court under seal. Augustus does not seem to have contemplated the possibility of conflicting responses being tendered from two or more jurists equally privileged. It was an awkward predicament for a judge to be placed in. Hadrian solved the difficulty by declaring that in such a case a judge should be entitled to use his own discretion. That on receiving a response with

[3] Gaius and Justinian, as in note 1.   [4] Seneca, *Epist.*, xliv. 27.

which he was dissatisfied he could go on calling for others until he got one to his mind, and then pronounce judgment in accordance with it on the ground that there was difference of opinion, is extremely unlikely. The more probable explanation of Hadrian's rescript is this,—that the number of patented responding counsel was very limited; that a judge, if he desired their assistance, was required by this rescript to consult them all (*quorum omnium*, &c.); that if they were unanimous, but only then, their opinion had force of statute (*legis vicem optinet*); and that when they differed the judge must decide for himself.

SECTION 60.—CONSTITUTIONS OF THE EMPERORS.[1]

Gaius and Ulpian concur in holding that every imperial constitution, whether in the shape of rescript, decree, or edict, had the force of statute. It may be that by the time of Ulpian that was the prevailing opinion; but modern criticism is disposed to regard the *dictum* of Gaius, written in the time of Antoninus Pius, as coloured by his Asiatic notions, and not quite accurate so far as the edicts were concerned. As supreme magistrate the emperor had the same *jus edicendi* that kings, consuls, and prætors had had before him, and used it as they did to indicate some course of action he meant to adopt and follow, or some relief he proposed to grant. His range, of course, was much greater than that of the prætors had been; for his authority endured for life, and extended over the whole empire and every department of government. But originally, and in principle, his successor on the throne was no more bound to adopt any of his edicts than a prætor was to adopt those of his predecessors. That it was not unusual for an edict to be renewed,

[1] Gai., i. 5; Ulp. in *Dig.*, i. 4, fr. 1, § 1; Mommsen, *Röm. Staatsrecht*, vol. ii. p. 843 *sq.*; Wlassak, *Krit. Studien zur Theorie der Rechtsquellen im Zeitalter d. klass. Juristen*, Graz, 1884; A. Pernice (crit. Wlassak), in *Z. d. Sav. Stift.*, vol. vi., *R.A.* (1885), p. 293 *sq.*; Karlowa, *Röm. RG.*, vol. i. § 85.

and that it occasionally happened that the renewal was not by the immediate successor of its original author, is manifest from various passages in the texts.[2] Very frequently, when its utility had stood the test of years, it was transmuted into a senatusconsult;[3] this fact proves of itself that an edict *per se* had not the effect of statute. But just as, according to Cicero, a prætorian edict that had held its place on the album through a long series of years came to be regarded as consuetudinary law, so it may have been with the imperial edicts; their adoption by a succession of two or three sovereigns, whose reigns were of average duration, may have been held sufficient to give them the same character; and, by a not unnatural process, unreflecting public opinion may have come to impute force of statute to the edict itself rather than to the *longa consuetudo* that followed on it, thus paving the way for the assertion by the sovereigns of the later empire of an absolute right of legislation, and for the recognition of the *lex edictalis* (§ 74) as the only form of statute.

The imperial rescripts and decrees (*rescripta, decreta*) had force of law (*legis vicem habent*) from the earliest days of the empire, and their operation was never limited to the lifetime of the prince from whom they had proceeded. But they were not directly acts of legislation. In both the emperor theoretically did no more than authoritatively interpret existing law, although the boundary between interpretation and new law, sometimes difficult to define, was not always strictly

---

[2] *E.g., Dig.,* xvi. 1, fr. 2 : "Et primo quidem temporibus divi Augusti, mox deinde Claudii, edictis eorum erat interdictum, ne feminae pro viris suis intercederent;" which indicates that the edict of Augustus on the subject had not been adopted by Tiberius or Caligula, but first renewed by Claudius. From *Dig.,* xxxviii. 6, 26, it appears that an edict of Augustus's, forbidding a man to disinherit a son who was a soldier, dropped on his death and was not renewed by his successors. See another illustration in *Inst.,* ii. 12, pr.

[3] As happened to the edicts referred to in the first part of last note; they formed the substance of the Vellean senatusconsult, at the instance of the emperor Claudius. According to Tacitus (*Ann.,* iv. 16), the senatusconsult of Tiberius's declaring that confarreation should no longer place a wife in subjection to her husband (*infra,* p. 346) was the renewal of an edict of Augustus's.

adhered to.[4] The rescript was an answer by the emperor to a petition, either by an official or a private party, for an instruction as to how the law was to be applied to the facts set forth; it usually came from the provinces, where the services of the patented counsel were not readily obtained; and, when from a private party, was often only in anticipation of litigation, and for his guidance as to whether or not he should embark on it. When the answer was in a separate writing it was usually spoken of as an *epistula;* when noted at the foot of the application its technical name was *subscriptio* or *adnotatio.* The decree was the emperor's ruling in a case submitted to him judicially; it might be when it had been brought before him in the first instance *extra ordinem* (p. 368), or when it had been removed by *supplicatio* from an inferior court in its earliest stage, or when it came before him by appeal. It was as a judge that the emperor pronounced his decree; but, proceeding as it did from the fountain of authoritative interpretation, it had a value far beyond that of the judgment of an inferior court (which was law only as between the parties), and formed a precedent which governed all future cases involving the same question. Those decrees and rescripts constituted one of the most important sources of the law during the first three centuries and more of the empire, and were elaborated with the assistance of the most eminent jurists of the day, the rescripts being the special charge of the *magister libellorum.* From the time of the Gordians to that of the abdication of Diocletian they were almost the only direct channel of the law that remained (§ 64).

[4] As instances may be mentioned Hadrian's rescript (*epistula*) introducing the "benefit of division" amongst co-sureties (Just., *Inst.*, iii. 20, 4), and the decree of Marcus Aurelius (known ever after as the *decretum divi Marci*) repressing and punishing self-help (*Dig.*, xlviii. 7, fr. 7).

CHAPTER SECOND.

JURISPRUDENCE.

SECTION 61.—LABEO AND CAPITO, AND THE SCHOOLS OF
THE PROCULIANS AND SABINIANS.[1]

THE names of M. Antistius Labeo and Ateius Capito occur very frequently in conjunction. They were for a time rivals in political life, Capito attaching himself to the court party, while Labeo inclined to range himself in opposition to the régime of the nascent monarchy. Submission, if not subservience, to authority, and unquestioning acceptance of the new order of things, was the characteristic of the one; a stout but sometimes quixotic independence the characteristic of the other. The attempt has often been made to trace a parallel between their respective modes of thought in politics and jurisprudence. But we do not know enough of Capito as a jurist to enable us to speak with any certainty as to his opinions. He is rarely referred to in the texts; whereas Labeo's was the name of greatest authority from the time of Augustus down to that of Hadrian. From the remains of his writings preserved in the Digest, it is easy to

---

[1] Mascovius, *De sectis Sabinianor. et Proculianor.*, Leips., 1728; Van Eck, "De vita moribus et studiis Labeonis et Capitonis," in Oelrichs' *Novus Thesaurus dissert. jurid.*, vol. i., tom. 2, (Bremen, 1771), p. 821 *sq.*; Dirksen, "Ueber d. Schulen d. Röm. Juristen," in his *Beiträge zur Kunde d. Röm. Rechts*, (Leipsic, 1825), p. 1 *sq.*; Bremer, as in § 59, note 2; Pernice, *M. Antistius Labeo*, 2 vols., Halle, 1873, 1878; Kuntze, *Excurse über Röm. Recht*, (2d ed., Leipsic, 1880), pp. 318-331; Schanz, "Die Analogisten und Anomalisten im Röm. Recht," in *Philologus* for 1883, p. 309 *sq.*; Roby, *Introduction*, chap. ix.; Karlowa, *Röm. RG.*, pp. 662 *sq.*, 677 *sq.*

see—as, in fact, we are told by Pomponius and Aulus Gellius—that he was a man of great general culture, well versed in the history and antiquities of the law, an acute dialectician, and in philosophy imbued to some extent with the teaching of the Stoics. In his exposition of the law he was as independent as in his political opinions, criticising with freedom the doctrines even of those who had been his instructors in jurisprudence, and guided in his own judgments by constant reference to the origin of an institution or a rule, and the object it was intended to effect. One of the most celebrated of his writings was his *Libri πιθανῶν* (*Probabilium*), a theoretical treatise, which was epitomised and annotated by Paulus two centuries later. Another work, his *Libri Posteriorum*, a more practical treatise on various branches of the *jus civile*, was abridged by Javolenus, and seems to have been of considerable authority. Besides these, Labeo was the author of commentaries on the pontifical law, the XII Tables, and the Edicts of the urban and peregrin prætors, as well as of a collection of responses. The estimation in which he was held by the jurists of the classical period, *i.e.*, from Hadrian to Alexander Severus, is to be measured, not so much by the comparatively small bulk of the excerpts from his writings preserved in the Digest (and which are almost exclusively from his *Libri πιθανῶν* and *Posteriorum*), as by the frequency of the mention of him by other authors. It is nothing uncommon to find his opinions, and particularly his definitions of terms of law, referred to ten, fifteen, or even twenty times in the course of the same title.

Labeo and Capito are said to have been the founders of the two schools or sects—both phrases are used in the texts —of the Proculians and Sabinians;[2] but it is Nerva and Proculus that Gaius always speaks of as the early repre-

---

[2] Pompon., in *Dig.*, i. 2, fr. 2, §§ 47-52.

sentatives of the one, Sabinus and Cassius as the representatives of the other.[3] Bremer's view,[4] that the schools were two rival teaching halls—*stationes jus publice docentium*,[5] admits of a good deal of argument in its support; for we are expressly told that Nerva and Proculus were pupils of Labeo's, and Masurius Sabinus, Javolenus Priscus, and Julian are all mentioned as professors as well as practitioners. Bremer suggests that the schools may have taken their names from Proculus and Sabinus, because they were the first to found permanent halls in which they began to teach the doctrines they had respectively received from their masters, and which became a sort of tradition with their disciples. To the question, what were the essential doctrinal differences between them? there is no satisfactory reply. Karlowa propounds the opinion, and backs it with many quotations that seem fairly to support it, that the Proculians preferred to abide by the *jus civile*, while the Sabinians had a greater predilection for the *jus gentium* and the speculative doctrines of natural law. But it would be easy to glean from the records of their controversies in the pages of Gaius[6] (who professed himself a Sabinian) quite as

---

[3] The following, according to Pomponius, was the succession:—PROCULIANS—1. M. Antistius Labeo (*temp.* Aug. and Tib.); 2. M. Cocceius Nerva (consul 22 A.D.); 3. Sempron. Proculus (*temp.* Claudius, &c.); 4. Nerva the younger (prætor 65 A.D., father of the emperor Nerva); 5. Longinus (of whom nothing more is known than that he filled a prætorship); 6. Pegasus (*temp.* Vespasian); 7. Juventius Celsus (*temp.* Vespasian and Domitian); 8. Neratius Priscus (*temp.* Domitian, Nerva, Trajan); 9. Juventius Celsus the younger (Domitian to Hadrian). SABINIANS—1. M. Ateius Capito (consul 5 A.D., died 21 A.D.); 2. Masurius Sabinus (*temp.* Tiberius and Nero); 3. C. Cassius Longinus (Tiberius to Vespasian); 4. Cælius Sabinus (*temp.* Vespasian); 5. Javolenus Priscus (Domitian to Hadrian); 6. Aburius Valens (*temp.* Hadrian?); 7. Tuscianus (*temp.* Hadrian?); 8. Salvius Julianus (Hadrian and Antoninus Pius). These were the successive heads of the two schools, according to the narrative of Pomponius. To judge by their reputation in later years, they must have been of very unequal merit; for of some there is no further mention.

[4] Bremer, p. 68 *sq.* [5] Gell., xiii. 13, 1.

[6] Most of them will be found collected in Elvers's *Promptuarium Gaianum*, (Göttingen, 1824), under the heads "Auctores diversae scholae" and "Nostri

many texts that would support the very reverse. Karlowa's view is not very consistent either with the estimation in which Labeo was held by the jurists of two hundred years later as an independent thinker who had thrown new light upon many branches of the law, or with the fact that the *Libri III de jure civili* of Sabinus were regarded by those same jurists as the most authoritative repertory of it in existence,—brief, no doubt, but nevertheless the basis of several voluminous *commentarii ad Sabinum*.

SECTION 62.—JULIAN, GAIUS, AND THE ANTONINIAN JURISTS.

It is impossible in a work of the dimensions of the present to mention more than a few of the men who built up the law of Rome in the period under consideration.[1] Labeo and Sabinus were the most eminent of the Julian period; the Flavian produced none to equal them. Under Hadrian and the Antonines the most distinguished names are those of Salvius Julianus, Pomponius, Africanus, Gaius, and Q. Cervidius Scævola. The first, who, according to Pomponius,[2] was in his time at the head of the Sabinian school, was by birth an African, and maternal grandfather of the emperor Didius Julianus. Under Hadrian and Antoninus Pius he filled the offices of prætor, consul, and *praefectus urbi*, and for a long time was the leading spirit in the imperial council. It was to him that Hadrian entrusted the task of consolidating the Edict. That, however, was a small matter compared with the work to which he devoted

praeceptores." Many more, gleaned from other quarters, will be found in Mascovius, and a considerable selection of them in Roby, p. cxxxi. *sq*.

[1] Accounts of the jurists of the so-called classical period are abundant. See Rudorff, *Röm. RG.*, vol. i. §§ 66-78 ; Roby, *Introduction*, chaps. x.-xv.; Karlowa, *Röm. RG.*, vol. i. §§ 89-91 ; Ferrini, *Fonti*, pp. 55 *sq*. On their sequence, see Fitting, *Ueber das Alter d. Schriften d. Röm. Juristen von Hadrian bis Alexander*, Basle, 1860.

[2] See § 61, note 2. Buhl, *Salvius Julianus*, vol. i. (Heidelb., 1886), pp. 11-134.

the best part of his life,—his *Digesta*.³ Labeo had been a pioneer, but in this great body of law Julian shows himself well advanced towards the citadel. In ninety books, following so far much the same order in which he arranged the Edict, he deals with both civil and prætorian law, illustrating his doctrines with hypothetical cases and fresh and lively questions and answers. There is probably none in the whole catalogue of Roman jurists whose dicta are so frequently quoted by his successors and even by his contemporaries.

Sextus Pomponius was a contemporary of Julian's, but survived him. His literary career, like Julian's and Gaius's, was prolonged, beginning in the reign of Hadrian and continuing through the twenty-three years of that of Antoninus Pius, and well on into that of Marcus Aurelius and Verus. His work was diversified,—archæological, historical, doctrinal, critical. His readings on Quintus Mucius Scævola (p. 264) were utilised by the jurists of the Severan period, and drawn on to some extent by Justinian's commissioners. So were his *Epistulae*, which seem for the most part to have been opinions given to consulting clients in a fuller and more argumentative and critical fashion than was usual in the *responsa* of patented counsel. Still more largely drawn upon in the compilation of the Digest were his writings on Sabinus. Singularly enough, his voluminous commentary on the Edict is not excerpted directly, although numerous references to it are preserved in extracts from the commentaries of Ulpian and Paul. He is most familiar to moderns in connection with his *Enchiridion*, from which a long passage is preserved in the Digest, sketching the external history of the law from the foundation of the City to the time of Hadrian, and which has been often referred to in the preceding pages.⁴

³ See Mommsen, "Ueber Julians Digesta," in the *Z. f. RG.*, vol ix. (1870), p. 82 *sq.*; Buhl, *l.c.*, p. 86 *sq.*
⁴ Many critics entertain the opinion that it is to some extent corrupt;

Likewise of the same period as Julian, and one of his friends, though probably younger, was Sextus Cæcilius Africanus, whom Gellius introduces in a colloquy with Favorinus about some of the antiquities of the XII Tables, but without his cognomen. His principal works were several books of Questions (*quaestiones*) and a still greater number of *Epistulae*. The former were liberally made use of by Justinian's commissioners, but the latter very sparingly. About the Questions there is this peculiarity,—that the case stated interrogatively and the answer to it, are very frequently connected by a verb in the third person, *ait, respondit*, &c., from which many jurists conclude that Africanus is giving not his own opinion but that of some other counsel, probably Julian. His writings are acute and exact, but sometimes obscure; the saying was common long ago—" Lex Africani, ergo difficilis."

Gaius must be placed somewhat later than Julian, Pomponius, and Africanus; for although he speaks of an event in the reign of Hadrian as occurring in his "own time," yet his literary activity only commenced under Antoninus Pius, continuing until after the death of Marcus Aurelius. Although of such repute in the fifth century as to be one of the five jurists put before all others in the Valentinian Law of Citations (§ 78), yet of his personal history we know nothing. He is but once (if at all) mentioned by a contemporary,[5] and never by any of his successors. Some eminent authorities are of opinion, from the internal evidence of his writings, that he must have been a provincial,

---

see in particular Osann, *Pomp. de origine juris frag.*, Giessen, 1848. Sanio has attempted to make out its indebtedness to Varro, in his *Varroniana in d. Schriften d. Röm. Juristen*, Leipsic, 1867.

[5] By Pomponius, in *Dig.*, xlv. 3, 39 : "quod Caius noster dixit." It is by no means certain that Pomponius was not referring to Caius Cassius Longinus, one of the heads of the Sabinian school,—"our master Cassius." No doubt Gaius was a Sabinian as well as Pomponius, and the "noster" may mean no more than fraternity; but the "dixit" suggests allusion to a predecessor rather than to a young contemporary.

and probably an Asiatic,[6] while others maintain as decidedly that Rome must have been his headquarters.[7] It cannot be disputed that he devoted a considerable amount of attention in his Institutions to peculiarities of the law that affected peregrins; and Karlowa suggests what so far conciliates the discordant views,—that he may have taught in Rome, but addressed his teaching especially to provincials residing there.[8] It was as a teacher and theoretical jurist that he excelled; indeed it is very doubtful whether he was a practitioner at all, and all but certain that he had not the *jus respondendi*. His famous work was his *Institutionum commentarii quattuor*; not a work of erudition or indicative of juridical powers of the highest order; but of great value as a compendium of the fundamental doctrines of the law, alike from the simplicity of its method, the interest of its historical illustration, and the precision and accuracy of its language. The excitement that followed the happy discovery of the manuscript of it in the year 1816 (p. 329), at the moment when the founders of the historical school of jurisprudence were coming to the front, and the enthusiastic gratitude men felt towards its author for the store of new material which it laid open to them, have led to his elevation to a higher pinnacle than his actual merits altogether warrant.

As a jurist Gaius cannot be put on the same level with Labeo or Julian, Ulpian or Papinian. It may be owing to his having been only in the second rank that his name never occurs in the pages of his contemporaries and successors; men who sat in the imperial council and responded

---

[6] *E.g.*, Mommsen, "Gaius ein Provincialjurist," in *Bekker und Muther's Jahrb.*, vol. iii. (1859), p. 1 *sq.*; Blume, in the *Z. f. RG.*, vol. iii. (1864), p. 452 *sq.*; Kuntze, *Der Provincialjurist Gaius wissenschaftlich abgeschätzt*, Leipsic, 1883.

[7] *E.g.*, Huschke, in the *Z. f. RG.*, vol. vii. (1868), p. 161 *sq.*, and in the introduction to his 4th edition of Gaius.

[8] Karlowa, *Röm. RG.*, vol. i. p. 722. See Roby, *Introduction*, p. clxxv. *sq.*

ex auctoritate principis were unlikely to quote one who, however skilful and successful as a teacher, yet had neither experience as a practitioner nor great reputation as a speculative jurist. All his writings seem to have had an educational aim,—his commentaries on the XII Tables, on the ædilian edict, the provincial edict, and the *Lex Julia et Papia Poppaea*, his selected titles from the urban edict, his monographs on testamentary trusts, dowries, verbal obligations, and the Tertullian and Orphitian senatusconsults, his *libri aureorum*, &c. The last-mentioned,—*Rerum quotidianarum sive aureorum libri VII*,—a repertory of the law on matters of everyday occurrence, seem to have borne a certain relation to his Institutions, travelling over the same ground but in greater detail, and taking up many of the matters which were not deemed suitable for the elementary treatise. The passages preserved in the Digest are models of exposition. But they display little constructive talent. In this respect Gaius compares unfavourably with Julian. His tread is firm where his ground is sure, but he manifests timidity and hesitation as he approaches controversy. Notwithstanding these defects, however, his Institutes cannot be too highly valued. Criticism may detect in them a few historical[9] and even some doctrinal errors; but these shrink into insignificance in view of the wealth of instruction about branches of the law of the republic and early empire which their pages afford.[10]

Q. Cervidius Scævola was later than Gaius. He seems to have commenced his career in the reign of Antoninus Pius, to have been in his prime in that of Marcus Aurelius, in whose council he sat,[11] and to have been still engaged in

---

[9] See Lotmar, *Krit. Studien in Sachen der Contravindication* (Munich, 1878), pp. 10-22, 53-57; Kuntze, as in note 2.

[10] The literature on the subject of Gaius is overwhelming; the latest treatise is that of Glasson, *Étude sur Gaius*, &c., 2d ed., Paris, 1885.

[11] From what Capitolinus says (*Marc.*, 11), it is probable that Scævola was one of the emperor's prætorian prefects.

his profession in the early years of Septimius Severus. He was that emperor's instructor in law, and at the same time had Papinian as a pupil. With his successors he had great reputation as a consulting counsel ; and many of his clients, to judge from his *Digesta* and *Quaestiones*, seem to have been in the Greek-speaking provinces. His Questions, otherwise responses, are very brief and pointed, and the answers sometimes without reasons. The same *species facti* —one may say the same case—that is recorded in them frequently reappears in his *Digesta*, but treated more fully and argumentatively. The latter work, however, is not exclusively devoted to case law, but contains a considerable amount of doctrinal exposition of a high order, that justifies the compliment paid to Scævola by Arcadius and Honorius as *prudentissimus jurisconsultorum*.[12]

SECTION 63.—PAPINIAN, ULPIAN, AND PAUL.

Æmilius Papinianus[1] is supposed to have been a native of Phœnicia. Trained under Scævola, he was already *advocatus fisci* under Marcus Aurelius, and became master of requests (*magister libellorum*; § 60) and afterwards prætorian prefect under Septimius Severus. He is said to have been connected with the latter emperor by marriage, and was certainly one of his most intimate and trusted friends. He accompanied Severus to Britain ; and an enactment in the Code, dated from York in the year 210, may not unreasonably be imputed to his pen.[2] The emperor before his death committed to him the charge of his two sons ; but he was unable to prevent the murder of the younger, and his refusal to defend the act led to his own assassination by order and in the presence of the elder.

[12] *Cod. Theod.*, iv. 4, 3, § 3.
[1] See Æl. Spart., *Carac.*, 8 ; Ev. Otto, *Papinianus, sire de vita*, &c., Leyden, 1718 ; Ruby, *Introduction*, p. cxci. *sq*. [2] *Cod.*, iii. 32 1.

The words put into his mouth in his answer to Caracalla—that to defend the murder of the innocent was to slay him afresh—were characteristic of Papinian, whose integrity and high moral principle were as remarkable as his eminence in law. It may be that the one helped the other; and the criticism has been passed upon him that, if he was the prince of jurists, it was because he knew better than any of his contemporaries how to subordinate law to morals. His principal works were his collections of *Quaestiones* (thirty-seven books) and *Responsa* (nineteen books). His younger contemporaries Ulpian and Paul seem to have been somewhat envious of his reputation, and to have annotated many of his opinions with considerable freedom. But posterity judged between them; and first Constantine in 321, and afterwards Theodosius and Valentinian in 426, refused to allow the "notes" to be cited in the tribunals in derogation of Papinian. Justinian is even more lavish in his encomiums on his genius than any of his predecessors on the throne; *splendidissimus, acutissimus, disertissimus, sublimissimus,* σοφώτατος, *merito ante alios excellens,* being amongst the epithets in which he indulges. Modern criticism, so fond of applying new standards to a man's measurements, endorses the verdict of antiquity in so far as it places him far above his fellows in respect of the liveliness of his conceptions of right and wrong. He has no equal in the precision with which he states a case, eliminating all irrelevancies of fact, yet finding relevancies of humanity that would have escaped the vision of most; and without parade, and as it were by instinct, applying the rule of law as if it lay on the surface and was patent to the world. No man was ever more worthy of the privilege of responding *ex auctoritate principis,* and no man ever displayed a higher sense at once of the power it conferred and the responsibility it imposed.

Domitius Ulpianus and Julius Paulus made their first

appearance in public life as assessors in the *auditorium* of Papinian and members of the council of Septimius Severus; and in the reign of Caracalla were the heads of two ministerial offices,—the records and the requests. Ulpian was of Tyrian origin; which may account for the intimate relations that arose between him and Alexander Severus, whose mother, Julia Mammæa, was from Phœnician Syria. Heliogabalus had deprived him of his dignities and expelled him from Rome; but on the accession of Alexander, then only about sixteen years of age, he was at once reinstated, became the emperor's guardian, was appointed prætorian prefect, and virtually acted as regent. His curtailment of the privileges conferred on the prætorian guard by Heliogabalus provoked their enmity; again and again he narrowly escaped their vengeance; till at last in the year 228, in the course of a riot between the soldiery and the populace, the former one night found their way into the palace whither Ulpian had fled for shelter, and slew him almost in the arms of the emperor. It is not surprising to find that the cares of government interfered with his literary work; for, great as it was, it seems almost entirely to have been executed before the accession of Alexander. There was a commentary on the *jus civile* ("*ad Sabinum*") in over fifty books; one on the Edict in more than eighty books; collections of Opinions, Responses, and Disputations; books of Rules and Institutions; treatises on the functions of the different magistrates, one of them (*de officio proconsulis libri X*) being a comprehensive exposition of the criminal law; besides monographs on various statutes, on testamentary trusts, and so forth. The characteristic of the greater treatises is doctrinal exposition of a high order, flavoured with judicious criticism, and marked by great lucidity of arrangement, style, and language; throughout they bear evidence of the extent of his indebtedness to his predecessors. The quasi-philosophical observations in which he indulges in his Institutions are superficial; but otherwise his compendia are models of conciseness, while free from inelegance. His works altogether have supplied to Justinian's Digest about a third of its contents, and his commentary on the Edict of itself nearly a fifth.

Paul, who seems to have been in youth a pupil and in riper years an admirer of Scævola's, had a literary career very much like that of Ulpian; it was extremely prolific until, as the latter's successor, he became Alexander's prætorian prefect, but happily was not altogether interrupted by the cares of government. The range of both jurists was much the same; Paul, however, contenting himself with a shorter commentary on Sabinus than Ulpian, though going far beyond the latter in the number of his monographs, some of which were devoted to the exposition of points of procedure. He was more many-sided than Ulpian, quite as acute, and perhaps more subtle. Modestine, who was a pupil of Ulpian's, speaks of the two as κορυφαῖοι τῶν νομικῶν; and some of the later emperors, oblivious of Labeo and Julian, bestow on Paul epithets that seem to give him rank only second to Papinian. But he failed in two qualities in which Ulpian excelled,—precision of statement and clearness of diction; and it is not surprising, therefore, to find that his writings contributed to the Digest only about a fifth of its bulk as against Ulpian's third.

SECTION 64.—MODESTINE AND THE POST-SEVERAN JURISTS.

Herennius Modestinus, a native of or closely connected with one of the Greek-speaking provinces, and a pupil of Ulpian's, merits special attention for no other reason than that he is put by the Valentinian Law of Citations (§ 78) on the same distinguished platform as Gaius, Papinian, Ulpian, and Paul. There are numerous extracts from his writings, some of them in Greek, preserved in the Digest;

but they leave the impression of their author's incapacity to take broad views and inclination towards hair-splitting. His career began in the reign of Caracalla, and continued through that of Alexander and into the turmoils that followed the extinction of the Severan dynasty. He is mentioned with esteem in a rescript of Gordian's of the year 239 ; and in an inscription of the year 244, (the year of the accession of Philip the Arabian), preserved in the Capitoline Museum, his name occurs as one of the arbiters in a question raised by a guild of fullers.[1] There are only four jurists of later date quoted in the Digest, and two of them (Hermogenian and Arcadius Charisius) are supposed to have flourished as late as the middle of the fourth century. With Modestine jural literature in the proper sense seems to have come to an end, and general opinion goes the length of affirming a complete eclipse of jural talent. This, however, is going too far. There are in Justinian's Code and elsewhere about 300 rescripts of Gordian's six years' reign ; the constitutions of the reign of Diocletian, half a century later, if the list of them in Hænel's Index[2] be correct, number about 1200 or 1300, far more than nine-tenths of them rescripts ; and even in some of the intermediate reigns, *e.g.*, those of Philip the Arabian and Valerianus and Gallienus, the number is not inconsiderable. Many of those rescripts are of great merit, and not inferior to the ordinary run of the Responses of an earlier period. This could not have been the case had jurisprudence passed on the death of Alexander Severus into such utter darkness as is commonly supposed. That there was a serious change for the worse is unquestionable ; otherwise there would hardly have been such a cessation of literary activity, contemporaneously with the discontinuance of the practice of responding. The latter is

[1] Printed in Bruns, p. 259.
[2] The Index Legum appended to Hænel's *Corpus leg. ab imp. rom. ante Justinianum latarum*, Leipsic, 1857.

to be accounted for by the growth of absolutism. It was no longer patented counsel that responded under imperial authority; the emperor himself was now more than ever resorted to as the fountainhead of authoritative interpretation; and the imperial consistory drew within it, to aid him in his labours, all that remained of the skilled representatives of jurisprudence.[3]

SECTION 65.—REMAINS OF THE JURISPRUDENCE OF THE PERIOD.

The principal repository of what remains of the jurisprudence of the first three centuries of the empire is the Digest of Justinian (§ 84), the imperial rescripts being largely embodied in various collections of the later empire, as well as in Justinian's Code. A considerable number of passages from the writings of Gaius, Papinian, Ulpian, and Paul are to be found also in the *Collatio*, the Vatican Fragments, and the *Consultatio* (§ 81). In addition to them we have from other quarters three texts of great importance,— the Institutes of Gaius, part of a work of Ulpian's, and Paul's Sentences, together with some lesser ones and a few isolated fragments.[1]

An abridgment of the Institutes of Gaius in two books is contained in the *Lex Romana Visigothorum* (§ 82).[2] It was well known to be an abridgment because of the existence of passages from the original text in the *Collatio* and in Justinian's Digest. It was also well known that the original had not only been compiled and employed by its author for educational purposes (although opinions differed very widely

---

[3] See on this subject Hofmann, "Der Verfall der röm. Rechtswissenschaft," in his *Krit. Studien im Röm. Rechte* (Vienna, 1885), p. 3 *sq*.

[1] See a connected account of the remains of the jurisprudence of the classical period in Karlowa, *Röm. RG.*, vol. i. § 92.

[2] First edited apart from the *Lex Romana* in 1525; the last edition is that of Böcking (Bonn, 1831), in the *Corp. jur. rom. antejustinianei*.

as to its date), but that it had been in use as the elementary text-book in law from the time of the establishment of the Constantinople school in 425 down to that of Justinian's reforms of 533. Great, therefore, was the regret that had often been expressed that so valuable a monument had been lost; and great consequently the rejoicing over the happy chance that unearthed a copy of it in the chapter library at Verona. Scipio Maffei, in the middle of last century, in describing some of its manuscript treasures, referred to and printed a stray leaf that dealt with the subject of interdicts; but it was not much noticed by lawyers, and was for the first time discovered (by Haubold) to be a passage from the long-lost Gaius in the year 1816. Almost at the same time, by a curious coincidence, Niebuhr, passing through Verona, and devoting a day or two to the library, came upon a palimpsest of the Epistles of St. Jerome, underneath which he detected what he conjectured to be a treatise of Ulpian's, but which Savigny, to whom Niebuhr communicated his discovery, along with the leaf *de interdictis* and a leaf from the palimpsest, at once pronounced to be the work of Gaius.[3] Further investigation revealed it to be the very copy of his Institutes from which the stray leaf referred to had been extracted,—a large quarto of 127 leaves, written apparently in the fifth century. Commissioners were at once deputed by the Berlin Academy to make a transcript, and in 1820 the work was printed under the editorship of Göschen. It was very incomplete; for some thirty pages of the MS. were entirely or to a great extent illegible, owing partially to the action of the chemicals on the parchment where the monks had destroyed the surface with pumice-stone. A revision of it was made two years later by Blume; unfortunately his reckless use of more powerful agents than Göschen had ventured to employ obscured far more than it revealed. Edition

---

[3] Savigny's account of the discovery, embodying Niebuhr's letter to him, is in the *Z. f. gesch. RW.*, vol. iii. (1817), p. 129 *sq.*

after edition of the text followed in tolerably rapid succession; each new editor offering his own contribution of conjectural readings towards amendment of errors and filling up of gaps. The wildness of some of their suggestions convinced the more reflecting of the necessity of bringing the critics back to the MS. itself. Böcking set to work to prepare a facsimile; but it was only of the transcripts made years before by Göschen and Blume.[4] This was insufficient; so the Berlin Academy again took the matter in hand, and commissioned Studemund to proceed to Verona and prepare a fresh transcript of the MS. itself. He spent there several months of 1866, 1867, and 1868; and when his transcript was completed a fount of type was cast for him at the expense of the Academy, representing as closely as possible the letters and other marks in the original, wherewith he was enabled in 1874 to produce his *Apographum*.[5] It is of the same size as the original, and represents line by line and letter by letter all that Studemund was able to decipher; doubtful words and letters being in fainter type, what Göschen had read (before Blume's chemicals had made passages undecipherable) being also in faint type but enclosed in square brackets, and those that no one had ever been able to make out being left blank. This magnificent and conscientious reproduction will probably remain the basis of every reliable edition of Gaius for many years to come.[6] But it has already received its first supplement,—the result

[4] *Gai Inst. Cod. Veron. Apographum ad Goescheni Hollwegi Bluhmii schedas compositum . . . publicavit* Ed. Böcking, Leipsic, 1866.

[5] *Gaii Institutionum Cod. Veron. Apographum . . . edid.* Guilelmus Studemund, Leipsic, 1874.

[6] There have been published since 1874, and based upon it, editions by Polenaar (Leyden, 1876), Krüger and Studemund jointly (Berlin, 1877, 2d ed., 1884), Huschke (his 4th, Leipsic, 1879), Muirhead (Edinburgh, 1880), Gneist (Leipsic, 1880), Dubois (Paris, 1881), Abdy and Walker (their 3d, Cambridge, 1885, which, however, contains no mention of the new readings published by Studemund in 1884). Dubois reproduced the *Apographum* more literally than the others. He offered no conjectural restitutions of his own, but appended in footnotes and frequently criticised those suggested by previous editors.

of a fresh inspection and chemical treatment of the MS. by Studemund and Krüger in the years 1878 and 1883, which has enabled them (1) to add considerably to the deciphered matter, and (2) to negative with certainty the accuracy of some of the restitutions of undeciphered passages previously proposed.[7]

In 1549 there were first published in Paris by Bishop Jean Dutillet, from a manuscript in his possession, what bore to be a portion of a work of Ulpian's. The MS. soon afterwards disappeared; but its identity with one presently in the Vatican Library is now generally admitted.[8] It opens with the words "Incipiunt tituli ex corpore Ulpiani." Modern criticism has satisfactorily established that the titles which follow are from an abridgment of Ulpian's *Liber sing. Regularum*, executed soon after the year 320, by simple excision of matter no longer applicable to the then state of the law, but without further corruption of the text.[9] It is a sort of *vade-mecum* for practitioners, rather than an institutional book; every line almost embodying a doctrine, in language of unparalleled perspicuity. It follows pretty much the order of Gaius; incorporating, however, various matters which he had purposely omitted, such as the law about dowries, the provisions of the Julian and Papia-Poppæan law, and so forth. Unfortunately a large part of it is lost, for the manuscript ends abruptly with the law of succession; so that we are deprived of the rules about obligations and actions, of which a few sentences are preserved elsewhere.

[7] *Supplementa ad Codicis Veron. Apographum Studemundianum conposuit* Guil. Studemund. They are printed in facsimile in the introduction to, and embodied in the text of, Krüger and Studemund's second students' edition of Gaius (Leipsic, 1884). This edition forms the first volume of Krüger, Mommsen, and Studemund's *Collectio librorum juris antejustiniani in usum scholarum*.

[8] Savigny, "Ueber d. Vatikanische MS. des Ulpian," in his *Verm. Schrift.*, vol. iii. p. 28 *sq*.

[9] Mommsen, "De Ulpiani Regularum libro singulari," in Böcking's 4th edition (Bonn, 1855); Krüger in the preface to his edition of Ulpian (as in note 10), p. 1 *sq*.

All the modern editions are based upon a facsimile of the Vatican MS. made in 1855.[10]

The collection which passes by the name of Paul's Sentences (*Julii Pauli libri V Sententiarum ad filium*) is in this sense a compilation,—that, while the whole of it is from the treatise so designated, yet its parts are collected from a variety of intermediate sources. The original, which was also a *vade-mecum* for practice, more detailed and more complete than Ulpian's, and arranged in the order of Julian's Edict, was held in the very highest estimation in the third and fourth centuries; and alike by an enactment of Constantine's of the year 327 and by the Valentinian Law of Citations of 426 was declared as authoritative as any imperial constitution.[11] The pre-eminence thus conferred upon the Sentences explains how it was they found a place in the *Lex Romana Visigothorum* (§ 82), but greatly abridged by the omission of all that the compilers judged to be no longer of practical value. Some of the later MSS. of the Visigothic collection contain passages which are not in the earlier ones; but the chief sources of the augment of the text are Justinian's Digest and the *Collatio*, the Vatican Fragments and one or two other collections also aiding to some extent. The result is a reconstruction of the five books, each divided into rubricated titles, altogether of about three times the bulk of the remains of Ulpian's Rules. This is so at least in Krüger's edition, where the additions from the Digest, &c.,

---

[10] *Ulpiani liber sing. Regularum Cod. Vat. exempl. cur.* Ed. Böcking, Leipsic, 1855. Of the subsequent editions may be mentioned Vahlen's (Bonn, 1856), Krüger's (in vol. ii. of the *Collectio*, &c., mentioned in note 7, Leipsic, 1878), Huschke's (in the 4th ed. of his *Jurisprudentia antejustiniana*, Leipsic, 1879, p. 547 *sq.*), Muirhead's (appended to his *Gaius*, Edinburgh, 1880), Gneist's (in the 2d ed. of his *Syntagma Institutionum*, Leipsic, 1880), and Abdy and Walker's (appended to their *Gaius*, 3d ed., Cambridge, 1885).

[11] Says the *Consultatio* (*infra*, § 81), vii. 3,—" . . . secundum sententiam Pauli juridici, cujus sententias sacratissimorum principum scita semper valituras ac divalis constitutio declarant." It was probably in consequence of the authority thus accorded to them that in one or two MSS. they are called *Pauli Receptae Sententiae.*

are printed as part of the text; some editors, however, as, for example, Huschke, content themselves with a simple reference to these in what they consider their appropriate places, and print *in extenso* no more than is found in the manuscripts of the Visigothic collection.[12]

Of less importance than the three treatises described above, though still of considerable value to the jurist, are the four following:—(1.) Some remains of the *Notae juris* of Valerius Probus, who was of the time of Nero, Vespasian, and Domitian,—explanations of the meanings of single letters occurring in laws and plebiscits, in the practice of the *jus civile*, in the *legis actiones*, and in the perpetual Edict. *A.T.M.D.O.*, for example, is interpreted—" aio te mihi dare oportere ; " *B.E.E.P.P.V.Q.I.*,—" bona ex edicto possideri proscribi venireque jubebo," and so on to the number of over 150 *notae*. The most authoritative edition is that of Mommsen, in Keil's collection of the *Grammatici Latini*.[13] (2.) *Volusii Macciani assis distributio*, a tractate on money, weights, measures, and the usual modes of dividing an inheritance, written in the time of Antoninus Pius or of Marcus Aurelius. Here also the authoritative edition is by Mommsen, in the Transactions of the Saxon Academy.[14] (3.) What is known as the *Fragmentum Dositheanum de manumissionibus*,—a passage from a school-book, dating from the year 207, which the master (Dositheus) was in the habit of setting to his pupils for translation. Its original is attributed by some to Pomponius, by others to Cervidius Scævola, by others again to Gaius, Ulpian, or Paul.[15] (4.) The so-

---

[12] The editions are numerous; but it is enough to refer to the two mentioned in the text. Krüger's (of 1878) is in vol. ii. of the *Collectio librorum*, &c., cited in note 7; and Huschke's in the *Jurisprudentia antejustiniana*, cited in note 10.

[13] Also printed in the *Collectio*, &c., p. 141 *sq.*, and Huschke, *l.c.*, p. 129 *sq.*

[14] Printed in Huschke, *l.c.*, p. 409 *sq.*

[15] Printed in vol. ii. of the *Collectio*, &c., p. 149 *sq.*, and in Huschke, *l.c.*, p. 422 *sq.* On the different opinions about it see Karlowa, *Röm. RG.*, p. 764 *sq.*

called *Fragmentum de jure fisci*. This was found by Niebuhr in the chapter library at Verona at the same time that he discovered the MS. of Gaius. There is difference of opinion as to its date and authorship; most critics attribute it to Paul; but Huschke thinks it Ulpian's, while some jurists regard it as not earlier than the time of Diocletian. It was first edited by Göschen in 1820, along with Gaius. Krüger made a new transcript of the MS. in 1868; his facsimile forms the basis of all the later editions.[16]

In addition to the above there exist a line or two from Pomponius about the indivisibility of servitudes, first published in 1536, from a MS. that had belonged to one of the Scaligers;[17] a sentence from the first book of Papinian's *Responsa* on the subject of agreements between husband and wife, which forms the conclusion of the *Lex Romana Visigothorum*;[18] a couple of parchment sheets much decayed, brought from Upper Egypt in the year 1878, and now in the Berlin Museum, which contain extracts from the fifth book of Papinian's *Responsa*, with some notes by Ulpian and Paul;[19] other four tattered parchments from the ninth book of Papinian's *Responsa*, obtained from Egypt about the same time, and now in the museum of the Louvre;[20] some passages from Ulpian's Institutions, discovered by Endlicher in 1835 in the imperial library at Vienna, on a parchment which formed the cover of a papyrus manuscript *De Trini-*

---

[16] *Fragmentum de jure fisci edidit Paulus Krueger*, Leipsic, 1868. See *Collectio*, &c., vol. ii. p. 162 *sq.*; Huschke, *l.c.*, p. 615 *sq.*

[17] *Collectio*, &c., vol. ii. p. 148; Huschke, *l.c.*, p. 146 *sq.*

[18] *Collectio*, &c., vol. ii. p. 157; Huschke, *l.c.*, p. 433.

[19] First communicated to the Berlin Academy by Krüger in 1879 and 1880; and since then, along with the parchment referred to in note 24, the subject of several papers, for the principal of which see references in Karlowa, *Röm. RG.*, pp. 765, 766, notes. It is remarkable that in the parchments the red letters of the rubrics are perfectly preserved, while the black letters of the text are to a great extent eaten out.

[20] First published by Dareste in 1883 in the *Nouv. Rev. Hist.*, p. 361 *sq.*, and since commented by Alibrandi, Huschke, Krüger, Esmein, &c.; see Karlowa, *l.c.*, p. 768, and *Nouv. Rev. Hist.*, vol. x. (1886), p. 219.

tate;[21] a passage from the second book of Paul's Institutions in Boethius on Cicero's Topics;[22] a couple of sentences of Modestine's, the one (from the first book of his Rules) published in 1573 by Pierre Pithou from a MS. of his father's, and the other taken from Isidore's *Differentiae*;[23] finally, a fragment of uncertain authorship dealing, *inter alia*, with the condition of dediticians, now in the Berlin Museum, having been obtained from Egypt along with the Papinianian parchments above mentioned.[24]

[21] *Collectio*, &c., vol. ii. p. 157 *sq.*; Huschke, *l.c.*, p. 601 *sq.* See also note of critical papers on them in Karlowa, *l.c.*, p. 772.
[22] *Collectio*, &c., vol. ii. p. 160; Huschke, *l.c.*, p. 546.
[23] *Collectio*, &c., vol. ii. p. 161; Huschke, *l.c.*, p. 626.
[24] Communicated to the Berlin Academy by Mommsen in 1879. See *supra*, note 19, and *infra*, § 66, note 2.

CHAPTER THIRD.

SUBSTANTIVE CHANGES.

SECTION 66.—CITIZENSHIP, JUNIAN LATINITY, AND PEREGRINITY.

ONE of the achievements of the legislation of Augustus was the recognition of a class of freemen intermediate between citizens and peregrins, who got the name of Junian latins.[1] It came about in this way. Augustus was of opinion, and doubtless rightly, that one of the causes that had contributed to the social and political corruption of the later republic was the degradation of the burgess-class by the admission into their ranks of enormous numbers of enfranchised slaves. Prior to his legislation every freedman regularly manumitted became a citizen as a matter of course, although not qualified for enrolment in any but one of the four urban tribes. The Aelia-Sentian law of 4 A.D. was passed in order to render the attainment of citizenship by manumission a matter of greater difficulty. Before its enactment there were three regular modes of enfranchisement (*legitimae manumissiones*) known to the law, viz., (1) entry of the slave's name in the census-list as a freeman, (2) formal act in presence of the prætor (*man. vindictâ*), and (3) testamentary grant of freedom; but there were also various irregular modes, such as a written declaration addressed to the slave

[1] *Fragm. Dosith.* (*supra*, p. 333), §§ 6-8; Vangerow, *Ueber die Latini Juniani*, Marburg, 1833; Cantarelli, "I Latini Juniani," in the *Archiv. Giurid.*, vol. xxix. (1882), p. 3 *sq.*, vol. xxx. (1883), p. 41 *sq.*; and the works cited *supra*, § 57, note 4.

by his owner, an invitation from the latter to the slave to
take a place at table, informal grant in presence of friends,
&c. Only the *legitimae manumissiones* could make the freedman a citizen, and that only if the manumitter was his
quiritarian owner; irregular manumissions, and even a regular
one proceeding from a mere bonitarian owner (p. 270), were
de jure ineffectual, although *de facto* enforced by prætorian
intervention.

The leading provisions of the amending enactment were
these :—(1) that all manumissions in fraud of creditors
should be null, with this qualification,—that an insolvent
might institute one of his slaves as his testamentary heir,
for the purpose of avoiding the disgrace of *post mortem*
bankruptcy; (2) that manumission by an owner under the
age of twenty should not have the effect of making the
freedman a citizen unless it was accomplished *vindictâ*, and
for reasons that had been held sufficient by a court of
inquiry established for the purpose; (3) that manumission
of slaves under thirty years of age, in order to make them
citizens, required to be under the same two conditions;
(4) that slaves who had suffered criminal punishment or
been otherwise disgraced should not under any circumstances become citizens on manumission, but should rank
only as dediticians, incapable of ever in any way attaining
citizenship, and subject to other serious disabilities both
in public and private life.[2] In aid, however, of a freedman
under thirty, whose want of citizenship was due to nothing
but the neglect of official approval of his manumission or
its performance otherwise than *vindictâ*, it was provided that
if he married a woman who was either a citizen, or a colonial
latin, or of his own class, declaring at the time, in presence
of a certain number of witnesses, that he was doing so in

---

[2] See Zubli, *De L. Aelia Sentia*, Leyden, 1861 ; Brinz, *Die Freigelassenen d.
L. Aelia Sentia u. das Berliner Fragment von d. Dediticiern*, Freiburg, 1884.
(The Fragment alluded to is that mentioned in the end of last section.)

terms of and in order to have the benefit of the statute, then, on a child of the marriage attaining the age of twelve months, he was entitled to go to the prætor or a provincial governor, and, on proof of the facts, obtain from him a declaration of citizenship, which enured to wife and child as well, if the former was not a citizen already.[3]

But a question not unnaturally presented itself as to what was the real condition of the manumittee before he had thus acquired citizenship. Was he slave or free ? It is usually said that he was *de jure* the former, but *de facto* the latter;[4] (although *de jure* slavery is hardly consistent with the recognition of the possibility of marriage between him and a woman who might even be a citizen). The Junia-Norban law of 19 A.D. was passed to settle the question.[5] It did so by declaring that the condition of those freedmen under thirty whose manumission had not been both sanctioned by the council and accomplished *vindictâ* was to be similar to that of the colonial latins (§ 51) ; and, partly by the Junian law itself and partly by subsequent legislation, the same status seems to have been conferred on all freedmen, except those falling under the class of dediticians, who failed to become citizens because of the irregularity of their enfranchisement. Hence arose that Junian latinity which figures so largely in the pages of Gaius and Ulpian. It had this advantage,—that it was convertible into citizenship in a variety of ways, *e.g.*, the exercise for a certain length of time of some trade, craft, or calling from which the community derived benefit, renewal of the enfranchisement in such a way as to overcome its defects, imperial grant, and so forth.[6] While

---

[3] This was technically *causae probatio ex lege Aelia Sentia* (Gai., i. 29) ; and to acquire citizenship in this way was *ex l. Aelia Sentia ad civitatem pervenire* (Gai., iii. 73).

[4] " Ex jure Quiritium servi, sed auxilio praetoris in libertatis forma servati " (Gai., iii. 56).

[5] There is controversy as to the date of the Junian law and its relation to the Aelia-Sentian one. See § 57, note 4.

[6] Gai., i. §§ 32-34 ; Ulp., iii. §§ 1-6.

a man remained a latin he had *commercium*, and therefore might be a party to a mancipation and hold property on a quiritarian title.[7] But he could not make a testament;[8] and, though he might lawfully be instituted heir or appointed a legatee under one,[9] yet the statute did not allow him to take the inheritance to which he had been instituted or the legacy bequeathed to him unless he converted his latinity into citizenship within a certain limited period.[10] Having no *potestas* over his children, they could not succeed him on his death either as *sui heredes* of the *jus civile* or *liberi* of the prætor's edict. But for the Junian law, conferring *de jure* freedom on the manumittee, there would have been no difficulty in determining what was to be done with his estate after his decease. Before its enactment he was still *de jure* a slave, and all that belonged to him in law no more than *peculium*, the property of his manumitter, to whom it reverted on the freedman's death. The Junian law expressly reserved the manumitter's right to it as a *quasi peculium;* he took his latin's estate on his death, not, however, as his heir, but as his owner, whose right in it had only been suspended during the freedman's lifetime.[11] This is the explanation of the memorable *dictum* of Justinian (who abolished Junian latinity), that, though a latin went through life as a freeman, yet with his last breath he gave up both life and liberty.[12]

It must have been between the years 212 and 217 that Caracalla published his constitution conferring citizenship

[7] Ulp., xix. 4.   [8] Gai., i. 23; Ulp., xx. 14.
[9] Ulp., xxii. 3.
[10] Gai., ii. §§ 110, 275; Ulp., xvii. 1, xxii. 3, xxv. 7. But he might, as a latin, take an inheritance or a legacy under a soldier's testament, or a testamentary trust gift even from a civilian.
[11] Gai., iii. 56.
[12] Just., *Inst.*, iii. 7, § 4. So fully recognised was the old owner's reversionary right, and so completely a vested interest, that he might transfer it *inter vivos* or bequeath it to a legatee (Gai., ii. 195). This is what is meant by *legatum latini* in the passage referred to.

on all the free inhabitants of the empire.[13] Far-reaching as were its consequences, the primary purpose was purely fiscal. Augustus had imposed a tax of five per cent. on inheritances and bequests, except where the whole succession was worth less than 100,000 sesterces, or the heir or legatee was a near kinsman of the deceased.[14] It was continued by his successors, and was very profitable, thanks to the propensity of the well-to-do classes for single blessedness, followed by testamentary distribution of their fortunes amongst their friends. But it affected only the successions of Roman citizens;[15] so that the great mass of the provincial population escaped it. Caracalla, being needy, not only increased it temporarily to ten per cent., but widened the area of its operation by elevating all his free subjects to the rank of citizens. The words of Ulpian are very inclusive,— "In urbe Romano qui sunt . . . cives Romani effecti sunt;" but there is considerable diversity of opinion as to their meaning, caused by the fact that peregrins are still mentioned by some of Caracalla's successors. The reasonable interpretation is that the enactment conferred citizenship on the Junian latins and on all the emperor's peregrin subjects except Aelia-Sentian dediticians; and the boon, as a matter of course, enured to their descendants. But it did not exclude the possibility of peregrins in the future, when persons who were not citizens became subject to Rome, as happened to some extent in the course of the third century. And although all the Junian latins living at the date of the enactment in virtue of it became citizens, the class must at once have begun to form again in consequence of manumissions that were not in all points in accordance with the

---

[13] Dio Cass., lxxvii. 9 ; Ulp., in *Dig.*, i. 5, fr. 17. Justinian (*Nov.* 78, *cap.* 5) attributes it erroneously to Antoninus Pius.

[14] The *lex Julia de vicesima hereditatum* of 6 A.D. See a paper on it by Bachofen, in his *Ausgewählte Lehren des Röm. Civilrechts* (Bonn, 1848), p. 322 *sq.*

[15] Plin., *Panegyr.*, §§ 36-39.

requirements of the Aelia-Sentian law. Limit Caracalla's constitution, however, as we may, there can be no question of its immense importance. By conferring citizenship on the provincial peregrins it subjected them in all their relations to the law of Rome, and qualified them for taking part in many transactions, both *inter vivos* and *mortis causa*, which previously had been incompetent for them. It did away with the necessity for the *jus gentium* as a separate positive system. Its principles and its doctrines, it is true, survived, and were expanded and elaborated as freely and successfully as ever; but they were so dealt with as part and parcel of the civil law of Rome, which had ceased to be Italian and become imperial.

SECTION 67.—CONCESSION OF PECULIAR PRIVILEGES TO SOLDIERS.

While the period with which we are dealing saw the substantial disappearance of the distinction between citizen and peregrin, it witnessed the rise of another,—that between soldiers and civilians (*milites, pagani*).[1] The peculiar position of a soldier, spending the best years of his life in camp, far away from home and kindred, with little or nothing in common with the private citizen who was occupied with the cares of his family, his possessions, and his merchandise, on the one hand subjected him to various disqualifications, and on the other entitled him to important indulgences. He could not, for example, acquire lands in the province in which he was serving; he could not fill any municipal office; neither could he become a surety for another, nor act for him as his attorney in a litigation. His service exempted him from undertaking a tutory; he was relieved from the consequences of mistake in law, while a private citizen, with

[1] Kuntze (*Cursus*, p. 648 *sq.*) devotes two or three chapters to the *jus militare*.

opportunities of obtaining advice, was relieved only against mistake of fact; if unsuccessful in a litigation, his adversary was not allowed to deprive him of his last penny; and on his discharge, and as a reward for his service, he often had a grant of *conubium* with any wife he chose to marry, even a latin or a peregrin.

But the most remarkable effluxes of the *jus militare* were the military testament and the *castrense peculium*. The first set at naught all the rules of the *jus civile* and the prætors' Edict alike as to the form and the substance of a testament. Julius Cæsar is said to have been the first to confer on soldiers the right to test without observing the requirements of the common law. His example was followed by Titus, Domitian, and Nerva, and from the time of Trajan the military testament became a recognised institution. "I will give effect," he says, "to the last wills of my faithful companions in arms, no matter how they have tested. Let them, therefore, make their testaments how they like, let them make them how they can; the bare will (*nuda voluntas*) of a testator shall suffice to regulate the distribution of his goods." [2] It might be in writing, by word of mouth, by the unspoken signs perhaps of a dying man; all that was required was the will so manifested as not to be mistaken.[3] And as a man could thus make his testament free from all fetters of form, so might he also rescind it, add to it, alter it, and renew it. More extraordinary still,—it was sustained even though its provisions ran counter to the most cherished rules of the common law. Contrary to the maxim that no man could die partly testate and partly intestate, a soldier might dispose of part of his estate by testament and leave the rest to descend to his heirs *ab intestato*.[4] Contrary to this other maxim—*semel heres semper heres*, he might give

---

[2] Ulp. in *Dig.*, xxix. 1, fr. 1, pr.
[3] Gai., ii. 109; Ulp., xxiii. 10; Just., *Inst.*, ii. 11, pr.
[4] *Inst.*, ii. 14, 5; *Dig.*, xxix. 1, 6.

his estate to A for life, or for a term of years, or until the occurrence of some event, with remainder to B.[5] Contrary to the general rule, a latin or peregrin, or an unmarried or married but childless person, might take an inheritance or a bequest from him as freely as a citizen with children.[6] His testament, in so far as it disposed only of *bona castrensia*, was not affected by *capitis deminutio minima*.[7] It was not invalidated by præterition of *sui heredes*,[8] nor could they challenge it because they had got less under it than their "legitim" (p. 250);[9] and it was not in the mouth of the instituted heir to claim his Falcidian fourth, even though nine-tenths of the succession had been bequeathed to legatees.[10] Finally, a later testament did not nullify an earlier one, if it appeared to be the intention of the soldier-testator that they should be read together.[11]

All this is remarkable, manifesting a spirit very different from that which animated the common law of testaments. True, it was a principle with the jurists of the classical period that the *voluntatis ratio* was to be given effect to in the interpretation of testamentary writings; but that was on the condition that the requirements of law as to form and substance had been scrupulously observed. But in the military testament positive rules were made to yield to the *voluntas* in all respects; the will was almost absolutely unfettered. Roman law in this matter gave place to natural law. One would have expected the influence of so great a change to have manifested itself by degrees in the ordinary law of testaments. Yet it is barely visible. In a few points the legislation of Constantine, Theodosius II., and Justinian relaxed the strictness of the old rules; but there was never any approach to the recognition of the complete supremacy of the *voluntas*. In the *Corpus Juris* the contrast between

[5] *Dig.* xxix. 1, 15, § 4.
[6] Gai., ii. §§ 110, 111.
[7] *Dig.*, xxviii. 3, 6, § 13; *Inst.*, ii. 11, 5.
[8] *Inst.*, ii. 13, 6.
[9] *Dig.*, v. ii. 27, § 1.
[10] *Dig.*, xxix. 1, 17, § 4.
[11] *Dig.*, xxix. 1, 19, pr.

the *testamentum paganum* and the *testamentum militare* was almost as marked as in the days of Trajan. The latter was still a privileged deed, whose use was confined to a soldier actually on service, and which had to be replaced by a testament executed according to the usual forms of law within twelve months after his retirement.[12]

The *peculium castrense* had a wider influence; for it was the first of a series of amendments that vastly diminished the importance of the *patria potestas* on its patrimonial side. In its origin it was nothing more than a concession by Augustus to a *filiusfamilias* on service of the right to dispose by testament of what he had acquired in the active exercise of his profession (*quod in castris adquisierat*).[13] But it soon went much further. Confined at first to *filiifamilias* on actual service, the privilege was extended by Hadrian to those who had obtained honourable discharge. The same emperor allowed them not merely to test on their *peculium castrense*, but to manumit slaves that formed part of; and a little step further recognised their right to dispose of it gratuitously *inter vivos*. By and by the range of it was extended so as to include not only the soldier's pay and prize, but all that had come to him, directly or indirectly, in connection with his profession,—his outfit, gifts made to him during his service, legacies from comrades, and so on. All this was in a high degree subversive of the doctrines of the common law; it may almost be called revolutionary. For it involved in the first place the recognition of the right of a person *alieni juris* to make a testament as if he were *sui juris;* and in the second place the recognition of a separate estate in a *filiusfamilias* which he might deal with independently of his *paterfamilias*, which could not be touched by the latter's creditors, and which he was not bound to collate (or bring into hotch-pot) on claiming a share of his father's succession. The radical right of the parent, how-

[12] *Inst.*, ii. 11, pr. [13] *Inst.*, ii. 12, pr.

ever, like that of a manumitter over his Junian freedman, was rather suspended than extinguished; for, if the soldier-son died intestate, the right of the *paterfamilias* revived; he took his son's belongings, not as his heir appropriating an inheritance, but as his *paterfamilias* reasserting his ownership of a *peculium*.[14] Thus did the law attempt to reconcile the privilege of the soldier while he lived with the prerogative of the family-head after his death.[15]

SECTION 68.—THE FAMILY.

All branches of the law of the family underwent modification during the period, but radical changes beyond those already mentioned were comparatively few. The legislative efforts of Augustus to encourage marriage, to which persons of position showed a remarkable distaste, have already been alluded to (p. 304). The relation of husband and wife still in law required no more for its creation than deliberate interchange of nuptial consent; although for one or two purposes the bride's home-coming to her husband's house was regarded as the criterion of completed marriage.[1] But it was rarely accompanied with *manus*. So repugnant was such subjection to patrician ladies that they declined to submit to confarreate nuptials; and so great consequently became the difficulty of finding persons qualified by confarreate birth to fill the higher priesthoods, that early in the

---

[14] This, however, was altered by Justinian's 118th Novel, under which a father taking any part of a deceased son's estate did so in the character of his heir; see *infra*, p. 418.

[15] The same principles were afterwards partially extended to the *peculium quasi-castrense*,—the earnings of a *filiusfamilias* in the civil or ecclesiastical service of the state; see *Inst.*, ii. 11, § 6; ii. 12, pr.

[1] The references to the necessity in certain cases of *ductio uxoris in domum mariti* have led some French writers to maintain that marriage was regarded by the jurists of the empire as a real rather than a consensual contract. But it was only when one of the parties had died or deserted before they had lived together, and the ordinary evidence of completed interchange of consent failed, that this proof had to be called in aid as a decisive fact and circumstance.

empire it had to be decreed that confarreation should in future be productive of *manus* only *quoad sacra*, and should not make the wife a member of her husband's family.[2] *Manus* by a year's uninterrupted cohabitation was already out of date in the time of Gaius; and although that by coemption was still in use in his time, it probably was quite unknown by the end of the period. Husband and wife therefore had their separate estates; the common establishment being maintained by the husband, with the assistance of the revenue of the wife's dowry (*dos*),—an institution which received much attention at the hands of the jurists, and was to some extent regulated by statute. Divorce was unfortunately very common; it was lawful even without any assignable cause; when blame attached to either side, he or she suffered deprivation to some extent of the nuptial provisions, but there were no other penal consequences.

The relaxation of the bond between parent and child in the case of a *filiusfamilias* who had adopted a military career has already been alluded to. But it was not in his case alone that it was manifest; for in all directions there was a tendency to place restrictions on the exercise of the *patria potestas*. This was due to a great degree to the hold that the doctrines of natural law were gaining within the Roman system; partly also to the fact that the emperors, having succeeded to the censorial *regimen morum*, allowed it freely to influence their edicts and rescripts. Exposure of an infant was still allowed;[3] but a parent was no longer permitted, even in the character of household judge, to put his son to death; in fact his prerogative was limited to moderate chastisement, the law requiring, in case of a grave offence that merited severe punishment, that he should hand his child over to the ordinary tribunals.[4] His right of sale,

[2] Gai., i. 136.
[3] The earliest absolute prohibition of it was by Valentinian and his colleagues in 374, *Cod.*, viii. 51, 2.
[4] Alex. Sev. in *Cod.*, viii. 46, 3.

in like manner, was restricted to young children, and permitted only when he was in great poverty and unable to maintain them;[5] while their impignoration by him was prohibited under pain of banishment.[6]

Except in the solitary case of a son who was a soldier, a *paterfamilias* was still recognised as in law the owner of all the earnings and other acquisitions of his children *in potestate*; but the old rule still remained that for their civil debts he was not liable beyond the amount of the fund he had advanced them to deal with as *de facto* their own (*peculium profecticium*), except when he had derived advantage from their contract, or had expressly or by implication authorised them to enter into it as his agents.[7] To the party with whom he had contracted a *filiusfamilias* was himself liable as fully as if he had been a *paterfamilias*,[8] with one exception, namely, when his debt was for borrowed money; in that case, with some very reasonable qualifications, it was declared by the notorious Macedonian senatusconsult (of the time of Vespasian) that the lender should not be entitled to recover payment, even after his borrower had become *sui juris* by his father's death.[9] Between a father and his emancipated son there was, and always had been, perfect freedom of contract; but so was there now between a father and his soldier-son in any matter relating to the *peculium castrense*, even though the son was *in potestate*. What is still more remarkable is that the new sentiment which was operating on the *jus civile* admitted the possibility of natural obligation between *paterfamilias* and *filiusfamilias* even in reference to the *peculium profecticium*; which, though incapable of direct enforcement by action, was yet to some extent recognised and given effect to indirectly.[10]

[5] Paul., *Sent.*, v. 1, § 1.
[6] Ibid.
[7] Gai., iv. §§ 69-74.
[8] *Dig.*, xliv. 7, 39.
[9] *Dig.*, xiv. 6, 1.
[10] See Savigny, *Das Obligationenrecht*, vol. i. (Berlin, 1851), pp. 49, 59.

In the matter of guardianship, while the tutory of pupils was carefully tended and the law in regard to it materially amended during the period under review, (particularly by a senatusconsult generally referred to as the *Oratio divi Severi*, prohibiting alienation of the ward's property without judicial authority),[11] that of women above the age of pupillarity gradually disappeared. This change, which was in harmony with the disappearance of the husband's *manus*, was aided by the Julian and Papia-Poppæan law (which made release from tutelage one of the rewards it offered to fruitful wives), and by a *Lex Claudia* abolishing the tutory-at-law of agnates; but really was an inevitable result of the recognition of the right of a woman to substitute for her tutor-at-law, for her testamentary tutor, or for him who had been appointed to the office by a magistrate, another of her own selection, who was expected to comply with her wishes, and whose co-operation was therefore a mere matter of form, and practically a farce.

The guardianship or curatory (*cura*) of minors above pupillarity owed its institution to Marcus Aurelius.[12] The Plætorian law of the middle of the sixth century of Rome had indeed imposed penalties on those taking undue advantage of the inexperience of minors, *i.e.*, persons *sui juris* under the age of twenty-five; and from that time the prætors were in the habit of appointing curators to act with such persons for the protection of their interests in particular affairs. But it was Marcus Aurelius that first made curatory a general permanent office, to endure in the ordinary case until the ward attained majority (twenty-five). The appointment was made on the application of the minor

[11] It is reproduced by Ulpian in *Dig.*, xxvii. 9, fr. 1, § 2. As Severus was in Asia at the time (195 A.D.), it must have been communicated to the senate in writing, which may account for the constant reference to the oration itself instead of the confirmatory senatusconsult.

[12] Capitolin., *in Marc.*, 10. See Savigny, *Verm. Schr.*, vol. ii. p. 321 *sq.*; Huschke, in *Z. f. g. R W.*, vol. xiii. p. 311 *sq.*

himself; but in practice there was this compulsitor upon him to petition for it,—that his tutor refused to proceed to account for his administration unless the ex-pupil had a curator conjoined with him in the investigation, and who might concur in granting the tutor his discharge, thus minimising the chance of its future challenge. The powers, duties, and responsibilities of such curators became a matter for careful and elaborate definition and regulation by the jurists, whose exposition of the law of guardianship, whether by tutors or curators, has found wide acceptance in modern systems of jurisprudence.

SECTION 69.—POSSESSION, PROPERTY, REAL RIGHTS,
AND OBLIGATIONS.

In all those branches of the law there was much more of organic development than radical change. Much was written about possession; but all incidentally, and chiefly in connection with the possessory interdicts and the law of usucapion or prescriptive acquisition of property. In all the long list of the writings of the jurists we find no reference to a single monograph on the subject; and as the principles of possession *quoad interdicta* and possession *quoad usucapionem* were by no means identical, and we have no absolute certainty that the compilers of Justinian's Digest were always careful to remember the distinction between them in arranging their excerpts, modern jurisprudence is anything but sure of what the general rules of possession *per se* really were.[1]

In the law of property (*dominium*) nothing new of any

---

[1] Savigny's great work on Possession (*das Recht des Besitzes*), first published in 1803, underwent great modification at his own hand in subsequent editions. Since then the books on the subject are innumerable. Bruns, Ihering, Bekker, Dernburg, and a host of eminent jurists have written upon it; and it is not too much to say that there is hardly one of Savigny's positions that has not been assailed, while many have been completely overthrown.

very great importance was introduced, with exception of the *caducum* of the Papia-Poppæan law as a mode of acquisition;[2] but many branches of the subject underwent careful elucidation, as, for example, the requisites of various natural modes of acquisition, and the relations between an owner and a party withholding from him his property, according as the detention was in good faith or in bad. Among real rights, considerable attention was given to the nature of usufruct, the modes of its constitution, and the relative positions of usufructuary and owner; and legislation devised a means of giving effect to a bequest of a usufruct of money, which, as it could not be used without being parted with, was theoretically incapable of being usufructed.[3] The modes of constitution alike of personal and prædial servitudes were much simplified, formal conveyance by mancipation or cession in court being dispensed with, and their creation by nothing more than pacts and stipulations, or even formless agreements followed by exercise of the right without objection from the owner of the servient estate, held to make them valid and effectual not only against the latter's heirs but even against a third party acquiring from him. Hypothec, a security over either real or personal estate, completed by simple agreement without any conveyance or change of possession, to a great extent supplanted the old and more formal *fiducia*; and the jurists in time succeeded in making it a most effectual real security, with every facility for reduction into possession and eventual sale of what had been hypothecated, no matter into whose hands it might have passed.

The law of obligations made immense strides during the period; but except in the expansion of the so-called *obligationes quasi ex contractu*, and the determination of the true ground of actionability of the so-called innominate con-

[2] Ulp., *Frag.*, tit. xvii. ; xix. § 17.
[3] For usufruct was the right to use and to appropriate the fruits or profits of a thing, preserving always its substance.

tracts, the results were mostly in the direction of definition and qualification of already existing doctrine, classification of already recognised grounds of liability, and simplification of current forms of engagement.

SECTION 70.—THE LAW OF SUCCESSION, AND PARTICULARLY TESTAMENTARY TRUSTS.

There were far more positive changes in the law of succession than either in that of property or in that of obligation. The rise and progress of the military testament has already been explained (p. 342). The testament of the common law was still ostensibly that *per aes et libram* (p. 167); but the practice of granting *bonorum possessio secundum tabulas* to the persons named as heirs in any testamentary instrument that bore outside the requisite number of seals, led, from the time of Marcus Aurelius, to the frequent neglect of the time-honoured formalities of the *familiae mancipatio* and *nuncupatio testamenti*. It was his enactment,[1] declaring that an heir-at-law should no longer be entitled to dispute the last wishes of a testator on the technical ground of non-compliance with the purely formal requirements of the law, that practically introduced what Justinian calls the prætorian testament.[2] That testamentary deeds were often very voluminous is manifest from the fragmentary remains of one or two of the first and second century. In the testament of one Dasumius, of the year 109,[3] for example, we have the usual institutions and substitutions of heirs, and a series of legacies (which he desires shall be paid free of duty), annuities, trust-gifts, and enfranchisements of slaves; together

[1] Gai., ii. 120.
[2] *Inst.*, ii. 10, 2. Justinian makes it the outcome of the prætorian Edict. This is not quite accurate; for under the edict a grant of *bonorum possessio secundum tabulas* might be defeated by a *hereditatis petitio* at the instance of a near agnate of the testator's, on the ground of defective execution (Gai., ii. 119).
[3] Bruns, *Fontes*, p. 228 *sq.*

with instructions about his funeral arrangements and the erection of a sepulchral monument to his memory, and a reservation of power to make alterations and additions by codicil.

About fifty years before the date of this testament an important change had been made in the law of legacies. There had been, and still continued to be, four different forms in which a legacy (*legatum*) could be bequeathed,[4] and which were attended with very different consequences so far as concerned the rights they conferred on legatees. To a great extent it was in the power of a testator to employ which he pleased; but his discretion was not altogether unlimited; for some peculiarity in the subject-matter of the bequest might make one or other of them inappropriate. For instance, while it was quite lawful for a testator to bequeath what belonged to a third party, yet he could do so validly only by imposing upon his heir the obligation of procuring it or else paying its value to the legatee (*legatum per damnationem*),—not by a direct gift to the latter (*legatum per vindicationem*). There were various other subtleties of this sort, whose disregard frequently caused the failure of a bequest. To remedy this, and in the same spirit that was animating the law in many other directions, namely, that a man's *voluntas* should if possible be respected notwithstanding technical defect in its manifestation, it was enacted by a senatusconsult of the time of Nero that, whenever a legacy other than one *per damnationem* was ineffectual in the particular form in which it had been bequeathed, it should be given effect to as if it had in fact been one *per damnationem*, which was in most respects the most favourable for a legatee.[5] The result, though not immediate, was the simplification of legacies, paving the way for their final equiparation with trust-gifts (*fideicommissa*).

[4] They are described in Gaius, ii. §§ 192-223.
[5] Gai., ii. §§ 197, 218 ; Ulp., xxiv. 11a.

These had been introduced in the time of Augustus;[6] not by statute, but by some innovator who desired to circumvent the rule of law which prevented him leaving either inheritance or bequest to an individual who had no *testamenti factio* with him.[7] It was a harsh rule when applied to the case of a citizen who had married a foreigner with whom he had no *conubium* ; for, as the issue of the marriage were not citizens like their father but peregrins like their mother,[8] they could neither succeed him *ab intestato* as his *sui heredes* or his agnates,[9] nor could he by testament either institute them as his heirs or make them his legatees. According to Theophilus,[10] amplifying an observation of Gaius's,[11] it was to meet this very case that the *fideicommissum* was first devised; a testator instituted as his heir a qualified friend on whom he could rely, and requested him, as soon as he had entered on the succession, to transfer the benefits of it to his peregrin children. He soon found imitators; and their number must rapidly have multiplied after the emperor, shocked at the perfidy of a trustee who had failed to comply with the request of his testator, remitted the matter to the consuls of the day, with instructions to do in it what they thought just. So quickly did the new institution establish itself in public favour, and so numerous did the questions become as to the construction and fulfilment of testamentary trusts, that before long it was found necessary to institute a court specially charged with their determination,—that of the *praetor fideicommissarius*.[12]

[6] *Inst.*, ii. 23, 1; ii. 25, pr.
[7] Ulp., xxii. 1.   [8] Gai., i. 67.
[9] They could not even have a claim as cognates under the prætorian rules: for the prætors followed the rule of the *jus civile* to this extent,—that they did not grant *bonorum possessio* to a person who had not *testamenti factio* with him whose succession was in question.
[10] Theoph., *Par. Inst.*, ii. 23, 1.   [11] Gai., ii. 285.
[12] Just., *Inst.*, ii. 23, 1. A special court was necessary for this reason,— that, because of the peculiar relation between the trustee and the beneficiaries,

Z

The employment of a trust as a means of benefiting those who were under disqualifications as heirs or legatees, as, for example, persons who had no *testamenti factio*, women incapacitated by the Voconian law (pp. 253, 288), unmarried and married but childless persons incapacitated by the Julian and Papia-Poppæan law (p. 304), and so on, was in course of time prohibited by statute ;[13] but that did not affect its general popularity. For, whether what was contemplated was a transfer of the universal *hereditas* or a part of it to the beneficiary (*fideicommissum hereditatis*), or only of some particular thing (*fideicommissum rei singularis*), a testamentary trust had various advantages over either a direct institution or a direct bequest (*legatum*). In theory the imposition upon the heir of a trust in favour of a beneficiary, whether it required him to denude of the whole or only a part of the inheritance, did not deprive him of his character of heir or relieve him of the responsibilities of the position; and at common law therefore he was entitled to decline the succession, often to the great prejudice of the beneficiary. In order to avoid such a mischance, and at the same time to regulate their relations *inter se* and towards debtors and creditors of the testator's, it became the practice for the parties to enter into stipulatory arrangements about the matter; but these were to some extent rendered superfluous by two senatusconsults, the Trebellian in the time of Nero, and the Pegasian in that of Vespasian,[14] which at once secured the beneficiary against the trustee's (*i.e.*, the heir's) repudiation of the inheritance, protected the latter from all risk of loss where he was trustee and nothing more, and

it would have been difficult to adjust an issue for remit to an ordinary *judex* formulating precisely the question between them ; consequently there was no such remit, the case being heard from first to last and finally disposed of by the *praetor fideicommissarius* himself, in what was called an *extraordinaria cognitio*. See *infra*, § 72.

[13] Gai., ii. §§ 285-287.

[14] For their provisions see Gai., ii. 252-259. They were amalgamated and simplified by Justinian, as described in *Inst.*, ii. 23, 7.

enabled the former to treat directly with debtors and creditors of the testator's and himself ingather the corporeal items of the inheritance.

It was one of the advantages of a trust-bequest, whether universal or singular, that it might be conferred in a codicil, even though unconfirmed by any relative testament.[15] The codicil (*codicilli*), also an invention of the time of Augustus, was a deed of a very simple nature. It was inappropriate either for disherison of *sui* or institution of an heir; but if confirmed by testament might contain direct bequests, manumissions, nominations of tutors, and the like; and whether confirmed or unconfirmed might, as stated, be utilised as a vehicle for trust-gifts. Latterly it was held operative even in the absence of a testament, the trusts contained in it being regarded as burdens on the heir-at-law (p. 423).

The most important changes in the law of intestate succession during the period were those accomplished by the Tertullian and Orphitian senatusconsults, fruits of that recognition of the precepts of natural law which in so many directions was modifying the doctrines of the *jus civile*. The first was passed in the reign of Hadrian, the second in the year 178, under Marcus Aurelius. Down to the time of the Tertullian senatusconsult a mother and her child by a marriage that was unaccompanied with *manus* stood related to each other only as cognates, being in law members of different families; consequently their chance of succession to each other was remote, being postponed to that of their respective agnates to the sixth or seventh degree. The purpose of the senatusconsult[16] was to prefer a mother to all agnates of her deceased child except father and brother and sister; father and brother excluded her; but with a sister of the deceased, and in the absence of father or brother, she shared equally. While there can be little doubt that it was natural considerations that dictated this amendment, yet its

[15] Ulp., xxv. 12.   [16] *Inst.*, iii. 3.

authors were too timid to justify it on the abstract principle of common humanity, lest thereby they should seem to impugn the wisdom of the *jus civile*; and so they confined its application to women who had the *jus liberorum*, i.e., to women of free birth who were mothers of three children and freedwomen who were mothers of four, thus making it ostensibly a reward of fertility.[17] The Orphitian senatus-consult [18] was the counterpart of the Tertullian. It gave children, whether legitimate or illegitimate, a right of succession to their mother in preference to all her agnates; and subsequent constitutions extended the principle, admitting them to the inheritance not only of their maternal grandparents but also of their paternal grandmother.

[17] This limitation to mothers of three or four children held its place till repealed by Justinian (see *tit. cit.*, § 4).
[18] *Inst.*, iii. 4.

CHAPTER FOURTH.

JUDICIAL PROCEDURE.

SECTION 71.—THE FORMULAR SYSTEM.[1]

THE ordinary procedure of the first three centuries of the empire was still two-staged; it commenced before the prætor (*in jure*), and was concluded before a *judex* (*in judicio*). But the *legis actiones* (§§ 33-37, 41) had given place to prætorian *formulae*. Under the sacramental system parties, and particularly the plaintiff, had themselves to formulate in statutory or traditional words of style the matter in controversy between them; and as they formulated, so did it go for trial to centumviral court or *judex* or arbiters, with the not infrequent result that it was then all too late discovered that the real point in the case had been missed. Under the formular system parties were free to represent their plaint and defence to the prætor in any words they pleased; the plaintiff asking for a *formula* and usually indicating the style on the *album* that he thought would suit his purpose, and the defendant demanding when necessary an exception, *i.e.*, a plea in defence, either prætorian or statutory, that without traversing the facts or law of the plaintiff's case, yet avoided his demand on grounds of equity or public policy. It was for the prætor to consider and determine whether the action or exception should or should not be granted (*dare, denegare actionem, exceptionem*), and if granted,

---

[1] See Keller, *Röm. CP.*, §§ 23-43 ; Bethmann-Hollweg, *Gesch. d. CP.*, vol. ii. §§ 81-87 ; Bekker, *Aktionen*, vol. i. chaps. 4-7, vol. ii. chaps. 15, 19, 20 ; Baron, *Gesch. d. R. R.*, vol. i. §§ 202-215 ; Buonamici, *Procedura*, vol. i. pp. 86-122.

whether it should be according to the style exhibited on the *album* (p. 255) or a modification of it. The result he embodied in a written and signed appointment to a judge, whom he instructed what he had to try and empowered to pronounce a finding either condemning or acquitting the defendant. This writing was the *formula*.

Although it was not until the early empire that this system of procedure attained its full development, yet it had its commencement two centuries before the fall of the republic. Gaius[2] ascribes its introduction and definitive establishment to the *Lex Aebutia*, probably of the second decade of the sixth century of the city, and two judiciary laws of the time of Augustus, all three referred to in a previous section (§ 44). The Aebutian law, of which unfortunately we know very little, is generally supposed to have empowered the prætors (1) to devise a simpler form of procedure for causes already cognizable *per legis actionem*, (2) to devise forms of action to meet cases not cognizable under the older system, and (3) themselves to formulate the issue and reduce it to writing. It was by no means so radical a change as is sometimes supposed. There were *formulae* employed by the prætor both in the procedure *per judicis postulationem* (§ 35) and in that *per condictionem* (§ 41). The difference between them and the *formulae* of the Aebutian system was this,—that the former were in part mere echoes of the statutory words of style uttered by the plaintiff, and that they were not written but spoken in the hearing of witnesses.

A large proportion of the personal actions of the formular system were evolved out of the *legis actio per condictionem*. The sequence of operations may have been something like this. Taking the simplest form of it, the action for *certa pecunia* under the Silian law, the first step was to drop the formal *condictio*[3] from which it derived its

[2] Gai., iv. 30. [3] Gai., iv. 18.

character of *legis actio*, thus avoiding a delay of thirty days; the plaintiff stated his demand in informal words, and, if the defendant denied indebtedness, the prætor straightway formulated a written appointment of and instruction to a judge, embodying in it the issue in terms substantially the same as those he would have employed under the earlier procedure:—" Titius be judge. Should it appear that N. N. ought to pay (*dare oportere*) 50,000 sesterces to A. A., in that sum, Judge, condemn N. N. to A. A.;[4] should it not so appear, acquit him." This was no longer the *legis actio per condictionem* but the *certi condictio* of the formular system. The *condictio triticaria* of the same system ran on the same lines: " Titius be judge. Should it appear that N. N. ought to give A. A. the slave Stichus, then, whatever be the value of the slave, in that condemn N. N. to A. A.," and so on. In both of these examples the *formula* included only two of the four clauses that might find place in it,[5]— an " intention " and a " condemnation." The matter of claim in both cases was certain,—so much money in one case, a slave in the other; but while in the first the condemnation also was certain, in the second it was uncertain. What if the claim also was uncertain,—say a share of the profits of a joint adventure assured by stipulation? It was quite competent for the plaintiff to condescend on a definite sum, and claim that as due to him; but it was very hazardous; for unless he was able to prove the debt to the last sesterce he got nothing. To obviate the risk of such failure, the prætors devised the *incerti condictio*, whose *formula* commenced with a " demonstration " or indication of the cause

---

[4] In the typical Roman styles of actions the plaintiff was usually called Aulus Agerius, and the defendant Numerius Negidius.

[5] Gaius enumerates them as the *demonstratio, intentio, adjudicatio,* and *condemnatio*, and describes their several functions in iv. §§ 39-43. Besides these, a *formula* might be preceded by a *praescriptio* (Gai., iv. §§ 130-137); and have incorporated in it fictions (§§ 32-38), exceptions (§§ 115-125), and replications, duplications, &c. (§§ 126-129).

of action, and whose "intention" referred to it and was conceived indefinitely : " Titius be judge. Whereas A. A. stipulated with N. N. for a share of the profits of a joint adventure, whatever it appears that N. N. ought in respect thereof to give to or do for A. A. (*dare facere oportere*), in the amount thereof condemn N. N.," and so on.[6] Once this point was attained, further progress was comparatively easy, the way being open for the construction of *formulae* upon illiquid claims arising from transactions in which the practice of stipulation gradually dropped out of use (p. 284) ; till at last the *bonae fidei judicia* were reached, marked by the presence in the "intention" of the words *ex fide bona*— "whatever in respect thereof N. N. ought in good faith to give to or do for A. A."

In the case of real actions, the transition from the *legis actiones* to the *formulae* followed a different course. The Aebutian law did not abolish the procedure *per sacramentum* when reference was to be to the centumviral court on a question of quiritarian right. In the time of Cicero, although the petitory formula was sometimes employed,[7] that court was still in full activity (§ 33, note 13); but by the time of Gaius it is doubtful if it was resorted to except for trial of questions of inheritance. In his time questions of property were raised either *per sponsionem* or *per formulam petitoriam*. The procedure by sponsion must be regarded as the bridge between the sacramental process and the petitory *vindicatio*. In the first as in the second the question of real right was determined only indirectly. The plaintiff required the defendant to give him his stipulatory promise to pay a nominal sum of twenty-five sesterces in

---

[6] This was specifically called the *actio ex stipulatu*, but really nothing more than a variety of the *condictio incerti*. The later actions on the consensual contracts, and on all the nominate real contracts except *mutuum*, in like manner had specific names, but in fact were just *incerti condictiones* in the larger sense of the phrase.

[7] See an example in Cic., *in Verr. II.*, ii. 12, § 31.

the event of the thing in dispute being found to belong to the former; and at the same time the defendant gave sureties for its transfer to the plaintiff, with all fruits and profits, in the same event. The *formula* that was adjusted and remitted to a judge *ex facie* raised only the simple question whether the twenty-five sesterces were due or not: the action was in form a personal, not a real one, and therefore appropriately remitted to a single *judex* instead of to the centumviral tribunal. But judgment on it could be reached only through means of a finding (*sententia*) on the question of real right; if it was for the plaintiff, he did not claim the amount of the sponsion, but the thing which had been found to be his; and if the defendant delayed to deliver it with its fruits and profits, the plaintiff had recourse against the latter's sureties.[8] The petitory *formula* was undoubtedly of later introduction and much more straightforward. Like the *certi condictio*, it contained only "intention" and "condemnation." It ran thus: "Titius be judge. Should it appear that the slave Stichus, about whom this action has been raised, belongs to A. A. in quiritary right, then, unless the slave be restored, whatever be his value, in that, Judge, you will condemn N. N. to A. A.; should it not so appear, you will acquit him."

The *formulae* given above, whether applicable to real or personal actions, are so many illustrations of the class known as *formulae juris civilis* or *in jus conceptae*. The characteristic of such a *formula* was that it contained in the "intention" one or other of the following phrases—*ejus esse ex jure Quiritium, adjudicari oportere*,[9] *dari oportere, dari fieri oportere*, or *damnum decidi oportere*.[10] Such a *formula* was em-

[8] Gai., iv. 91-96.
[9] Employed only in the divisory actions, *i.e.*, for dividing common property, partitioning an inheritance, or settling boundaries; the demand was that the judge should adjudicate (or award in property) to each of the parties such a share as he thought just.
[10] Employed in certain actions upon delict, where the old penalties of death,

ployed where the right to be vindicated or the obligation to be enforced had its sanction in the *jus civile*, whether in the shape of statute, consuetude, or interpretation. Where, on the other hand, the right or obligation had its sanction solely from the prætors' edict, *formulae* so conceived were inappropriate and incompetent. The actions employed in such cases were *actiones juris honorarii*, and these either *actiones utiles*, or *actiones in factum*. The first were adaptations of actions of the *jus civile* to cases that did not properly fall within them; the second were actions entirely of prætorian devising, for the protection of rights or redress of wrongs unknown to the *jus civile*.[11]

Of the *actiones utiles* some were called *actiones ficticiae*. Resort to a fiction is sometimes said to be a confession of weakness, and adversely criticised accordingly. But every amendment on the law is an admission of defect in what is being amended; and it was in sympathy with the spirit of Roman jurisprudence, when it found an action too narrow in its definition to include some new case that ought to fall within it, rather, by feigning that the new case was the same as the old, to bring it within the scope of the existing and familiar action, than to cause disturbance by either altering the definition of the latter or introducing an entirely new remedy. A *bonorum possessor* (p. 291) held a position unknown to the *jus civile*; he was not an heir, and therefore not entitled off-hand to employ the actions competent to an heir, either for recovering the property of the defunct or proceeding against his debtors. The prætor could have

slavery, or talion had in practice been transmuted into money payments, and the defendant consequently called upon to make a settlement in that way.

[11] In a few instances (not satisfactorily explained) there was both civil and prætorian remedy for the same wrong; for Gaius observes (iv. 45) that in commodate and deposit failure of the borrower or depositary to return the thing lent to or deposited with him gave rise to actions that might be formulated either *in jus* or *in factum*. In the same section he gives the styles of *actiones depositi in jus* and *in factum conceptae*; their comparison is instructive.

had no difficulty in devising quite new actions to meet his case; but he preferred the simpler expedient of adapting to it those of an heir, by introducing into the *formula* a fiction of civil heirship.[12] So he did with the *bonorum emptor* or purchaser of a bankrupt's estate at the sale of it in mass by his creditors. *Emptio bonorum* was a purely prætorian institution,[13] and the prætor, if he had thought fit, could easily have fortified the purchaser's acquisition by giving him prætorian remedies for recovering the property and suing the debtors of the bankrupt; but here again he followed the simpler course of giving him, as if he were a universal successor, the benefit of an heir's actions by help of a fiction of heirship.[14] A peregrin could not sue or be sued for theft or culpable damage to property, for the XII Tables and the Aquilian law applied only to citizens; but he could both sue and be sued under cover of a fiction of citizenship.[15] A man who had acquired a *res mancipi* on a good title but without taking a conveyance by mancipation or surrender in court, if he was dispossessed before he had completed his usucapion, could not sue a *rei vindicatio* for its recovery, for he was not in a position to affirm that he was quiritarian owner; neither, for the same reason, could a man who in good faith and on a sufficient title had acquired a thing from one who was not in a position to alienate it. But in both cases the prætor granted him what was in effect a *rei vindicatio* proceeding on a fiction of completed usucapion,[16]—the extremely useful Publician action referred to in a previous section (§ 52).

These are examples of *actiones ficticiae*,—actions of the *jus civile* adapted by this very simple expedient to cases to which otherwise they would have been inapplicable, and that formed one of the most important varieties of the

[12] Gai., iv. 34.   [13] Gai., iii. §§ 77-81.
[14] Gai., iv. 35. Theophilus (*Par. Inst.*, iii. 12) calls the *bonorum emptor* πραιτώριος διάδοχος (prætorian successor) of the bankrupt.
[15] Gai., iv. 37.   [16] Gai., iv. 36.

actiones utiles. Quite different was the course of procedure in the *actiones in factum*, whose number and varieties were practically unlimited, although for the most part granted in pursuance of the prætor's promise in the edict that under such and such circumstances he would make a remit to a *judex* (*judicium dabo*),[17] and formulated in accordance with the relative skeleton styles also published on the album. A great number of them came to be known by special names, as, for example, the *actio de dolo, actio negotiorum gestorum, actio hypothecaria, actio de pecunia constituta, actio vi bonorum raptorum, actio de superficie,* &c., the generic name *actio in factum* being usually confined to the innominate ones. Their *formulae,* unlike those in *jus conceptae,* submitted no question of legal right for the consideration of the judge, but only a question of fact, proof of which was to be followed by a condemnation. That of the *actio de dolo,* for example, ran thus : " Titius be judge. Should it appear that, through the fraud of N. N., A. A. was induced to convey and give up possession of his farm (describing it) to N. N., then, Judge, unless according to your order N. N. restores it, you will condemn him in damages to A. A.; if it shall not so appear, you will acquit him."

The words *nisi arbitratu tuo restituat* in this *formula* are an illustration of a qualification of the *condemnatio* of frequent occurrence in certain classes of actions. Under the formular system a judge, in condemning a defendant, had no alternative but to do so in money;[18] the amount being sometimes definitely fixed in the *formula,* sometimes limited to a maximum, and sometimes left entirely to his discretion.[19] But it frequently happened, especially in actions for

[17] Examples: "Si quis negotia alterius . . . gesserit, judicium eo nomine dabo " (*Dig.,* iii. 5, 3, pr.) ; " Quae dolo malo facta esse dicentur, si de his rebus alia actio non erit et justa causa esse videbitur, judicium dabo " (*Dig.,* iv. 3 1, § 1) ; " Nautae caupones stabularii quod cujusque salvum fore receperint, nisi restituent, in eos judicium dabo " (*Dig.,* iv. 9, 3, 1) ; " Quod quis commodasse dicetur, de eo judicium dabo " (*Dig.,* xiii. 6, 1, pr).
[18] Gai., iv. 48.   [19] Gai., iv. §§ 50, 51.

restitution or exhibition of a thing, that pecuniary damages might not be the most appropriate result of the procedure; and so the judge was empowered, once the plaintiff had made out his case, to determine what, in all the circumstances, and in fairness and equity, would be sufficient satisfaction by the defendant.[20] It is possible that in some instances this discretionary power may have been conferred on the judge in such general words as "nisi arbitratu tuo N. N. A° A° satisfaciat;" but in actions for restitution or exhibition, if satisfaction was not given voluntarily, it was usually specific performance that was ordained, under such qualifications as to mode, time, and place as the judge thought proper. It was only when default was made in obeying his order that the judge proceeded to condemnation in damages, the amount being assessed by the plaintiff himself under oath. Actions in which such a discretionary power was conferred on the judge were called arbitrary (*actiones arbitrariae*). It is noteworthy that the list of them given by Justinian[21] contains none but prætorian actions. But it is not therefore to be inferred that in actions of the *jus civile* a judge had no such discretion. On the contrary, Gaius says that it was his duty to acquit a defendant who made satisfaction to the plaintiff at any time after litiscontestation.[22] There was no question that he was bound to do so *ex officio* in a *bonae fidei* action; and the doubt of the Proculians whether he was bound or even entitled to do so in those that were *stricti juris* created no real difficulty, as it was apparently the practice in actions of that sort, when the complaint was of non-restitution, to

---

[20] "Permittitur judici ex bono et aequo secundum cujusque rei, de qua actum est, naturam aestimare, quemadmodum actori satisfieri oporteat" (Just., *Inst.*, iv. 6, § 31).

[21] *Inst.*, *l.c.* The passage in which Gaius probably dealt with them is almost entirely illegible in the Verona MS.; it is page 227, and would come between §§ 114 and 115 of book iv.

[22] Gai., iv. 114.

introduce the words *nisi restituat*. This did not, it is true, empower the judge to determine what, short of restitution, might in the circumstances be deemed sufficient satisfaction to the plaintiff; but it authorised, if not compelled, him to abstain from condemning a defendant who had made full restitution.[23]

Another clause that was very frequently incorporated in a *formula* was what was known as an exception (*exceptio*),— a plea in defence that excluded condemnation on grounds of equity or public policy, even when the plaintiff had clearly established the matter of fact and law embodied in his *intentio*. Thus, suppose A. to have given B. his stipulatory promise for 1000 sesterces, and B. to have thereafter informally agreed not to sue upon the debt: the agreement, as a mere *nudum pactum*, was of no moment according to the *jus civile*, and so was no *ipso jure* bar to an action at B.'s instance,—it had not affected the *dare oportere*. Such an action, however, in face of the agreement, involved a breach of faith on B.'s part, which the prætor could not tolerate. He had announced in his *album* that he would give effect to any informal pact honestly entered into, that neither contravened a statute nor wronged either of the parties to it;[24] and so, when B. applied for a *formula*, A. was entitled to have inserted in it an instruction to the judge that condemnation was to be conditional on A.'s failure to prove the alleged *pactum de non petendo* (" si inter A. A. et N. N. non convenit ne ea pecunia peteretur ").[25] So where it was alleged that the money promised was in repayment of a loan that in fact had never been advanced; that the promise had been induced by fraudulent misrepresentations, extorted by intimidation, or given under excusable error of fact; that the matter had been compromised, and so on,—in all these cases

[23] On the *actiones arbitrariae* and the judge's *arbitrium*, see Lenel, *Beiträge*, p. 80 *sq.*; Sohm, *Inst. d. R. R.*, p. 136 *sq.*
[24] Ulp., *lib. 4 ad edict.*, in *Dig.*, ii. 14, fr. 7, § 7.
[25] Gai., iv. 119.

the exception formulated by the prætor was the assertion of the equity of the *jus honorarium* in derogation of the strictness of the *jus civile*. Sometimes a defendant, instead of condescending on a particular fact which might have entitled him to a specific exception, deemed it more for his advantage to have words inserted in the formula which reserved to him the right to plead any unfair dealing on the part of the plaintiff that in equity disentitled him to demand condemnation; this was the so-called *exceptio doli (generalis)*,—" si non in ea re quid dolo malo A¹ A¹ fiat." It was held to be implied in all *bonae fidei* actions,—" exceptio doli inest bone fidei judiciis;" the *quidquid dare facere oportet ex fide bona* of their "intention" entitled the judge, without any exception formally pleaded, to take into consideration any suggestion by the defendant of unfair conduct on the part of the plaintiff.[26]

It is unnecessary to go into any explanation of the consequences of defects in the *formula*; or of the procedure *in jure* before it was adjusted, or *in judicio* afterwards; or of appeal for review of the judgment by a higher tribunal; or of execution (which was against the estate of the judgment-debtor, and took the form of incarceration only when his goods could not be attached). Enough has been said to show how elastic was this procedure, and how the prætorian *formulae*, in conjunction with the relative announcements in the Edict, supplied the vehicle for the introduction into the law of an immense amount of new doctrine. The system was fully developed before Julian's consolidation of the Edict; and the statutory recognition which the latter then obtained did nothing to impair its efficiency.

[26] On the subject of exceptions see Lenel, *Ueber Ursprung u. Wirkung d. Exceptionen*, Heidelb., 1876, and literature there referred to; Sohm, *Inst. d. R. R.*, p. 141 *sq*. The latter explains very distinctly and in short compass the nature of exceptions founded on statute, such as the Velleian and Macedonian senatusconsults, and the function of the exception in *actiones in factum*.

SECTION 72.—PROCEDURE "EXTRA ORDINEM."[1]

The two-staged procedure, first *in jure* and then *in judicio*, constituted the *ordo judiciorum privatorum*. Early in the empire, however, it became the practice in certain cases for the magistrate to abstain from adjusting a *formula* and making a remit to a *judex*, and to keep the cause in his own hands from beginning to end. This course was adopted sometimes because the claim that was being made rested rather on moral than on legal right, and sometimes in order to avoid unnecessary disclosure of family misunderstandings. Thus the earliest questions that were raised about testamentary trusts were sent for consideration and disposal to the consuls; apparently because, in the existing state of jurisprudence, it was thought incompetent for a beneficiary to maintain in reference to the heir (who had only been *requested* to comply with the testator's wishes) that he was bound in law to pay him (*dare oportere*) his bequest. Had the difficulty arisen at an earlier period and in the heyday of the constructive energy of the prætors, they would probably have solved it with an *actio in factum*. As it was, it fell to the emperors to deal with it, and they adopted the method of *extraordinaria cognitio*; the jurisdiction which they in the first instance conferred on the consuls being before long confided to a magistrate specially designated for it,—the *praetor fideicommissarius*. Questions between tutors and their pupil wards in like manner began to be dealt with *extra ordinem*, the cognition being entrusted by Marcus Aurelius to a *praetor tutelaris*; while fiscal questions in which a private party was interested went to a *praetor fisci*, whose creation was due to Nerva. Claims for aliment between parent and child or patron and freedman rested on

[1] See Keller, *Röm. CP.*, § 81; Bethmann-Hollweg, *Gesch. d. CP.*, vol. ii. § 122; Bekker, *Aktionen*, vol. ii. chap. 23; Baron, *Gesch. d. R. R.*, vol. i. § 220; Buonamici, *Procedura*, p. 398 *sq.*

natural duty rather than legal right; they could not therefore well be made the subject-matter of a *judicium*, and consequently went for disposal to the consuls or the city prefect, and in the provinces to the governor. Questions of status, especially of freedom or slavery, at least from the time of Marcus Aurelius, were also disposed of *extra ordinem*; and so were claims by physicians, advocates, and public teachers for their *honoraria*, and by officials for their salaries, the Romans refusing to admit that these could be recovered by an ordinary action of location. In all those extraordinary cognitions the procedure began with a complaint addressed to the magistrate, instead of an *in jus vocatio* of the party complained against; it was for the magistrate to require the attendance of the latter (*evocatio*) if he thought the complaint relevant. The decision was a *judicatum* or *decretum* according to circumstances.

SECTION 73.—JURAL REMEDIES FLOWING DIRECTLY FROM THE MAGISTRATE'S IMPERIUM.[1]

Great as were the results for the law of the multiplication and simplification of *judicia* through the formular system, it may be questioned whether it did not benefit quite as much from the direct intervention of the prætors in certain cases, in virtue of the supreme power with which they were invested. It manifested itself principally in the form of (1) interdicts; (2) prætorian stipulations; (3) *missio in possessionem*; and (4) *in integrum restitutio*.

1. The interdicts[2] have already been referred to as in use under the *régime* of the *jus civile* (p. 218); but their number

---

[1] Keller, §§ 74-80; Bethmann-Hollweg, vol. ii. §§ 98, 119-121; Bekker, vol. ii. chaps. 16-18; Baron, vol. i. §§ 216-219.

[2] In addition to the authorities in last note, see K. A. Schmidt, *Das Interdiktenverfahren d. Röm. in geschichtl. Entwickelung*, Leipsic, 1853; Machélard, *Théorie des interdits en droit romain*, Paris, 1864; Buonamici, *Procedura*, pp. 420-480.

and scope were vastly increased under that of the *jus honorarium*. The characteristic of the procedure by interdict was this,—that in it the prætor reversed the ordinary course of things, and instead of waiting for an inquiry into the facts alleged by a complainer, provisionally assumed them to be true, and pronounced an order upon the respondent which he was bound either to obey or show to be unjustified. The order pronounced might be either restitutory, exhibitory (in both cases usually spoken of in the texts as a decree), or prohibitory:—restitutory when, for example, the respondent was ordained to restore something he was alleged to have taken possession of by violent means, remove impediments he had placed in the channel of a river, and so on; exhibitory, when he was ordained to produce something he was unwarrantably detaining, *e.g.*, the body of a freeman he was holding as his slave, or a will in which the complainer alleged that he had an interest; prohibitory, as, for example, that he should not disturb the *status quo* of possession as between the complainer and himself, that he should not interfere with a highway, a watercourse, the access to a burial-place, and so forth. If the respondent obeyed the order pronounced in a restitutory or exhibitory decree, there was an end of the matter. But frequently, and perhaps more often than not, the interdict was only the commencement of a litigation, facilitated by sponsions and restipulations, in which the questions had to be tried (1) whether the interdict or injunction was justified, (2) whether there had been breach of it, and (3) if so, what damages were due in consequence. The procedure, therefore, was often anything but summary.

In the possessory interdicts *uti possidetis* and *utrubi* in particular it was extremely involved; due to some extent to the fact that they were double interdicts (*interdicta duplicia*), *i.e.*, addressed indifferently to both parties. Gaius says,[3] but, as most jurists think, without adequate grounds for it,

[3] Gai., iv. 148.

that they had been devised as ancillary to a litigation about ownership, and for the purpose of deciding which of the parties, as possessor, was to have the advantage of standing on the defensive in the *rei vindicatio*.[4] That they were so used in his time, as in that of Justinian,[5] cannot be doubted. But it is amazing that they should have been, for they were infinitely more cumbrous than the *vindicatio* to which they led up.[6] Take the interdict *uti possidetis*, (which applied to immovables, as *utrubi* did to movables). Both parties being present, the prætor addressed them to this effect: " I forbid that one of you who does not possess the house in question to use force to prevent him who does possess it from continuing to do so as at present, provided always that his possession is due neither to clandestine or forcible exclusion of his adversary, nor to a grant from him during pleasure." It is manifest that this decided nothing; it was no more than a prohibition of disturbance of the *status quo*; it left the question entirely open which of the parties it was that was in possession, and which that was forbidden to interfere. The manner of its explication was somewhat singular. Each of the parties was bound at once to commit what in the case of one of them must have been a breach of the interdict, by a pretence of violence offered to the other (*vis ex conventu*);[7] each of them was thus in a position to say to the other— " We have both used force; but it was you alone that did

[4] If that had been their original purpose, they must have been unknown as long as the *rei vindicatio* proceeded *per sacramentum*; for in the sacramental real action both parties vindicated, and both consequently were at once plaintiffs and defendants (*supra*, § 34, note 5).

[5] *Inst.*, iv. 16, 4. But long before the time of Justinian they had been greatly simplified, and really converted into an action, though retaining the old name.

[6] See the (imperfect) description of the procedure in Gai., iv. §§ 148-152, 160, 166-170.

[7] So Gaius calls it: it was probably the same thing as the *vis moribus facta* referred to by Cicero, *Pro Cacc.*, 1, § 2; 8, § 22. See Kappeyne van de Copello, " Ueber das *vim facere* beim *interdictum uti possidetis*," in his *Abhandl. zum Röm. Staats- und Rechtslehre* (Stuttgart, 1885), pp. 115 *sq*.

it in defiance of the interdict, for it is I that am in· possession." The interim enjoyment of the house was then awarded to the highest bidder, who gave his stipulatory promise to pay the rent to his adversary in the event of the latter being successful in the long-run; penal sponsions and restipulations were exchanged upon the question which of them had committed a breach of the interdict; and on these, four in number, *formulae* were adjusted and sent to a *judex* for trial. If the procedure could not thus be explicated, because either of the parties declined to take part in the *vis ex conventu*, or the bidding, or the sponsions and restipulations, he was assumed to be in the wrong, and, by what was called a "secondary" interdict, required at once to yield up his possession or detention, and to abstain from disturbing the other in all time coming.[8] Whatever we may think of the action-system of the Romans in the period of the classical jurisprudence, one cannot help wondering at a procedure so cumbrous and complex as that of their possessory interdicts.

2. A prætorian stipulation[9] was a stipulatory engagement imposed upon a man by a magistrate or judge, in order to secure a third party from the chance of loss or prejudice through some act or omission either of him from whom the engagement was exacted or of some other person for whom he was responsible. Although called prætorian, because the cases in which such stipulations were exigible were set forth in the Edict, yet there can be no question that they originated in the *jus civile;* in fact they were just a means of assuring to a man in advance the benefit of an action of the

[8] Kappeyne van de Copello (p. 166 *sq.*) holds that the secondary interdict (*int. secundarium*) was not a contumacial procedure, but one in which the party declining *vim facere*, &c., (because he knew he could not establish lawful possession in his own person), was still entitled to appear as defendant, and require his adversary to prove *his* possession as the foundation of a restitutory or prohibitory decree·.

[9] To the authorities in note 1 add Schirmer, *Ueber die prätorischen Judicialstipulationen*, Greifswald, 1853 ; Buonamici, *Procedura*, p. 499 *sq.*

jus civile, whereby he might obtain reparation for any injury suffered by him through the occurrence of the act or omission contemplated as possible. Ulpian classified them [10] as cautionary (*cautionales*), judicial, and common. The first were purely precautionary, and quite independent of any action already in dependence between the party moving the magistrate to exact the stipulation and him on whom it was desired to impose it. There were many varieties of them, connected with all branches of the law; for example, the *cautio damni infecti,* security against damage to a man's property in consequence say of the ruinous condition of his neighbour's house, the *cautio usufructuaria* that property usufructed should revert unimpaired to the owner on the expiry of the usufructuary's life interest, the ædilian stipulation against faults in a thing sold, and so forth. In all these cases the stipulation or *cautio* was a guarantee against future loss or injury, usually corroborated by sureties, and made effectual by an action on the stipulation in the event of loss or injury resulting. Judicial stipulations, according to Ulpian's classification, were those imposed by a judge in the course of and with reference to an action in dependence before him, as, for example, the *cautio judicatum solvi* (that the defendant would satisfy the judgment), the *cautio de dolo* (that a thing claimed in the action would not be impaired in the meantime), and many others. Common were such as might either be imposed by a magistrate apart from any depending action or by a judge in the course of one; such as that taken from a tutor or curator for the faithful administration of his office, or from a procurator that his principal would ratify what he was doing.

3. *Missio in possessionem* was the putting of a person in possession either of the whole estate of another (*missio in bona*) or of some particular thing belonging to him (*missio in rem*). The first was by far the most important. It was

[10] *Dig.,* xlvi. 5, 1.

resorted to as a means of execution, not only against a judgment-debtor, but also against a man who fraudulently kept out of the way and thus avoided summons in an action, or who, having been duly summoned, would not do what was expected on the part of a defendant; against the estate of a person deceased to which no heir would enter, thus leaving creditors without a debtor from whom they could enforce payment of their claims; and also against the estate that had belonged to a person who had undergone *capitis deminutio* (§ 29), if the family-head to whom he had subjected himself refused to be responsible for his debts. *Missio in rem* was granted, for example, when a man refused to give *cautio damni infecti*; the applicant was then put in possession of the ruinous property for his own protection.

4. *In integrum restitutio*,[11] reinstatement of an individual, on grounds of equity, in the position he had occupied before some occurrence that had resulted to his prejudice, was one of the most remarkable manifestations of the exercise of the *imperium*. It was not that the individual in question, either directly by action or indirectly by exception, obtained a judgment that either rendered what had happened comparatively harmless or gave him compensation in damages for the loss he had sustained from it, but that the magistrate —and it could only be the prætor, the urban or prætorian prefect, a provincial governor, or the emperor himself—at his own hand pronounced a decree that as far as possible restored the *status quo ante*. It was not enough, however, to entitle a man to this extraordinary relief that he was able to show that he had been taken advantage of to his hurt, and that no other adequate means of redress was open to him; he required in addition to be able to found on some subjective ground of restitution, such as minority, or, if he was of full age, intimidation which could not be resisted,

---

[11] In addition to the authorities in note 1, see Savigny, *System*, vol. vii. §§ 315-343; Buonamici, *Procedura*, p. 480 *sq.*

mistake of fact, fraud, absence or the like. What should be held to amount to a sufficient ground of restitution, either objective or subjective, was at first left very much to the discretion of the magistrate; but even here practice and jurisprudence in time fixed the lines within which he ought to confine himself, and made the principles of *in integrum restitutio* as well settled almost as those of the *actio quod metus causa* or the *actio de dolo*.

PART V.

THE PERIOD OF CODIFICATION.

Diocletian to Justinian.

PART V.
THE PERIOD OF CODIFICATION.
Diocletian to Justinian.

———

CHAPTER FIRST.
HISTORICAL EVENTS THAT INFLUENCED THE LAW.

SECTION 74.—SUPREMACY OF THE EMPERORS AS SOLE LEGISLATORS.

FROM the time of Diocletian downwards, the making of the law was exclusively in the hands of the emperors. The senate still existed, but shorn of all its old functions alike of government and legislation. The responses of patented jurists were a thing of the past. It was to the imperial consistory alone that men looked for interpretation of old law or promulgation of new.

In the reign of Diocletian rescripts (p. 313) were still abundant; but the constitutions in the Theodosian and Justinianian Codes that date from the time of Constantine downwards are mostly of a wider scope, and of the class known as general or edictal laws (*leges generales, edictales*). It would be wrong, however, to infer that rescripts had ceased; for Justinian's Code contains various regulations as to their form, and the matter is dealt with again in one of his Novels. The reason why so few are preserved is that they were no longer authoritative except for the parties to whom they were addressed. This was expressly declared by the Emperors Arcadius and Honorius in 398, in reference to those in answer to applications for advice from officials; and it is not unreasonable to assume that a limitation of the same sort had been put at an earlier date on the authority of those addressed to private parties. Puchta is of opinion that the enactment of Honorius and Arcadius applied equally to *decreta* (p. 314); for this reason, —that during this period matters of litigation did not come under the cognisance of the emperors except on appeal, and that under the new arrangements of Constantine the judgment of affirmance or reversal was embodied in a rescript addressed to the magistrate from whom the appeal had been taken. The rule of Arcadius and Honorius was renewed in 425 by Theodosius and Valentinian, who qualified it, however, to this extent,—that if it contained any distinct indication that the doctrine it laid down was meant to be of general application, then it was to be received as an edict or *lex generalis*. To this Justinian adhered in so far as rescripts in the old sense of the word were concerned; but declared that his judgments (*decreta*) should be received everywhere as laws of general application, and that so should any interpretation given by him of a *lex generalis*, even though elicited by the petition of a private party.

The imperial edicts, adjusted in the consistory, were usually addressed to the people, the senate, or some official civil, military, or ecclesiastical, according to the nature of their subject-matter. The mode of publication varied; but when sent down to an official it was his duty to see to the matter. After the partition of the empire, as each Augustus had the power of legislating for the whole empire, constitutions that affected the interests of both East and West were frequently the result of consultation; at other times there was a communication of a new law by pragmatic sanction from its author to his colleague, the latter by edict ordering its publication if thought expedient. In style the edicts compare very unfavourably with the senatusconsults and rescripts of the second and third century, being uniformly verbose and in many cases obscure. It is not in the least surprising that the compilers of the *Lex Romana Visigothorum* thought them to stand in need of an "*interpretatio;*" the pity is that the latter is itself so far from clear.

SECTION 75.—ESTABLISHMENT OF CHRISTIANITY AS THE STATE RELIGION.[1]

A disposition has sometimes been manifested to credit nascent Christianity with the humaner spirit that began to operate on some of the institutions of the law in the first century of the empire, but which in a previous section (§ 55) has been ascribed to the infiltration into the *jus civile* of doctrines of the *jus naturale*, the product of the philosophy of the Stoa. The teaching of Seneca did quite as much, nay, far more, to influence it then than the lessons that were taught in the little assemblies of the early converts. It would be a bold thing to say that, had Christianity never gained its predominance, that spirit of natural right would not have continued to animate the course of legislation, and to evoke, as years progressed, most of those amendments in the law of the family and the law of succession that were amongst the most valuable contributions of the imperial constitutions to the private law. It may well be that that spirit was intensified and rendered more active with the growth of Christian belief; but not until the latter had been publicly sanctioned by Constantine, and by Theodosius declared to be the religion of the state, do we meet with incontestable records of its influence. We find them in enactments in favour of the Church and its pro-

[1] Troplong, *De l'influence du christianisme sur le droit civil des Romains*, Paris, 1843 (and subsequently); Merivale, *The Conversion of the Roman Empire* (Boyle Lectures for 1864), London, 1864, particularly Lect. 4 and notes to it in the Appendix.

perty, and of its privileges as a legatee; in those conferring or imposing on the bishops a supervision of charities and charitable institutions, and a power of interfering in matters of guardianship; in the recognition of the efficacy of certain acts done in presence of two or three of the clergy, and thereafter recorded in the church registers; in the disabilities as to marriage and succession with which heretics and apostates were visited, and in a variety of minor matters. Of greater importance were three features for which it was directly responsible,—the repeal of the caduciary provisions of the Papia-Poppæan law (p. 304), the penalties imposed upon divorce, and the institution of the bishop's court (*episcopalis audientia*).

The purpose of the Caduciary Law was to discourage celibacy and encourage fruitful marriages; but legislation in such a spirit could not possibly be maintained when celibacy had come to be inculcated as a virtue, and as the peculiar characteristic of a holy life. The penalties alike of *orbitas* and *coelibatus* were abolished by Constantine in the year 320.

The legislation about divorce, from the first of Constantine's enactments on the subject down to those of Justinian, forms a miserable chapter in the history of the law. Not one of the emperors who busied himself with the matter, undoing the work of his predecessors and substituting legislation of his own quite as complicated and futile, thought of interfering with the old principle that divorce ought to be as free as marriage, and independent of the sanction or decree of a judicial tribunal. Justinian was the first that, by one of his Novels, imposed a condition on parties to a divorce of common accord (*communi consensu*), namely, that they should both enter a convent, otherwise it should be null; but so distasteful was this to popular feeling, and so little conducive to improvement of the tone of morals within the conventual precincts, that it was repealed by his successor.

What wonder, with such unqualified freedom of divorce, that Jerome should tell us he had seen in Rome a man living with his twenty-first wife, she having already had twenty-two husbands; or that we should have a bishop of Amasia, some thirty or forty years before Justinian, declaring that men changed their wives just as they did their clothes, and that nuptial beds were removed as often and as easily as market-stalls! The legislation of Justinian's predecessors and the bulk of his own were levelled at one-sided repudiations, imposing penalties, personal and patrimonial, (1) upon the author of a repudiation on some ground the law did not recognise as sufficient,—and the lawful grounds varied from reign to reign,—and (2) upon the party whose misconduct gave rise to a repudiation that was justifiable. Into the details, however, it is unnecessary to enter.[2]

The bishop's court (*episcopale judicium, episcopalis audientia*)[3] had its origin in the practice of the primitive Christians, in accordance with the apostolic precept, of submitting their differences to one or two of their brethren in the faith, usually a presbyter or bishop, who acted as arbiter.[4] On the establishment of Christianity the practice obtained legislative sanction; Constantine giving the bishop's court concurrent jurisdiction with the ordinary civil courts where both parties preferred the former, and by a later enactment going so far as to empower one of the parties to a suit to remove it to the ecclesiastical tribunal against the will of the other. For various reasons, and amongst them the ignorance of the ordinary judges and the costs of litigation in the civil courts, advantage was taken of this power of resorting to the bishop to an extent which seriously interfered with the proper discharge of his spiritual functions; so that Honorius judged it expedient to revert to the

[2] See Wächter, *Ueber Ehescheidungen bei den Römern* (Stuttgart, 1822), p. 184 *sq.*

[3] Bethmann-Hollweg, *Gesch. d. CP.*, vol. iii. § 139.

[4] Cox's *First Century of Christianity* (London, 1886), p. 226 *sq.*

original rule, and, at least as regarded laymen, to limit the right of resort to the episcopal judicatory to cases in which both parties consented. The procedure was of much the same nature as a reference to arbitration; the bishop's finding was not a judgment but a *definitio;* and, if not voluntarily implemented, had to be made operative by aid of the civil magistrate. It is impossible to say with any approach to exactitude what effect this intervention of the clergy as judges in ordinary civil causes—for they had no criminal jurisdiction—had on the development of the law; but it can hardly have been without some influence in still further promoting the tendency to subordinate act and word to will and *animus*, to deal leniently with technicalities, and to temper the rules of the *jus civile* with equity and considerations of natural right.

SECTION 76.—SOCIAL AND AGRARIAN CHANGES.

There were two amid the many social and economical changes of the period that had a material bearing on the private law,—the introduction of the principle of heredity into most trades, occupations, and professions, and the extension of the colonate or servitude of the glebe. The consequences of the first, however, are too special to be discussed with advantage.

As regards the colonate (*colonatus*),[1] it seems to have become the normal condition of the *plebs rustica* all over the

[1] The earlier literature is referred to and criticised in Heisterbergck, *Die Entstehung des Colonats*, Leipsic, 1876. He omits reference to the important work of Elia Lattes, *Studi storici sopra il contratto d' Enfiteusi nelle sue relazioni col Colonato*, Turin, 1868, of which chaps. ii. and iii. are devoted to the colonate. Of later date than Heisterbergck may be noted Marquardt, *Röm. Staatsverwalt.*, vol. ii. p. 232 *sq.*; Fustel de Coulanges, "Le Colonat Romain," in his *Recherches sur quelques problèmes d'histoire*, Paris, 1881; Mommsen, "Ueber d. Dekret des Commodus f. den *saltus Burunitanus*," in *Hermes*, vol. xv. p. 408 *sq.*; Humbert's article "Colonus," in Daremberg and Saglio's *Dict. des Antiquités Grecques et Romaines*, part ix. (1884), p. 1322 *sq.*; Karlowa, *Röm. RG.*, vol. i. p. 918 *sq.*

empire,—personal freedom, but perpetual servitude to the soil (*servi terrae ipsius*). There is much controversy as to its origin. The truth seems to be that conditions nearly resembling it, and out of which it may be said to have been evolved, existed in different parts of the empire long before there was any general legislation on the subject; and that those conditions, regulated to a great extent by local custom or special imperial mandate, must be ascribed to different causes in different places. There is evidence that in Egypt there existed something very like the colonate even before it had passed under Roman domination; that in some parts of Africa slaves were enfranchised on condition of perpetual attachment to the land that had been their *peculium*; that into the western provinces there were repeated importations of barbarian prisoners who were distributed amongst the great landowners as *coloni*; and that very often the small yeomen placed themselves in the same position in relation to some great landowner for the sake of his protection, or were by him compelled so to submit themselves. It was a state of matters which those at the head of affairs, with their recollection of the disastrous fate of the *latifundia* of Italy, had good reason to encourage; for it moderated the mischiefs of great estates by ensuring that they would be peopled by freemen, whose poll-tax increased the revenue, and whose own interests afforded the best guarantee for their doing all they could to make their little holdings productive.

According to the very numerous constitutions in the Theodosian and Justinianian Codes that regulate the position of the *coloni*, they were freemen, subject to capitation, and inscribed in the census list in the page appropriated to the landowner under whom they held and from whom their poll-tax was collected; it is in reference to their liability to it that they are frequently spoken of as *adscripticii, tributarii, censiti*. They were liable also to military service when their lord was called upon to furnish recruits; but they were not entitled voluntarily to enlist, for that was to desert their service. From his lord the *colonus* held a small farm, for a rent payable sometimes in money but usually in kind, but which the former had no power to augment. With fixity of rent he had also a sort of fixity of tenure; his lord (*dominus, possessor, patronus*) could not sell him apart from his holding, nor his holding without him; but it was lawful for an owner of two estates, if one was insufficiently furnished with tenants, to replenish it from the other, provided that in so doing he did not separate a man from his wife and young children. If a *colonus* fled, his lord, when he recovered him, might put him in chains; and against any third party detaining him the lord had a right of action as if the *colonus* were really a slave. This, however, he was not; for, with permission of his lord, which sometimes had to be paid for, he might contract a lawful marriage that gave him *potestas* over his children; he might hold property of his own, even lands, in respect of which he was entered in the census lists and liable for land-tax as proprietor in his own right; and on his death what belonged to him passed to his heirs by testament or on intestacy, and only on their failure fell to his lord. Alienation *inter vivos*, as a rule, was competent only with the lord's consent, the belongings of the *colonus* being in a manner no more than *peculium ;* but a privileged class known as *liberi coloni*, who either themselves or their ancestors had originally been citizens of free birth, were not subject to this restriction.

Once a class of *coloni* had been created on an estate, it was perpetuated and recruited by birth (for the condition was hereditary), by prescription, by a freeman's marriage with an *adscripticia*, and by the reduction of able-bodied mendicants to that condition as a penalty. Once a *colonus*, ever a *colonus*, was almost literally true. For a time it was held that if a born *colonus* had *de facto* for thirty years lived in independence, he thereby acquired *de jure* the status of a free Roman citizen; but this was disallowed by Justinian, who, possibly out of consideration for the interests of agriculture, refused to admit the possibility of a man's escape from the bonds that tied him to the soil except by his elevation to the episcopate, and provided always he had taken orders with the consent of his lord.

SECTION 77.—ABANDONMENT OF THE "FORMULAR" SYSTEM OF PROCEDURE.[1]

The formular system, with its remit from the prætor to a sworn *judex* who was to try the cause, was of infinite advantage to the law; for the judgment was that of a free and independent citizen, untrammelled by officialism, fresh from some centre of business, and in full sympathy with the parties between whom he had to decide. Such a system was incompatible with the political arrangements of Diocletian and Constantine; and it is with no surprise that we find the former of those sovereigns instructing the provincial governors that in future, unless prevented by pressure of business (or, according to a later constitution of Julian's, when the matter was of trifling importance), they were themselves to hear the causes brought before them from first to last, as was already the practice in the *extraordinariae cognitiones* (§ 72). The remit in exceptional cases was not, as formerly, to a private citizen, but to what was called a *judex pedaneus*, probably a matriculated member of the local bar, (whom, however, the parties might decline if they could agree upon a referee of their own selection); and for a time his delegated authority was embodied in a *formula* after the old fashion. But even this exceptional use of it did not

[1] Wieding, *Der Justinianeische Libellprocess*, Vienna, 1865; Bethmann-Hollweg, *Gesch. d. CP.*, vol. iii. (1866); Muther (rev. Wieding), in the *Krit. VJS.*, vol. ix. (1867), pp. 161 sq., 329 sq.; Wieding, in same journal, vol. xii. (1870). p. 228 sq.; Bekker, *Aktionen*, vol. ii. chaps. 23, 24; Baron, *Gesch. d. R.R.*, vol. i. p. 448 sq.; Buonamici, *Procedura*, p. 408 sq.

long survive; for an enactment by the two sons of Constantine, conceived in terms the most comprehensive, declared fixed styles to be but traps for the unwary, and forbade their use in any legal act whatever, whether contentious or voluntary. The result was not only the formal disappearance of the distinction between the proceedings *in jure* and *in judicio*, but the practical disappearance also of the distinctions between actions *in jus* and *in factum*, and *actiones directae* and *utiles;* the conversion of the interdict into an *actio ex interdicto;* admission of power of amendment of the pleadings; condemnation in the specific thing claimed, if in existence, instead of its pecuniary equivalent; and execution accordingly by aid of officers of the law.

In Constantinople the jurisdiction in civil matters was in the prefect of the city and the minor judges, to wit, the *praefectus annonae* and the prætors; in Rome it was in the hands of the same officials, and concurrently with them the *vicarius urbis*. In the provinces it was in the governors; but with a limited competence in the municipal magistrates and the defenders of towns. The vicars and prætorian prefects acted as courts of the first instance only exceptionally; but the latter had eventually the same power as the emperor of citing any person to their tribunal, whatever his proper *forum*.[2] In addition, there were many special *fora* for privileged parties or causes, to which it is unnecessary to refer. From the minor judges there was appeal to the superior ones, and from these again to the emperor. A process was full from first to last of intervention by officials. The *in jus vocatio* of the Twelve Tables—the procedure by which a plaintiff himself brought his adversary into court, was a thing of the past. In the earlier part of the period the proceedings commenced with the *litis denuntiatio* introduced in the time of Marcus Aurelius and remodelled by Constantine; but under Justinian (though probably begun

[2] Willems, *Droit publ. Romain* (4th ed., Paris, 1880), p. 620.

before his reign) the initial step was what was called the *libellus conventionis*. This was a short and precise written statement addressed by the plaintiff to the court, explaining (but without detail) the nature of the action he proposed to raise and the claim he had to prefer; which was accompanied with a formal undertaking to proceed with the cause and follow it out to judgment, under penalty of having to pay double costs to the defendant. If the judge was satisfied of the relevancy of the libel, he pronounced an interlocutor (*interlocutio*) ordaining its service on the respondent. This was done by an officer of court, who cited him to appear on a day named, usually at a distance of two or three months. The defendant, through the officer, put in an answer (*libellus contradictionis*), at the same time giving security for the proper maintenance of the defence and eventual satisfaction of the judgment. On the day appointed the parties were first heard on any dilatory pleas, such as defect of jurisdiction; if none were offered, or those stated repelled, they then proceeded to expound their respective grounds of action and defence, each finally making oath of his good faith in the matter (*juramentum calumniae*), and their counsel doing the same.

From this point, which marked the *litis contestatio* or joinder of issue, the procedure was much the same as that *in judicio* under the formular system. But in all cases in which the demand was that a particular thing should be given or restored, and the plaintiff desired to have the thing itself rather than damages, execution was specific and effected through officers of the law (*manu militari*). Where, on the other hand, the condemnation was pecuniary, the usual course was for the judge, through his officers, to take possession of such things belonging to the defendant as were thought sufficient to satisfy the judgment (*pignus in causa judicati captum*), and which were eventually sold judicially if the defendant still refused to pay; the *missio in bona* (p.

373) of the classical period was rarely resorted to except in the case of insolvency.

SECTION 78.—THE VALENTINIANIAN "LAW OF CITATIONS."[1]

This famous enactment, the production of Theodosius II., tutor of the youthful Valentinian III., was issued from Ravenna in the year 426, and addressed to the Roman Senate. It ran thus:—

"We accord our approval to all the writings of Papinian, Paul, Gaius, Ulpian, and Modestine, conceding to Gaius the same authority that is enjoyed by Paul, Ulpian, and the rest, and sanctioning the citation of all his works. We ratify also the jurisprudence (*scientiam*) of those earlier writers whose treatises and statements of the law any of the aforesaid five have made use of in their own works,—Scævola, for example, and Sabinus, and Julian, and Marcellus,—and of all others whom they have been in the habit of quoting as authorities (*omniumque quos illi celebrarunt*); provided always, as their antiquity makes them uncertain, that the texts of those earlier jurists are verified by collation of manuscripts. If divergent *dicta* be adduced, that party shall prevail who has the greatest number of authorities on his side; if the number on each side be the same, that one shall prevail which has the support of Papinian; but, whilst he, most excellent of them all, is to be preferred to any other single authority, he must yield to any two. (Paul's and Ulpian's notes on his writings, however, as already enacted, are to be disregarded.) Where opinions are equal, and none entitled to preference, we leave it to the discretion of the judge which he shall adopt."

This constitution has always been regarded as a signal proof of the lamentable condition into which jurisprudence had sunk in the beginning of the fifth century. Constantine, a hundred years earlier, had condemned the notes of Ulpian and Paul upon Papinian. Claiming, as the later emperors did, to be the only authoritative mouthpieces of the law, it was not an unreasonable stretch of their prerogative to declare that the criticism of the two younger jurists, not-

---

[1] *Theod. Cod.*, i. 4, 3; Puchta, in the *Rhein. Museum f. Jurisprud.*, vol. v. (1832), p. 141 *sq.*, and in his *Verm. Schrift.* (Leipsic, 1851), p. 284 *sq.*; Sanio, in his *Rechtshistor. Abhandl. u. Studien* (Königsberg, 1845), p. 1 *sq.*; Karlowa, *Röm. RG.*, vol. i. p. 933 *sq.*; Roby, *Introduction*, p. lxxxiv., *sq.*

withstanding that they had enjoyed the *jus respondendi ex auctoritate principis*, should not derogate from the authority of their more eminent predecessor. There were no longer any living jurists to lay down the law (*jura condere*) ; and if it was to be gathered from the writings of those who were dead, it was well that the use of them should be regulated as was done by Constantine. The Valentinian law proceeded so far in the same direction. It made a selection of the jurisconsults of the past whose works alone were to be allowed to be cited : Papinian, Paul, Ulpian, and Modestine, the four latest patented counsel of any distinction ; Gaius, of authority previously only in the schools, but whose writings were now approved universally, notwithstanding that he had never possessed the *jus respondendi;* and all the earlier jurists whose *dicta* those five had accepted.[2] But it went yet a step further ; for it declared all of them, with the sole exception of Papinian, to be of equal authority, and degraded the function of the judge in most cases, so far at least as a question of law was concerned, to the purely arithmetical task of counting up the names which the industry of the advocates on either side had succeeded in adducing in support of their respective contentions. It is probable that, from the days of Hadrian down to those of Alexander Severus, when the emperor in his council had to frame a rescript or a decree, its tenor would be decided by the vote of the majority; but that was after argument and counter-argument, which must in many cases have modified first impressions. Taking the votes of dead men, who had not heard each other's reasons for their opinions, was a very different process. It may have been necessary ; but it can have been so only because a living jurisprudence had no existence,— because the constructive talent of the earlier empire had entirely disappeared.

[2] This seems to be the natural reading of the enactment ; although some are of opinion that it was intended to sanction the citation of those passages only of the earlier jurists that were referred to by any of the five.

CHAPTER SECOND.

ANTEJUSTINIANIAN COLLECTIONS OF STATUTE AND JURISPRUDENCE.

SECTION 79.—THE GREGORIAN AND HERMOGENIAN CODES.[1]

THE first of these codes was a collection of imperial rescripts (with a few edicts, &c.) made by one Gregorianus in the very end of the third century, and probably at the instigation of Diocletian, though whether in East or West, critics are unable to decide. It is believed to have contained fifteen or sixteen books, subdivided into titles, arranged after the order of the Edict. Our acquaintance with its contents is derived principally from Alaric's Breviary (p. 398), and the *Collatio*, the Vatican Fragments, and the *Consultatio* (pp. 395–397), although there can be little doubt that most of the rescripts in Justinian's Code are taken from it without acknowledgement. The collection of Hermogenianus, also of rescripts, seems to have been a supplement to the earlier one, but, so far as appears, arranged only in titles. As the latest enactment in it is of the year 365, the probability is that it was published about that time. Both codes, although the work of private parties, received statutory recognition from Theodosius and Valentinian in their commission for preparation of a collection of edictal law; and from the language of Justinian in reference to them there is reason to believe that in the courts they were regarded as authoritative, even to the ignoring of all rescripts not embodied in

---

[1] Huschke, "Ueber den Gregorianus u. Hermogenianus Codex," in the *Z. f. RG.*, vol. vi. (1867), p. 283 *sq.*; Karlowa, *Röm. RG.*, vol. i. pp. 940 *sq.*, 959 *sq.*

them. Their latest editor is the younger Haenel, in the *Corpus Juris Romani Antejustiniani* (Bonn, 1837); he has gathered about seventy constitutions that stood in the first, and about thirty that stood in the second. But how small a proportion this bears to their original contents is manifest when we take note of the 1200 or 1300 rescripts of Diocletian and Maximian alone which we find in the Justinianian Code, and which can hardly have been obtained from any other source than the Gregorian and Hermogenian collections. They seem to have been still a subject of exposition in the law-school of Beirout in the early years of Justinian; for comments upon them by Eudoxius and Patricius, who taught there, are preserved amongst the scholia of the Basilica (p. 431).

SECTION 80.—THE THEODOSIAN CODE AND POST-THEODOSIAN NOVELS.[1]

Three years after publication of the "Law of Citations" (§ 78) Theodosius nominated a commission of nine members to initiate the preparation of a body of law, which, if his scheme had been carried into execution, would have rendered that of Justinian unnecessary. In a constitution some ten years later he explains the motives that had actuated him,—that he saw with much concern the poverty-stricken condition of jurisprudence, and how very few men there were who, notwithstanding the prizes that awaited them, were able to make themselves familiar with the whole range of law; and that he attributed it very much to the multitude of books and large mass of statutes through which it was dispersed, and which it was next to impossible for any ordinary mortal to master. His scheme was eventually to compile one single code from materials derived alike from the writings of the jurists, the Gregorian and Hermogenian

[1] See Karlowa, *Röm. RG.*, vol. i. pp. 943 *sq.*, 960 *sq.*

collections of rescripts, and the edictal laws from the time of Constantine downwards. His language leaves no doubt that it was his intention to have the general code very carefully prepared, so as to make it a complete exponent of the law in force, which should take the place of everything, statutory or jurisprudential, of an earlier date. The collection of edicts which he directed his commissioners to prepare, and which was to contain all that had not been displaced by later legislation, even though some of them might be obsolete by disuse, was to be the first step in the execution of his project. For some reason or other nothing followed upon this enactment; and in 435 a new commission of sixteen members was nominated to collect the edicts, but with nothing said in their instructions about anything ulterior. It was completed in three years, and published at Constantinople early in the year 438, with the declaration that it should take effect from 1st January following; and a copy was communicated to Valentinian, who ordained that it should come into force in the West from 12th January 439.

The arrangement of the Theodosian Code is in sixteen books, subdivided into titles, in which the constitutions are placed in chronological order. They cover the whole field of law, private and public, civil and criminal, fiscal and municipal, military and ecclesiastical. The private law is in the first five books. Until the present century, these were known only by the excerpts from them in the *Lex Romana Visigothorum*; whereas the last eight books were published *in extenso* by Dutillet as long ago as 1550, from a manuscript of the Code itself, and books 6, 7, and 8 by Cujas a few years later from another manuscript. It was upon the Code as thus restored that Jac. Gothofredus wrote his six folios of commentary,—a work of stupendous industry and erudition, which remains of the highest importance as illustrative of the public law and administration of the period. Between the years 1820 and 1840 a large number of constitutions belonging to the first five books were recovered by Amedeo Peyron, Baudi di Vesme, Cardinal Mai, Clossius, and Haenel, mostly from palimpsests in the University Library at Turin; all these were incorporated in the edition of the Code contributed by Haenel to the (Bonn) *Corpus Jur. Rom. Antejust.*[2] There are still, however, many deficiencies; Haenel estimates that about 450 of the constitutions of the first five books are lost.

The imperial edicts subsequent to the publication of the Theodosian Code got the name of Novels (*novellae constitutiones*). There were many such published in both divisions of the empire, and for a time communicated from one emperor to the other. The first recorded transmission— it was of a considerable batch of constitutions—was by Theodosius himself to Valentinian in the year 447; Marcian seems to have followed his example, as long as Valentinian was alive; but Leo bestowed his favours only on Anthemius. It is probable that Valentinian sent his Novels to Theodosius and Marcian; but it does not appear that the practice was followed by his successors, although a considerable number were published in the Western empire by Maximus, Majorian, Severus, and Anthemius. But, whether communicated or not, none of the Western Novels seem to have been adopted in the East, for there is not one of them in the Justinianian Code. They are preserved partly in manuscripts and partly (in abridgement) in the Breviary; and are usually published (as in Haenel's edition) as an appendix to the Theodosian Code.

SECTION 81.—THE " COLLATIO," THE VATICAN FRAGMENTS, AND THE " CONSULTATIO."

These three were unofficial collections. (1.) The *Collatio Legum Mosaicarum et Romanarum*, otherwise *Lex Dei quam*

[2] *Codex Theodosianus. Ad LIV libror. manuscriptor. et prior. edition. fidem*

Dominus praecepit ad Moysen,[1] is a parallel of divine and human law, the former drawn from the Pentateuch, and the latter from the writings of Gaius, Papinian, Paul, Ulpian, and Modestine, rescripts from the Gregorian and Hermogenian Codes, and one or two later general enactments. Its date is probably about the year 390, but its authorship is unknown. It was first published by P. Pithou in 1573, and has been often re-edited; the most critical version being that of Blume (Bonn, 1833), and the latest that of Huschke in his *Jurisprudentia Antejustiniana*. (2.) The Vatican Fragments were discovered by Mai in a palimpsest in the Vatican in 1820. What was the title of the book to which they originally belonged it is impossible to say; but it was evidently a book of practice, compiled in the Western empire, and of very considerable dimensions. The extant fragments deal with the law of sale, usufruct, dowries, donations, tutories, and processual agency. They are drawn from the writings of Papinian, Ulpian, and Paul, the two collections of rescripts, and a few general enactments, the latest dating from the year 372. The compilation may be of about the same antiquity as the *Collatio*; although Mommsen is disposed to ascribe it to the time of Constantine, and to assume that the enactment of 372 was introduced by a later hand. It is printed in Huschke's collection of Antejustinianian law; but the authoritative text is that of Mommsen, submitted, along with a facsimile of the MS., to the Berlin Academy in 1859.[2] (3.) The *Consultatio* (*veteris cujusdam*

recognov. et annot. crit. instruxit Gust. Haenel, Bonn, 1842. Krüger, in 1868, 1869, and 1878, prepared a facsimile of the Turin palimpsests, which was published in the Transactions of the Royal Academy of Berlin in 1879. He promises a new edition of the Code for the 3d vol. of his, Mommsen's, and Studemund's *Collectio libror. juris antejustiniani*.

[1] See a paper by Huschke in the *Z. f. gesch. RW.*, vol. xiii. (1846), p. 1 *sq.*; a second by Dirksen (published originally in 1846), in his *Hinterlass. Schriften* (Leipsic, 1871), vol. ii. p. 100 *sq.*; and a third by Rudorff, in the *Abhandl. d. K. Akademie d. Wissensch. zu Berlin*, 1868, p. 265 *sq.*

[2] The text is reprinted in a small volume published at Bonn in 1861, and since then in Weidmann's collection of Latin and Greek authors.

jurisconsulti consultatio)[3] was first published by Cujas in 1577 from a manuscript (now lost) that had come to him from his friend Antoine Loysel. It seems to be part of a collection of answers upon questions of law submitted for the opinion of counsel, and is of value for the fragments it contains from Paul's Sentences and the three Codes. It is thought to have been written in France in the end of the fifth or beginning of the sixth century.

SECTION 82.—THE ROMANO-BARBARIAN CODES.

This title is usually applied to three collections compiled in Western Europe after it had thrown off the sovereignty of Rome. They are—

1. The *Edictum Theodorici*, compiled at the instance of Theodoric, king of the Ostrogoths, during his residence in Rome in the year 500. Its materials were drawn from the writings of the jurists (principally the Sentences of Paul), the Gregorian, Hermogenian, and Theodosian Codes, and the later Novels; all reduced into 154 sections, with no systematic arrangement, but touching upon all branches of the law, public and private, especially criminal law and procedure. It was professedly intended to apply to all Theodoric's subjects, both Goths and Romans; but it is pretty generally admitted that this idea cannot have been fully realised, and that in some matters, *e.g.*, the law of the family, Gothic customs must still have continued to prevail.[1]

---

[3] See Rudorff, "Ueber d. Entstehung d. Consultatio," in the *Z. f. gesch. RW.*, vol. xiii. (1846), p. 50 *sq.*, and Huschke, in his preface to it in his *Jurisprud. antejustiniana*, p. 797 *sq.*

[1] See Savigny, *Gesch. d. R. R.*, vol. ii. p. 172 *sq.*; Glöden, *Das Röm. Recht im Ostgothischen Reiche*, Jena, 1843 ; Stobbe, *Gesch. der deutsch. Rechtsquellen* (Leipsic, 1860-64), vol. i. p. 94 *sq.* The text was first published in 1579, from a MS. of Pithou's, in an appendix to Cassiodorus's *Variarum Libri XII*, and is in most collections of the *Leges Barbarorum* ; that in Pertz's *Monum. Germ. hist., Leges*, vol. v., is by Blume. The last separate edition is that of Rhon, *Comment. ad Edict. Theodorici*, Halle, 1816.

2. The *Lex Romana Visigothorum* or *Breviarium Alaricianum* was a much more ambitious and important collection. It was compiled by commissioners appointed by Alaric II., king of the Western Goths, with approval of the bishops and nobles, published at Aire in Gascony in the year 506, the original deposited in the treasury, and compared and certified copies sent down to all the greater officials of the kingdom, with instructions to allow no other law to be used within their jurisdictions on pain of death. In accordance with their commission the compilers selected their material partly from *leges* (statute law) and partly from *jus* (jurisprudential law); taking what they considered appropriate, without altering the text except in the way of excision of passages that were obsolete or purely historical. For the *leges* they utilised some 400 of the 3400 enactments (according to Haenel's estimate) of the Theodosian code, and about 30 of the known 104 post-Theodosian Novels; for the *jus*,— the Institutes of Gaius, Paul's Sentences, the Gregorian and Hermogenian rescripts, and the first book of Papinian's Responses (a single sentence). All of these, except Gaius, were accompanied with an "interpretation," which resembles the *interpretatio* of the XII Tables in this respect,—that it is often not so much explanatory of the text as qualificative or corrective. Gaius is in an Epitome in two books, believed to have been only a reproduction of an abridgement already current, and dating from about the beginning of the fifth century. The Breviary exercised very considerable influence in Europe generally. This is traceable, for example, in the *lex Salica*, in the Capitularies, and in the collections of styles of the early middle age; and there is no question that, until the rise of the Bologna school in the twelfth century, it was from it, rather than from the books of Justinian, that Western Europe acquired its scanty knowledge of Roman law.[2]

[2] See Savigny, vol. ii. p. 37 *sq.*; Haenel's *Prolegomena*; Stobbe, vol. i. p.

3. The *Lex Romana Burgundionum*, formerly, owing to a mistake of a transcriber, called *Papianus*. This is the collection which King Gundobald, in publishing in 501 his code of native law (*lex Burgundionum* or *Gundobada*), had promised should be prepared for the use of his Roman subjects. Its date, and even whether it was promulgated by him or his son Sigismund, are uncertain: owing to the incorporation in it of certain passages bearing a close resemblance to some of the "interpretations" in the Breviary, many jurists think it must be of later date than 506; but it is quite possible that the interpretations in question were borrowed by the compilers of both collections from an earlier source. The Romano-Burgundian Code deals with private law, criminal law, and judicial procedure, distributed through forty-seven titles, and arranged very much after the order of the Gundobada, from which it has a few extracts. Its statutory Roman sources are the same as those of the Breviary; the jurisprudential authorities referred to are Gaius and Paul, the latter in his Sentences, and the former (only three times altogether) in some other book than his Institutes. In form it is not, like the Breviary or the Justinianian Digest and Code, a collection of extracts, but a consecutive and homogeneous compilation, something between a text-book and a code, with only occasional quotation of the writer's authorities in this way—" secundum legem Theodosiani, lib. ix.," " secundum legem Novellam," " secundum Pauli sententiam," &c.[3]

65 *sq.*; Karlowa, *Röm. RG.*, vol. i. p. 976 *sq.* The Breviary was first published *in extenso* by Sichard (Basle, 1528); but the authoritative edition is that of Haenel,—*Lex Rom. Wisigothorum ad LXXII libror. manuscriptor. fidem recognovit . . . Gust. Haenel*, Berlin, 1847.

[3] See preface to Barkow, *Lex Romana Burgundionum*, Greifswald, 1824; Savigny, vol. ii. p. 9 *sq.*, and vol. vii. (addition by Merkel), p. 30 *sq.*; Blume, " Ueber den burgundischen Papianus," in Bekker and Muther's *Jahrb. des gem. Rechts*, vol. ii. (1858), p. 197 *sq.*; Karlowa, *Röm. RG.*, vol. i. p. 983 *sq.* The first edition was by Cujas in 1566; the best is that of Blume, in Pertz's *Monum. Germ. hist., Leges*, vol. iii. (1863), p. 505; the handiest that of Barkow (as above).

Section 83.—Oriental Collections.

A few years ago there was discovered in the convent on Mount Sinai a bundle of papyrus leaves which seemed to contain part of a treatise on Græco-Roman law. Their finder, Dr. Bernardakis, made a transcript, which he forwarded to Dareste in Paris, by whom they were published in 1880. Since then they have been re-edited by Zachariæ v. Lingenthal, Alibrandi, and Krüger; and may possibly be still further elucidated after a revision and, if practicable, photographic reproduction of the originals. They have proved to be parts of a commentary on *Ulpianus ad Sabinum*, written after the Theodosian Code, but before that of Justinian, and therefore between 439 and 529. The scholiast, who seems to have intended his book rather for educational than practical purposes, and may have been of the school of Beirout, makes use not only of the Theodosian, but also of the Gregorian and Hermogenian Codes, drawing frequently upon the last, and, as Krüger observes, creating the impression that it must have been of greater proportions than is usually supposed; and amongst the jurists to whom he refers are Marcian, Florentine, Paul, and Modestine. The *papyri* have thrown new light upon a few questions of historical jurisprudence, and it is possible that still more may be derived from them.[1]

Under the title of *Leges Constantini Theodosii et Leonis* there are extant, in Syrian, Arabic, and Armenian, in the British Museum, the Bodleian, and the National and Royal libraries of Paris, Berlin, and St. Petersburg, manuscripts of a collection of Syro-Roman law, dating from about the year 476, which was recently published by Bruns and Sachau

[1] See Dareste, in the *Nouv. Rev. Hist.*, vol. iv. (1880), p. 643 *sq.*; Alibrandi, in the *Studi e documenti di storia e diritto*, vol. iii. (1882), p. 30 *sq.*; Krüger in the *Z. d. Sav. Stift. (R.A.)*, vol. iv. (1883), p. 1 *sq.*; Karlowa, *Röm. RG.*, vol. i. p. 985 *sq.*

under the title of *Syrisch-Römisches Rechtsbuch*.[2] It is the opinion of Bruns that all the versions are from a Greek original of which no trace survives, but which he thinks must have been compiled in Syria itself. As a repertory of Roman law it is of little or no value; interesting no doubt as showing how, notwithstanding all the efforts of legislation, the law might become corrupted and degraded in the provinces by commixture with native custom, and to some extent by the ignorance of the jurists; but adding scarcely a single iota to our knowledge of pure Roman doctrine.

[2] *Syrisch-Römisches Rechtsbuch aus dem fünften Jahrhundert . . . herausgegeben, übersetzt, u. erlautert von Dr K. G. Bruns u. Dr E. Sachau*, Leipsic, 1880. See review by Bluntschli, in the *Krit. VJS. f. Rechtswissensch.*, N.F., vol. iii. (1880), p. 548 sq. ; also Karlowa, *Röm. RG.*, vol. i. p. 987 sq. A Syrian version, from a British Museum MS., had been published, with a Latin translation, by the Dutch theologian and orientalist, Dr. Land, in his *Anecdota Syriaca* (Leyden 1862) ; but as, from want of acquaintance with law, it was not up to the mark, the edition of Bruns and Sachau was undertaken at the instigation and cost of the Berlin Academy. Some particulars are given by von Hube, in the *Z. d. Sav. Stift.* (*R.A.*), vol. iii. p. 17 sq., of a translation of the Law Book into Georgian in the 17th century, and from that into Russian in 1813 and 1823.

CHAPTER THIRD.

THE JUSTINIANIAN LAW.

SECTION 84.—JUSTINIAN'S COLLECTIONS AND HIS OWN LEGISLATION.

"FLAVIUS ANICIUS JUSTINIANUS, surnamed the Great, the most famous of all the emperors of the Eastern Roman empire, was by birth a barbarian, native of a place called Tauresium in the district of Dardania, a region of Illyricum, and was born, most probably, on May 11, 483. His family has been variously conjectured, on the strength of the proper names which its members are stated to have borne, to have been Teutonic or Slavonic. The latter seems the more probable view. His own name was originally Uprauda. Justinianus was a Roman name which he took from his uncle Justin who adopted him, and to whom his advancement in life was due. Of his early life we know nothing except that he came to Constantinople while still a young man, and received there an excellent education. Doubtless he knew Latin before Greek; it is alleged that he always spoke Greek with a barbarian accent. When Justin ascended the throne in 518 A.D., Justinian became at once a person of the first consequence, guiding, especially in church matters, the policy of his aged, childless, and ignorant uncle, receiving high rank and office at his hands, and soon coming to be regarded as his destined successor. On Justin's death in 527, having been a few months earlier associated with him as co-emperor, he succeeded without opposition to the throne."[1]

Of his great projects at home and abroad none was attended with so much success as his scheme for making an authoritative collection of the law. Ambitious to carry out a reform more complete even than that which Theodosius had planned but failed to execute (p. 393), he took the first step towards it little more than six months after the death of his uncle, in the appointment of a commission to prepare a collection of the statute law. It was published in April 529 ; and in rapid succession there followed his Fifty Decisions (529-532), his Institutes (21st November 533), his Digest of excerpts from the writings of the jurists (16th December 533), and the revised edition of his Code, in which he incorporated his own legislation down to date (16th November 534). From that time until his death in 565 there followed a series of Novels (*novellae constitutiones*), which were never officially collected, and of which probably many have been lost.

The first intimation of his scheme was contained in a constitution addressed to the senate, of date 13th February 528.[2] There is reason for believing that he had already planned the compilation of all the collections we now possess, and he may even have had in view an eventual general codification in the modern sense of the word. But this constitution contained no hint of anything beyond a collection of statute law (*leges*),—of all that was worth preserving in the Gregorian, Hermogenian, and Theodosian Codes, and the later enactments of his imperial predecessors.

[1] From Professor Bryce's article " Justinian " in the *Encyclopædia Britannica*, vol. xiii. p. 792 *sq.* ; to which, and to another article with the same title in the third volume of Smith's *Dictionary of Christian Biography*, from the pen of the same learned writer, the reader is referred for an account of the emperor's administration of the empire, his ecclesiastical policy, and his wars and foreign policy generally. For the present those who would go more fully into his history must consult the pages of Gibbon.

[2] *Const.* " Haec quae necessario," which forms the 1st preface to the Code.

He informed the senate that for its compilation he had nominated a commission of ten members, mostly ministers of state, but including Theophilus, who was a professor at Constantinople, and two barristers of distinction. They were instructed to reject all enactments that had gone into disuse and all that they considered of no practical value; and were authorised to abridge those they accepted, and make such alterations in their language as they considered necessary or expedient. The work was completed in little more than a year, and officially ratified, under the name of *Justinianeus Codex*, by a constitution of 7th April 529, addressed to Menna, one of the prætorian prefects.[3] The emperor therein declared that the new collection was in future to be regarded as the sole repertory of statute law throughout the empire, reference to the earlier collections being expressly prohibited; and that those of its provisions that had originally been addressed to individuals, and that hitherto had ranked only as rescripts, were now to be received with all the authority of general enactments (*leges edictales*). As for the statutory enactments of the republic and the senatusconsults of the early empire, these had long ceased to be referred to as authoritative monuments of legislation; they were recognised only in the form in which they had been embodied in the writings of the jurisconsults, and were regarded as part of the *jus* or jurisprudential law rather than of the *leges* or statute law.

It was to this jurisprudential law (*vetus jus*) that Justinian turned his attention in the next place. Notwithstanding the limitation imposed by the Valentinian "Law of Citations" (§ 76), in bulk it was excessive and in quality unequal, while in certainty it left much to be desired; and it therefore seemed to the emperor expedient that it should be thoroughly sifted and reduced into more manageable compass. In this scheme he was seconded, if not prompted, by Tribonian, who had become Quæstor of the Royal Palace, and

[3] *Const.* "Summa rei publicae,"—the 2d preface to the Code.

whose name will ever be associated with Justinian's as that of the master-spirit of the latter's law-reforms. There can be little doubt that Tribonian was the real author of the constitution, addressed to himself,[4] in which the lines were laid down upon which the new collection was to be constructed. Under the name of *Digesta* or *Pandectae*, divided into fifty books, each subdivided into titles, and arranged generally after the order of topics in the Julian consolidation of the Edict, it was to embody such a selection of extracts from the writings of those of the old jurists whose authority had been recognised by earlier sovereigns[5] as would afford an exposition of so much of the law still in observance as had not been already promulgated in the recently completed collection of statutes. To aid him in the execution of the work Tribonian was empowered to appoint such coadjutors as he thought fit. While he and they were required on the one hand, in testimony of their strict adherence to the general design, to insert at the head of each extract the name of its author and the particular treatise of his from which it was taken, they had on the other hand a very large discretion in their choice of materials and in their mode of dealing with them. The Valentinian law had forbidden any reference to the notes of Ulpian and Paul upon the writings of Papinian, and had declared that, where there was difference of opinion amongst the jurists, that of the latter (unless there was a majority against him) was to prevail; but the compilers of the Digest were relieved from any such restrictions, and authorised to use their own judgment as to which of two or more conflicting *dicta* should be preferred. Fur-

[4] *Const.* "Deo auctore" of 15th December 530, in the preface to the Digest, and again in *Cod.* i. 17, 1.

[5] "Antiquorum prudentium, quibus auctoritatem conscribendarum interpretandarumque legum sacratissimi Principes praebuerunt" (*Const. cit.*, § 4). This description included not only those who had enjoyed the *jus respondendi ex auctoritate principis* (*supra*, § 59), but also those not so privileged (such as Gaius), whose writings enjoyed imperial sanction under the "Law of Citations" (§ 76).

thermore, they were empowered to delete superfluities and redundancies, to alter expressions, and even to interpolate a word or phrase where it was deemed expedient; for the design of the emperor was to publish, not a historical view of the law, but an authoritative statement of it as it then stood, which should be beyond controversy and everywhere be received as definitive.

Tribonian associated with himself sixteen colleagues, of whom four were law-professors, and eleven were members of the bar. Even before they had commenced their labours Tribonian had discovered that there were moot points in the law which could be satisfactorily settled only by imperial authority; and as the work progressed more and more of them became apparent. All controversy in regard to them was set at rest by a series of enactments of Justinian's in the years 529–32, which got the name of "the Fifty Decisions" (*Quinquaginta Decisiones*),[6] and which there is some reason for supposing formed a collection by themselves before their incorporation in the second edition of the Code.[7]

When the Digest was nearing its completion another work was taken in hand, which had been foreshadowed in the constitution "Deo auctore."[8] This was the little volume so well known under the name of Justinian's Institutes (*Justiniani Institutiones*),—an elementary treatise for the use of students. Its preparation was entrusted to Tribonian, Theophilus, and Dorotheus; but seems to have been really accomplished by the two last, who were professors in Constantinople and Beirout respectively. Its foundation, according to the emperor's instructions, was the Institutes of Gaius, which had long been the introductory text-book

---

[6] "Nostras constitutiones, per quas, suggerente nobis Triboniano, . . . antiqui juris altercationes placavimus" (Just., *Inst.*, i. 5, § 3).

[7] "Sicut libro L constitutionum invenies:" in the Turin Gloss on the Institutes, in Savigny, *Gesch. d. R.R.*, vol. ii. p. 452.

[8] *Const. cit.*, § 11. See also *Const.* "Tanta," § 11, (in pref. to *Dig.* and in *Cod.* i. 17, 2), and *proem. Inst.*

in the law-schools. In its preparation its compilers had a much freer hand than in the Digest. They were enjoined to expunge everything that was antiquated, and to introduce whatever in their judgment was necessary to make the little book a faithful though elementary exposition of Justinianian law. In this way the detailed accounts in Gaius of institutions that before the time of Justinian had gone out of date, all disappeared, a brief reference to them being introduced only here and there; some rules and definitions were incorporated from the *Libri VII rerum quotidianarum* of Gaius, and the elementary works of Marcian, Ulpian, Florentine, and other classical jurists; and a great body of new matter was inserted displaying the amendments of the later emperors, among which special prominence was given to the legislation of Justinian himself. The way in which this was done is objectionable, and mars the work as a whole; for in form the emperor is the relator; and it is unpleasant to have him parading so frequently his own wisdom, humanity, and beneficence, and drawing comparisons between himself and his predecessors, all to his own advantage.

The Institutes were published on the 21st November 533; the Digest or Pandects (*Digesta, Pandectae*) followed on the 16th December of the same year. Three constitutions of that date announced its completion,—one, known as "Tanta," ratifying the work, which was addressed to the senate and the world; another, known as "Δέδωκεν," which was substantially a Greek version of the first; and the third, known as "Omnem rei publicae," addressed specially to the professors in the law-schools.[9] Three years had sufficed to reduce the mass of the old jurisprudence (*jus vetus*) to about one-twentieth of its bulk. This had been facilitated by a division of labour; the commissioners having formed themselves into three sections, to each of which were con-

[9] All three are printed in the preface to the Digest; the "Tanta" also in *Cod.* i. 17, 2.

fided all the books of a particular class,—those bearing on the *jus civile* to the first, those bearing on the *jus honorarium* to the second, and those not properly rangeable under either of those heads to the third.[10] The matter selected by those three sections seems then to have been submitted either to the whole commission or an editorial committee, at whose hands it was distributed under appropriate rubrics, and submitted to a second revision, in which manifest superfluities were expunged,[11] contrarieties removed,[12] and expressions varied or words interpolated so as to adapt the doctrine to the altered state of the law.[13] The whole was then arranged in seven parts and fifty books. The division into seven parts was made apparently in view of a readjustment of the course of study in the schools;[14] that into books was in compliance with the emperor's instructions in the "Deo auctore," and was not accomplished without some humouring of the subject-matter.[15] Each book, with the exception of the three on legacies, contains a greater or smaller number of rubricated

[10] It was Blume that, from internal evidence, discovered the *modus operandi* of the commissioners, which explains the otherwise confusing arrangement of the extracts in the several titles. His paper is in the *Z. f. gesch. RW.*, vol. iv. (1820) p. 257 *sq.* An account of the results at which he arrived will be found in Roby, *Introduction*, p. xlvi. *sq.*

[11] All this was in accordance with the instructions contained in *Const.* "Deo auctore," §§ 7-10.

[12] Justinian, in *Const.* "Tanta," § 15, denies that any contradictions are to be found in the Digest. But there are not a few passages in it which not all the skill of the civilians has yet been able to reconcile.

[13] Such alterations and interpolations are often spoken of as "Tribonian's emblems" (*emblemata Triboniani*). It is only in regard to a very few of the Digest extracts that we have the means of judging how far the text was manipulated; but a comparison of some of these with the presumably original versions of them preserved in the Vatican Fragments and elsewhere is given by Mr. Roby in his *Introduction*, chapter v., and is very instructive.

[14] On this division, see Justinian himself in *Const.* "Tanta" and "Δέδωκεν," §§ 2-8; Eyssenhardt, *Justinians Digesten nach Drittheilen, Partes, Büchern, Titeln, u. Fragmenten* (Leipsic, 1845), p. 44 *sq.*; Roby, *Introd.*, p. xxix. *sq.*

[15] In order to eke out the fifty, the matter of legacies had to be spread over three books (xxx.-xxxii.), often called the 1st, 2d, and 3d books *de legatis*, none of them subdivided into titles.

titles; these again contain each a varying number of laws or fragments, some of no more than a word or two that serve as a connecting-link between what precedes and follows, others filling two or three pages; and all but the shortest of those fragments are subdivided into paragraphs.[16] Each law, or rather fragment, is an excerpt from some treatise of an earlier jurist; and this, in compliance with Justinian's instructions, is invariably quoted at the commencement.[17] The nature of the books laid under contribution has been indicated in previous sections (§§ 61-64) in commenting on the literary activity of the jurists of the earlier empire. Their number was very considerable, but all from the pens of thirty-nine writers. The earliest is Quintus Mucius Scævola (p. 264), not to be confounded with Q. Cervidius Scævola (p. 322); he is the only jurist of the republic from whose works any direct extract is preserved. The latest are Hermogenian and Arcadius Charisius (p. 327), who are supposed to have flourished about the middle of the fourth century after Christ. The most largely utilised is Ulpian; he furnishes about one-third of the whole Digest, the greater part being from his Commentary on the Edict. Paul supplies about one-sixth of the whole; and next in importance, so far as the bulk of their contributions is concerned, come Papinian, Julian, Pomponius, Q. Cervidius Scævola, Gaius, and Modestine.[18]

The order of sequence of the books and titles in the Digest is at the first sight somewhat incomprehensible, and from a modern point of view anything but satisfactory. It

[16] This explains the now usual method of citation: *Dig.* xi. 7, fr. 8, § 3, or sometimes fr. 8, § 3, *Dig.*, *de religiosis* (xi. 7).

[17] As, in the fragment referred to in last note,—" Ulpianus, libro xxv. ad Edictum."

[18] In Hommel's *Palingenesia libror. juris veterum* (3 vols., Leipsic, 1767) the extracts from each author are collected, re-arranged according to the books of his from which they were taken, and printed consecutively; and the order given above is determined by the number of pages of the *Palingenesia* which the contributions of each of those jurists occupy.

is not a systematic exposition either of the rights of individuals or of the law by which they were regulated, but rather of the magisterial and judicial measures employed for their protection and vindication. The method is substantially that adopted by Julian in his consolidation of the Edict (p. 307). This was in accordance with Justinian's instructions; and for those for whom his collection was destined was not without its advantages. But it is at first a little perplexing to a modern to find (for example) the matter of pacts or agreements dealt with in the second book, real and consensual contracts in books 12-19, but stipulations postponed to the forty-fifth; to find property dealt with in the sixth book, and its exposition resumed in the forty-first; to see the disabilities of minors explained in the second book, but guardianship introduced only in the twenty-sixth and twenty-seventh. All this, however, has its historical explanation.[19] The order of sequence of the fragments in the individual titles was also somewhat perplexing until the key was supplied by Blume (*supra*, p. 408). In many titles the ground seems to be gone over a second and often a third time. One is disposed to think that this might to a great extent have been avoided had the final revision been more deliberate. But expedition was one of the things at which Tribonian aimed; as witness the allowance of no more than a fortnight between the pub-

[19] See Roby, *Introduction*, pp. xxxi.-xlvi. He observes (p. xxxiii.): "The Digest is a handbook for practitioners, not a systematic treatise for students. It treats of who are judges, who are plaintiffs, and how they can get defendants into court, what matters are actionable, the effect of a judgment and the means of enforcing it, and then other remedies, such as injunctions and recognisances" (*i.e.*, interdicts and prætorian stipulations). "Matter necessary for the explanation of the various actions is prefixed, often in separate titles, and cognate matter is sometimes appended in other titles." (*E.g.*, the law of espousals, marriage, dowries, dotal settlements, and the matrimonial relation generally, is grouped round the discussion of the *actio rei uxoriae*.) "It is the insertion of these prefatory and explanatory titles and occasional digressions which often prevents a student from catching the main lines of the arrangement."

lication of this great body of law and its coming into force all over the empire. So, to save time, the matter appropriate to any particular title, as brought up by each of the three sections into which the commission had been divided, as a rule was thrown into it as it stood, the largest contribution usually getting precedence; the revisers were content to leave mere repetitions undisturbed, and to expunge only what was irrelevant or contradictory. In the title *locati* (*Dig.* xix. 2), for example, there are in all 62 fragments. The first 38, with four or five exceptions, constitute what is called the Sabinianian group,—the contribution of the section that dealt with works on the *jus civile;* fragments 39–52 constitute the so-called Edictal group, contributed by the section entrusted with the treatise on the *jus honorarium*; fragments 53–56 form the so-called Papinianian group,— the contribution of the third section; while the remainder mostly belong to what recent editors regard as an appendix to all three. The same mode of treatment is observable all through the Digest, although every now and then may be noticed the interpolation of an Edictal or Papinianian fragment in the middle of a series of Sabinianian ones, or *vice versa*, when it is necessary as a qualification of or an addition to what precedes.[20]

Soon after the publication of the Digest, Justinian commissioned Tribonian, Dorotheus, and two or three others to prepare a new edition of the Code of statute-law of 529. This had become necessary in consequence of the numerous amendments introduced by the emperor during the six years he had filled the throne. The terms of the commission are not preserved, but the scope of it is indicated in the constitution " Cordi nobis " of 16th November 534,[21] whereby the new collection was ratified under the name of *Codex Justini-*

[20] See *supra*, note 10.
[21] It is addressed to the senate, and will be found in the preface to the Code.

aneus repetitae praelectionis. This is the edition that we now possess. Owing to the entire disappearance of all copies of the earlier one it is impossible to say with certainty whether or not they proceeded on the same lines; but from the emphasis that the emperor, in the constitution referred to, puts on the phrase *repetita praelectio*, it is more than probable that the only changes consisted in the deletion of what had ceased to be law,[22] and the introduction of some four hundred enactments of Justinian himself, including the *Quinquaginta Decisiones* (p. 406). The arrangement follows that of the Edict rather more closely than does the Digest. The division is into twelve books, whose relation to the Digest is roughly this:—

Part i. of Digest = Books 1, 2 of Code.
,, ii. ,, = Book 3 ,,
,, iii. ,, = ,, 4 ,,
,, iv. ,, = ,, 5 ,,
,, v. ,, = ,, 6 ,,
,, vi. ,, = ,, 7 ,,
,, vii. ,, = Books 8–12 ,,

The Code, however, especially in Books 1 and 9–12, contains much in reference to political, ecclesiastical, criminal, municipal, fiscal, and military institutions, that has no counterpart in the Digest. Each book is subdivided into titles, much more numerous than in the jurisprudential collection; and each title contains a greater or smaller number of laws (*leges*), the longer ones being subdivided into paragraphs.[23] In compliance with Justinian's instructions the laws in the titles are arranged chronologically; the name of the emperor from whom each proceeded, and the body or individual to whom it was addressed, are mentioned at the head of it (*inscriptio*), and the place and time of its issue (if known) at the end (*subscriptio*). The collection contains

[22] Either by accident or design one or two enactments were deleted which are founded on in the Institutes; for example, in ii. 10, § 11, and ii. 20, § 27.

[23] Hence the usual mode of citation,—*Cod.* vi., 23, *l.* 21, § 5, or sometimes *l.* 21, § 5, *C. de testament.* (vi. 23).

between 4600 and 4700 enactments, of which more than the half were originally rescripts. The latter have manifestly been much abridged; and comparison with corresponding versions in the Theodosian Code shows that even the constitutions of Constantine and Theodosius have often been considerably curtailed. The earliest in the collection is a rescript of Hadrian's, and the latest a law of Justinian's dated about a fortnight before the Code was published. Anton. Verus and Marc. Aurelius (the *Divi Fratres*) are responsible for about 180, Commodus for about 190, Sept. Severus and Caracalla for about the same number, Caracalla alone for nearly 250, Alexander Severus for about 450, Gordian III. for more than 270, Diocletian and Maximinian for more than 1200, Constantine for over 200, Valentinian II., Theodosius I., and Arcadius for about the same number, Valentinian II. alone for nearly 170, Arcadius for about 180, Theodosius II. for about 190, and Justinian for about 400.[24]

The name of Novels (*novellae constitutiones post Codicem*), is given to the enactments of Justinian subsequent to the publication of the Code. They are mostly in Greek, some in both Greek and Latin, and a very small number of peculiarly local interest in Latin alone. The greater number relate to public and ecclesiastical affairs; but some of those dealing with the private law, especially those reforming the law of intestate succession, are of the very highest importance. They do not seem ever to have been officially collected, and only about 170 have been preserved.[25]

Taking his enactments in the Code and his Novels together, we have of Justinian's own legislation not far short

[24] The figures are from Deurer's *Aeussere Gesch. u. Inst. de R.R.* (Heidelb. 1849), p. 174. There are chronological lists in Haenel's *Corp. leg. ab imperatorib. rom. ante Justinianum latarum* (Leipsic, 1857), and in an appendix to Krüger's edition of the Code.

[25] See Biener's *Geschichte der Novellen Justinians*, Berlin, 1824. A complete account of the sources from which those extant have been obtained may be expected in the Prolegomena to Schoell's edition of the Novels now in course of publication (see p. 439).

of six hundred constitutions. Diocletian's contributions to the Code are more than twice as numerous, but most of them professed to be nothing more than short declaratory statements of pre-existing law; whereas Justinian's, apart from his Fifty Decisions, were mostly reformatory enactments, many of those in the Novels as long as an average Act of Parliament, and dealing with diverse matters under the same rubric. They cover the whole field of law, public and private, civil and criminal, secular and ecclesiastical. It cannot be said that they afford pleasant reading; they are so disfigured by redundancy of language, involved periods, and nauseous self-glorification. But it is undeniable that several of those dealing with the private law embody reforms of great moment and of most salutary tendency. The emperor sometimes loved to pose as the champion of the simplicity and evenhandedness of the early law (*antiquum statum renovantes sancimus*, &c.), at others to denounce it for its subtleties (*antiquae subtilitatis ludibrium expellentes*); sometimes he allowed himself to be influenced by his own extreme asceticism, and now and again we detect traces of subservience to the imperious will of his consort; but in the main his legislation was dictated by what he was pleased to call *humanitas* so far as the law of persons was concerned, and by *naturalis ratio* and public utility so far as concerned that of things. The result was the eradication of almost every trace of the old *jus Quiritium*, and the substitution for it, under the name of *jus romanum*, of that cosmopolitan body of law which has contributed so largely to almost every modern system.

SECTION 85.—CHANGES IN THE LAW OF THE FAMILY.

With the Christian emperors the last traces disappeared of the old conception of the *familia* as an aggregate of persons and estate subject absolutely to the power and dominion of its head. *Manus*, the power in a husband over his wife and her belongings, was a thing of the past; they stood now on a footing of equality before the law; perhaps it might be more accurate to say, at least with reference to the Justinianian legislation, that the wife was the more privileged of the two in respect both of the protection and indulgence the law accorded her. With *manus* the old confarreation and coemption had ceased, marriage needing nothing more than simple interchange of consent,[1] except as between persons of rank or when the intention was to legitimate previous issue; in the latter case a written marriage settlement was required,[2] and in the former either such a settlement, or a marriage in church before the bishop and at least three clerical witnesses, who granted and signed a certificate of the completed union.[3] Second marriage, which the Julian and Papia-Poppæan law enjoined upon widows under fifty, was discountenanced by Theodosius and his successors, and latterly entailed forfeiture of the *lucra nuptialia* of the first, in favour of the children who were the issue of it.[4] The legislation of the Christian emperors on the subject of divorce, largely contributed to by Justinian in his Novels, has already (p. 382) been referred to.[5] In regard to the *dos* many new provisions were introduced, principally for curtailing the husband's power of dealing with it while the marriage lasted, enlarging the right of the wife and her heirs in respect of it, and simplifying the means of recovering it from the husband or his heirs when the marriage was dissolved.[6] Between the time of Constantine and that of Theodosius and Valentinian it had become

[1] Theod. and Valent., in *Cod.* v. 4, 22; Just. in *Nov.* cxvii, *cap.* 4.
[2] Just., in *Cod.* v. 27, 10, pr.   [3] Just., in *Nov.* cxvii, *capp.* 4, 6.
[4] Grat., Valent., and Theod., in *Cod.* v. 9, *l.* 3; Leo and Anthem., *cod. tit.*, *l.* 6; Just., *cod. tit.*, *l.* 10, and in *Nov.* xxii, *capp.* 21-28.
[5] There is an important enactment of Theod. and Valent. in *Cod.* v. 17, 8. Justinian deals with the subject *eod. tit.*, *ll.* 10-12, and in Novels xxii, cxvii, cxxvii, and cxxxiv.
[6] See Just., *Cod.* v. 12, *ll.* 29-31; v. 13, *l. un.*

the practice for a man to make a settlement on his intended wife of a provision which was to remain his property (but without the power of alienation) during the marriage, but to pass to her on his predecease; it got the name of *donatio ante nuptias*, or sometimes, as being a sort of return for the *dos*, *antipherna*. The earliest legislation about it was by the last-mentioned emperors; Zeno and Justin followed suit; and Justinian, in Code and Novels, published five or six enactments for its regulation. The general result was that wherever a *dos* was given or promised on the part of the wife, there a *donatio* was to be constituted on the part of the husband; that if one was increased during the marriage, a corresponding increase was to be made to the other; that it might be constituted after the marriage without infringing the rule prohibiting donations between husband and wife, (which caused Justinian to change its name to *donatio propter nuptias*); that the wife might demand its transfer to her (as she could that of the *dos*) on her husband's insolvency, but under obligation to apply its income to the maintenance of the family; and that, on the dissolution of the marriage by her husband's death or by a divorce for which he was in fault, she had ample remedies for reducing it into possession.[7]

The change in the complexion of the relations between husband and wife under the Christian emperors, however, was insignificant when compared with that which had overtaken the relation between parent and child. Justinian in his Institutes reproduces the boast of Gaius that nowhere else had a father such power over his children as was exercised by a Roman *paterfamilias*.[8] True it is that the *patria potestas* in name still held a prominent place in the Justinianian collections; but it had been shorn of most of the prerogatives that had characterised it during the republic. To

---

[7] See *Inst.* ii. 7, § 3, and tit. *Cod. de don. ante nupt.* (v. 3).
[8] *Inst.* i. 9, § 2.

expose a new-born child was forbidden under penalties.[9] To take the life of a grown-up one—unless it was a daughter slain with her paramour in the act of adultery [10]—was murder;[11] for the domestic tribunal, with the judicial power of life and death in the *paterfamilias* as its head, had long disappeared. For the same reason a parent could no longer sell his child as a slave; at least he could do so only when the child was an infant, and he in such extreme poverty as to be unable to support it.[12] Even the right to make a noxal surrender of his son to a party who had suffered from the latter's delict had silently become obsolete,—so greatly had altered sentiment, in sympathy with legislation, curtailed the power of the *paterfamilias* over those in his *potestas*.[13] All that remained of it in the latest Justinianian law was no more than is sanctioned in most modern systems as natural emanations of the paternal relationship,—the rights of moderate chastisement for offence, of testamentary nomination of guardians, of giving a *filiusfamilias* in adoption, of pupillary substitution (enlarged by Justinian), and of withholding consent from the marriage of a child, (subject to magisterial intervention if done unreasonably). How the right of the *paterfamilias* over the earnings and acquisitions of his children was modified by the recognition of the *peculium castrense vel quasi* has been shown in a previous section (p. 344). But the modification was carried to such an extent by the Christian emperors as finally to negative the father's ownership altogether, except as regarded acquisitions that were the outcome of funds advanced by him to his *filiusfamilias* for his separate use (*peculium profecticium*).[14] Of some of the child's acquisitions his father had, down to the time of Justinian, the life-interest and right of administration; but by his legislation even these might be

[9] Valent., Val., and Grat., in *Cod.*, viii. 51, *l*. 2; Just., *eod. tit.*, *l*. 3.
[10] *Dig.*, xlviii. 5, fr. 20, fr. 22, §§ 2, 4. [11] Const., in *Cod.*, ix. 17, *l. un.*
[12] Const., in *Cod.*, viii. 46, 10, and iv. 33, 2.
[13] *Inst.*, iv. 8, § 7. [14] Just., *Inst.*, ii. 9, § 1; *Cod.*, vi. 61, 6.

excluded at the pleasure of the persons from whom the acquisitions had been derived.[15] By the classical law, the father's radical right in his son's *peculium castrense* revived on the latter's death; for if he died intestate the former appropriated it, not as his son's heir, but as an owner whose powers as such had been merely temporarily suspended.[16] But, by one of the chapters in the famous Novel on the law of intestate succession, even this prerogative of the *paterfamilias* was abolished, and all a child's belongings except his *peculium profecticium* recognised as his own in death as well as in life, so that, if any of them should pass to his parent on his intestacy, it should only be by title of inheritance and in the absence of descendants.[17]

In every other branch of the law of the family the same reforming spirit was manifested. Adoption was no longer followed in all cases by a change of family for the adoptee, but only when the adopter was in fact one of his parents, such as a paternal or maternal grandfather,—when there was a natural *potestas* to underlie and justify the civil one.[18] The modes of legitimation of children born out of wedlock, especially that by subsequent marriage of the parents, first introduced by Constantine,[19] were regulated, and the extent of the rights of the legitimated issue carefully defined.[20] Emancipation was simplified, and the old procedure by sales and manumissions, which degraded the child too much to the level of a slave, dispensed with.[21] Tutory at law was opened to the pupil's nearest kinsmen, whether on the father's side or the mother's;[22] and the mother herself, or the child's grandmother, might be allowed, under certain

---

[15] *Nov.* cxvii, *cap.* 1, *pr.*
[16] Ulp., in *Dig.*, xlix. 17, 2.
[17] *Nov.* cxviii, *cap.* 1.
[18] Just., in *Cod.*, viii. 47, 10.
[19] *Cod.*, v. 27, 5.
[20] Just., in *Cod.*, v. 27, *ll.* 10, 11; *Nov.* xii, *cap.* 4; lxxiv, *praef.*, *capp.* 1, 2; lxxxix, *capp.* 8-10.
[21] Just., *Cod.*, viii. 48, 6.
[22] Just., *Cod.*, vi. 58, 15, § 4; *Nov.* cxviii, *cap.* 5.

conditions, to act as its guardian.[23] Slavery was often converted into the milder condition of colonate (§ 75); but even where this did not happen, the rights of owners were not allowed to be abused; for slaves were permitted to claim the protection of the magistrate, and cruelty by a master might result in his being deprived of his human property.[24] Kinship that had arisen between two persons when one or both were slaves (*servilis cognatio*) was recognised as creative not only of disabilities but of rights.[25] The modes of manumission were multiplied, and the restrictions of the legislation of the early empire (p. 337) abolished;[26] and a freedman invariably became a citizen, Junian latinity (p. 339) and dediticiancy being no longer recognised.[27]

SECTION 86.—THE LAW OF PROPERTY AND OBLIGATION.

In the law of property the principal changes of the Christian empire were the simplification of the forms of conveyance, the extension of the colonate, the introduction and regulation of emphyteusis, and the remodelling of the law of prescription. Simplification of the forms of conveyance was necessary only in the case of *res mancipi*, for *res nec mancipi* had always passed by delivery. From the Theodosian Code it is apparent that movable *res mancipi* usually passed in the same way from very early in the period; and that for the mancipation of lands and houses—for *in jure cessio* had disappeared with the formular system —a *solemnis traditio*, a written instrument and delivery following thereon, and both before witnesses, was gradually substituted.[1] Of this there is no trace in the Justinianian Code. For the emperor abolished all remains of the distinc-

---

[23] This had been allowed even before the time of Justinian. See the enactment of Valent., Theod., and Arcad., in *Cod.*, v. 35, 2. See also *Nov.* cxiv.
[24] *Inst.*, i. 8, 2.   [25] *Inst.*, iii. 6, 10.   [26] *Inst.*, i. 5, 1.
[27] *Cod.*, vii. 5, vii. 6; *Inst.*, i. 5, 3.
[1] Theod., Arcad., and Honor., in *Theod. Cod.*, ii. 29, 2, §§ 1, 2.

tion between *res mancipi* and *nec mancipi*, between full ownership, bonitarian ownership, and *nudum jus Quiritium*, placing movables and immovables on a footing of perfect equality so far as their direct conveyance was concerned.[2] But as regarded the possession required of an alienee to cure any defect in the conveyance, he made a marked difference between them. For, amalgamating the old positive usucapion of the *jus civile* with the negative "prolonged possession" (*longi temporis possessio*) that had been introduced in the provinces (probably by the provincial edict), he declared that possession on a sufficient title and in good faith should in future make the possessor legal owner of the thing possessed by him, provided that the possession of himself and his author had endured uninterruptedly for three years in the case of a movable, and in the case of an immovable for ten years if the party against whom he possessed was resident in the same province, or for twenty if he resided in another one.[3]

The effects of the extension of the colonate have already been referred to (§ 75). The same causes that had led to it induced the introduction of emphyteusis;[4] an institution which had previously existed in some of the Eastern provinces when independent, and which came to be utilised first by the emperors, then by the Church, and afterwards by municipalities and private landowners, for bringing into cultivation the large tracts of provincial land belonging to them which were unproductive and unprofitable through want of supervision on the spot. One somewhat like it had long existed both in Italy and in some of the western provinces under the name of *ager vectigalis*,—an inheritable lease for a long term of years, usually from a municipality, which gave the grantee rights much greater than those of an ordinary

---

[2] *Cod.*, vii. 31. [3] *Inst.*, ii. 6, *pr*; *Cod.*, vii. 31.
[4] On emphyteusis, see Lattes (as in § 75, note 1), chaps. i. and iii.; François *De l'emphytéose*, Paris, 1883.

tenant; but this Justinian assimilated to emphyteusis. The nature and conditions of the latter were carefully defined by Zeno and amended by Justinian himself.[5] The *emphyteuta*, as the grantee of the right was called, did not become owner; the granter still remained *dominus*, all that the grantee enjoyed being a *jus in re aliena*, but *de facto* so extensive as hardly to be distinguishable from ownership. It conferred upon him and his heirs a perpetual right in the lands included in the grant, in consideration of a fixed annual payment to the lord (*canon*) and due observance of conventional and statutory conditions; but he was not entitled to abandon it, or able to free himself of the obligations he had undertaken, without the lord's consent. The latter was entitled to hold the grant forfeited if the *canon* fell into arrear for three years (in church lands for two), or if the land-tax was in arrear for the same period, or if the *emphyteuta* allowed the lands to deteriorate, or if he attempted to alienate them (*alienare meliorationes* as the text says) without observance of statutory requirements. These were that he should intimate an intended alienation and the name of the proposed alienee to the lord, so that the latter, before giving his assent, might satisfy himself that he would not be a loser by the transaction; and if the alienation was to be by sale, he had to state the price fixed, so as to give the lord the opportunity of exercising his statutory right of preemption at the same figure. If those requirements were complied with, and the lord, himself declining to purchase, had no reasonable objection to the proposed alienee, he was not entitled to resist the alienation, provided a payment (*laudemium*) was made to him of two per cent. of the sale price in consideration of his enforced consent.

The changes in the law of obligation were more superficial than those in the law of property, and consisted principally

[5] Zeno, in *Cod.*, iv. 66, 1; Just., *cod. tit.*, *ll.* 2, 3; *Nov.* vii, *cap.* 3, § 2; *Nov.* cxx, *capp.* 6, 8.

in the simplification of formalities, and in some cases their entire abolition. To describe them, however, would necessitate details which would here be out of place.

SECTION 87.—CHANGES IN THE LAW OF SUCCESSION.

The changes made in the law of succession by Justinian's Christian predecessors, especially Theodosius II. and Anastasius, were far from insignificant; but his own were in some directions positively revolutionary. The testament *per aes et libram* of the *jus civile* (pp. 167 *sq.*) probably never obtained any firm footing in the East; for it was only by Caracalla's constitution conferring citizenship on all his free subjects that provincials generally acquired *testamenti faetio*; and by that time a testament bearing externally the requisite number of seals had been recognised as sufficient for a grant of *bonorum possessio*, unchallengeable by the heirs-at-law, even though they were able to prove that neither *familiae mancipatio* nor *testamenti nuncupatio* had intervened.[1] Hence the universal adoption of what Justinian calls the prætorian testament;[2] which, however, underwent considerable reform at the hands of the emperors, notably in the requirement (in the ordinary case) of signature by the testator and subscription by the witnesses. There was much hesitating legislation on the subject before the law was finally established as it stands in the Justinianian books;[3] and even at the last we find it encumbered with many exceptions and reservations in favour of testaments that were merely deeds of division by a parent among his

[1] Gai., ii. §§ 119, 120 ; Ulp., xxiii. 6, xxviii. 6.
[2] *Inst.*, ii. 10, 2.
[3] The leading provisions are in the title of the Code *de testamentis* (vi. 23). The testator's subscription was required by an enactment of Theodosius II. of the year 439 (*Cod.*, vi. 23, 21). The subscriptions of five witnesses (as well as their seals) had been required by Arcad. and Honor. (*Theod. Cod.*, iv. 4, 3, §§ 1, 2), who declared they were following a rule of Constantine's. It was Theodosius in (439) that reverted to the old number of seven.

children, testaments made in time of plague, testaments recorded in books of court, testaments intrusted to the safekeeping of the emperor, and so forth. Codicils had become deeds of such importance as, in the absence of a testament, to be dealt with as imposing a trust on the heir-at-law;[4] it was therefore thought expedient to refuse effect to them unless attested by at least five witnesses.[5] And a most important step in advance was taken by Justinian in the recognition of the validity of an oral *mortis causa* trust; for he declared that if it should be represented to a competent judge that a person on his deathbed had by word of mouth directed his heir-at-law to give something to the complainant, the heir should be required either on his oath to deny the averment or to give or pay what was claimed.[6]

In the matter of intestacy there was long a halting between two opinions,—a desire still further to amend the law in the direction taken by the prætors and by the legislature in the Tertullian and Orphitian senatusconsults (p. 355 *sq.*), and yet a hesitancy about breaking altogether from the time-hallowed principle of agnation.[7] Justinian in his Code went far beyond his predecessors, making a mother's right of succession independent altogether of the *jus liberorum* ;[8] extending that of a daughter or sister to her descendants, without any deduction in favour of agnates thus excluded ;[9] admitting emancipated collaterals and their descendants as freely as if there had been no *capitis deminutio* ;[10] applying to agnates the same *successio graduum* that the prætors had allowed to cognates,[11] and so forth. But it was by his Novels, and especially the 118th and 127th, that he revolutionised the system, by eradicating agnation altogether, and settling the canons of descent—which were the same for

[4] *Inst.*, ii. 23, 10 ; ii. 25, 1.   [5] Theod., in *Cod.*, vi. 36, 8, § 3.
[6] *Cod.*, vi. 42, 32 ; *Inst.*, ii. 23, § 12.
[7] Examples in *Inst.*, iii. 1, 15 ; iii. 3, 5 ; iii. 5, 1.
[8] *Cod.*, viii. 58, 2.   [9] *Cod.*, vi. 55, 12.   [10] *Cod.*, vi. 58, 15, § 1.
[11] *Cod.*, vi. 4, *l.* 4, § 20 ; *Inst.*, ii. 2, § 7.

real and personal estate—solely on the basis of blood kinship, whether through males or females, and whether crossed or not by a *capitis deminutio minima* (pp. 127 *sq.*) First came descendants of the intestate, male and female alike, taking *per capita* if all were of the nearest degree, *per stirpes* if of remoter ones. Failing descendants, the succession passed to the nearest ascendants, and, concurrently with them, brothers and sisters of the full blood and (by Nov. 127) the children of any that had predeceased. Where there were ascendants alone, one-half of the succession went to the paternal line and one-half to the maternal; where there were ascendants and brothers and sisters, or only brothers and sisters, the division was made equally *per capita;* when children of a deceased brother or sister participated it was *per stirpes.* In the third class came in brothers and sisters of the half blood or by adoption, and their children; the partition here was on the same principle as in the second class. The fourth class included all other collaterals according to propinquity, and without distinction between full and half blood; the primary division was *per stirpes,* but all of the same branch took *per capita.*

A reform effected by Justinian by his 115th Novel ought not to pass unnoticed, for it rendered superfluous all the old rules about disherison and præterition of a testator's children (p. 171 *sq.*), practically abolished *bonorum possessio contra tabulas* (p. 291), and established the principle that a child had, as a general rule, an inherent and indefeasible right to be one of his father's heirs in a certain share at all events of the *hereditas,* and that a parent had the same right in the succession of his child if the latter had died without issue. The enactment enumerated certain grounds upon which alone it should be lawful for a parent to disinherit his child or a child his parent; declaring that in every case of disherison the reason of it should be stated in the testament, but giving leave to the person disinherited to dispute and disprove the facts when the testament was opened. If a child who had not been disinherited—and one improperly disinherited was eventually in the same position—was not instituted to some share, however small, of his parent's *hereditas*, he was entitled to have the testament declared null in so far as the institutions in it were concerned, thus opening the succession to himself and the other heirs-at-law, but without affecting the minor provisions, such as bequests, nomination of tutors, &c. ; and if the share to which he was instituted was less than his legitim (*legitima* or *debita portio*), he was entitled to an action in supplement. The legitim, which under the practice of the centumviral court had been one-fourth of the share to which the child would have been entitled *ab intestato*, was raised by Justinian (by his 18th Novel) to one-third at least, and one-half where there were five or more entitled to participate. He did not allow challenge of the will to be excluded, as in the earlier *querela inofficiosi testamenti* (p. 249), because the testator had made advances to his child during his life or left him a legacy which quantitatively equalled the legitim ; his idea was that a child was entitled to recognition by his parent *as one of his heirs*, and that without cause to deny him that position was to put upon him an affront which the law ought not to tolerate.

Amongst the other beneficial changes effected by Justinian or his immediate predecessors may be mentioned the assimilation as far as possible of *hereditas* and *bonorum possessio*, so that the latter might be taken like the former without formal petition for a grant of it ;[12] the equiparation of legacies and singular trust-gifts,[13] and the application of some of their rules to *mortis causa* donations ;[14] the extension of the principle of " transmission " to every heir without

[12] Const., in *Cod.*, vi. 9, 9.
[13] Just., in *Cod.*, vi. 43, 2, § 1 ; *Inst.*, ii. 20, § 3.
[14] Just., in *Cod.*, viii. 56, 3 ; *Inst.*, ii. 7, § 1.

exception, so that, if he died within the time allowed him for considering whether or not he would accept (*tempus deliberandi*), his power of acceptance or declinature passed to *his* heirs, to be exercised by them within what remained of the period :[15] the introduction of entry under inventory (*cum beneficio inventarii*), which limited the heir's responsibilities, and rendered unnecessary the nine or twelve months of deliberation;[16] and the application of the principle of collation to descendants generally, so that they were bound to throw into the mass of the succession before its partition every advance of importance they had received from their parent in anticipation of their shares.[17]

[15] Just., in *Cod.*, vi. 30, *l.* 19, *l.* 22, § 13.
[16] Just., in *Cod.*, vi. 30, 22.
[17] Leo, in *Cod.*, vi. 20, 17 ; Just., *eod. tit.*, *ll.* 19, 20 ; *Nov.* xviii, *cap.* 6.

CHAPTER FOURTH.

THE JUSTINIANIAN LAW-BOOKS.

SECTION 88.—THEIR USE IN THE COURTS AND IN THE SCHOOLS.[1]

ALTHOUGH the Institutes were primarily intended to serve as a text-book in the schools, yet it was expressly declared that they and the Digest and Code should be regarded as just so many parts of one great piece of legislation and all of equal authority; and that, although Digest and Code were but collections of legislation and doctrine that had proceeded originally from many different hands, yet they were to be treated with the same respect as if they had been the work of Justinian himself. But, while everything within them was to be held as law, nothing outside them was to be looked at, not even the volumes from which they had been collected; and so far did this go that, after the publication of the revised Code, neither the first edition of it nor the Fifty Decisions were allowed to be referred to. If a case arose for which no precedent was to be found, the emperor was to be resorted to for his decision, as outside his collections the only fountain of the law. To preserve the purity of the texts,—for which Justinian would have done well to have followed the example of Alaric, who had copies of his Breviary prepared and certified in the chancery, and then distributed through the country,—he forbade the use of

---

[1] See Heimbach's *Prolegomena Basilicorum* (Leipsic, 1870), book i. chap. i. §§ 1-6, chap. ii. §§ 1, 2.

conventional abbreviations (*sigla*) in making transcripts, visiting an offender with the penalties of falsification (*crimen falsi*). Literal translations into Greek were authorised, and indeed very necessary for many of his subjects; and so were παράτιτλα or summaries of the contents of individual titles, (although the jurists read the word less strictly). Commentaries and general summaries were forbidden under heavy penalties, as an interference with the imperial prerogative of interpretation ; but the prohibition does not seem to have been enforced, as we have accounts and remains not only of translations, but of commentaries, notes, abridgements, excerpts, and general summaries, even in Justinian's lifetime. Dorotheus, Anatolius, and Thalelæus were all amongst those to whom his collections were specially addressed, and two of them were engaged in their preparation; yet the first was author of a translation of the Digest with notes; the second made an abridgement of the Code ; and the third translated it with annotations. Julian, too, who made a Latin abridgement of the Novels in 556, probably at the instance of Justinian himself, has been identified with an *Anonymus* often referred to in the scholia of the Basilica, as the author of an annotated translation of the Digest. All of these, it is true, were professors (*antecessores*), and their productions may have been intended primarily for educational purposes; but there can be little doubt that they soon passed into the hands of the practitioners and were used without scruple in the courts.

In the early empire the teaching[2] of the law was free ; and it may have been first in the time of Diocletian that state recognition was accorded to the schools of Rome and Beirout, and not until considerably later that it was extended to those of Constantinople, Alexandria, and Cæsarea. That of Rome seems still to have subsisted while Italy was in the

[2] See Heimbach as in last note ; Amos, *History and Principles of the Civil Law* (London, 1883), p. 102 *sq.*; Karlowa, *Röm. RG.*, p. 1022 *sq.*

hands of the Ostrogoths; but Justinian suppressed those of Alexandria and Cæsarea, and prohibited the public teaching of law elsewhere than in the other three, under heavy pecuniary penalties. The course of study prior to Justinian's reforms ran over five years, the last two being given to private reading. The students of the first year—*dupondii* they were called—were taken through the Institutes of Gaius and four separate books of his (*libri singulares*) on dowries, tutories, testaments, and legacies. Those of the second (*edictales*) and third (*Papinianistae*) were exercised in the Edict or probably Ulpian's commentary on it, and the latter (in addition) in eight of the nineteen books of Papinian's Responses. In the fourth the students (then called λύται) read Paul's Responses, and in the fifth (προλύται) the imperial constitutions. Justinian still enjoined a five years' course, but prescribed that the teaching should be entirely from his own collections. The men of the first year—whom he relieved of their old nickname, and honoured with the title of *novi Justinianei* (Justinian's freshmen)—were to be instructed in the Institutes and the first part (books 1–4) of the Digest; those of the second year in either the second (books 5–11) or the third part (books 12–19) of the Digest, along with four of the last fourteen books of parts iv. and v., of which one should be on the law of dowries, one on tutories, one on testaments, and one on legacies; those of the third year in that one of parts ii. and iii. of the Digest which had not been taken up in the second, together with the first three books of the fourth part; those of the fourth year were to read privately the remaining ten books of parts iv. and v.; while those of the fifth were to read the Code of imperial constitutions, leaving the sixth and seventh parts (books 37–50) of the Digest to be read after the course was completed, as opportunity presented itself. As already observed, it is not improbable that the instruction thus prescribed was conveyed through the medium of translations and annotated summaries of the Justinianian books. A Greek paraphrase of the Institutes, usually attributed to Theophilus, a professor in Constantinople and one of Justinian's commissioners, is commonly supposed to have been used by him in his prelections. It embodies much more historical matter than is to be found in the Institutes; but its value has been very differently rated by different critics. Its latest editor, Ferrini,[3] who puts a high estimate on it, is of opinion that the original of it was a paraphrase of Gaius, which was remodelled after the plan of Justinian's Institutes, and had their new matter incorporated in order to adapt it to the altered conditions; but he doubts if there be any sufficient authority for ascribing it to Theophilus. If he be right in assuming it was really a redaction of Gaius, the historical explanations will be received with all the more confidence.

SECTION 89.—FATE OF THE JUSTINIANIAN BOOKS IN THE EAST.[1]

The literary work indicated in the first part of last section was continued throughout the sixth century by various writers, of whom Heimbach gives some account in his Prolegomena. But the next three were comparatively barren; the only thing worth noting being the Ἐκλογὴ τῶν νόμων ἐν συντόμῳ γενομένη of Leo the Isaurian in 740, professedly an

---

[3] *Institutionum graeca paraphrasis Theophilo antecessori vulgo tributa. Ad fid. libror. manuscriptor. recensuit* E. C. Ferrini. 2 vols., Berlin, 1884, 1885, (second not yet completed).

[1] Zachariae, *Historiae juris Graeco-Romani delineatio*, Heidelberg, 1839; Montrueil, *Histoire du Droit Byzantin*, 3 vols., Paris, 1843-46; Prolegomena to Heimbach's edition of the Basilica (6th vol. of *Basilicorum libri LX* . . . *Restituit* C. G. E. Heimbach, 6 vols., Leipsic, 1833-70, with a supplement to books 15-19 by Zachariae in 1846); Zachariae von Lingenthal, *Jus Graeco-Romanum*, (a collection of Byzantine treatises of the second order,) 7 vols. Leipsic, 1856-84; Zachariae v. Ling., *Gesch. d. Griech.-Röm. Rechts* (doctrine), 2d ed., Berlin, 1877; Rivier, *Introd. hist. au droit romain* (2d ed., Brussels, 1881), p. 545 sq.; Amos (as in § 88, note 2), p. 392 sq.

abstract of the whole Justinianian law amended and rearranged, but which was repealed by Basil the Macedonian on account of its imperfections and its audacious departure from the law it pretended to summarise. The last-named emperor, with his son Leo the Philosopher, set themselves in the end of the ninth and beginning of the tenth centuries to the production of an authoritative Greek version of the whole of the Justinianian collections and legislation, omitting what had become obsolete, excising redundancies, and introducing such of the post-Justinianian legislation as merited preservation. The result was the Basilica (τὰ Βασιλικά, i.e., νόμιμα), which was completed in the reign of Leo, though probably issued in a preparatory stage in the reign of Basil, (who also published a sort of institutional work, the Πρόχειρον, which was revised and republished by Leo under the name of 'Επαναγωγὴ τοῦ νόμου). The Basilica are in sixty books, subdivided into titles, following generally the plan of the Justinianian Code, but with the whole law on any particular subject arranged consecutively, whether borrowed from the Digest, the Code, or the Novels. Leo's son, Constantinus Porphyrogenetus, made an addition to it in the shape of an official commentary collected from the writings of the sixth-century jurists,—the so-called Παράγραφαι τῶν παλαιῶν, which are now spoken of as the *Scholia* to the Basilica, and have done good exegetical service for modern civilians. The Basilica retained their statutory authority until the fall of the Byzantine empire in 1453. But long before that they had practically been abandoned; and not a single complete copy of them exists. Their place was taken by epitomes and compendia, of which several are printed in Zachariae's collection, the last being the 'Εξάβιβλος of Const. Harmenopulus of 1345,[2] "a miserable epitome of the epitomes of epitomes," as Bruns calls it, which survived the

[2] *Harmenopuli manuale legum seu Hexabiblos. Recensuit* G. E. Heimbach, Leipsic, 1851.

vicissitudes of the centuries, and finally received statutory authority in the new kingdom of Greece in the year 1835, in place of the Basilica which had been sanctioned in 1822.

SECTION 90.—THEIR FATE IN THE WEST.

Before the rise of the Bologna school it was to a very much greater extent from the Romano-Barbarian Codes (§ 79) than from the books of Justinian that Central and Western Europe derived their acquaintance with Roman law. Theodoric's Edict can have had little influence after Justinian's recovery of Italy, and the Romano-Burgundian law was no doubt gradually displaced by the Breviary (*Lex Rom. Visigothorum*) after Burgundy had fallen into the hands of the Franks; but the Breviary itself found its way in all directions in France and Germany, penetrating even into England, to a great extent through the agency of the Church. There must, however, have been other repertories of Roman law in circulation; as witness a testament made in Paris in the end of the seventh century, preserved by Mabillon, in which the testator uses the old formula of the *jus civile*,—" ita do, ita lego, ita testor, ita vos Quirites testimonium mihi perhibetote,"—words that are not to be found either in the Visigothic or the Justinianian collections.

In his pragmatic sanction of the year 554 Justinian anew accorded his imperial sanction to the *jura* and *leges, i.e.,* the Digest and Code, which he says he had long before transmitted to Italy; at the same time declaring that his Novels were to be of the same authority there as in the East. Two years after this came Julian's Latin epitome of them, not improbably prepared by command of the emperor himself. That they all came at once to some extent into use is beyond question; for there is preserved in Marini's collection the testament of one Mannanes, executed at Ravenna in the reign of Justinian's immediate successor, Justin II., in which the requirements of both Code and Novels are scrupulously observed. Of other monuments of the same period that prove the currency of the Justinianian law in Italy, several are referred to by Savigny in the second volume of his History of the Roman Law in the Middle Ages; among which may be mentioned the Turin Gloss of the Institutes, which Fitting ascribes to about the year 545, and two little pieces known as the *Dictatum de consiliariis* and the *Collectio de tutoribus*, which form an appendix to some manuscripts of Julian's Epitome of the Novels, and may possibly have been from his pen. The invasion of the Lombards, the disturbance they caused in Italy for 200 years, and the barrier they formed between it and the rest of Europe, militated against the spread of the Justinianian law northwards; but it was taught without much interruption in Ravenna, the seat of the exarchs, to which—but this is doubtful—the school (*studium*) of Rome, revived by Justinian, is said to have been transferred. By the Lombards, as their savagery toned down, the Roman law was recognised to this extent,— that they allowed it to be applied to Romans within their territory; and it is said to have even been taught in Pavia, which they had established as their capital. Their overthrow by Charlemagne opened an outlet for it beyond Italy; and in the ninth century there is evidence that the Justinianian books, or some of them, were already circulating in the hands of the clergy in various parts of Europe. Yet there are very few remains of any literature indicating much acquaintance with them. Almost the only pieces worth mentioning are the so-called *Summa Perusina*, an abridgement of the first eight books of the Code, ascribed to the ninth century; the *Quaestiones ac Monita* on the Lombardic Laws, drawn mostly from the Institutes, but with a few texts from the Digest, the Code, and Julian's Epitome, and supposed to have been written early in the eleventh century; the *Brachylogus*, an abbreviated revision of Justinian's

Institutes, with references to his other books, which is thought to have been written in France (Orleans ?), according to Fitting between 999 and 1002, but according to other authorities nearer the end of the eleventh century; and *Petri exceptiones legum romanarum*, a systematic exposition of the law in four books, written in the south of France early in the latter half of the eleventh century, and mostly compiled from Justinianian sources.

It was in the very end of the eleventh century or the beginning of the twelfth that at Bologna, and under one Irnerius, who appears not to have been a professional jurist but originally a teacher of letters, the study of Roman law began somewhat suddenly to attract students from all parts of southern Europe. The only parts of the Justinianian legislation that had hitherto made any great way,—and that through the action of the clergy,—were the Institutes, the Code, and the Novels. The first, from its elementary character, had very naturally commended itself; the Code, with its opening title on the Trinity and its second on Holy Church, and the Novels with their abundant legislation on matters ecclesiastical, were in many respects charters of the Church's privileges and prized accordingly; but the Digest, the work of pagan jurists, had been practically ignored. The Code and the Novels, however, with their modicum of wheat concealed in such a quantity of chaff, offered little attraction to laymen of intelligence; and when a copy of a portion of the Digest, with its infinitely purer diction and clear and incisive reasoning, came into the hands of Irnerius, it must have been for him as a new revelation. The text of it seems to have reached him by instalments; at least this is the reasonable explanation of its division by the Glossarists—as Irnerius and his successors of the Bologna school were called, from the *glossae*, notes marginal and interlinear, with which they furnished it—into three parts, *Digestum Vetus* (books 1 to 24, tit. 2), *Infortiatum*, and *Digestum Novum* (books 39 to the end) ; the general idea being that after first the old and then the new Digest had come to light, the connecting link unexpectedly turned up, and got in consequence the somewhat singular name by which it continued to be known for centuries. The whole collection was by the Glossarists distributed in five volumes ; the fourth containing the first nine books of the Code, and the fifth, called *volumen parvum legum*, containing the Institutes, a Latin translation of 134 of the Novels known as the *Authenticum*, and the last three books of the Code (which had been recovered subsequently to the others). With those five volumes, the teaching that accompanied them, and the *glossae, summae, casus, brocardica*, &c., with which they were enriched from the rise of the school with Irnerius till its close with Franciscus Accursius in 1260, Roman jurisprudence began a new career, which it would carry me beyond the scope of this little book to attempt to trace even in meagrest outline.[1]

SECTION 91.—THE PRINCIPAL MANUSCRIPTS, TEXTS, AND EDITIONS OF THE JUSTINIANIAN BOOKS.

Of the whole *Corpus Juris Civilis*, as the collected body of the Justinianian law was first styled by Denis Godefroi (Gothofredus) in 1583, very few MSS. are known to exist. There is one in Copenhagen, but it is not of great antiquity or any

[1] The great authority on the matter of this section is still Savigny's *Gesch. d. Röm. Rechts im Mittelalter*, 7 vols., 2d ed., Heidelberg, 1834-51 ; but much additional light has been thrown on it by Merkel, Stintzing, Blume, Fitting, Bruns, Mommsen, Krüger, Ficker, Rivier, Conrat (Cohn), and others, whose writings, mostly in periodicals, are too numerous to mention. On the early traces of Roman law in Britain, see Amos (as in § 88, note 2), p. 443 sq. ; Caillemer, *Le Droit Civil dans les provinces Anglo-Normandes*, Caen, 1883 ; Scrutton, *The Influence of the Roman Law on the Law of England*, Cambridge, 1885. A tractate by Leonard, *Beiträge zur Geschichte des Römischen Rechts in England*, (Heidelb. 1868), is of little value ; it is mostly compiled from Selden's *Ad Fletam dissertatio*, Savigny's *Geschichte*, and Wenck's *Magister Vacarius, primus juris Romani in Anglia Professor*, Leipsic, 1820.

critical value. It is said that a second exists (or existed) in the Dominican library at Würzburg, gifted to it by the Emperor Frederick Barbarossa, and a third in a convent library at Prague; but the mention in the *Catalogus MSS. Angliae et Hiberniae* of the existence of a fourth in the cathedral library at Salisbury is founded on a misapprehension. Of printed editions, on the other hand, it may be said with certainty that there is but one book of which there is a greater multitude,—the Holy Bible.

Of the Institutes the manuscripts are numerous, the earliest mere fragments, and but one of the ninth (or more probably tenth) century complete,—the *Codex Bambergensis;* the great majority are of the fourteenth century, and some still later. The earliest edition was that of Peter Schoeffer (Mayence, 1468), with the Accursian gloss; the first unglossated one was published in Paris in 1511; and the most authoritative one at the present day, being the result of a collation of the best manuscripts, is that of Krüger, first published in 1867. The texts of Schrader (1832) and Huschke (1868) rank next in importance.

There is but one complete manuscript of the Digest of earlier date than the rise of the Bologna school,—the famous *Codex Florentinus,* formerly in Pisa, but now one of the most valued treasures of the Lorenzian Library in Florence. Of this MS. a minute description is given by Brencmann in his *Historia Pandectarum* (Utrecht, 1722), and a more critical one by Mommsen in the preface to the first volume of his greater edition of the Digest (Berlin, 1866). It is a very beautiful codex, dating from the sixth or seventh century, written, if not in Constantinople, at all events in Greece, with a good many corrections by later hands. It is free from abbreviations,—the *sigla* which Justinian had forbidden; and has neither numeration of the consecutive fragments, nor spaces between the words, nor punctuation except at the end of sentences. The inscriptions are always preserved, and the Greek passages written with even greater accuracy than the general text. Also of great antiquity, and probably not much younger than the Florentine, are the Pommersfeld and Naples codices; but they are mere fragments,—the first a papyrus containing part of the first title of the forty-fifth book, and the second a palimpsest containing part of the tenth book. A manuscript in the Royal Library at Berlin, which dates from the ninth century, contains part of the ninth book. ·No other known codices go beyond the commencement of the school of the glossarists. With very few exceptions, they contain not the whole Digest, but only one of its Bolognese divisions,—either the *Dig. Vetus*, the *Infortiatum*, or the *Dig. Novum;* not more than six or eight are as old as the eleventh or twelfth century; while about 500 are known of later date. These last for the most part contain the Accursian gloss; and it is characteristic of them that they do not give the inscriptions in full,—*i.e.*, the indications of the books of the old jurists from which the passages had been excerpted,—and sometimes omit them altogether; and that they omit the Greek words and sentences, or substitute for them a current Latin translation. Of the texts, three are distinguished by the civilians,—the Pisan, the Vulgate, and the Noric. The first is that of the Florentine manuscript. The Vulgate is that which was adopted by the glossarists, and which is to be found, more or less variated, in all the manuscripts from the thirteenth century downwards. Mommsen is of opinion that, while the (Pisan or) Florentine formed the basis of the Bologna text, yet the glossarists must have been in possession of another manuscript of perhaps equal antiquity, though possibly incomplete, from which they corrected the former with great advantage. The *lectio Norica* or *Haloandrina* is a mixed text due to Gregorius Haloander (Metzler), the result of a collation of the Florentine with some of the oldest Vulgate MSS., aided largely by arbitrary conjecture, which was published by him at Nuremberg in 1529. The *editio princeps*, curiously enough, was of the *Infortiatum*, at Rome, in 1475; the *Dig. Vetus* and *Novum* followed in the ensuing year at Perusina and Rome respectively. All three were prints of the Bologna text, with the Accursian gloss. Haloander's edition of 1529, which was of the whole Digest, was unglossated. So was the magnificent reproduction of the Florentine Pandects by the Torellis in 1553, under the sanction of several crowned heads, and amongst them King Edward VI. From that time, and down to the middle of the present century, most unglossated editions—the latest glossated one dates from 1627—were a combination of all three texts, the Florentine predominating, but conjectural readings gradually multiplying. The uncertainty which thus resulted induced Mommsen to undertake the preparation of the edition (2 volumes, Berlin, 1866–70) which is now on all hands accepted as authoritative. It is substantially the reading of the Florentine from a new collation prepared for the purpose, checked only by the three fragments above referred to and a small number of the very earliest Bologna codices, and, where necessary, by the Basilica and its scholia; conjectural emendations being very sparingly admitted, and usually relegated to footnotes.

Of the Code there exist three incomplete ante-glossarist manuscripts. Irnerius seems to have had originally only the first nine books, for the three last (*tres libri*) formed part of the *Volumen* according to the Bologna arrangement. They all fared somewhat badly; for comparatively early the inscriptions and subscriptions and all the Greek constitutions came to be omitted. Into the Code as they had it the glossarists introduced what they called *Authenticae*,—notes of the alterations made on the law by Justinian's Novels; also some constitutions of the Emperors Frederick I. and II., which are quite out of place. The authoritative edition, prepared from the best manuscripts, with restitution of all that the glossarists had excised, is that of Krüger (Berlin, 1877).

The Novels, as already observed, were never collected officially. For several centuries they were known in Italy only through Julian's Latin Epitome of some 125 of them. Another Latin version, which is thought to have been also of the time of Justinian, was accepted by the glossarists (*versio vulgata*), and obtained the name of *Authenticum,*— "that sanctioned as law."[1] This they divided into twelve *Collationes*; in nine of them ranging those laws which they glossated as of practical value (*authenticae ordinariae*), the rest (the *authenticae extraordinariae* or *extravagantes*) being placed in the other three and unglossated. In the sixteenth century two Greek manuscripts were discovered, which form the basis of the now accepted collection; one in Florence, which was published by Haloander in 1531, the other in Venice, published in 1558 by Henry Scrimgeour, the first Scotsman who obtained European distinction as a civilian. The last edition is that of Zachariae von Lingenthal (2 vols., Leipsic, 1882). Another by Rudolf Schoell is in course of publication; it is meant to rank with the Digest by Mommsen, and the Institutes and Code by Krüger, as the completion of a trustworthy presentation of the whole *Corpus Juris Civilis.*

[1] *Authenticum Novellarum Constitutionum Justiniani versio vulgata quam recensuit.* G. E. Heimbach, 2 vols., Leipsic, 1851, with elaborate *prolegomena* and other critical apparatus.

APPENDIX.

NOTE A. (See § 9, *in fine.*)

REFERENCES in the pages of the lay writers to the action of the *cognati* and *adfines* must be received with caution. For instance, in their accounts of the *caristia* or *cara cognatio*, an annual festival that immediately followed the *parentales dies* and the *feralia*, and at which all the members of a family assembled to renew the bonds of goodwill and affection over a common repast in presence of the domestic *lares*, Ovid (*Fast.*, ii. 617 *sq.*) and Valerius Maximus (ii. 1, § 8) speak of it as a reunion of the *cognati* and *adfines* generally, to the exclusion of all third parties. But as the feast was held everywhere on the same day and was kept up till night, and as both men and women might be nearly connected by blood or marriage with half-a-dozen families or more, it is clear that the cognation and affinity that qualified for participation in it must have stopped short of that sixth degree to which they usually extended. It is only by assuming that the gathering was exclusively of wife, sons, unmarried daughters, and wives and children of sons, around the table of the head of the house, that the account of it becomes comprehensible. His sons and their children and his unmarried daughters were undoubtedly cognates of his, and his wife and daughters-in-law *adfines* in the wider sense of the word; but what a small proportion probably of those entitled to those designations. It may be that in other cases in which *cognati* and *adfines* are spoken of a similar limitation is necessary.

NOTE B. (See § 14, note 4.)

Gaius (i. 113) describes *coemptio* as an imaginary sale and purchase *per aes et libram*, in presence of a *libripens* and five citizen witnesses; but unfortunately the final words in the MS.—"a [=asse] emit eum mulierem, cujus in manum convenit"—do not indicate with certainty which of the parties was the nominal seller and which the nominal purchaser. Comparative jurisprudence shows so many examples of bride-capture developing into bride-purchase, that many jurists rush to the conclusion that, as the story of the Sabine rape, the *hasta coelibaris*, the pretended forcible tearing of the bride from her mother, &c., point to a time when capture was in vogue, and as Gaius defines *coemptio* as an imaginary sale, there must have been an intermediate stage in which there was a real purchase of the bride from her father or guardian, of which *coemptio* was a modified survival; that in it consequently the bridegroom was the purchaser, the bride's *paterfamilias* or guardian the seller, and the bride herself the object of sale. That there may have been such an intermediate stage is more than probable; but the coemption of the texts does not represent it.

The following points are to be noted: (1) *Emere* in old Latin did not necessarily mean to purchase for a substantial money price, but simply to take, receive, or acquire; see Festus v. *Redemptores* (Bruns, p. 286), Paul. Diac. vv. *Abemito* and *Emere* (Bruns, pp. 262, 267); (2) though *coemptio* was a mancipation, yet this was used for many other purposes besides actual sale and conveyance of a *res mancipi*, *e.g.*, the execution of a testament and the effecting of a donation, adoption, or emancipation; the touching of the scales with a piece of copper (and later a coin) in the presence of witnesses was but the solemnity employed to mark the completion of the act, whose nature and purpose were defined in the contemporaneous spoken words; (3) that Cicero and Gaius never use the word *coemere*, but always *coemptionem facere*, a phrase they apply exclusively to the bride, *coemptionari* and *coemptionator* being applied to the bridegroom; (4) that Servius, speaking of *coemptio*, says (*in Aen.*, iv. 103, Bruns, p. 322), "Mulier atque vir in se quasi coemptionem faciunt," and (*in Georg.*, i. 31, Bruns, p. 324) "Se maritus et uxor invicem coemebant;" (5) that Boethius (*in Cic. Top.*, ii. 3, § 14, Bruns, p. 320), quoting Ulpian as his authority, says, "Sese in coemendo invicem interrogabant," &c.; (6) that Isidore (*Orig.* v. 24, § 26, Bruns, p. 327) says, "Se maritus et uxor invicem emebant, ne videretur uxor ancilla;" (7) that Nonius Marcellus, v. *Nubentes* (Bruns, p. 312), says that in ancient times a woman marrying carried three pieces of money, one for her husband *tamquam emendi causa*, and the others for his domestic and compital *lares*.

In presence of all these authorities it seems impossible to accept either the prevalent opinion that the bridegroom alone was purchaser, or that entertained by Hölder (*Die Römische Ehe*, Zurich, 1874, p. 20 *sq.*), that this position was taken solely by the bride, the bridegroom being the object of purchase. Reciprocal purchase, or rather, as Boethius puts it, the acquiring of each other as *paterfamilias* and *materfamilias* respectively, and that under pretence of purchase, seems to have been the true nature of the transaction. The objection usually urged against this view—that a man could not sell *himself*—is of very little weight. Why could he not do so as well as the bride? It is said she did not do so; that if a *filiafamilias*, she was sold by her father, and if *sui juris*, by her tutors. But the last part of the explanation is inconsistent with what is stated both by Gaius (i. 190) and Ulpian (xi. 25), that tutors never acted *for* their full-grown female wards, but only sanctioned the latters' acts,—a rule to which coemption formed no exception (Gai., i. 115, 195) ; and even the first part of it is contradicted by a statement of Paul's in a passage preserved in the *Collatio* (iv. 2, 2),—that, when a *filiafamilias* passed *in manum mariti*, the act was her own, her father being no more than *auctor*. That a man could not go through the form of selling himself *per aes et libram*, however, is a proposition that is unsupported by any authority ; the extent of the truth is that he could not so sell himself into slavery or *quasi* slavery ; and Gaius says expressly (i. 123) that neither of these was implied by the words used in coemption.

On these grounds I am disposed to think that there is an omission in the text of the MS. of Gaius, and that the latter ought to read somewhat to this effect,—" asse [emit vir mulierem, quam in manum recipit (see Gai., ii. 98), et invicem] emit eum mulier, cujus in manum convenit." Huschke's opinion is similar ; in his last (4th) edition of Gaius he has " asse emit eum [mulier et is] mulierem, cujus in manum convenit." The objection to this reading is that, as *vir* does not occur in the previous part of the sentence, *eum* and *is* have no antecedent.

NOTE C. (See § 31, note 3.)

Considerable confusion has been caused as to the meaning of the word *nexum* by some definitions of it by writers of the later republic, preserved by Varro, *De L. L.*, vii. 105 (Bruns, p. 308) and Festus v. *Nexum* (Bruns, p. 274). In reading them it must be kept in view that Mamilius (as quoted by Varro) and Aelius Gallus (as quoted by Festus) are not speaking of a *person* making himself *nexus* by copper and scales,—for that practice was abolished by the Poetilian law of 428 U.C. (*supra*, p. 161),—but of a thing being bonded (*obligata*) in that way. The phrase *res nexa* is quite common in the classical law, as applied to something impledged or hypothecated to a creditor ; see Ulp., in *Dig.*, xliii. 4, fr. 1, § 4, Antoninus (Caracalla), in *Cod.*, viii. 19, 2, Alex. Sever., in *Cod.*, viii. 27, 2. When a thing was given as a security *per aes et libram* it was called *fiducia* (*supra*, p. 140 *sq.*), and it is this that Q. Mucius Scævola (Varro, as above) appears to have had in view when correcting Mamilius ; he limits the word *nexum* to a thing over which a *nexus* was created *per aes et libram*, and excludes from it an ordinary mancipatory conveyance of property,—a limitation and exclusion of which Varro approves. It may be objected that a *fiducia*, although undoubtedly intended only as a security, was in form transferred to the creditor in property. But the money lent to a borrower *per aes et libram* also became his property, and yet it was called *nexum aes*. The borrowed money and the thing given as *fiducia*, therefore, were in much the same position : both became the property of the receiver, but with an obligation of return ; if the one was properly called *nexum aes*, why should not the other be *res nexa?* The final, and unfortunately corrupt, sentence in the passage of Varro refers to the case of the debtor who, in the earlier law, made himself *nexus*, and has little or no connection with what precedes it. (See on this subject the observations of Prof. Nettleship in the *Journal of Philology*, vol. xii. (1883), p. 198 *sq.*)

NOTE D. (See § 34, note 12.)

In the early sacramental procedure each party had to deposit his stake before he could be heard on the question at issue ; but afterwards he only gave security for its payment in the event of a judgment declaring him to have been in the wrong. Ihering ("Reich und Arm im altröm. Civilprozess," in his *Scherz und Ernst*, p. 175 *sq.*) regards this change of practice as a signal triumph of popular legislation. He maintains that not only the tendency but the motive of the arrangements of the judicial procedure, both by sacrament (§ 34) and *manus injectio* (§ 36), were to throw obstacles in the way of a poor man asserting or defending his rights, by making deposit of a considerable sum of money in the one case, and the finding of a *vindex* in the other, a condition precedent of his plaint or defence ; that both these procedures were instruments for defeating the ends of justice when a rich man set himself in opposition to a poor one. This was in time amended in the case of *manus injectio* by allowing the party against whom it was employed to defend himself in most cases *in propria persona, i.e.*, without a *vindex;* and in that of the sacramental procedure by its being held sufficient for the parties to give sureties for the *summa* or *poena sacramenti*, which was exacted only from him who was eventually unsuccessful. Ihering ascribes the latter amendment to a law partially preserved by Festus (Bruns, p. 43), passed on the proposal of one L. Papirius, a tribune of the people, and which cannot have been earlier than the sixth century, appointing three officials to collect and adjudicate upon sacramental penalties (*sacramenta exigunto judicantoque*) ; and he understands by these words that not only were they to exact the penalties, but that, disregarding the figures of 500 or 50 *asses* which had been named in the *provocatio*, they were to determine in each particular case what the amount should be. He identifies this Papirian law with one of the same name mentioned by Pliny (*H. N.*, 33, § 46), but which most recent writers assign to the year 665, reducing the weight of the copper *as* to half an ounce ; (it had been reduced in 485 from 1 lb. to 4 oz., about 513 to 2 oz., and in 537 to 1 oz.) He thus makes the *lex Papiria* a statute of considerable scope, at once postponing the collection of the *sacramentum* until the end of the suit, empowering the *IIIviri capitales* to say what should be its amount, and facilitating its payment by reducing the value of the *as*. But the purpose of this last provision is more likely to have been the alleviation of the position of borrowers; and as regards the other two, the text preserved by Festus seems rather to indicate that the new officials in exaction and judgment—and what is meant by the *judicanto* is far from clear—were to follow already existing practice. Be this as it may, and the date of the change earlier than that assigned to it by Ihering, there can be no question of its importance or doubt of the benefit it must have conferred on poor litigants.

NOTE E. (See § 34, note 19.)

Varro, *De L. L.*, v. 180 (Bruns, p. 303), says that even after the *summa sacramenti* had been converted into money, it was deposited *ad pontem*,—some bridge, he does not say which, where there was a sacred "pound." (Curiously enough, the Irish spelling of "pound" is "pont;" Skeate's *Etym. Dict.*, v. "Pound.") A most ingenious and plausible explanation was suggested by Danz in 1867, in the *Z. f. RG.*, vol. vi. p. 359. Recalling the facts that there had been discovered in the Tiber-island *sacella* of Jupiter Jurarius and Dius Fidius, the two deities to whom solemn oaths were usually addressed, and that the island was spoken of as "inter duos pontes," because connected with both banks of the river by bridges bearing no particular names, he suggested that the island may have been the spot to which disputants resorted to make their *sacramenta*, and that the cattle, sheep, or money were deposited in a place for the purpose before the bridge was crossed. Much the same explanation was offered by Huschke two years later in his book *Das alte römische Jahr* (Breslau, 1869), p. 360, apparently without being aware of Danz's speculation. He adds, on the authority of the Iguvine Tables, that while bullocks were offered to Jupiter, only sheep were offered to Dius Fidius. The island, he thinks, must have been selected as neutral ground, to which all parties might have access, and which obviated intrusion into the temples of the two gods on the Capitol and Quirinal respectively. And it is to its use as the scene of the sacramental procedure that he attributes its name of "holy island," rather than to the fact of its having been the seat of the temple of Æsculapius. Huschke recurs to and enforces this view in his *Multa und Sacramentum* (1874), p. 410, where he does refer to Danz's paper.

NOTE F. (See § 36, note 11.)

Another argument in favour of the view that the *aeris confessi* of the XII Tables referred to nexal debt occurred to me after the text was in type. It is derived from the language of cap. lxi. of the *Lex Coloniae*

Juliae Genetivae of the year of Rome 710 (Bruns, p. 111) : " Judicati jure manus injectio esto.... Vindex arbitratu II viri quive jure dicundo praerit locuples esto. Ni vindicem dabit judicatumve faciet, secum ducito. Jure civili vinctum habeto," &c. The *aeris confessi* of the Tables does not reappear ; but no one contends that the *manus injectio* authorised by the colonial statute did not apply to the *in jure confessus*. If it did apply to him, it must have been because he was included in the term *judicatus*. The *aeris confessi* no doubt was omitted because it applied to nexal debtors, against whom *manus injectio* had been prohibited by the Poetilian law.

NOTE G. (See § 36, note 20.)

" The idea of responsibility (*Haftung*) is primarily one of answering with life and limb ; in primitive times responsibility in any other way is inconceivable. Hence the debtor who does not pay falls straightway into the hands of his creditor, who may hold him as a slave, may sell him into slavery, may kill him. But this last alternative is ere long subjected to some modification. The members of the body have very soon each its own value put upon it, in order that for every case of injury there may be a fixed and certain composition. This point reached, a creditor must no longer cut from his debtor's body more than necessary—than is a proper equivalent for the wrong he has sustained ; and, if there be several concurring creditors, none must cut more than corresponds to his own claim. So we find it put in the extant remains of old Scandinavian law. In contrast it may be said to have been a step in advance when the Roman XII Tables made an end of this detestable calculation, by declaring that in such a case it should be of no moment whether one or more creditors cut away more or less than his or their proper share ; they might hack their debtor in pieces just as they pleased ; the law was no longer to be encumbered with details : *si plus minusve secuerunt se fraude esto*. So long as the sequence of ideas in the world's history was undiscovered, this provision of the Tables was naturally beyond comprehension. And yet it is somewhat surprising that no one should have lighted on the meaning of it when one thinks of all the hypotheses that have been suggested to explain it, but that really explain nothing ; hypotheses so multitudinous that there fails from the list of them this only,—that the ancient Romans must have been *anthropophagi !*

" It is a step further in advance when the law stops short of killing a debtor, and contents itself with pains and tortures. In the invention of such punitive devices mankind has given signal proofs of its ingenuity, —expulsion from the body social, infamy in every shape, corporal punishment, incarceration. All these fell to the lot of the unfortunate debtor. If he was dead, his creditor seized even his poor remains. To deprive a debtor's body of a peaceful grave was a custom among the Egyptians that survived into the Christian period. Even as late as the sixth century the emperors had to interfere to suppress this horrible abuse ; and the legends alike of East and West held him in honour who ransomed an insolvent's corpse and gave it decent burial.

"In my work '*Shakespeare vor dem Forum der Jurisprudenz*,' I have shown in detail how those gruesome customs gradually disappeared,—how the development of the law step by step removed the foundations of the system ; and it is enough to refer to what is there said. I have shown there also the conservative element that for many a long year held that development of the law in check. The severities that attended insolvency were perpetuated through the medium of contract. When the old consequences of insolvency no longer resulted by direct operation of law, creditors began to make sure of them by clauses embodied in their agreements. If a debtor was no longer to fall *ipso jure* into the hands of his creditor, it was necessary that he should expressly impledge himself. He pledged his body, his freedom, his honour, even the salvation of his soul. The clause inserted in the contract might prescribe forfeiture by the debtor of a pound of flesh,—a figure that has become typical for all times through the genius of the great dramatist. Or it might be one whereby the debtor subjected himself, in the event of non-payment, to some indignity, or to outlawry, or even to excommunication," &c., &c. Kohler, *Das Recht als Culturerscheinung*, Würzburg, 1885, p. 17 *sq.*

NOTE H. (See § 53, note 15.)

Gaius says that, while it was on all hands admitted that there could be transcription of a book-debt from one person to another only between citizens, it was a matter of dispute in the empire whether there might not be transcription from thing to person even between peregrins, seeing it proceeded on an antecedent liability under a *juris gentium* obligation. One might suppose from the anecdote told by Cicero (*De Off.*, iii. 14, §§ 58–60) of C. Canius and Pythius, the Syracusan banker, that it was in use by peregrins in his time, (unless indeed Pythius, though living in a province, was in fact a citizen). It affords a capital illustration of the effect of the *nomen*. Hearing that Canius was in search of a country-house, Pythius, who owned one, invited him to dine with him a day or two afterwards. In the meantime he bespoke some fishermen to be then in the bay (which was finless) with some boats well filled with fish, which, on a given signal, they were to bring ashore before the eyes of his guest, as if just caught ; while he arranged with some huntsmen to be in the vicinity, well furnished with game, which they were to bring to the house while Canius was sipping his wine, pretending it had been newly killed in the woods. The bait took. A place with such attractions was just what Canius wanted. Would Pythius sell it? He might have any price he liked; and so on, and so on, until Pythius made pretence of reluctant consent. Naturally, Canius had not the money with him; but the astute Pythius knew very well that if he left the price standing until his guest had discovered the fraud, he would never have any chance of fingering it. So he produced his books and transcribed the debt at once: *nomina facit, negotium conficit*. He thereby made Canius his debtor, not for the price of a house and grounds, but for money booked against him, recoverable by an *actio certae creditae pecuniae;* and as the *exceptio* and *actio doli* had not yet been invented, there was no means by which Canius could plead the fraud as an equitable defence, or have reparation for the deceit of which he had been the victim.

INDEX.

ACCEPTILATION, 277.
Accrual (*adcretio*) amongst heirs, 176.
Actiones, Classes of: *a. arbitrariae*, 364 *sq.; bonae fidei*, 285 *sq.*, 360; *ficticiae*, 362 *sq.; in factum*, 364; *juris honorarii*, 362; why prætorian actions had to be raised within a year, 256; *a. stricti juris*, 199, 285; *utiles*, 362; practical disappearance of some of those distinctions in later empire, 388.
Actiones, Legis, see "*Legis actiones*."
Actiones, Particular: *a. auctoritatis*, 136 *sq.; de dolo*, 364; *depensi*, 166; *depositi*, 142 n. 8, 362 n. 11; *de rationibus distrahendis*, 148; *de tigno juncto*, 148; *empti* (its successive phases), 284 *sq.; ex stipulatu*, 274, 283, 360; *familiae erciscundae*, 166, 176; *fiduciae*, 141 *sq.; furti* (the various actions of the XII Tables), 147; *Pauliana*, 250; *Publiciana*, 269 *sq.*
Adcretio (accrual) amongst heirs, 176.
Addictio debitoris in *manus injectio*, 207; distinction between *judicati* and *addicti, ibid.* n. 17; no *addictio* in case of nexal debtors, 155, 158; status of *addicti*, 209; provisions of Poetilian law in reference to them, 161.
Aditio hereditatis, 175; *tempus deliberandi*, 426; entry *cum beneficio inventarii, ib.*
Adjudication, 145, 361 and n. 9.
Adoption,—its purpose originally, 29; n. of a *paterfamilias*, see "Adrogation;" n. of a *filiusfamilias*, 30, 119 *sq.*; effect, 30, 129; Justinianian amendments, 418.
Adrogation (or adoption of a *paterfamilias*),—its purpose, 29; how accomplished, 30; incompetent to plebeians in regal period, 48; effects, 130 n. 4, 131, 176.
Adsertor libertatis (in status-actions about freedom or slavery), 196.
Ædiles, Curule, their institution, 88; their edicts, 258.
Ædiles, Plebeian, 84, 85 and n. 5.
Aelianum, Jus, 262 and n. 10.
Aes et libram, Origin of the *negotium per*, 58; conveyance *per*, see "Mancipation;" loan *per*, see "*Nexum*;" marriage *per*, see "*Coemptio;*" *solutio per*, 60 n. 16; testament *per*, see "Testament;" justification of the procedure *per acs et libram*, 62. n. 25, 68 *sq.* and n. 12.
Aes con/cssum of XII Tables meant nexal loan, 157, 203 *sq.*, 445 *sq.*
Aes rude, 59.
Aes signatum of Serv. Tullius, 59 and notes 12, 14.
Africanus, Sext. Cæc., 320.
Agency, 272.
Ager publicus, 90–92.
Ager rectigalis, 420.
Agnates and Agnation, as distinct from the *gens*, unknown in regal period, 43 and n. 3; agnatic tutory and inheritance invented by Decemvirs to meet necessities of the plebeians, 122 *sq.*, 172 *sq.*; who were agnate, 123 *sq.* and notes 8, 10; relation dissolved by *capitis deminutio*, 130, 174; tutory of agnates under XII Tables, 124; their succession, 172; limitations put upon it, 173, 288, 292 *sq.*; a *successio graduum* amongst them first admitted by Justinian, 423; preference of agnates over cognates entirely abolished by his Novels, *ib.*

2 F

Agrarian legislation of republic, 91 sq.
Alaric's Breviary (*Lex Rom. Visigoth.*), 398.
Album, The prætor's, 254, 357.
Amicitia, 110.
Antestatus, 290 n. 9.
Aquilian stipulation, 274.
Aquilius Gallus, 264.
Arbitria and *judicia*, 198 sq.; *arbitrium litis aestimandae*, 195.
Auctorem laudare, 190 n. 10.
Auctoritas and *Auctoritatis actio*, 136 sq.; limited to two years, 138.
Auctoritas patrum (in legislation), 85.
Authenticae in Code, 438.
Authenticum (Bolognese version of Novels), 435, 439.

BANKRUPTCY, — the Rutilian edict about it, 250; how post-mortem b. avoided, 175.
Barter, its conversion into sale, 280.
Basilica, The, 431.
Bernardakis's Sinaitic papyri, 400.
"*Bina jugera*," The, of Varro and Pliny, 36 sq.
Bishops' courts, — their institution, jurisdiction, and procedure, 383 sq.
Blood-feud, its early suppression, 53.
Bologna and the Glossarists, 434 sq.
"*Bona paterna avitaque*," 32, 126.
Bonae fidei action, — what involved in, 285 sq.; *intentio* of, 360; *exceptio doli* superfluous in, 367.
Bonae fidei possessio, 271.
"*Bonam copiam jurare*," 162.
Boni mores as a regulative of public and private order, 21.
Bonitarian ownership (*in bonis habere*) of *res mancipi*, 41 n. 9; a result of Publician edict, 268 sq.; distinction between it and Quiritarian ownership abolished by Justinian, 420.
Bonorum, Emptio, see "*Emptio bonorum.*"
Bonorum possessio, 289-294; nature and probable origin, 289; *b. p. secundum tabulas*, 289 sq.; *b. p. contra tabulas*, 291 sq.; its practical abolition by later Justinianian law, 424; *b. p. ab intestato*, 292 sq.; the prætorian order of intestate succession and admission of cognates, 293 sq.; how *b. p.* obtained, 294, 425; refused in absence of *testamenti factio*, 353;

immediate effect, 291; heir's actions granted to *bonorum possessor* under fiction of heirship, 362 sq.
Brachylogus, The, 433.
Breviarium Alaricianum, 398.
Burgundionum, Lex Romana, 399.
Byzantine jurisprudence, 430-432.

"CAPITE *poenas dabat*" of decemviral *manus injectio*, 207 sq.
Capitis deminutio: meaning of *caput*, 126; degrees of *c. d.*, 127; *c. d. minima* in particular, 127-129; its consequences, 129-131; not involved in *servitium* of *nexus*, 159.
Capito and Labeo, 315 sq.
Caracalla's general grant of citizenship, 339 sq.
Carvilius Ruga and his divorce, 248 note.
Cassian treaty of 262 u.c., 223.
Cattle and sheep as media of exchange, 58 and n. 7.
Cautio damni infecti, 373; *c. de dolo, ib.; c. judicatum solvi, ib.; c. praedibus praediisque*, 149; *c. usufructuaria*, 373.
Censors, Institution of, 88; their *regimen morum*, 222 sq. and n. 9.
Centumviral court,—its creation, composition, and functions, 75 sq.; c. causes, 185 sq. and n. 13, 360; *centumviralis hasta*, 75 n. 9.
Certi condictio, 359.
Cessio bonorum, 96, 160.
Cessio in jure, see "*In jure cessio.*"
Christianity, Establishment of,—its influence on the law generally and specially, 381-384.
Cicero's book *de jure civili in artem redigendo*, 263 n. 11.
Citations, Valentinian law of, 390 sq.
Citizen and non-citizen under *jus civile*, 107-113; citizen's *conubium*, *commercium*, and *actio*, 108; his capacity generally, 127; he alone could make a testament, 48 n. 13; Caracalla's general grant of citizenship, 339 sq.
Clientage in regal period, 8 sq.; how affected by XII Tables, 114.
Codex, Gregorianus, 392.
Codex, Hermogenianus, 392 sq.
Codex, Justinianeus, the 1st edit., 403 sq.; *J. Cod. repetitae praelectionis*, 411-413; its relation to the Digest,

412; its sources, 413; MSS. and editions, 438.
Codex, Theodosianus, 393 sq.
Codices accepti et expensi, 276.
Codicils, Introduction of, as adjuncts to testaments, 355; latterly effectual though standing alone, 423; witnesses required, *ib*.
Coemptio,—origin of, 64; nature, 65, 441 sq.; how dissolved, 117 and n. 7; Gaius' account of, 441 sq.; c. *fiduciae causa*, 44 n. 6, 141 and n. 36.
Cognates (kinsmen generally),—their position among plebeians prior to XII Tables, 35 sq.; by Tables preference given to agnates in tutory and succession, 122 sq., 172 sq.; by prætors c. admitted to succession on intestacy on failure of agnates, 293, provided they had *testamenti factio* with deceased, 353 n. 9; who included among *cognati* of edict, 294; c. put by Justinian on a par with agnates, 424; the word *cognati* in the pages of the lay writers, 441.
Cognatio, Servilis, 419.
Collatio Legum Mosaicar. et Romanar., 395.
Collation by *emancipati* admitted to *bonor. possessio contra tabulas*, 292; its extension in Justinianian law, 426.
Collectio de tutoribus, 433.
Colonatus (servitude of the glebe), 384-387.
Colonial latinity, 265 sq.
Comitia tributa,—its institution and organisation, 85 sq.
Commerce, Growth of, after first Punic war,—its influence on the law, 239 sq.
Commercium, 109 and n. 6; its concession by treaty to non-citizens, 111, 113; enjoyed by colonial and Junian latins, 265, 339.
Compounding for capital or corporal punishment, 71 sq., 106, 361 n. 10.
Concilium plebis,—its legislative competency, 84, 86.
Condictio, 232 sq.; c. *causa data causa non secuta*, 280 sq.; *certi c.*, 359; *incerti c.*, 359 sq.; c. *triticaria*, 232, 235, 359.
Condictionem, Legis actio per, 230-235.
Confarreatio,—a patrician marriage-ceremony, 26; incompetent to ple-

beians, 34, 64; how dissolved, 117; declared creative of *manus* only *quoad sacra*, 346.
Confessio in jure, 203-205, 446.
Consensual contracts, 278-286.
Consilium domesticum, 32, 36, 117, 248.
Consortium (amongst heirs), 45 and n. 7, 176.
Constitutions, The imperial, in earlier empire, 312-314; *edicta*—their character then, 312 sq.; *rescripta* and *decreta*, 313 sq.; the i. c. in later empire, 379 sq.
Consuetude, see "Custom."
Consulate,—effects of its institution, 81-83.
Consultatio veteris jurisconsulti, 397.
Contract, Law of, in regal period and early republic, 49 sq., 150-165; insufficiency of bare agreement to create c., 150; omnipotence of word and form, *ib.*; what if bare agreement fortified with oath or appeal to *Fides*, 50, 165; the formal contracts of the early *jus civile*, 151; *nexum* in particular, see "*Nexum;*" development of the law of c. in the latter half of the republic, 271-287; verbal c., see "*Sponsio*" and "Stipulation;" literal, 275 sq.; real, 286 sq.; consensual, 163, 278-286; innominate, 350.
Conubium, 25, 108, 109 n. 6; the essential pre-requisite of *justae nuptiae* and *patria potestas*, 118 n. 10; not enjoyed by plebeians in regal period, 34, 64; the Canuleian law, 87; c. with non-citizens by treaty, 111 sq.; none between citizens and colonial or Junian latins, 265, 339.
Corpus Juris Civilis, 435; MSS., texts, and editions, 436 sq.
Coruncanius, Tib., 262.
Credita pecunia, 276.
Cretio hereditatis, 175.
Crime and private wrong, Line between, at first not well defined, 71; criminal offences in early regal period, 51 sq.
"*Cum nexum faciet mancipiumque*," &c., 137 n. 21, 169, 280, 281 n. 23.
Curatory of lunatics, spendthrifts, &c., in patrician Rome, 121; under XII Tables, 126; c. of minors established by Marc. Aurelius, 348 sq.
Custom or consuetude, Early, 20; importance of c. as a factor of the law at

all times, 258; the making of custom, 259-261.

"DAMNAS *esto*," 153 and n. 7.

"*Damnum decidi oportere,*" 361 and n. 10.

Debt, Law of, in early republic, 92-96; treatment of nexal debtors, see "*Nexum;*" of judgment debtors, see "*Manus injectio;*" their incarceration in later law, 212.

Decemviri, Judices, of Valerio-Horatian laws, 76, 84 *sq.*, 219 *sq.*

Decemviri legibus scribundis, 97.

Decemviri litibus judicandis, 76 and n. 14.

Decreta, Imperial, in early empire, 313 *sq.;* their authority enhanced by Justinian, 380.

Decretum divi Marci (punishing self-help), 314 note.

Dediticiancy, Aelia-Sentian, 337; abolished by Justinian, 419.

Delatio hereditatis, 174.

Delegation, 278 and n. 16.

Deliberandi, Heir's *jus,* 426.

Demonstratio of *formula,* 359.

Depensum, 166.

Deposit,—the action *in duplum* of XII Tables, 142 n. 38; the *formulae in jus* and *in factum* of the prætorian system, 362 n. 11.

Dictatum de consiliariis, 433.

Diffarreatio, 117.

Digest, Justinian's instructions for its preparation, 404 *sq.;* its compilation, 406; its completion, 407 *sq.;* the sources drawn upon, 409; order of sequence of books, titles, and fragments, 409-411; *dig. vetus, infortiatum,* and *dig. novum,* 434; MSS., texts, and editions, 436-438.

Diocletian, multitude of his rescripts, 327, 393; excellence of many of them, 327.

Disherison of children, see "Testament."

Distress, see "*Pignoris capio.*"

Divorce in regal period, 27 n. 11; in early republic, 116 *sq.*; formula of d., 117; increasing frequency of d. in later republic, 248; d. in the classical period, 346; legislation of later empire, 382 *sq.;* that of Justinian in his Novels, 415.

Dolo, Actio de, 364.

Domestic *consilium,* 32, 36, 117, 248.

Dominium bonitarium of *res mancipi,* see "Bonitarian ownership."

Dominium ex jure Quiritium, meaning, 40; applied to *res nec mancipi* as well as *res man.,* 132 and n. 3; civil and natural modes of acquiring, 133; *nudum jus Quiritium,* 270 and n. 13; abolition by Justinian of distinctions between *d. ex j. Q., d. bonitarium,* and *nudum jus Quir.,* 420.

Domum ductio in *manus injectio,* 207, 210 n. 31.

Donatio propter nuptias, 416.

Dos and *Dotis dictio* of early *jus civile,* 116 and n. 4, 150; *d. d.* of classical law, 116 n. 4; the *lex Maenia de dote,* 248 note; Justinian's legislation about *dos,* 415.

Dositheï Fragmentum de manumissionibus, 333.

Dualism in institutions of early law, 5.

Ductio uxoris in domum mariti, 345 n. 1.

EDICTS of the Emperors, their character in early empire, 312 *sq.;* the edicts or *leges edictales* of the later empire, 379 *sq.*

Edicts of the Magistrates, 253-258; antiquity of practice of publishing edicts, 253; those of urban prætor, 253-257; spoken of as *viva vox jur. civilis,* 255; their aim, *ib.* n. 5; *edicta repentina* and *perpetua,* 253; *ed. tralaticia,* 254; gradual enlargement of *e. t.,* 255; *e.* proper and app. of styles, 255; forms of edictal provisions, 256; *e.* of peregrin prætors, provincial governors, and curule ædiles, 257 *sq.*

Edictum perpetuum (consolidated) of Salvius Julianus, 307-310; history, 307; what embodied in it, 308; arrangement, 309.

Edictum Theodorici, 397.

Editions of Institutes, 436; of Digest, 438; of Code, *ib.;* of Novels, 439.

Emancipation,—early procedure in, 62 n. 25; Justinianian simplification, 418; was *a capitis deminutio,* 128; was it originally meant as a boon to child or a penalty on parent? 118 *sq.;* its result in law, 25, 129; put an end to *patria potestas* and agnation, 174; father not required testamentarily to institute or disinherit emancipated child, 292, but prætor gave latter *bonor. poss. contra tabulas* on condition of collation, *ib.*; by *jus civile* he had no right of succession on intestacy either direct or collateral, 174, 292; by edict *unde liberi* prætors admitted him to intestate succession of parent along with unemancipated children, 293, and later imperial legislation admitted him collaterally as if never *capite minutus*, 423.

Emblemata Triboniani, 408 n. 13.

Emphyteusis,—its introduction, 420; amendments of Zeno and Justinian, 421.

Emptio bonorum, 363; actions granted to *b. emptor* under fiction of heirship, *ib.*

Episcopalis audientia (bishop's court), —institution, jurisdiction, and procedure, 383 *sq.*

Epistula Hadriani introducing *beneficium divisionis*, 314 note.

Equity, 247, 257.

Eviction, Warranty against, in mancipation, 135-138, 279; did it arise *ipso jure?* 137; the *stipulatio duplae*, 283; liability for e. eventually held implied in sale, 285.

Exceptions, 366 *sq.*; *ex. doli*, 367; unnecessary in a *bonae fidei judicium, ib.*; *ex. rei venditae et traditae*, 250, 269; *ex. non numeratae pecuniae*, 250.

Execution under system of *legis actiones*, see "*Manus injectio;*" under formular system, 367; under system of later empire, 389.

Exheredatio (disherison) of children, see "Testament."

Expensilatio (literal contract), 275-278.

Expiatio, 53.

Exposure of children, law of Romulus, 28; XII Tables, 118; prohibited by Valentinian, 346 n. 3; prohibition renewed by Justinian, 417.

Extraordinaria cognitio, 368 *sq.*

FAMILIA, meanings, 24 and n. 2; *familia pecuniaque*, 64, 66 n. 5; *familiae emptor*, 66, 167-169; *familiae mutatio*, see "*Capitis deminutio;*" *sacra familiae*, see "*Sacra.*"

Family, The,—its organisation in regal period, 24 *sq.*; its legal aspects, 26 *sq.*; its domestic aspects, 30 *sq.*; the plebeian f. as compared with the patrician, 34 *sq.*; law of the f. under the XII Tables, 115 *sq.*; the f. in the later republic, 248 *sq.*; changes in the early empire, 345 *sq.*; law of the f. in the Justinianian legislation, 414-419.

Fas, 15-18; little of it in XII Tables, 104.

Fideicommissa (*mortis causa* trusts).— what led to their introduction, 241, 353; universal and singular *f.*, 354; relative positions of heir (trustee) and beneficiary, *ib.*; regulation by Trebellian and l'egasian senatusconsults, *ib.*; equiparation of singular *f.* with legacies, 425; oral *f.* by a person on deathbed declared binding on heir *ab intestato*, 423.

Fides,—deification by Numa, 22 *sq.*; appeal to *F.* a safeguard of obligation, 50, 165; its seat in the right hand, 50 n. 2.

Fiducia, 139-143; mancipatory *lex fiduciae*, 140; purposes of *f.*, 141 *sq.*; *actio fiduciae*, 141; *usureceptio fiduciae*, 142 *sq.*; fiduciary coemption, 44 n. 6, 141 and n. 36.

Filiusfamilias and *paterfamilias*, see "*Patria potestas.*"

Fisci, Fragmentum de jure, 334.

Flavianum, Jus, 262.

Florentine MS. of Digest, 436.

Forcti sanatesque (of XII Tables), 111 n. 12.

Foreigners, Influx of, after first Punic war,—its influence on the law, 239 *sq.*; capacities and disabilities of f., see "Non-Citizens."

Form, Conservatism of R. L. in matters of, 151; all forms had their historical utilitarian explanation, *ib.*

Formular system of procedure, 357-367; its introduction, 244 *sq.*; its characteristic, 245, 357; the Aebutian and Julian laws, 244 *sq.*, 358; transition from the *legis actiones*,— in personal actions by the simplification of the procedure *per condictionem*, 358-360, and in *vindicationes* by the introduction of that *per sponsionem*, 360, paving the way for the *formula petitoria*, 361; parts of a *formula* 359 n. 5; *formulae in jus*

and *in factum conceptae*, 361 *sq.*; *intentiones* of former, 361; *actiones utiles*, 362; *act. ficticiae*, 362 *sq.*; *act. in factum*, 364; *act. arbitrariae*, 364 *sq.*; *exceptiones*, &c., 366 *sq.*; elasticity of the system, 367; its abandonment in the later empire, 387 *sq.*
Fragmenta Vaticana, 396.
Fragmentum de jure fisci, 334.

GAIUS, 320–322; his Institutes and the Verona codex, 328-331.
Gens,—Organisation of, in regal Rome, 6 *sq.*; how far affected by XII Tables, 113 *sq.*; gentile settlements, 38; jurisdiction of *g.*, 70, 223; its tutorial and curatorial functions, 33, 121, 124 *sq.* and n. 15; how far its sanction necessary to marriage of *sui juris* female member, 114; its right of succession in regal period, 43; by XII Tables postponed to agnates, 172.
Gentium, Jus, of Rome, 240.
Glossarists, The, and their treatment of the Justinianian books, 434 *sq.*
Græco-Roman jurisprudence, 430–432.
Greece, Decemviral mission to, 97.
Greek law in XII Tables, 98.
Gregorian Code, 392 *sq.*
Guardianship, see "Tutory" and "Curatory."
Guilds, Numa's, 11.

HARMENOPULI *Manuale*, 431.
Hasta, Centumviralis, 75 n. 9.
Hercules, The *ara maxima* of, 50.
Hereditas (see "Succession"), — its delation by testament, see "Testament;" on intestacy, see "Intestate Succession;" necessary and voluntary heirs, 174; *ipso jure* vesting of *h.* in former, *ib.*; acceptance by latter, see "*Aditio*;" accrual (*adcretio*) amongst heirs, 176; *heres eadem persona cum defuncto*, 177; heir's liability for deceased's debts, *ib.*; its limitation by entry under inventory, 426; heir's liability for family *sacra*, see "*Sacra familiae.*"
Heredium, 36 *sq.*; was it alienable? 39 *sq.*
Hermogenian Code, 392 *sq.*
Herus, derivation and meaning, 40 n. 7.
Homo sacer, see "*Sacer esto.*"

Hospitium, 110 *sq.*
Hostis, see "Non-Citizen."
Husband and Wife, Law of, among patricians of regal period, 25-27, 31; among plebeians, 34 *sq.*, 44 *sq.*; under XII Tables, 115-117; in later republic, 248; in early empire, 303 *sq.*, 345 *sq.*; in later empire, 382 *sq.*, 415 *sq.*
Hypothec, 267 *sq.*, 350.

IMPERIUM, magisterial,—quasi-judicial intervention in virtue of it, 218 *sq.*, 369 *sq.*
Imprisonment for debt after Poetilian law, 160.
"*In bonis*" tenure of *res mancipi*, see "Bonitarian ownership."
Incerti conductio, 359 *sq.*
Ingratitude,—its consequences in law, 22 n. 2.
Inheritance, see "*Hereditas.*"
In integrum restitutio, 374 *sq.*
In jure cessio, 144, 189 n. 9; involved no warranty of title, 136.
In jus vocatio of XII Tables, 184.
Institutes, Justinian's, 406 *sq.*; MSS., texts, and editions, 436.
Institutio and *instructio*, 263 n. 12.
Intentio of formula, 359-361.
Interdictio igni et aquae, 54 n. 13.
Interdiction of spendthrift, 32, 114, 126, 219 n. 2.
Interdicts under *jus civile*, 218; under prætorian rules, 369-372; characteristic, 370; varieties, *ibid.*; *uti possidetis* and *utrubi*, 371 *sq.*
Interpretatio of republic, 100, 101 n. 3, 262.
Intestate succession (see "Succession"), Law of, among patricians in regal period, 43 *sq.* (and see "*Sui heredes*" and "*Gens*"); among plebeians, 48; i. s. of agnates, after *sui heredes* but before *gens*, introduced by XII Tables, 172 *sq.* (and see "Agnates and Agnation"); artificiality of rules of *jus civile* as to i. s. of agnates, 173, 292; prætorian amendments, 293; admission of cognates, 293 *sq.* (and see "Cognates"); admission of i. s. as between mother and child, 355 *sq.*; Justinian's amendments on law of i. s. in his Code, 423; amendments by his 118th and 127th Novels, 424; rights, &c., of heir *ab*

intestato, see "*Hereditas*," "*Bonor. Possessio.*"
Inventarii, Heir's entry *cum beneficio*, 426.
Iruerius and the Glossarists, 434 sq.
Italicum, Jus, 267 n. 3.

JUDEX, The single,—an institution of Serv. Tullius's, 77 ; his position, 260 ; his disappearance, 387.
Judicati,—manus injectio against, 205 sq. ; distinction between *j.* and *addicti*, 207 n. 17.
Judices decemviri of Valerio-Horatian laws, 76, 84 sq., 219 sq.
Judicia and *arbitria*, 198 sq.
Judicial procedure,—the arrangements of Serv. Tullius, 73-77 ; procedure *per legis actiones*, 181-217, 232-235 ; j. p. outside the *legis act.*, 217-225 ; j. p. *per formulas*, 244 sq., 357-367 ; j. p. *extra ordinem*, 368 sq. ; quasi-judicial p. in virtue of the *imperium*, 369-375 ; j. p. *per libellum conventionis*, 387 sq. ; j. p. in the bishops' courts, 383 sq.
Judicis postulationem, Leg. actio per, 197-201.
Judicium de moribus, 249.
Julianus, Salvius, 318 sq. ; his consolidation of the prætorian edict, 307 sq.
Junian latinity, 338 sq. ; abolished by Justinian, 419.
Juramentum calumniae, 389.
Jurgia and *lites*, 73 note, 199.
Jurisdiction in regal period, 69-72 ; *jurisdictio* of magistrate and *judicium* of judge during republic and early empire, 184 sq. ; who invested with ordinary j. in later empire, 388 ; j. of bishops, 383 sq.
Jurists of later republic, 262 sq. ; honourable position held by professional j. in early empire, 302 ; notices of the most eminent, 315-327.
Jus, primitive meaning, 18 ; its embodiments, 20 ; its prevalence in XII Tables over *fas*, 104 ; meaning of j. in later law, 404.
Jus Aelianum, 262 and n. 10.
Jus civile, j. gentium, and *j. naturale* distinguished, 240 n. 4.
Jus Flavianum, 262.
Jus gentium. The Roman, 240 sq.
Jus Italicum, 267 n. 3.

Jus Latii, 265.
Jus liberorum, 304, 356, 423.
Jus naturale in early empire, 298-301; distinguished from *jus gentium*, 299 ; its characteristics and fundamental principles, 299-301 ; illustrations, 300.
Jus nexi mancipiique, 111 and n. 12.
Jus novum, 306.
Jus Quiritium, Nudum, 270 and n. 13.
Jus respondendi, see "*Responsa prudentium.*"
Jus vitae necisque of *paterfamilas*, 29 ; its restriction in the early empire, 346 ; its complete disappearance in Justinianian law, 417.
Justae nuptiae, see "Marriage."
Justinian, 402 ; chronology of his collections, 403 ; his first Code of statute-law, 403 sq. ; commission to compile Digest, 404-406 ; his "*quinquaginta decisiones*," 406 ; his Institutes, 406 sq. ; publication of the Digest, 407 ; second edition of his Code, 411 ; his Novels, 413 ; characteristics of his own legislation, 414 ; his law-books in the courts and schools, 427-430 ; their fate in the East, 430 ; their transmission to Italy, 432 ; their fate in the West, 432-435.

KINGS, their criminal jurisdiction, 69 sq. ; origin of their civil jurisdiction, 72 sq.

LABEO and Capito, 315 sq.
Land, Early distribution of, 36 sq. ; the public lands, 90-92.
Latinity,—colonial, 266 ; Junian, 338 sq. ; *legatum latini*, 339, n. 12 ; Junian l. abolished by Justinian, 419.
Laudatio auctoris (in a *rei vindicatio*), 190 n. 10.
Laudemium (in emphyteusis), 421.
Law-schools, The Roman, 428 ; course of study, 429.
Legacies (*legata*),—meaning of *legare*, 46 n. 8, 167 n. 1 ; restrictions on a testator's freedom of bequeathing l., 253 note, 288 ; the various forms of l., 352 ; the *Sc. Neronianum, ib.* ; equiparation (by Justinian) of l. with singular trust-gifts, 425.
Leges generally ; *Leges regiae*, 20 sq. ;

ll. sacratae, 83, *sq.*; *leges* (comitinl) displaced by senatusconsults, 306; *ll. generales* or *edictales* of later empire, 379 *sq.*; *ll. datae* as distinguished from *ll. latae*, 306; *ll. mancipii*, 139 *sq.* (See "*Lex.*")

Leges, Particular: *L. Aebutia*, 244 *sq.*, 358; *L. Aelia Sentia*, 336 *sq.*; *L. Apuleia*, 253 note; *L. Aquilia, ib.*; *L. Aternia Tarpeia*, 193 n. 18; *L. Atilia*, 252 n. 2; *L. Atinia*, 253 n.; *L. Calpurnia*, 232, 235; *L. Canuleia*, 87; *L. Cicereia*, 253 n.; *L. Cincia de donis*, 252 n. 2; *L. Claudia* (*de tut. mulier.*), 305, 348; *L. coloniae Juliae Genetivae*, 161 and n. 32, 445 *sq.*; *L. Cornelia* (*de sponsorib.*), 253 n.; *L. de imperio Vespasiani*, 305; *L. XII Tabularum*, see "Twelve Tables;" *L. Falcidia*, 250 n. 3, 253 n., 288; *L. Fufia Caninia*, 304; *L. Furia de sponsu*, 253 n.; *L. Furia testamentaria*, 213, 288; *L. Hortensia*, 86, 96; *L. Julia de adult. coercendis*, 303; *L. Julia de maritand. ordinib.*, 303; *L. Julia et Papia Popiaea*, 303 *sq.*, 382; *Ll. Julia et Titia*, 252 n. 2; *Ll. Juliae judiciariae*, 305, 358; *L. Junia Norbana*, 304, 338 *sq.*; *Ll. Liciniae Sextiae*, 87 *sq.*, 92, 95; *L. Maenia de dote*, 248; *L. Malacitana*, 306 and n. 9; *L. Marcia*, 213; *L. metalli Vipascensis*, 306 and n. 10; *L. Papiria* (*de sacrament. exigundis*), 444; *L. Pinaria*, 190 n. 11; *L. Placetoria*, 253 n., 348; *L. Poetilia Papiria*, 95, 160-162, 212; *L. Publilia* (415 u.c.), 85 *sq.*; *L. Publilia de sponsorib.*, 166, 206 n. 16; *L. Regia*, 305 n. 8; *L. Rubria*, 257; *L. Salpensana*, 306 and n. 9; *L. Silia*, 230 *sq.*; *L. Terentilia*, 89 *sq.*; *Ll. Valeriae Horatiae*, 84 *sq.*; *L. Vallia*, 213; *L. Voconia*, 44 n. 5, 253 n., 288.

Legis actiones generally, 181-186; meaning of *lege agere*, 183 n.; varieties of *l. a.*, 182; character and purpose, 183; *in jus vocatio*, 184; magistrate *in jure, ib.*; *litis contestatio, ib.*; judge *in judicio*, 185; centumviral court, *unus judex* and *tres arbitri*, 185 *sq.* See "*Sacramentum*," "*Judicis postulatio*," "*Condictionem*, *L. A. per*," "*Manus injectio*," "*Pignoris capio*."

Legislation in regal period, 20; in earlier republic, 83-86; in later republic, 252; l. of senate in place of *comitia*, 306; emperors sole legislators, 379 *sq.*

Legitim (*portio legitima*), introduction of, 250 and n. 3; Justinianian law as to, 425.

Legitimate birth, rule of XII Tables, 117.

Legitimation in Justinianian law, 415, 418.

Legitimus, meaning, 123.

Lex, meanings, 19 n. 7; etymology, *ib.*

Lex Dei or *Collatio Leg. Mosaicar. et Romanar.*, 395 *sq.*

Lex Rom. Burgundionum, 399.

Lex Rom. Visigothorum, 398; earliest channel of Roman law in Central and Western Europe, 432.

Libellus conventionis and procedure of later empire, 388 *sq.*

"*Liberi*" of prætorian succession on intestacy,—who included, 293.

Libripens in mancipation, 58 and n. 10.

Literal contract, 275 *sq.*, 447 *sq.*

Literature and philosophy, Spread of, after first Punic war,—how it influenced the law, 247.

Literature, Jurisprudential, of classical period, 316-326, 328-335.

Lites and *jurgia*, 73 n., 199.

Litigation, Reckless or dishonest,— how checked, 217 n.

Litis contestatio in *legis actiones*, 184, 191; under formular system, 359; under that of the *libellus conventionis*, 389.

Litis denuntiatio, 388.

Loan *per aes et libram*, see "*Nexum*;" l. of the *jus gentium* (see "*Mutuum*"), 286 *sq.*; impignoration of the borrower himself or his services in security, 155, 447.

Longi temporis possessio remodelled by Justinian, 420.

Lunatics, Curatory of, 121, 125.

MAECIANI *Assis distributio*, 333.

Mancipation (*mancipium*, *mancipatio*): meaning of *mancipare*, and rationale of m., 61 *sq.* and n. 25, 68 *sq.* and n. 12; Gaius's description of it, 57; its origin, 58; its regulation by Serv. Tullius, 58-60; its employment for creation of marital *manus* (see "*Co-*

INDEX. 457

emptio"), 65, and in testamentary dispositions (see "*Testament*"), 65 *sq.*; originally a real sale and transfer, 60, 134; with coined money became an imaginary sale,—really a formal conveyance, 134 *sq.*; m. the appropriate form of conveyance of *res mancipi*, 135; could *res nec mancipi* pass by it? 143; ceremonial, original and modified, 60, 134; was there a formula recited by both parties? 137 *sq.*; effects of m., 135 *sq.*; in particular,—warranty against eviction, 135-138; *leges mancipii* engrafted on the business per *aes et libram*, 139 *sq.*, 66 n. 6; last mention of m., as still in use as a conveyance, 135 n. 9; substitution for it of *solemnis traditio* in conveyance of immovable *res mancipi*, 419; simple tradition substituted for it by Justinian in all cases, 420.
Mancipi, Res, see "*Res mancipi*."
Mancipium, various meanings, 62. (See "Mancipation.")
Manumission, Modes of, 336 *sq.*; amendments of Aelia-Seutian law, 337 *sq.*; of *L. Junia Norbana*, 338 *sq.*; of Justinianian legislation, 419.
Manus,—its extensive meaning in early law, 24 n. 3, 40, 61 and n. 21; husband's m. over wife, 26 *sq.*; *in manum conventio* by confarreation (see "*Confarreatio*"), *ib.*; by coemption (see "*Coemptio*"), 65; by a year's uninterrupted cohabitation as husband and wife (*usus*), 115 *sq.*; modes of dissolution, 117; *in manum conv.* was a *cap. deminutio minima*, 131, involving a universal acquisition for the husband, 176, without liability under the *jus civile* for his wife's debts, 131, though otherwise under prætorian rules, *ib.*; unpopularity of marital *manus* in early empire, 345 *sq.*, and its eventual entire disappearance, 415; fiduciary *manus*, 44 n. 6, 141 and n. 36.
Manus consertio (in sacramental action *in rem*), 188 *sq.* and n. 6.
Manus injectionem, Leg. Act. per,— Gellius's description of it, 201 *sq.*; against whom employed, 203 *sq.*; procedure against a *nexus*, 157 *sq.*; against a *judicatus* or judgment-debtor, 205 *sq.*; "*capite poenas dabat*"—meaning, 208 *sq.*; "*partis secanto*"—meaning, 209 *sq.*; Kohler's view, 446 *sq.*; attempted reconstruction of provisions of XII Tables about *m. i.*, 211 and n. 34; effect of Poetilian law on *m. i.*, 161, 212 *sq.*; *m. i. pro judicato*, 213; *m. i. pura, ib.*
Manuscripts of *Corpus Juris Civilis*, 435 *sq.*; of Institutes, 436; of Digest, 436 *sq.*; of Code, 438; of Novels, 439.
Marriage: the *justae nuptiae* of the patricians of the regal period, 26; plebeians had no *j.* n. before the time of Serv. Tullius, 64,—only *matrimonia*, 34 *sq.*, 115; plebeian *j. n.* accomplished by *coemptio*, 65; the Canuleian law sanctioning intermarriage of the orders, 87; *non justae nuptiae* or *juris gentium* m. of the early empire, 241; its effects, *ib.*, 353; the *manus*-less *justae nuptiae* of the empire, 345; was *ductio uxoris in domum mariti* essential to its completion? *ib.* n. 1; requisites of m. in Justinianian law, 415; second marriages, *ib.*
Materfamilias, who so called, 31 and n. 22; *mf.* as distinguished from *uxor*, 115 n.
Matrimonium, original meaning, 35.
Minors, Curatury of, 348 *sq.*
Missiones in possessionem, 373 *sq.*
Modestinus, Herennius, 326 *sq.*
Money: media of exchange before money coined, 58; *aes rude*, 59; *aes signatum* of Serv. Tullius, *ib.* and notes 12, 14; coinage of Decemvirs, 134; successive reductions in weight of the *as*, 444.
Morals, Decline of, in latter half of republic,—how it influenced the law, 248 *sq.*
Moribus, Judicium de, 249.
Movables,—was there any property in them in regal period? 40 *sq.*
Mutuum, 286 *sq.*

NATURAL law, see "*Jus Naturale;*" n. 1. older than civil, 41.
Naturalis ratio, 301.
Nexum and *Nexus*,—occasional ambiguity of words, 154; Mamilius, Quint. Mucius, and Ael. Gallus on their meaning, 443 *sq.*; *nexum* a contract of loan of money *per aes et libram*, 152-162; its position before

Serv. Tullius, 67; his regulation of it, 68; the ceremonial after coined money in use, 152 *sq.*; its effects, 154 *sq.*; *manus injectio* by creditor sanctioned by XII Tables under words "*aeris confessi*," 203 *sq.*, 446; subsequent *domum ductio*, but without *addictio*, 155 *sq.*, 158, 205 *sq.*; status of *nexus* in detention, 93, 158 *sq.*; *nexi vincti solutique*, 162 n. 35; *nexi liberatio*, 156 and n. 17; abuses of *nexum* and maltreatment of the *nexi*, 93-95, 160; consequent prohibition of *nexum* by the Poetilian law, 95, 160; provisions of the statute for relief of existing *nexi*, 161 *sq.*

Nomen arcarium, 276; *n. transscripticium*, 275 *sq.*, 447 *sq.*

Non-citizens,—their position under the *jus civile*, 107-113; under the influence of the *jus gentium*, 265 *sq.*; *peregrinus*, 109 n. 8; recuperatory procedure between citizens and non-citizens, 223 *sq.*; fictitious actions to or against peregrins under prætorian system, 363; colonial and Junian latins, see "Latinity."

Novels (*novellae constitutiones*), Post-Theodosian, 395; Justinian's, 413; Julian's Latin epitome of them, 428, 432; their MSS., texts, and editions, 439.

Noxae deditio, 120 *sq.*; *n. d.* of *filiusfamilias* unknown in Justinianian law, 417.

Nudum jus Quiritium, 270 and n. 13.

Numa's guilds, 11.

Nuncupata, Verba, in mancipation, 139 *sq.*

OATH as safeguard of obligation, 50, 165; reference to o., 233 n. 2.

Obligation, Law of, under XII Tables, 149-166; prominence of o. *ex delicto*, 149, 165; paucity of those *ex contractu* (see "Contract"), 149; by XII Tables many breaches of contract punished as offences, 165; o. *ex re*, 166; o. to restore unjustifiable gains, 272 and n. 2.

Oratio principis initiating Sct., 306.

Osculi, Jus, 26 n. 7.

PANDECTAE, see "Digest."

Papinianus, Æmilius, 323 *sq.*

Parent and Child,—the relation when latter *in potestate*, see "*Patria potestas;*" when emancipated, see "Emancipation;" when issue of *non justae nuptiae* (or *juris gentium* marriage), 241, 353; p. and c. in Justinianian law, 416-418.

Parricidium, 53 n. 11.

"*Partis secanto*" of decemviral legislation against insolvent debtors, 209 *sq.*; Kohler's view of it, 446 *sq.*

Patented counsel, Responses of, see "*Responsa prudentium.*"

Paterfamilias, 24 *sq.*, 127.

Patria potestas,—its origin in custom, 118; its nature, 27 *sq.*, 31 *sq.*, 127; resulted from *justae nuptiae* (see "Marriage"), 118 and n. 10, adoption (see "Adoption" and "Adrogation"), 29, and legitimation of children by a mistress, 418, but not from *non justae nuptiae* (or *juris gentium* marriage), 241; how p. p. came to an end, 24 *sq.*, 32, 128 *sq.* (see also "Emancipation"); provisions of XII Tables in reference to it, 118 *sq.*; domestic jurisdiction of *paterfamilias*, 32, 70, 222 *sq.*; limited liability of *pf.* for debts of *filiusfamilias* under prætorian rule, 272; relaxation of *p. p.* by introduction of *peculium castrense*, 344 *sq.*; further relaxations of classical period, 346 *sq.*; remains of *p. p.* in Justinianian law, 416-418.

Patricians, their position in early law, 6 *sq.*; meaning of *patricii*, 35 n. 31; the p. family in regal period, 24 *sq.*; the p. order of succession, 43 *sq.*; the strife between p. and plebeians, 82 *sq.*

Patron and client, see "Clientage."

Patron and freedman, see "Manumission;" p.'s right of succession to f., 294 note.

Paulus, Julius, 326; his *Sententiae*, 332.

Peculium profecticium, 347; *p. castrense*, 344 *sq.*; *p. quasi-castrense*, 345 n. 15; the *peculia* of *filiifamilias* in Justinianian law, 417 *sq.*; the 118th Novel on the *p. castrense vel quasi*, 418.

Pecunia credita, 230 *sq.*, 276.

Peregrinus, see "Non-Citizen."

Personality,—only *paterfamilias* had complete, 127; *quoad jus civile* those

subject to him were representatives of his *persona*, ib.
Petri Exceptiones Leg. Romanar., 434.
Pignoris capionem, Leg. Act. per,—its nature, 214; when employed, 164 and n. 38, 215; effect, 216.
Pignus, 148 n. 65, 267; *p. in causa judicati captum*, 389.
Plebeians, The, of early Rome, 9 *sq.*; their position, 12; their domestic relations in regal period, 34 *sq.*; had no *justae nuptiae* before time of Serv. Tullius, 64,—only *matrimonia*, 34 *sq.*, 115; afterwards got *justae nuptiae* by coemption, 65, and *manus* by *usus*, 115; early distributions of land among them, 38; their order of intestate succession in regal period, 48 *sq.*; their substitute for a testament, 65; strife between them and patricians, 82 *sq.*; attainment of general equality of private rights by XII Tables, 99; right of intermarriage with the patricians by the Canuleian law, 87, and eventually, by a series of statutes, substantial political equality, 83-88.
Plebiscita, 84, 252; ranked with *leges*, 86.
Pomponius, Sextus, 319.
Pontiffs,—their judicial and quasi-judicial functions, 72 *sq.*, 77 note, 221 *sq.*; their functions in adrogations, 30, in matters of testament, 47, and in the *actio sacramento*, 191 *sq.*; their *interpretatio*, 261 *sq.*
Possessio, Bonae fidei, 271.
Possessio, Bonorum, see "*Bonor. Poss.*"
Possession, Roman law of, somewhat uncertain, 349 and note.
Possessionem, Missio in, 373 *sq.*
Possessiones, 90 *sq.*
Postulatio, Judicis, see "*Jud. post.*"
Praedes litis et vindiciarum in sacramental procedure, 191, 194 *sq.*
Prætors: institution of the prætorship, 88; office of the urban p., 242; the peregrin p., 243; their edicts, see "Edicts of the Magistrates;" the p. not specially the mouthpieces of equity, 257; prætorian amendments often the product of years, 289.
Prætorian stipulations, 274, 372 *sq.*
Primogeniture,—no privilege of, 45.
Procedure, see "Judicial procedure."

Proculians and Sabinians, 316 *sq.*
Prodigus, see "Spendthrift."
"Promise,"—possible etymology, 50 n. 2.
Property originally included in *manus*, 40, 131; early law of p., 36 *sq.*; p. civil and natural, 41; was there any p. of movables in regal period? 40 *sq.*; law of p. under XII Tables, 131-149; offences against p. in XII Tables, 146-148; changes in law of p. in later republic, 266-271; the law of p. in the Justinian legislation, 419-421. (See "*Dominium ex jure Quiritium*," "Bonitarian ownership.")
Propinquity, computation of degrees, 124 n. 13.
Provincial conquests,—how they influenced the law, 245 *sq.*; p. governors,—their edicts, 258; p. land, 266.
Prudentium, Responsa, see "*Resp. prud.*"
Publician edict and action, 268-271, 363.
Pupils, Tutory over, see "Tutory."

QUAESTIONES *ac monita*, Lombardic, 433.
Querela inofficiosi testamenti, 249 *sq.*, 288; substantially displaced by Justinian's legislation, 425.
Quiritarian right,—origin of king's jurisdiction in questions of, 72 *sq.*; Q. ownership, see "*Dominium ex jure Quiritium.*"
Quiritium, Meum est ex jure,—significance, 131 *sq.*

RAUDUSCULUM, 60.
Ravenna, reported transfer of Roman law-school to, 433.
Real contracts, 286 *sq.*
Recuperatio by treaty with foreigners, 111, 113; its nature, 223 *sq.*; its employment *inter cives*, 225.
Regal period,—elements of population, 3-13; regulatives of public and private order, 14-23; institutions of private law anterior to Serv. Tullius, 24-55; Servian reforms, 56-77.
Religion and morals, Decline of, in latter half of republic,—how it influenced the law, 248 *sq.*
Remancipation, 117.
Rescripta, Imperial, 313 *sq.*; their diminished authority in later empire,

379 sq.; Justinian's declaration as to them, 380.
Res mancipi and *nec mancipi*,—distinction due to Serv. Tullius, 57; meaning of *r. m.*, 62; what were *r. m.*, 63; why so called, *ib.*; consequence of defective conveyance of *r. m.*, 41 n. 9; *in bonis* tenure of *r. m.*, *ib.*, 268, 270; *r. n. m.* might be held *ex jure Quiritium*, 132; could *r. n. m.* pass by mancipation? 143; distinction abolished by Justinian, 420.
Responsa prudentium, 310-312; origin of *jus respondendi*, 310 sq.; form and value of *r.*, 311 sq.; their regulation by Hadrian, 312; out of use after middle of third century, 327.
Restitutio, In integrum, 374 sq.
Revenge, Blood, 52 sq.; vestiges of it in XII Tables, 106.
Romano-barbarian Codes, 397 sq.
Roscio com., Cicero *pro*, 275.
Rutilian bankruptcy arrangements, 161 n. 30, 250.

SABINE rape, 26 n. 6.
Sabini libri III de jure civili, 318.
Sabinians and Proculians, 316 sq.
Sacer esto and *Sacratio capitis*, 17, 53 sq.
Sacra familiae,—importance of perpetuating, 25 and note 5; heir's liability for, 178.
Sacramentum, Leg. actio per,—general idea, 187; procedure in vindication of land, 187-191; the *manus consertio*, 188 sq.; the *sacramento provocatio*, 190 sq.; the deposit *ad pontem*, 191, 445, for which *praedes sacramenti* substituted, 191, 444; what it all meant, 73, 192-194; effect of judgment, 194 sq.; sacramental procedure in other cases, 195-197.
Sacratae, Leges, 83 sq.
Sale, Stages in the history of, 163-165, 279-286; the decemviral provision that property of thing sold should not pass till price paid, 133 and n. 4, 135.
Satisdatio secundum mancipium, 282.
Scaevola, Q. Cervid., 322 sq.
Scaevola, Quint. Mucius, P. f. 263.
Seals to testaments, &c., 170, 290, n. 9.
Secession of plebeians, First, 83; second, 84; third, 96.

Sectio bonorum, 210.
Self-help in regal period, 51, 71 sq.; remains of it in XII Tables, 105; the *decretum divi Marci*, 314 note.
Senatusconsults take place of *leges*, 306; already numerous in time of Claudius, 305.
Senatusconsults, Particular: *Sc. Macedonianum*, 347; *Sc. Orphitianum*, 356; *Sc. Pegasianum*, 354; *Sc. Tertullianum*, 355; *Sc. Trebellianum*, 354; *Sc. Vellacanum*, 313, n. 3.
Servilis cognatio, 419.
Servitude of the glebe, see "*Colonatus.*"
Servitudes in XII Tables, 148; creation of s. by pacts and stipulations, 267 and n. 7; s. in classical period, 350.
Servius Sulpicius Rufus, 264.
Servius Tullius,—his reforms, 56-77; institution of *census*, 56; consequences, 57 sq.; his amendments on the course of justice, 69-77; his fifty laws about contracts and crimes, 67, 74, 89.
Sex: originally no privilege of s. in succession of *sui heredes*, 44; but females practically under fetters, *ib.*; disabilities imposed on them by Voconian law, 288; limitation by "interpretation" of their right of succession as agnates, 173, 288; praetorian relief, 294; Justinianian equalisation, 423.
Sinaitic papyri, Bernardakis's, 400.
Slaves: domestic position of s. in regal period, 33; provisions of XII Tables in reference to them, 120 sq.; slave *jure civili* a thing, *jure naturali* a person, 127; limited liability of owner for debts of a., 272; improved position of s. in Justinianian law, 419; enfranchisement of s., see "Manumission."
Soldiers, Exceptional privileges of, 341 sq.; *testamentum militare*, 342 sq.; *peculium castrense*, 344 sq.
Solutio per aes et libram, 60 n. 16, 156 and n. 17.
Spendthrift, Interdiction of, 32, 114, 126, 219 n. 2.
Sponsio,—derivation of word, 228; confined to citizens, 228, 273 and n. 7; heir of *sponsor* at one time not bound, 228 n. 7. (See "Stipulation.")

Sponsio et restipulatio tertiae partis, 230 sq.
Sponsionem, Procedure in real actions *per,* 360 sq.
Stationes jus publice docentium, 317.
Statu liberi, 120.
"*Status condictusve dies cum hoste,*" 224.
Stipulation,—its introduction, 226-229; derivation of word, 227; theories as to origin of s., 227 sq.; forms,— *sponsio* (σπένδειν and σπονδή), *promissio,* &c., 228 sq.; a formal contract, 229; its expansion in latter half of republic, 273-275; *stipulatio habere licere,* 282 sq.; *s. duplae, ib.*; *s. Aquiliana,* 274; prætorian stipulations, 372 sq.
Stoics, Philosophy of the,—its influence on the law, 247 note.
Succession, Universal, to the living,—by *in manum conventio,* see "*Manus*;" by adrogation, see "Adrogation;" by *bonorum emptio,* see "*Emptio bonorum :*" to the dead,—by inheritance, see "*Hereditas,*" testamentary, see "Testament," or on intestacy, see "Intestate succession;" by *usucapio pro herede,* see "*Usucapio pro herede;*" by *bonorum possessio,* see "*Bonor. poss.;*" by trust, see "*Fideicommissa.*"
Sui heredes,—who included amongst a man's, 174; real nature of their succession, 48 and n. 11; by *jus civile* and prætorian rules testator had either to institute or disinherit them, 171; consequences of prœterition, 291; the Justinianian law on prœteritition and disherison, 424 sq.; voidance of a testament by subsequent emergence of *s. h.* who had not been provided for, 171; under *jus civile, s. h.* had the first place on intestacy, 43, 48, 172; had no preference over emancipated children in prætorian or imperial intestate succession, 293; no privilege of males or of primogeniture among *s. h.,* 44, 45; they were necessary heirs, 174, and took *per stirpes,* 175.
Sui juris, 124 and n. 12.
Summa Perusina, 433.
Suretyship, 272.
Syrian collection of Ante-Justinianian law, 400 sq.

TALION in XII Tables, 106.
Terminus, worship of, 37.
Testament (see "Succession"),—what? 168; only a citizen could make a t., 48 n.13; original incapacity of women to do so, 44 n. 6; the t. *calatis comitiis,* 47, 167; the t. *in procinctu factum,* 47; difficulty experienced by plebeians in making a t., 65; their makeshift for it, 65 sq.; the t. *per aes et libram* in its inchoate condition, 167-169; its second and third stages, 169 sq.; necessity of testator's instituting or disinheriting *sui heredes,* see "*Sui heredes ;*" how he had to deal with emancipated children, see "Emancipation;" instituted heir required to have *testamenti factio* with testator, 363; substitutions, 175; subsidiary provisions, 351; the so-called prætorian t., *ib.*; the t. of the Justinianian law, 422; J.'s legislation about disherison, prœteritition, &c., 424 sq.; rights, &c., of heir, &c., under or in opposition to a testament, see "*Hereditas,*" "*Bonor. Possessio ;*" *querela inofficiosi testamenti,* see "*Querela ;*" *testamentum militare,* 342 sq.; testamentary trusts, see "*Fideicommissa ;*" codicils, see "Codicils."
Texts of Institutes, 436; of Digest, 437; of Code, 438; of Novels, 439.
Theft and its forms and actions, 147 sq.
Theodorici, Edictum, 397.
Theodosian Code, 393 sq.; Post-Theodosian Novels, 395.
Theophilus's Paraphrase of the Institutes, 430.
Tignum junctum, 132, 148.
Transmission (*transmissio*) of heir's *jus adeundi,*—Justinian's amendment, 425 sq.
Tribonian, 404 sq.; his "emblems," 408 n. 13.
Tribunate, Institution of, 83; functions of tribunes, 83 sq., 94.
Trinoctialis usurpatio, 35 n. 33, 116.
Turin Gloss on Institutes, 433.
Tutory over Pupils in regal period, 33, 121; t. of male agnates (*tutela legitima*) introduced by XII Tables, 124; *tut. leg.* ended by *capitis deminutio,* 130; the office of a tutor, 125; the *actio de rationibus distrahendis,*

148; removal of tutor as suspect, 219; regulation of t. over p. by *oratio divi Severi*, 348; tutory-at-law opened to cognates, and exceptionally even to females, 418.
Tutory over Women in patrician Rome, 33, 121; its justification, 33 n. 26; tutory of agnates, 124; fiduciary t., 44 n. 6; *tutela legitima* of agnates abolished by *l. Claudia*, 305; entire disappearance of t. over w. in later classical law, 348.
Twelve Tables,—the complaints that evoked them, 88 *sq.*; their compilation, 97; sources, 98; remains, 99 *sq.*; reconstruction, 101 *sq.*; arrangement and most authoritative versions, 103 n. 5; general characteristics, 103 *sq.*

ULPIANUS, Domitius, 325; *Fragmenta Ulpiani*, 331.
Usucapio, The, of XII Tables, 145 *sq.*; amended in latter half of republic, 267; remodelled by Justinian, 420.
Usucapio pro herede,—origin, 48 *sq.*; nature, 179 *sq.*, 142 n. 41.
Usufruct and quasi-usufruct, 350.
Usureceptio fiduciae, 142 *sq.*
Usury, Laws to repress, 94 *sq.*
"*Uti legassit suae rei ita jus esto*,"—original application, 167; extension, 171.

Uxor and *materfamilias*,—distinction 115 note.

VADIMONIUM, 150, 280 n. 2.
Valentinian "Law of Citations," 390 *sq.*
Valerius Probus,—his "*Notae Juris*," 333.
Vatican Fragments, 396.
Vectigalis, Ager, 420.
Vengeance, Private, in early law, 52 *sq.*
Verba nuncupata in a mancipation, 139 *sq.*
Vesting of an inheritance, 174 *sq.*
"*Veteres*" of later republic, 263 *sq.*
Vindex in *manus injectio* against a judgment-debtor, 206 and notes; no room for him in *m.i.* against a nexal debtor, 158.
Vindicare, meaning, 192 n. 15.
Vindicatio, Rei: per sacramentum, 187–196; *per sponsionem*, 360 *sq.*; *per formulam petitoriam*, 361.
Vindicta in sacramental real action, 189; in manumission, 337.
"*Vis civilis et festucaria*" (Gell.), 193.
Visigothorum, Lex Romana, 398.

WARRANTY against eviction in mancipation, 135 *sq.*; did it arise *ipso jure?* 137.
Women, see "Sex," "Testament," "Tutory over women."

THE END.

PRINTED BY BALLANTYNE, HANSON AND CO.
EDINBURGH AND LONDON.

www.ingramcontent.com/pod-product-compliance
Lightning Source LLC
Chambersburg PA
CBHW021427300426
44114CB00010B/687